Contents at a Glance

WEEK I   **5**

1   What Is XML and Why Should I Care?   7
2   Anatomy of an XML Document   21
3   Using XML Markup   37
4   Working with Elements and Attributes   55
5   Checking Well-formedness   73
6   Creating Valid Documents   93
7   Developing Advanced DTDs   121

WEEK II   **149**

8   XML Objects: Exploiting Entities   151
9   Checking Validity   173
10   Creating XML Links   195
11   Using XML's Advanced Addressing   215
12   Viewing XML in Internet Explorer   227
13   Viewing XML in Other Browsers   267
14   Processing XML   291

WEEK III   **307**

15   Event-Driven Programming   309
16   Programming with the Document Object Model   343
17   Using Meta-Data to Describe XML Data   361
18   Styling XML with CSS   375
19   Converting XML with DSSSL   411
20   Rendering XML with XSL   453
21   Real World XML Applications   495

APPENDIXES   **525**

   A   Glossary   527

   B   XML Resources   533

       Index   555

Simon North
Paul Hermans

Simon C.

SAMS
Teach Yourself

XML

in 21 Days

SAMS

A Division of Macmillan Computer Publishing
201 West 103rd St., Indianapolis, Indiana, 46290 USA

Sams Teach Yourself XML in 21 Days

Copyright © 1999 by Sams

International Standard Book Number: 1-57521-396-6

Library of Congress Catalog Card Number: 97-69126

Printed in the United States of America

First Printing: March 1999

01   00   4

Trademarks

Warning and Disclaimer

EXECUTIVE EDITOR
Tim Ryan

ACQUISITIONS EDITOR
Steve Anglin

DEVELOPMENT EDITOR
Jon Steever

PROJECT EDITOR
Carol Bowers

COPY EDITORS
Sean Medlock
Howard Jones

INDEXERS
Bruce Clingaman
Chris Barrick

PROOFREADERS
Kim Cofer
Mary Ellen Stephenson

TECHNICAL EDITOR
Bill Bruns

SOFTWARE DEVELOPMENT SPECIALIST
Adam Swetnam

INTERIOR DESIGN
Gary Adair

COVER DESIGN
Aren Howell

LAYOUT TECHNICIANS
Ayanna Lacey
Heather Hiatt Miller
Amy Parker

Contents

INTRODUCTION   **1**

How This Book Is Organized 1

This Book's Special Features 4

WEEK I   **5**

1 WHAT IS XML AND WHY SHOULD I CARE?   **7**

The Web Grows Up 8

Where HTML Runs Out of Steam 9

So What's Wrong with…? 11

SGML 12

Why Not SGML? 13

Why XML? 13

What XML Adds to SGML and HTML...15

Is XML Just for Programmers? 16

Summary 18

Q&A 18

Exercise...19

2 ANATOMY OF AN XML DOCUMENT   **21**

Markup 21

A Sample XML Document..28

    The XML Declaration (Line 1)...29

    The Root Element (Lines 2 through 23) 30

    An Empty Element (Line 13) 31

    Attributes (Lines 7 and 22) 31

Logical Structure..32

Physical Structure 33

Summary 35

Q&A 35

Exercises 36

3 USING XML MARKUP   **37**

Markup Delimiters 37

Element Markup 38

Attribute Markup 39

Naming Rules 42

Comments 43

Character References 44

Predefined Entities 44

Entity References 45
    Entity Declarations 45
    The Benefits of Entities...46
    Some of the Dangers of Using Entities...47
    Avoiding the Pitfalls 47
    Synchronous Structures 48
    Where to Declare Entities 49
CDATA Sections 50
Processing Instructions 52
Summary 52
Q&A 53
Exercises 54

4 WORKING WITH ELEMENTS AND ATTRIBUTES   55
Markup Declarations..56
Element Declarations 57
    Empty Elements...58
    Unrestricted Elements 58
Element Content Models 58
    Element Sequences 59
    Element Choices 59
    Combined Sequences and Choices 60
Ambiguous Content Models..60
    Element Occurrence Indicators 62
    Character Content 63
    Mixed Content Elements 64
Attribute Declarations..64
Attribute Types 65
    String Attribute Types 65
    Tokenized Attribute Types..66
    Enumerated Attribute Types 67
    Attribute Default Values 67
Well-Formed XML Documents 68
Summary 69
Q&A 70
Exercises 70

5 CHECKING WELL-FORMEDNESS   73
Where to Find Information on Available Parsers 74
Checking Your XML Files with expat 74
    Installing expat 75
    Using expat 75
    Checking a File Error by Error 75

Checking Your XML Files with DXP 81
   Installing DXP...81
   Using DXP..82
   Checking a File Error by Error 82
Checking Your Files Over the Web Using RUWF 84
   Using RUWF 84
Checking Your Files Over the Web Using Other Online Validation Services 85
   Using XML Well-formedness Checker....................................85
   Using XML Syntax Checker from Frontier 86
Summary..88
Q&A 89
Exercises 90

6 CREATING VALID DOCUMENTS   **93**

XML and Structured Information..94
Why Have a DTD at All? 97
DTDs and Validation...98
Document Type Declarations 99
Internal DTD Subset..100
Standalone XML Documents 100
Getting Sophisticated, External DTDs 103
   System Identifier 103
   Public Identifier 104
Developing the DTD..105
   Modifying an SGML DTD 105
   Developing a DTD from XML Code 106
Creating the DTD by Hand..108
   Identifying Elements 109
   Avoiding Presentation Markup 109
   Structure the Elements...111
   Enforce the Rules 112
   Assigning Attributes 113
Tool Assistance 113
A Home Page DTD...114
Summary..117
Q&A 118
Exercises 119

7 DEVELOPING ADVANCED DTDs   **121**

Information Richness 122
Visual Modeling 124
XML DTDs from Other Sources 128
Modeling Relational Databases 130
Elements or Attributes?..132

Saving Yourself Typing with Parameter Entities 133
Modular DTDs 134
Conditional Markup 136
Optional Content Models and Ambiguities 137
Avoiding Conflicts with Namespaces..139
A Test Case 140
Summary..146
Q&A 147
Exercises 147

WEEK II   **149**

8 XML OBJECTS: EXPLOITING ENTITIES   **151**

Entities 151
    Internal Entities 153
    Binary Entities..154
    Notations 155
Identifying External Entities..158
    System Identifiers 158
    Public Identifiers 159
Parameter Entities 161
Entity Resolution 161
Getting the Most Out of Entities 163
Character Data and Character Sets 165
    Character Sets 165
Entity Encoding 166
Entities and Entity Sets..167
Summary..170
Q&A 170
Exercises 171

9 CHECKING VALIDITY   **173**

Checking Your DTD with DXP 174
    Walkthrough of a DTD Check with DXP 174
Checking Your DTD with XML for Java 183
    Installing XML for Java 183
    Using XML for Java 183
    Walkthrough of a DTD Check with XML for Java 184
Checking Your XML Files with DXP 184
    Walkthrough of an XML File Check with DXP 185
Checking Your XML Files with XML for Java 189
    Walkthrough of an XML File Check with XML for Java 189

Summary 190

Q&A 190

Exercises 191

10 Creating XML Links

195

Hyperlinks..196

Locators...198

Link Elements 198

Simple Links 199

Extended Links 199

Extended Link Groups..204

Inline and Out-of-Line Links 205

Link Behavior 207

Link Effects 207

Link Timing 208

The `behavior` Attribute 209

Link Descriptions 210

Mozilla and the `role` Attribute...211

Attribute Remapping...213

Summary 213

Q&A 214

Exercises 214

11 Using XML's Advanced Addressing

215

Extended Pointers 216

Documents as Trees 216

Location Terms 218

Absolute Terms 219

Relative Terms 219

Selection 221

Selecting by Instance Number...222

Selecting by Node Type 222

Selection by Attribute 223

Selecting Text 223

Selecting Groups and Ranges (`spans`) 224

Summary 224

Q&A 224

Exercises 225

12 Viewing XML in Internet Explorer

227

Microsoft's Vision for XML 228

Viewing XML in Internet Explorer 4 228

Overview of XML Support in Internet Explorer 4 228

Viewing XML Using the XML Data Source Object...........................229

Viewing XML Using the XML Object API 238
Viewing XML via MS XSL Processor 244
Viewing XML in Internet Explorer 5 248
Overview of XML Support in Internet Explorer 5 248
Viewing XML Using the XML Data Source Object.....................................248
Viewing XML Using the XML Object API 249
Viewing Embedded XML 254
Viewing XML Directly 257
Viewing XML with CSS 259
Viewing XML with XSL..261
Summary 263
Q&A 263
Exercises 264

13 VIEWING XML IN OTHER BROWSERS   **267**

Viewing/Browsing XML in Netscape Navigator/Mozilla/Gecko 268
Netscape's Vision for XML...268
Viewing XML in Netscape Navigator 4 269
Viewing XML in Mozilla 5/Gecko 269
Viewing XML with DocZilla 279
Viewing XML with Browsers Based on Inso's Viewport Engine 279
Features of the Viewport Engine 279
How it Works...280
Summary 288
Q&A 288
Exercises 289

14 PROCESSING XML   **291**

Reasons for Processing XML..291
Delivery to Multiple Media...292
Delivery to Multiple Target Groups 294
Adding, Removing, and Restructuring Information 296
Database Loading 297
Reporting 297
Three Processing Paradigms..298
An XML Document as a Text File 298
An XML Document as a Series of Events 298
XML as a Hierarchy/Tree 302
Summary 304
Q&A 304
Exercise...305

WEEK III   **307**

15 EVENT-DRIVEN PROGRAMMING   **309**

Omnimark LE 309
    What Is Omnimark LE? 310
    Finding and Installing Omnimark LE 310
    How Omnimark Works 310
    Running Omnimark LE 311
    Basic Events in the Omnimark Language 311
    Looking Ahead 316
    Input and Output 318
    Other Features 318
    An Example of an Omnimark Script 318
    More Information 330
SAX 330
    The Big Picture 331
    Some Background on OO and Java Concepts 331
    The Interfaces and Classes in the SAX Distribution 332
    An Example 335
    Getting Our Conversion Up and Running 338
    Other Implementations 340
    Building Further on SAX 340
Summary 341
Q&A 341
Exercises 341

16 PROGRAMMING WITH THE DOCUMENT OBJECT MODEL   **343**

Background 343
The Specification 344
    Structure 344
    The Interfaces 345
    Interface Relationships 345
    The Node Object 347
    The NodeList Object/Interface 350
    The NamedNodeMap Object 351
    The Document Object 352
    The Data Object 354
    The Other Objects 355
An Example of Using the DOM 355
Implementations of the DOM 357
The Future of the DOM 357

Summary 358
Q&A 358
Exercises 358

17 USING META-DATA TO DESCRIBE XML DATA   361

What's Wrong with DTDs? 362
XML-Data 363
Resource Description Framework 364
Document Content Description 368
XSchema 369
Architectural Forms 370
Summary 372
Q&A 372
Exercises 372

18 STYLING XML WITH CSS   375

The Rise and Fall of the Style Language 376
Cascading Style Sheets 378
XML, CSS, and Web Browsers 379
XML, CSS, and Internet Explorer 379
XML, CSS, and Mozilla 387
    Getting Mozilla 388
    Displaying XML Code in Mozilla 388
Cheating 392
Embedding CSS in XSL 395
CSS Style Sheet Properties 399
    Units..399
    Specifying CSS Properties 400
    Classes 401
    ID Attributes 401
    CSS1 Property Summary..401
Summary 408
Q&A 408
Exercises 409

19 CONVERTING XML WITH DSSSL   411

Where DSSSL Fits In 412
A DSSSL Development Environment 413
    Installing jade 413
    Running jade 414
    jade Error Messages 417
    Viewing jade Output 418

First Steps in Using jade..418
    XML to RTF and MIF Conversion 419
    XML to HTML Conversion 422
Basic DSSSL..425
    Flow Objects 425
    Flow Object Characteristics 429
    Flow Object Tree 431
    Element Selection 433
    Construction Rules 433
Cookbook Examples..434
    Prefixing an Element...434
    Fancy Prefixing 438
    Tables..440
    Table of Contents..442
    Cross References 446
Summary..450
Q&A 451
Exercises 451

20 RENDERING XML WITH XSL   453

XSL1..454
XSL2..455
Template Rules 459
    Matching an Element by its ID 461
    Matching an Element by its Name 461
    Matching an Element by its Ancestry 461
    Matching Several Element Names 462
    Matching an Element by its Attributes 462
    Matching an Element by its Children 463
    Matching an Element by its Position 463
    Wildcard Matches 464
    Resolving Selection Conflicts 464
    The Default Template Rule 465
Formatting Objects 466
    Layout Formatting Objects 466
    Content Formatting Objects 467
Processing 471
    Direct Processing...471
    Restricted Processing...474
    Conditional Processing 474
    Computing Generated Text 476
    Adding a Text Formatting Object 477

Numbering 477
Sorting 479
Whitespace..481
Macros...481
Formatting Object Properties 482
Avoiding Flow Objects 490
Summary 492
Q&A 492
Exercises 493

21 REAL WORLD XML APPLICATIONS   **495**

The State of the Game 496
Mathematics Markup Language 498
Structured Graphics 506
WebCGM 508
Precision Graphics Markup Language 509
Vector Markup Language 513
Behaviors 517
Action Sheets..518
CSS Behavior 519
Microsoft's Chrome 521
Summary 522
Q&A 522
Exercises 523

WEEK IV   **525**

A GLOSSARY   **527**

B XML RESOURCES   **533**

Books 533
Online Resources 535
Articles..535
Applications...537
Standards 540
Information Sources 543
Software Packages...543
Software Companies 548
DSSSL..549
SGML 550
Usenet Groups 551
Mailing Lists...552
Test Data 553

INDEX   **555**

About the Author

Simon North originally hails from England, but thinks of himself as more of a European. Fluent in several European languages, Simon is a technical writer for Synopsys, the leading EDA software company, where he documents high-level IC design software. This puts him in the strange situation of working for a Silicon Valley company in Germany while living in The Netherlands.

Simon has been working with SGML and HyTime-based documentation systems for the past nine years, but was one of the first to adopt HTML. His writing credits include contributions on XML and SGML to the Sams.Net books *Presenting XML*, *Dynamic Web Publishing Unleashed*, and *HTML4 Unleashed, Professional Reference Edition*. Simon can be reached at north@synopsys.com (work) or sintac@xs4all.nl (or through his books Web page at http://www.xs4all.nl/~sintac/books.html).

Paul Hermans is founder and CEO of Pro Text, one of the leading SGML/XML consultant firms and implementation service providers in Belgium.

Since 1992 he has been involved in major Belgian SGML implementations. Previously he was head of the electronic publishing department of CED Samsom, part of the Wolters Kluwer group. He is also the chair of SGML BeLux, the Belgian-Luxembourgian chapter of the International SGML Users' Group.

Dedications

From Simon North:

To the thousands of givers in the online community without whose dedication, hard work, generosity, and selflessness the Internet would be just a poor, sad reflection of everyday life.

From Paul Hermans:

To Rika for bringing structure into my life and to my parents for caring.

Acknowledgements

From Simon North:

To all the folks at Sams for giving me the chance to write this book and for allowing me to make it the book I wanted it to be. To all my colleagues at Synopsys who made my working life so pleasant and gave me the enthusiasm and energy to survive the extra workload. Most of all, to my long-suffering wife Irma without whose willingness to spring into the breach and assume most of my parental responsibilities this book just wouldn't have been possible.

From Paul Hermans:

I would like to thank Simon North for giving me the opportunity to put some of my knowledge on paper. Furthermore I would like to acknowledge all the people at Sams Publishing who helped bring this book to completion.

Tell Us What You Think!

As the reader of this book, *you* are our most important critic and commentator. We value your opinion and want to know what we're doing right, what we could do better, what areas you'd like to see us publish in, and any other words of wisdom you're willing to pass our way.

As the Executive Editor for the Java team at Macmillan Computer Publishing, I welcome your comments. You can fax, email, or write me directly to let me know what you did or didn't like about this book—as well as what we can do to make our books stronger.

Please note that I cannot help you with technical problems related to the topic of this book, and that due to the high volume of mail I receive, I might not be able to reply to every message.

When you write, please be sure to include this bookís title and author as well as your name and phone or fax number. I will carefully review your comments and share them with the author and editors who worked on the book.

Fax: 317-817-7070

Email: webdev@mcp.com

Mail: Mark Taber, Executive Editor
          Web Development Team
          Macmillan Computer Publishing
          201 West 103rd Street
          Indianapolis, IN 46290 USA

Introduction

XML started as an obscure effort driven by a small group of dedicated SGML experts who were convinced that the world needed something more powerful than HTML. Although XML hasn't yet taken the world by storm, in its quiet way it is poised to revolutionize the Internet and usher in a new age of electronic commerce.

Until recently, the non-technical Internet user has largely written off XML as being more of a programmers' language than a technology that applies to us all. Nearly two years after XML's inception, there is still no real mainstream software support in the form of editors and viewers. However, just as with HTML, as the technology becomes adopted, the tools will start to arrive. Netscape and Microsoft have already given us a taste of what is to come.

Sams Teach Yourself XML in 21 Days teaches you about XML and its related standards (the XSL style language, XLink and XPointer hyperlinking, XML Data, and XSchema, to name just a few), but it doesn't stop there. As you follow the step-by-step explanations, you will also learn how to *use* XML. You will be introduced to a wide range of the available tools, from the newest to the tried and tested. By the time you finish this book, you'll know enough about XML and its use within the available tools to use it immediately.

How This Book Is Organized

Sams Teach Yourself XML in 21 Days covers the latest version of XML, its related standards, and a wide variety of tools. Some features of the tools will have been enhanced or expanded by the time you read this, and new tools will certainly have become available. Keep this in mind when you're working with the early versions of some of the software packages. If something doesn't work as it should, or if you feel that there is something important missing, check the Web sites mentioned in Appendix B, "XML Resources," to see if a newer version of the package is available.

Sams Teach Yourself XML in 21 Days is organized into three separate weeks. Each week brings you to a certain milestone in your learning of XML and development of XML code.

In the first week, you'll learn a lot of the basics about XML itself:

- On Day 1, you'll get a basic introduction on what XML is and why it's so important. You will also see your first XML document.
- On Day 2, you will dissect an XML document to discover exactly what goes into making usable XML code. You will also create your first XML document.

- On Day 3, you'll go a little further into the basics of XML code. You'll learn about elements, comments, processing instructions, and using CDATA sections to hide XML code you don't want to be processed.

- On Day 4, you will learn more about markup and elements by exploring attributes. You'll also learn the basics of information modeling and some of the ground rules of Document Type Definition (DTD) development. You will learn how to work with DTDs without having to go as far as creating valid XML code, and you will discover how much you can already achieve by creating well-formed XML documents.

- On Day 5, you'll reach an important milestone. You will learn how to put together everything you have learned so far and produce well-formed XML documents. You will be introduced to some basic parsing tools and then learn how to check and correct your XML documents.

- On Day 6, you will learn all about DTDs, their subsets, and how they are used to check XML documents for validity.

- On Day 7, you'll delve even further into the treacherous waters of DTD development and learn some of the major tricks of the trade that open the doors to advanced XML document construction.

Week two takes you into the "power" side of XML authoring:

- On Day 8, you will learn about entities and notations, and how to import external objects such as binary code and graphics files into your XML documents.

- On Day 9, you'll arrive at the next major milestone. You will be introduced to a couple of the leading XML parsers, and you'll learn how to validate your XML documents and recognize and correct some of the most common errors.

- On Day 10, you will discover the power of XML's linking mechanisms. Using practical examples, you will learn how you can use XML links to go far beyond HTML's humble features.

- On Day 11, you will continue to explore XML's linking mechanisms. You will learn how you can link to ranges, groups, and indirect blocks of data inside both XML and non-XML data.

- On Day 12, with much of the theory already in your grasp, you will learn how you can actually display the XML code you've written in Microsoft's Internet Explorer 5.

- On Day 13, you will continue the hands-on work of Day 12 by learning how to display the XML code you've written in Mozilla, Netscape's Open Source testbed for the development of future versions of its Web browser software.

- On Day 14, you will learn the basics of XML document processing. You will be introduced to the principles of tree-based and event-driven processing and learn when and how to apply them.

Week three takes you beyond XML authoring and teaches you how to process XML and HTML code.

- On Day 15, you will learn more about event-driven processing. You will learn how to download, install, and use two of the leading tools: Omnimark and SAX.

- On Day 16, going several steps further, you will learn how to use the Document Object Model (DOM) to gain programmatic access to everything inside an XML document.

- On Day 17, you will temporarily turn your back on XML code as a means of coding documents and examine how it's used to code data. You will learn why a DTD sometimes isn't enough, and you'll be introduced to some of the most important XML schemas.

- On Day 18, you will return to using XML for documents and explore how the Cascading Style Sheet language (CSS), originally intended for use with HTML, can be used just as easily with XML code. With the aid of practical examples, you will learn how you can legitimately use CSS code to render XML code. If that doesn't work, you'll also learn a few tricks to fool the browser into doing what you want it to do.

- On Day 19, you will learn the basics of DSSSL, the style language for rendering and processing SGML code. You will learn how easy it can be to use DSSSL to transform not just SGML code, but also XML and HTML code. With the help of numerous examples, you will also learn how to convert XML code into HTML and RTF, and how to convert HTML into RTF or even FrameMaker MIF using jade.

- On Day 20, you will be briefly introduced to earlier versions of the XML style languages before concentrating on XSL. Using the very latest XSL tools, you will learn how to create your own XSL style code and display the results.

- On Day 21, you will learn the basics of MathML, the mathematics application of XML, as well as the various initiatives to describe graphics in XML. (No book on XML would be complete without some mention of its applications.) Using practical examples, you will be introduced to VML and see how you can already use it in Microsoft Internet Explorer, versions 4 and 5. Finally, you will take a peek at some of the new developments that are just around the corner, such as Office 2000, CSS behaviors, and Microsoft's Chrome.

The end of each chapter offers common questions and answers about that day's subject matter and some simple exercises for you to try yourself. At the end of the book, you will find a comprehensive glossary and an extensive appendix of XML resources containing pointers to most of the software packages available, whether mentioned in this book or not, and pointers to the most important sources of further information.

This Book's Special Features

This book contains some special features to help you on your way to mastering XML.

Tips provide useful shortcuts and techniques for working with XML. Notes provide special details that enhance the explanations of XML concepts or draw your attention to important points that are not immediately part of the subject being discussed. Warnings highlight points that will help you avoid potential problems.

Numerous sample XML, DSSSL, XSL, HTML, and CSS code fragments illustrate some of the features and concepts of XML so that you can apply them in your own document. Where possible, each code fragment's discussion is divided into three components: the code fragment itself, the output generated by it, and a line-by-line analysis of how the code fragment works. These components are indicated by special icons.

Each day ends with a Q&A section containing answers to common questions relating to that day's material. There is also a set of exercises at the end of each day. We recommend that you attempt each exercise. You will learn far more from doing yourself than just seeing what others have done. Most of the exercises do not have any one answer, and the answers would often be very long. As a result, most chapters don't actually provide answers, but the method for finding the best solution will have been covered in the chapter itself.

Week 1

1 What is XML and Why Should I Care? 7

2 Anatomy of an XML Document 21

3 Using XML Markup 37

4 Working with Elements and Attributes 55

5 Checking Well-formedness 73

6 Creating Valid Documents 93

7 Developing Advanced DTDs 121

1

2

3

4

5

6

7

DAY 1

What Is XML and Why Should I Care?

Welcome to *Sams Teach Yourself XML in 21 Days*! This chapter starts you on the road to mastering the *Extensible Markup Language* (*XML*). Today you will learn

- The importance of XML in a maturing Internet
- The weaknesses of HTML that make it unsuitable for Internet commerce
- What SGML, the Standard Generalized Markup Language is and XML's relation to it
- The weaknesses of other tag and markup languages
- What XML adds to both SGML and HTML
- The advantages of XML for non-programmers

The Web Grows Up

Love them or hate them, the Internet and the World Wide Web (WWW) are here to stay. No matter how much you try, you can't avoid the Web playing an increasingly important role in your life.

The Internet has gone from a small experiment carried out by a bunch of nuclear research scientists to one of the most phenomenal events in computing history. It sometimes feels like we have been experiencing the modern equivalent of the Industrial Revolution: the dawning of the Information Age.

In his original proposal to CERN (the European Laboratory for Particle Research) management in 1989, Tim Berners-Lee (the acknowledged inventor of the Web) described his vision of

> …a universal linked information system, in which generality and portability are more important than fancy graphics and complex extra facilities.

The Web has certainly come a long way in the last ten years, and I sometimes wonder what Berners-Lee thinks of his invention in its present form.

The Web is still in its infancy, however. Use of the Web is slowly progressing beyond the stage of family Web pages, but the dawn of electronic commerce (e-commerce) via the Internet has not yet broken. By e-commerce, I do not mean being able to order things from a Web page, such as books, records, CDs, and software. This kind of commerce has been going on for several years, and some companies—most notably Amazon.com— have made a great success of it. My definition of e-commerce goes much deeper than this. Various new initiatives have appeared in recent years that are going to change the way a lot of companies look at the Web. These include

- Using the Internet to join the parts of distributed companies into one unit
- Using the Internet for the exchange of financial transaction information (credit card transactions, banking transactions, and so on)
- The exchange over the Internet of medical transaction data between patients, hospitals, physicians, and insurance agencies
- The distribution of software via the Web, including the possibility of creating zero-install software and of modularizing the massive suites of software in programs such as Microsoft Word so that you only load, use, and pay for the parts that you need

Note

Every time you visit a Web site that supports Java, JavaScript, or some other scripting language, you are in fact running a program over the Web. After you've finished with it, all that's left in your Web browser's cache is possibly a few scraps of code. Several software companies—including Microsoft—want to distribute software in this way. They'd gain by constantly generating new income from their software, and you would benefit by only having to pay for the software you used at the time that you used it, and only for as long as you used it.

Whereas most of these applications are impossible using *Hypertext Markup Language (HTML)*, XML can make all these applications (and many more) real possibilities. In a sense, XML is the enabling technology that heralds the appearance of a new form of Internet society. XML is probably the most important thing to happen to the Web since the arrival of Java.

So why can XML do what HTML can't? Read on for an explanation.

Where HTML Runs Out of Steam

Before we look at all the weaknesses of HTML, let's get one thing clear: HTML has been, and still is, a fantastic success.

Designed to be a simple tagging language for displaying text in a Web browser, HTML has done a wonderful job and will probably continue to do so for many years to come. It is no exaggeration to say that if there hadn't been HTML, there simply wouldn't have been a Web. Although Gopher, WAIS, and Hytelnet, among others, predated HTML, none of them offered the same trade-off of power for simplicity that HTML does.

Although HTML might still be considered the killer Internet application, there have been a lot of complaints leveled against it. Furthermore, people are now realizing that XML is superior to HTML. Following are some of the most frequently cited complaints against HTML (but many of them aren't really legitimate, as you will see from my comments):

- **HTML lacks syntactic checking: You cannot validate HTML code.**

    Yes and no. There are formal definitions of the structure of HTML documents—as you will learn later, HTML is an SGML application and there is a document type definition (DTD) for every version of HTML.

Note

> The *document type definition (DTD)* is an SGML or XML document that describes the elements and attributes allowed inside all the documents that can be said to conform to that DTD. You will learn all about XML DTDs in later chapters.

There are also some tools (and one or two Web sites) readily available for checking the syntax of HTML documents. This begs the question of why more people don't validate their HTML documents; the answer is that the validation is really a bit misleading. Web browsers are designed to accept almost anything that looks even slightly like HTML (which runs the risk that the display will look nothing like what you expected—but that's another story). Strangely enough, the only tag that is compulsory in an HTML document is the TITLE tag; equally strangely, this is one of the least common tags there is.

- **HTML lacks structure.**

  Not really. HTML has ordered heading tags (H1 to H6), and you can nest blocks of information inside DIV tags. Browsers don't care what order you use the headings in, and often the choice is simply based on the size of the font in which they are rendered. This isn't HTML's fault. The problem lies in how HTML code is used.

- **HTML is not content-aware.**

  Yes and no. Searching the Web is complicated by the fact that HTML doesn't give you a way to describe the information content—the semantics—of your documents. In XML you can use any tags you like (such as <NAME> instead of <H3>), but using attributes in tags (such as <H3 CLASS="name">) can embed just as much semantic information as custom tags can. Without any agreement on tag names, the value of custom tags becomes a bit doubtful. To worsen matters, the same tag name in one context can mean something completely different in another. Furthermore, there are the complications of foreign languages—seeing <inkoopprijs> isn't going to help very much if you don't know that it's Dutch for "purchase price."

- **HTML is not international.**

  Mostly true. There were a few proposals to internationalize HTML, and most particularly to give it a way of identifying the language used inside a tag.

- **HTML is not suitable for data interchange.**

  Mostly true. HTML's tags do little to identify the information that a document contains.

1

- **HTML is not object-oriented.**

  True. Modern programmers have been making a long and difficult transition to object-oriented techniques. They want to leverage these skills and have such things as inheritance, and HTML has done very little to accommodate them.

- **HTML lacks a robust linking mechanism.**

  Very true. If you've spent a few hours on the Web, you've probably encountered at least one broken link. Although broken links are the curse of Web managers the world over, there is little that can be done to prevent them. HTML's links are very much one-to-one, with the linking hard-coded in the source HTML files. If the location of one target file changes, a Webmaster may have to update dozens or even hundreds of other pages.

- **HTML is not reusable.**

  True. Depending on how well-written they are, HTML pages and fragments of HTML code can be extremely difficult to reuse because they are so specifically tailored to their place in the web of associated pages.

- **HTML is not extensible.**

  True but unfair. This is a bit like saying that an automobile makes a better motor vehicle than a bicycle. HTML was never *meant* to be extensible.

So what's really wrong with HTML? Not a lot, for everyday Web page use. However, looking at the future of electronic commerce on the Web, HTML is reaching its limits.

So What's Wrong with...?

All right, if HTML can't handle it, what's wrong with TeX, PDF, or RTF?

TeX is a computer typesetting language that still flourishes in scientific communities. In the early 1980's, there were online databases that returned data in TeX form that could be inserted straight into a TeX document. Adobe owns the *PDF* (Adobe Acrobat) standard, but it is fairly well documented. *RTF* is the property of Microsoft and, as many Windows Help authors will tell you, it is poorly documented and extremely unreliable. The RTF code created by Word 97 is not the same as the code created by Word 95, for example, and in some areas the two versions are completely incompatible.

All of these formats suffer from the same weaknesses: they are proprietary (owned by a commercial company or organization), they are not open, and they are not standardized. By using one of these formats, you risk being left out in the cold. Although the market represents a strong stabilizing force (as seen with RTF), when you place too much reliance on a format over which you have no control and into which you have little insight, you are leaving yourself open to a lot of problems if and when that format changes.

SGML

I'm going to try to avoid teaching you as much as I can about SGML. Although it can be helpful to know a little about it, in many ways you're probably better off not knowing anything about it at all. The problem with learning too much about SGML is that when you move to XML you'd have to spend most of your time forgetting a lot of the things you'd just learned. XML is different enough from SGML that you can become an expert in XML without knowing a thing about SGML.

That said, XML is very much a descendant of SGML, and knowing at least a little about SGML will help put XML in context.

The *Standard Generalized Markup Language (SGML)*, from which XML is derived, was born out of the basic need to make data storage independent of any one software package or software vendor. SGML is a *meta language*, or a language for describing markup languages. HTML is one such markup language and is therefore called an SGML application. There are dozens, maybe even hundreds, of markup languages defined using SGML. In XML, these applications are often called *markup languages*—such as the *hand-held device markup language (HDML)* and the *FAQ markup language (QML)*.

In SGML, most of these markup languages haven't been given formal names; they are simply referred to by the name of their document type definition (DocBook), their purpose (LinuxDOC), their application (TEI), or even the standard they implement (J2008— automobile parts, Mil-M-38784—US Military).

By means of an SGML declaration (XML also has one), the SGML application specifies which characters are to be interpreted as data and which characters are to be interpreted as markup. (They do not have to include the familiar < and > characters; in SGML they could just as easily be { and } instead.)

Using the rules given in the SGML declaration and the results of the information analysis (which ultimately creates something that can easily be considered an information model), the SGML application developer identifies various types of documents—such as reports, brochures, technical manuals, and so on—and develops a DTD for each one. Using the chosen characters, the DTD identifies information objects (elements) and their properties (attributes).

The DTD is the very core of an SGML application; how well it is made largely determines the success or failure of the whole activity. Using the information elements defined in the DTD, the actual information is then marked up using the tags identified for it in the application. If the development of the DTD has been rushed, it might need continual improvement, modification, or correction. Each time the DTD is changed, the

1

information that has been marked up with it might also need to be modified because it may be incorrect. Very quickly, the quantity of data that needs modification (now called *legacy data*) can become a far more serious problem—one that is more costly and time-consuming than the problem that SGML was originally introduced to solve.

You are already getting a feel for the magnitude of an SGML application. There are good reasons for this magnitude: SGML was built to last. At the back of the developers' minds were ideas about longevity and durability, as were thoughts of protecting data from changes in computer software and hardware in the future.

SGML is the industrial-strength solution: expensive and complicated, but also extremely powerful.

Why Not SGML?

The SGML on the Web initiative existed a long time before XML was even considered. Somehow, though, it never really succeeded. Basically, SGML is just too expensive and complicated for Web use on a large scale. It isn't that it *can't* be used—it's that it *won't* be used. Using SGML requires too much of an investment in time, tools, and training.

Why XML?

XML uses the features of SGML that it needs and tries to incorporate the lessons learned from HTML.

Note

> One of the most important links between XML and SGML is XML's use of a DTD. On Day 17, "Using Meta-Data to Describe XML Data," you will learn more about the developments that are underway to cut this major link to SGML and replace the DTD with something more in keeping with the data-processing requirements of XML applications.

When the designers of XML sat down to write its specifications, they had a set of design goals in mind (detailed in the recommendation document). These goals and the degree to which they have already been met are why XML is considered better than SGML:

- XML can be used with existing Web protocols (such as HTTP and MIME) and mechanisms (such as URLs), and it does not impose any additional requirements. XML has been developed with the Web in mind—features of SGML that were too difficult to use on the Web were left out, and features that are needed for Web use either have been added or are inherited from applications that already work.

- XML supports a wide variety of applications. It is difficult to support a lot of applications with just HTML; hence, the growth of scripting languages. HTML is simply too specific. XML adopts the generic nature of SGML, but adds flexibility to make it truly extensible.

- XML is compatible with SGML, and most SGML applications can be converted into XML. In the foreseeable future, the SGML standard will be amended to make XML applications fully backward-compatible.

- It is easy to write programs that process XML documents. One of the major strengths of HTML is that it's easy for even a non-programmer to throw together a few lines of scripting code that enable you to do basic processing (and there's an amazing variety of scripting languages available). HTML even includes some features of its own that enable you to carry out some basic processing (such as forms and CGI query strings). XML has learned a lesson from HTML's success and has tried to stay as simple as possible by throwing out a lot of SGML's more complex features. XML processing applications are already appearing in Java, SmallTalk, C, C++, JavaScript, Tcl, Perl, and Python, to name just a few.

- The number of optional features in XML has been kept to an absolute minimum. SGML has many optional features, so SGML software has to support all of them. It can be argued that there isn't actually a single software package that supports all of SGML's features (and it's difficult to imagine an application that actually needs all of them). This degree of power immediately implies complexity, which also means size, cost, and sluggishness. The speed of the Web is already becoming a major concern; it's bad enough to wait for a document to download, but if you had to wait ages for it to be processed as well, XML would be doomed from the start.

- XML documents are reasonably clear to the layperson. Although it is becoming increasingly rare, and even difficult, for HTML documents to be typed in manually, and XML documents weren't intended to be created by human beings, this remains a worthy goal. Machine encoding is limited in longevity and portability, often being tied to the system on which it was created. XML's markup is reasonably self-explanatory.

Given the time, you can print out any XML document and work out its meaning—but it goes further than this. A valid XML document

  - Describes the structural rules that the markup attempts to follow

  - Lists any external resources (external entities) that are part of the document

  - Declares any internal resources (internal entities) that are used within the document

- Lists the types of non-XML resources (notations) used and identifies any helper applications that might be needed
  - Lists any non-XML resources (binaries) that are used within the document and identifies any helper applications that might be needed
- The design of XML is formal and concise. The Extended Backus-Naur Format (EBNF) was used as the basis of the XML specification (a method well understood by the majority of programmers). Information marked up in XML can be easily processed by computer programs. Better still, by using a system that is familiar to computer programmers and is almost completely unambiguous, it is reasonably easy for programmers to develop programs that work with XML.
- XML documents are easy to create. HTML is almost famous for its ease of use, and XML capitalizes on this strength. In fact, it is actually even easier to create an XML document than an HTML document. After all, you don't have to learn any markup tags—you can create your own!

What XML Adds to SGML and HTML

XML takes the best of SGML and combines it with some of the best features of HTML, and adds a few features drawn from some of the more successful applications of both. XML takes its major framework from SGML, leaving out everything that isn't absolutely necessary. Each facility and feature was examined, and if a good case couldn't be made for its retention, it was scrapped. XML is commonly called a *subset* of SGML, but in technical terms it's an *application profile* of SGML; whereas HTML uses SGML and is an application of SGML, XML is just SGML on a smaller scale.

From HTML, XML inherits the use of Web addresses (URLs) to point to other objects. From *HyTime* (a very sophisticated application of SGML, officially called *ISO/IEC 10744 Hypermedia/Time-based Structuring Language*) and an academic application of SGML called the *Text Encoding Initiative* (*TEI*), XML inherits some other extremely powerful addressing mechanisms that allow you to point to parts and ranges of other documents rather than simple single-point targets, for example.

XML also adds a list of features that make it far more suitable than either SGML or HTML for use on an increasingly complex and diverse Web:

- **Modularity**—Although HTML appears to have no DTD, there is an implied DTD hard-wired into Web browsers. SGML has a limitless number of DTDs, on the other hand, but there's only one for each type of document. XML enables you to leave out the DTD altogether or, using sophisticated resolution mechanisms, combine multiple fragments of either XML instances or separate DTDs into one compound instance.

- **Extensibility**—XML's powerful linking mechanisms allow you to link to material without requiring the link target to be physically present in the object. This opens up exciting possibilities for linking together things like material to which you do not have write access, CD-ROMs, library catalogs, the results of database queries, or even non-document media such as sound fragments or parts of videos. Furthermore, it allows you to store the links separately from the objects they link (perhaps even in a database, so that the link lists can be automatically generated according to the dynamic contents of the collection of documents). This makes long-term link maintenance a real possibility.

- **Distribution**—In addition to linking, XML introduces a far more sophisticated method of including link targets in the current instance. This opens the doors to a new world of *composite documents*—documents composed of fragments of other documents that are automatically (and transparently) assembled to form what is displayed at that particular moment. The content can be instantly tailored to the moment, to the media, and to the reader, and might have only a fleeting existence: a virtual information reality composed of virtual documents.

- **Internationality**—Both HTML and SGML rely heavily on ASCII, which makes using foreign characters very difficult. XML is based on Unicode and requires all XML software to support Unicode as well. Unicode enables XML to handle not just Western-accented characters, but also Asian languages. (On Day 8, "XML Objects: Exploiting Entities," you will learn all about character sets and character encoding.)

- **Data orientation**—XML operates on data orientation rather than readability by humans. Although being humanly readable is one of XML's design goals, electronic commerce requires the data format to be readable by machines as well. XML makes this possible by defining a form of XML that can be more easily created by a machine, but it also adds tighter data control through the more recent XML schema initiatives.

Is XML Just for Programmers?

Having read this far, you might think that XML is only for programmers and that you can quite happily go back to using HTML. In many ways you'd be right, except for one important point: If programmers can do more with XML than they can with HTML, eventually this will filter down to you in the form of application software that you can use with your XML data. To take full advantage of these tools, however, you will need to make your data available in XML. As of yet, support for XML in Web browsers is incomplete and unreliable (you will learn how to display XML code in Mozilla and Internet Explorer 5 later on), but full support will not take long.

In the meantime, is XML just for programmers? Definitely not! One of the problems with HTML is that all the tags are optional, so you have to be somewhat familiar with all of them in order to make the best choice. Worse, your choice will be affected by the way the code looks in a particular browser. But XML is extensible, and extensibility works both ways—it also means you can use less rather than more. Instead of having to learn more than 40 HTML tags, you can mark up your text in a way that makes a lot more sense to you and then use a style sheet to handle the visible appearance. Listing 1.1 shows a typical XML document that marks up a basic sales contact entry.

LISTING 1.1   A SIMPLE XML DOCUMENT

```
1: <?xml version="1.0"?>
2:   <contacts>
3:     <contact>
4:       <name>
5:         <first>John</first>
6:         <last>Belcher</last>
7:       </name>
8:       <address>
9:         <street>Pennington 13322</street>
10:        <city>Washington</city>
11:        <state>DC</state>
12:        <zip>66522</zip>
13:      </address>
14:      <tel>555 1276</tel>
15:      <fax>555 9983</fax>
16:      <mobile>887 8887 7777</mobile>
17:      <email>jb@southside.com</email>
18:    </contact>
19:  </contacts>
```

As Listing 1.1 suggests, you can make your markup very rich in information (semantic content). The great thing about XML is that you can adapt it to your needs. When you need less you can use less, as demonstrated by Listing 1.2. (It would hardly be in keeping with all the other computer language-oriented books in the world if we didn't include some kind of "Hello World" example.)

LISTING 1.2   "HELLO WORLD" IN XML

```
1: <?xml version="1.0"?>
2:   <greeting>
3:     <salutation>Hello</salutation>
4:     <target>World!</target>
5:   </greeting>
```

XML is already becoming the preferred language for interfacing between databases and the Web, and it is becoming an important method for interchanging data between computers and computer applications. However, at the level of "ordinary" Web document authoring, XML still has a lot to offer. The wonderful thing about XML is that it can actually be even simpler than HTML! You can decide what tags you'll need and how many, and you can choose names that either mean something sensible to you or to your readers. Instead of producing documents containing meaningless jumbles of H1, H2, P, LI, UL, and EM tags, you can say what you really mean and use CHAPTER, SECTION, PARAGRAPH, LIST.ITEM, UNNUMBERED.LIST, and IMPORTANT. This doesn't just make your documents more meaningful, it makes them more accessible to other people. Tools (such as search engines) will be able to make more intelligent inquiries about the content and structure of your documents and make meaningful inferences about your documents that could far exceed what you originally intended.

Summary

On this first day, you were introduced to XML as a markup language in abstract terms. You saw why XML is needed by the rapidly maturing Internet and its commercial applications. You were also given a very brief overview of why XML is seen as the solution to publishing text and data through the Internet, rather than SGML or HTML.

Just as medical students start their education by dissecting corpses, tomorrow you will dissect the anatomy of an XML document to determine what it is made of.

Q&A

Q Is XML a standard, and can I rely on it?

A XML is recommended by a group of vendors, including Microsoft and Sun, called the World Wide Web Consortium (W3C). This is about as close to a standard as anything on the Web. The W3C has committed itself to supporting XML in all its other initiatives. Also, in the regular standardization circles, the SGML standard is being updated so that XML can rely on the support and formality of SGML.

Q Do I need to learn SGML to understand XML?

A No. It might help to know a little about SGML if you're going to get involved in highly technical XML developments, but no knowledge of SGML is needed for most XML applications.

Q I know SGML; how difficult will it be for me to learn XML?

A If you already have some experience with SGML, it will take less than a day to convert your knowledge to XML and learn anything extra you'll need to know. However, you'll need the discipline to unlearn some of the things you were doing with SGML.

Q I know HTML; how difficult will it be for me to learn XML?

A This depends on how deep your knowledge of HTML is and what you intend to do with XML. If all you want to do with XML is create Web pages, you can probably master the basics in a day or two.

Q Will XML replace SGML?

A No. SGML will continue to be used in the large-scale applications where its features are most needed. XML will take over some of the work from SGML but will never replace it.

Q Will XML replace HTML?

A Eventually, yes. HTML has done a wonderful job so far, and there is every reason to believe it will continue to do so for a long time to come. Eventually, though, HTML will be rewritten as an XML application instead of being an SGML application—but you are unlikely to notice the difference.

Q I have a lot of HTML code; should I convert it to XML? If so, how?

A No. Existing HTML code can be expressed very easily in XML syntax. It will also be possible to include HTML code in XML documents, and vice versa. However, it is not quite so simple to convert an HTML authoring environment into an XML one. Currently there are no XML DTDs for HTML. Until there are, it's easier to create the HTML code using HTML (or SGML) tools and then convert the finished code.

Exercise

1. You've already seen what a basic XML document looks like. Mark up a document that you'd like to use on the Web (something personal, like a home page or the tracks on a CD).

DAY 2

Anatomy of an XML Document

Just as student doctors begin their medical training by dissecting a human body and learning the nature and relation of the parts before they learn how to treat them, this exploration of XML begins with an examination of a small XML document with all its parts identified. Today you will

- Learn about a short XML document and its components
- Examine the difference between markup and character data
- Explore logical and physical structures

Markup

Before cutting into the skin of XML, as it were, let's quickly take a small step back and review one of the most basic concepts—markup. Yesterday, you learned about a couple of markup languages and some of the detailed features of a few implementations, such as TeX, but what exactly is markup?

At its most simple, *markup* involves adding characters to a piece of information that can be used to process that information in a particular way. At one end of the scale, it could be something as basic as adding commas between pieces of data that can be interpreted as field separators when the information is imported into a database program. At its most complex, it can be an extremely rich meta-language such as the Text Encoding Initiative (TEI) SGML DTD. The TEI DTD makes it possible to mark up transcriptions of historical document manuscripts to identify the particular version, the translation, the interpretation, comments about the content, and even a whole library of additional information that could be of use to anyone carrying out academic work related to the manuscript.

What actually constitutes the markup and what doesn't is a matter that has to be resolved by the software—the *application*. Compare the WordPerfect code for a single sentence shown in Listing 2.1 with the same sentence in Microsoft's RTF format shown in Listing 2.2.

LISTING 2.1   WORDPERFECT CODE

```
ŸWPC)_   _   °Ÿ_ 2 x_   _ _   B   _ (   J   _ ¨ _   r   Z   -_ _ ¦ x
Times New Roman  (TT) Courier New  (TT) _ X__Ù_C Ù_\__ _ Pé "6Q___
_ _ Ù__Ù_d ?_6_X_   __@… DèQ___
°?_ 2 C_   _ <   ™_   _ [   Ê_  ??   A_  _ _   A_
Ÿ__ ?ÙÈ?phoenix _   _ _Ÿ—_   Ù_C Ù_\__              _ Pé "6Q___
__   _— At its most simple, markup is simply ad
Simon North Simon North    °?_ 2   _¥  u_
Default Paragraph Fo _Default Paragraph Font __.   .
—_   X_P Ù_\__   _ Pé "6Q___   _—"_   _ _ "
_ _"—_   Ù_C Ù_\__   _ Pé "6Q___ __
_—_ 8_8 ‹_‹  _—-   _ _ _ _-"
__ _"At its most simple, markup is simply adding
characters to a piece of information. —_
Ù_d ?_6_X_   __@… DèQ_____  _—
```

LISTING 2.2   MICROSOFT WORD RTF CODE

```
{\rtf1\ansi\ansicpg1252\uc1 \deff0\deflang1033
\deflangfe1033{\fonttbl{\f0\froman\fcharset0\fprq2
{\*\panose 02020603050405020304}Times New Roman;}
{\f2\fmodern\fcharset0
\fprq1{\*\panose 02070309020205020404}Courier New;}}
{\stylesheet{
\widctlpar\adjustright \fs20\cgrid \snext0 Normal;}
{\*\cs10 \additive Default Paragraph Font;}}{\info{\title
simple}{\edmins1}{\nofpages1}{\nofwords0}{\nofchars0}{\nofcharsws0}
{\vern89}}
```

```
\widowctrl\ftnbj\aenddoc\formshade\viewkind4\viewscale100
\pgbrdrhead\pgbrdrfoot \fet0\sectd \linex0\endnhere\sectdefaultcl
{\*\pnseclvl9\pnlcrm\pnstart1\pnindent720\pnhang{\pntxtb ()}
{\pntxta )}}
\pard\plain
\widctlpar\adjustright
\fs20\cgrid {At its most simple, markup is simply adding chara}
{cters to a piece of information.}
{\f2 \par }}
```

2

You could claim that WordPerfect and RTF codes aren't really markup as such, but they are. They certainly aren't what most people would think of as markup, and they aren't as readable as the markup you will encounter in the rest of this book, but they are just as much markup as any of the XML element tags you will encounter. These codes are in fact a form of *procedural* markup, which is used to drive processing by a particular application.

Obviously, there's no point in expecting WordPerfect code to be usable in Microsoft Word, and it would be just as unreasonable to expect WordPerfect to work with Microsoft RTF code (even though they can import each other's documents). These two examples of markup are proprietary, and any portability between applications should be considered a bonus rather than a requirement.

SGML is intended to be absolutely independent of any application. As pure markup, it often is independent, and the SGML code that you produce in one SGML package is directly portable to any other SGML application. (You might not be able to do much with it until you've added some local application code, but that's another story.) Life isn't quite that simple, though. Within the context of SGML, the word *application* has taken on a meaning of its own.

An SGML application consists of an SGML declaration and an SGML DTD. The SGML declaration establishes the basic rules for which characters are considered to be markup characters and which aren't. For example, the SGML declaration could specify that elements are marked up using asterisks instead of the familiar angle brackets (*book* instead of <book>). The DTD can then introduce all sorts of additional rules, such as *minimization* rules that allow markup to be deduced from the context, for example.

Going one step further, you could use the markup minimization rules and the element models defined in the DTD to create a document that contained only normal English words. When processed (parsed) by the SGML software, the beginnings and ends of the elements the document contained would be implied and treated as though they were explicitly identified. Compare Listing 2.3, which uses all the minimization techniques that SGML offers in as single document (it is highly unlikely that such extreme mini-mization would ever be used for real!) with Listing 2.4, which shows the same code without any minimization.

 Note

The code shown in these two listings is available, without line numbers, on this book's file download Web page. Go to http://www.mcp.com/ and click the Product Support link. On the Product Support page, enter this book's ISBN (1-57521-396-6) in the space provided under the heading Book Information and click the Search button.

LISTING 2.3   TAG MINIMIZATION

```
1:  <p>SGML uses markup to identify the
2:  <em/logical/ structure of a document
3:  rather than its <em/physical/ appearance.
4:  Tags can be minimized using
5:  <it/tag omission/,
6:  <it/short tags/,
7:  <it/ranked elements/ and,
6:  <it/data tags/.
7:  <p>and these can <b<em/all/</> be
8:  used at the same time.</p>
```

LISTING 2.4   THE UNMINIMIZED VERSION

```
1:  <section number="4"><p>SGML uses markup to identify the
2:  <em>logical</em> structure of a document
3:  rather than its <em>physical</em> appearance.
4:  Tags can be minimized using</p>
5:  <list type="unordered"><li><it>tag omission</it>,</li>
6:  <li><it>short tags</it>,</li>
7:  <li><it>ranked elements</it>, and</li>
6:  <li><it>data tags</it>.</li></list>
7:  <p>and these can <bold><em>all</em></bold> be
8:  used at the same time.</p></section>
```

Obviously, you need some pretty high-powered software to take advantage of these advanced features, not to mention the time and effort it takes to learn to write code like this. Also, considering the amount of divergence between SGML applications that this represents, even discounting the different elements that would be found in the separate applications, it's unlikely that SGML code from one application could be used in another application. It would be similar to converting from WordPerfect to Microsoft RTF, except that you'd be completely on your own.

In the face of this complexity, HTML takes a much simpler, more practical approach. Take a look at Listing 2.5, which shows some HTML that is intentionally full of "mistakes."

INPUT   **LISTING 2.5   BAD HTML CODE**

```
1: This is a pseudo HTML file. It has a less than (<) &amp;
2: a greater than (>) symbol in it but they aren't &hf;
3: <em>really</em> used as markup at all.
4: <p>
5: <P>All the browser really does is look for the tags
6: it recognizes, so that if it finds a tag that it isn't
7: setup to interpret like <point><font color="red">
8: this</font></point> one, it will simply ignore it.
```

If you enter this text and view it in a Web browser, you might see something like the display shown in Figure 2.1. (There is really no guarantee that your particular browser will show something that looks anything like this!)

OUTPUT

FIGURE 2.1

This is how Netscape displays the bad code from Listing 2.5.

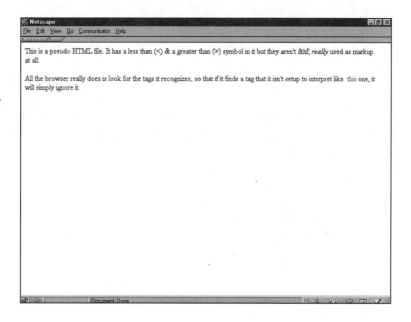

As you can see from Figure 2.1, the Web browser tries to make sense of the markup it sees by comparing it to the tags that it *expects* to see. If there is a match, you get the prescribed appearance. If there is no match but the markup was meant to be interpreted as a special character or as a range of text that required special treatment (such as the <point> tag), the browser ignores it. If the markup was possibly not markup at all (the freestanding < and > symbols), the browser treats them as character data and displays them as if they were normal characters.

SGML and HTML almost represent two extremes. There is a very vague continuum between content-oriented markup and presentation-based markup. (We are getting a little ahead of ourselves here because this delves into DTD development, which is covered much later in the book.) SGML's markup is generic. It is primarily intended to be *content-oriented*—it says nothing about how something should be displayed, but rather identifies the nature or purpose of pieces of text. It *can* be used for either or both.

NEW TERM There are a lot of names for the various types of markup, and little agreement about how to use those names correctly. The most technically accurate term for content-oriented markup is *semantic markup*, in which the names of elements describe what the elements are rather than what they do, what they are used for, or how they are to be processed. Digging deeper, however, formatting instructions can be considered a form of semantics, and so I shall keep to the possibly less accurate but more neutral term *content-oriented*.

HTML's markup, however, is a use of SGML that is purely presentation-based and really has little to do with the information contained in its documents. This isn't really HTML's fault, but rather a result of the loose way it is used. For example, if a rigid hierarchy was applied to the order in which levels of headings were used, so that an H2 always came after an H1 and they were all properly nested within each other, HTML could be quite content-oriented. If you went as far as adding classes and types to all the HTML elements in a file, you could actually turn it into a very rich piece of content-oriented markup. However, the real world is not so perfect, and any possible semantic value to be gained from organizing heading levels would be negated by their willful and random use solely on the grounds of their font size on a browser. If you doubt that HTML is purely presentational, however, ask yourself what kind of semantic information the <HR> (horizontal rule) element conveys.

So where does XML fit in? Well, somewhere in the middle. Remembering that XML is meant to be unambiguous and free of options, XML's rules for distinguishing between markup and content are very simple:

1. The start of markup is identified by either the less-than symbol (<) or the ampersand character (&).

2. Three other characters are also treated as markup characters: the greater-than symbol (>), the apostrophe or single quote, ('), and the (double) quotation mark (").

3. If you want to use any of the preceding special characters as normal characters, you must "escape" them by using the general entities that represent them. The replacements you should use are shown in Table 2.1.

New Term To *escape* a character means to conceal it from a subsequent software package or process. It is often used in computing terms to refer to prefixing certain characters in programming languages with a special character string to prevent them from being interpreted as special characters. Originally the ESC (escape) character string was used to prefix commands sent to the printer itself to control such things as the font or page size and distinguish the command strings from printable characters.

4. Everything that is not markup is content (character data).

TABLE 2.1 THE PREDEFINED GENERAL ENTITIES

Character	Replacement
&	&
'	'
>	>
<	<
"	"

The rules for interpretation are somewhat closer to HTML's than SGML's, but unlike HTML, markup characters aren't treated as normal characters if they can't be interpreted sensibly as markup. When these rules are combined with the other rules about the structure of XML documents, which you will learn later, the results are always predictable—even if they aren't always what you want.

What kind of markup do you use XML for? The answer is really quite logical. XML is *extensible*, and it is also a generic markup language, so it can be content-oriented, presentation-oriented, or both. But there's one major difference between how XML and HTML approach physical appearance: The final appearance of the XML code is not determined by the Web browser, but is specified by the attached style.

2

NEW TERM Like SGML (and unlike HTML), XML is not a markup language but a language for defining markup languages. Therefore, you can extend any XML markup language as the need arises, rather than having to always use the same fixed elements over and over again as you do with HTML. XML is truly *extensible*: It has no predefined list of elements, and you can name and use the elements according to the needs of the application.

A Sample XML Document

Listing 2.6 shows the XML code for a Web home page. This is a very simple example, but it contains all the important parts that you will find in nearly all XML documents.

As with all other listings in this book, the lines are numbered for ease of identification. The numbers are not part of the XML code, and you should leave them out if you type in this code yourself.

INPUT LISTING 2.6 XML CODE FOR A SIMPLE WWW HOME PAGE

```
1:  <?xml version="1.0"?>
2:  <home.page>
3:    <head>
4:      <title>
5:        My Home Page
6:      </title>
7:      <banner source="topbanner.gif"/>
8:    </head>
9:    <body>
10:     <main.title>
11:       Welcome to My Home Page
12:     </main.title>
13:     <rule/>
14:     <text>
15:       <para>
16:         Sorry, this home page is still
17:         under construction. Please come
18:         back soon!
19:       </para>
20:     </text>
21:   </body>
22:   <footer source="foot.gif"/>
23: </home.page>
```

OUTPUT Figure 2.2 shows what the code from Listing 2.6 looks like in Internet Explorer 5.

FIGURE 2.2

The XML code for a simple home page (in Internet Explorer 5).

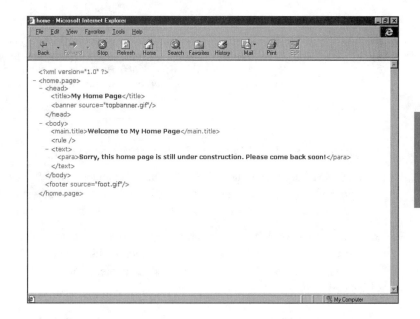

2

Note

The current versions of the leading Web browsers (the beta preview, release 2, of Internet Explorer 5 and the August 1998 build of the Mozilla source code) cannot display the XML code shown in Listing 2.6 without it being radically changed. The display in Figure 2.2 is less than optimal because IE5 needs either an XSL or a CSS style sheet to give the XML something other than the default rendering shown here. An explanation of how to do this is given on Day 12, "Viewing XML in Internet Explorer."

The XML Declaration (Line 1)

The XML declaration identifies what follows it as XML code. It states which version of the XML standard the code complies with, and it specifies whether the document can be treated as a standalone document (it can) or whether a DTD must also be retrieved in order to make full sense of the contents.

The XML declaration is in fact a *processing instruction* (identified by the ? at its start and end), but for now it's enough to just treat it as a standard declaration.

Tip The XML declaration is not strictly compulsory (the fact that the document is XML code can also be announced by the Web server in the same way that is often done for HTML documents). However, you should get into the habit of including such a declaration because it increases the portability of your code.

The Root Element (Lines 2 through 23)

Each XML document must have only one root element, and all the other elements must be completely enclosed in that element. Line 2 identifies the start of the <home.page> element (the start tag), and line 23 identifies the end of the element (the end tag).

Note that unlike HTML, in which a <P> tag might often be used as a sort of formatting instruction to insert a blank line between paragraphs of text, in XML an element normally consists of three things: a start tag, content (either text or other elements), and an end tag.

Note An XML element doesn't always have content. Empty elements, such as the IMG element in HTML that simply points to an external graphics file through its SRC attribute, obviously have no content. An empty element might have an end tag, but it can have a special form of start tag that allows an explicit end tag to be omitted.

Also note that the name you use in the element start tag must exactly match the name you use in the end tag. If you want to use an odd combination of cases to increase the legibility of long names (for example, ThisIsAnIntelligibleName), you must be very careful to exactly match the case usage in both the opening and the closing tag.

Tip XML is case sensitive, recognizing the difference between uppercase letters (A–Z) and lowercase letters (a–z). In applications that aren't case sensitive, mixed-case characters are usually converted—*folded* into one case or the other. The ASCII character set usually folds to uppercase characters. Unicode usually folds to lowercase characters. XML has to account for this, and for the fact that it might have to deal with languages in which the case folding is uncertain. Therefore, XML defaults to lowercase (and the XML declaration also has to be in lowercase). It is a good idea to keep all your markup in lowercase too, even though this can reduce the readability of your code.

An Empty Element (Line 13)

Empty elements are a special case in XML. In SGML and HTML, it is obvious from the DTD's definition of an empty element that it is empty and has no comment. XML, in keeping with its developers' design goals, requires you to be much more explicit. Indeed, you might not use a DTD at all, so it could be hard to decide whether an element is or should be empty. Therefore, empty elements have to be very clearly identified as such. To do so, there is a special empty tag close delimiter, />, as in the following:

```
<empty_element/>
```

To maintain a certain degree of backward-compatibility with SGML (until such time as the SGML standard is updated to allow the use of empty-tag close delimiters), and to make the conversion of existing SGML and HTML code into XML a little easier (a process called *normalization*, which adds end tags to all elements and is supported by a lot of SGML tools), you can use an end tag instead of the special empty tag close delimiter. The element declaration

```
<graphic source="file.gif"/>
```

is therefore interchangeable with

```
<graphic source="file.gif"></graphic>
```

Attributes (Lines 7 and 22)

Element tags can include one or more optional or mandatory attributes that give further information about the elements they delimit.

Attributes can only be specified in the element start tag. The syntax for specifying an attribute is

```
<element.type.name attribute.name="attribute.value">
```

If elements were nouns, attributes would be adjectives. We could therefore say

```
<fruit taste="sharp">
```

or even

```
<problem size="huge" cause="unknown" solution="run.away">
```

An attribute can only be specified in an element start tag.

In direct contrast to SGML and HTML, in which multiple declarations are considered to be fatal errors, XML deals with multiple declarations of attributes in a unique manner. If an element appears once with one set of attributes and then appears again with a different set of attributes, the two sets of attributes are merged. The first declaration of an attribute for a particular element is the only one that counts, and any other declarations are ignored. The XML processor might warn you about the appearance of multiple declarations, but it is not required to do so and processing can continue as normal.

Note

An XML processor is a software package, library, or module that is used to read XML documents. The XML processor makes it possible for an XML application, such as a formatting engine or a viewer, to access the structure and content of an XML document.

Logical Structure

In the earlier discussion of HTML markup, you learned about the conceptual differences in markup between XML (and SGML) and HTML. HTML uses its tags as if they were style switches. The start tag turns a feature on, such as underlining, and an end tag turns it off again. XML uses its start tags and end tags as containers. Together, the start tag, the content, and the end tag all form a single element. Elements are the building bricks out of which an XML document is assembled. Each XML document must have only one root element, and all the other elements must be *perfectly nested* inside that element. This means that if an element contains other elements, those elements must be completely enclosed within that element.

Let's look at what this means for the simple example in Listing 2.6. If you sketch out the structure of the elements in this XML document, you'll obtain the kind of tree structure of elements shown in Figure 2.3.

As you can see from Figure 2.3, the document has a sort of tree-like structure, with the root element (<home.page>) at the top of the tree (or the base, depending on how you look at it). All the elements that are inside this element are neatly contained within each other. An XML document must contain one and only one root element, and there must not be any elements that are either partially or completely outside, before or after, that element.

To make it easier to refer to the relationships between elements and to elements with respect to other elements, you could say that an element is the *parent* of the elements that it contains. The elements that are inside an element are called its *children*. Elements that share the same parent element are called *siblings*.

In the simple example shown in Figure 2.3, <home.page> is the parent of all the other elements, <text> is the parent of <para>, <title> is a child of <head>, and <title> and <banner> are siblings. Going down the element tree, each child element must be fully contained within its parent element. Sibling elements may not overlap.

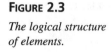

FIGURE 2.3

The logical structure of elements.

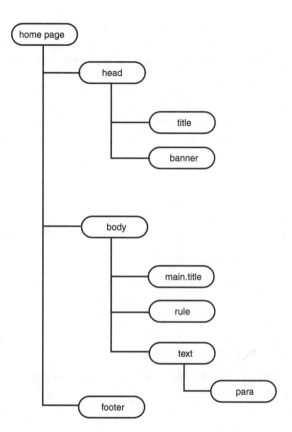

2

The arrangement of the elements in an XML document is called the *logical structure*. As you will see next, an XML document also has a physical structure. In order to be usable (technically, in order to be *well-formed*), the logical and physical structure of an XML document must be *synchronous*; they must be completely and properly nested inside each other.

Physical Structure

One of the key concepts in XML is that of the *entity*. To really understand XML, you need to understand what entities are. There are various types of entities, and the entities are far more important than the elements in determining how the XML processor deals with the XML code. You will learn about entities in some detail later, but for now it is enough to think of an entity as a physical storage unit. It's an object, although in fact most entities can usually be thought of as being separate computer files.

NEW TERM   An *entity* is essentially a unit of information, but in the official terms of the
            XML language specification, an entity is a *storage object*. This object might be
an element or an XML ENTITY object (normally an unparsed external file).

The main entity that you work with all the time, although you will hardly ever even
notice that it's there, is the document entity. As you have seen, this document (or root)
entity is logically divided into elements. (There are other logical components covered
later, but for now it is enough to concentrate on the elements.)

Entities can reference other entities and can cause them to be included in the XML document. Surprisingly enough, you've already seen some entities. The entities listed in Table
2.1 that you used to escape markup characters in normal text are in fact internal entities,
but more on those later. For now, let's examine the basic reference to a graphics file that
is common in HTML Web pages, and the derivative example in Listing 2.6 (line 7):

```
<banner source="topbanner.gif"/>
```

The banner element's source attribute refers to an external entity (not contained in the
current document), which is an external graphics file. If this were HTML code, the
graphic would appear on your Web browser at this point in the document. In XML terms,
this graphics file is called an *unparsed entity*; the XML processor ignores the content of
the entity and passes it on to the application.

XML is a little stricter than HTML about the inclusion of external graphics files. As you
will learn later, XML allows you to specify the *notation* or format that the graphic is in,
but it can also include more than just a simple graphic. This is where a lot of problems
start!

XML can include entities that contain XML code, text, HTML code—almost anything.
Depending on how the referenced entity is identified, if it too was a piece of XML code,
it could be processed (parsed) by the XML processor as if that XML code had been in
the original document (root entity) and not in an external file. To further complicate matters, that XML entity could then reference another entity, and so on to infinity. Apart
from the practical problems that this might cause (just imagine trying to open a small
document and getting several thousand linked pages!), this creates special problems
when the included entities also contain markup.

Just as the arrangement of the elements gives a logical structure, so the arrangement of
the entities gives a physical structure. Now, suppose that an included entity also contains
elements. This doesn't seem like such a problem on the surface, but it certainly does
become a problem if the included entity contains elements with the same element type
names as elements in the root (or other) entities, and if it is important to the application
to distinguish the differences. This problem is solved by a mechanism called *namespaces*
that will be discussed later on Day 7, "Developing Advanced DTDs."

Besides element conflicts, suppose that you had opened an element in the root entity (your XML document) and referenced an external entity. Again, not a problem; it's a normal thing to do. But suppose that the external entity contained an end tag for the element you just opened. Suddenly your whole logical structure would be ruined.

To limit the occurrence of these problems, the logical and physical structures of XML entities must be synchronous; logical entities cannot cross physical entity boundaries, and physical entities must be fully enclosed (nested) within logical entities. Sometimes it can be hard to work out whether this is the case, and when it *isn't* the case, it can cause a lot of problems. This requirement is unique to XML and for authors coming from either SGML or HTML. It is probably the most difficult point to grasp and the most common source of mistakes.

2

Summary

This chapter looked at an XML document as an object constructed of various components. You've learned about markup and the distinction that XML makes between markup and character data. You have also learned how XML documents have both a logical and a physical structure, and you've seen the connection between these and XML's elements and entities.

Q&A

Q Why is XML case sensitive, whereas SGML and HTML are not?

A XML is designed to work with applications that might not be case sensitive and in which the case folding (the conversion to just one case) cannot be predicted. Rather than make dangerous assumptions, XML takes the safest route and opts for case sensitivity.

Q Why are Web browsers so loose in interpreting markup?

A This was a conscious decision aimed at making the Web easy to use. Rather than enforce a lot of rules concerning HTML code, the decision was made to accept everything and ignore anything that can't be interpreted.

Q Why doesn't XML allow tag minimization?

A XML processors are meant to be simple to create (and consequently inexpensive and fast). This means that they must not be asked to perform complicated processing, such as storing their current context and then looking ahead to see where the current element ends. Therefore, tagging has to be 100 percent explicit, thereby avoiding the processing overhead created by tag minimization.

Q What purpose do the predefined entities serve?

A Officially, they give you an easy way to escape XML delimiters. Unofficially, they mean you have no excuse for trying to use the delimiter characters as normal characters. Generally, they make it simpler for an XML processor because the delimiters can always be treated as delimiters and never as normal characters (although there are a few exceptions).

Q Why must elements be properly nested?

A Again, this is a question of avoiding processing overhead. If the XML processor has to remember which elements have been opened but not yet closed, it will have to store this information somewhere. This means memory (or disk) storage has to be used, which means more processing, more complexity, and less speed. This is one of many examples in XML in which a bit of (enforced) coding discipline can save a lot of programming effort.

Exercises

1. Mark up the following email message to identify its information content:

   ```
   From: Simon North <north@synopsys.com>
   To: Nick <sintac@xs4all.nl>
   Subject: Hi
   Hi Nick, this is just a quick message
   to say I got the material. Thanks.
   ```

2. Now mark up the same message to identify its appearance:

   ```
   From: Simon North <north@synopsys.com>
   To: Nick <sintac@xs4all.nl>
   Subject: Hi
   Hi Nick, this is just a quick message
   to say I got the material. Thanks.
   ```

3. Compare your two marked-up messages. Give two reasons why one type of markup could be more useful than the other.

DAY 3

Using XML Markup

Yesterday, in "Anatomy of an XML Document," you learned about the main features of XML markup for elements and entities. Today's chapter will expand on this, and you'll also learn about the following:

- Attributes
- Entity references and how to use them as shortcuts
- How to include comments in your code
- What CDATA sections are and how they are used
- Processing instructions

Markup Delimiters

Yesterday you learned about XML's markup characters in fairly general terms. Now it's time to get a little more technical and examine the exact details of XML's markup declarations.

Table 3.1 identifies the parts of XML's element tags. When the details get a bit more technical, it will be helpful if you're familiar with these parts. (Although you don't need to commit them to memory!)

TABLE 3.1 THE PARTS OF AN ELEMENT TAG

Symbol	Description
<	Start tag open delimiter
</	End tag open delimiter
foo	Element name
>	Tag close delimiter
/>	Empty tag close delimiter

It is worth remembering that, whereas HTML simply relies on recognizing prepro-grammed tags, XML is triggered by these specific parts of the element tags, and the XML processor's behavior and what it expects to see next are directly controlled by the named symbols.

Element Markup

XML is concerned with element markup. This might sound like an obvious point to make, but it is worth repeating because it indicates a deeply rooted conceptual difference between XML as a markup language and an arbitrary tag language. As you have already seen, HTML often tends toward being a tag language rather than a markup language. This is a direct consequence of Web browsers being so intentionally lenient in accepting bad markup.

Instead of XML's tags being markers that indicate where a style should change or a new line should begin, XML's element markup is composed of three parts: a start tag, the contents, and the end tag. This is shown in Table 3.2. The start tag and end tag should be treated like wrappers, and when you think of an element, you should have a mental picture of a piece of text with both tags in place.

TABLE 3.2 THE PARTS OF AN ELEMENT

Symbol	Name	Description
<foo>	Start tag	At the start of an element, the opening tag
text	Content	In the middle of an element, its content
</foo>	End tag	At the end of an element, the closing tag

Note that the element name that appears in the start tag must be exactly the same as the name that appears in the end tag. For example, the following would be wrong:

```
<simple.element>This element won't close!</simple.Element>
```

Caution The first versions of XML, before it became a full-blown proposal, were not case sensitive. There are still some XML software packages in circulation that are not case sensitive and will not signal an error if you mix up cases. For conformity with XML requirements, you must be careful to keep your use of upper- and lowercase consistent.

Attribute Markup

As you learned yesterday, attributes are used to attach information to the information contained in an element. The general form for using an attribute is

```
<!element.name property="value">
```

or

```
<!element.name property='value'>
```

The technical description of the markup of this attribute specification is given in Table 3.3.

TABLE 3.3 SPECIFYING AN ATTRIBUTE

Symbol	Description
<	Start tag open delimiter
element.name	Element name
property	Attribute name
=	Value indicator
"	Literal string delimiter
'	Alternative literal string delimiter
value	Value of the attribute
>	Start tag close delimiter

Note that an attribute value must be enclosed in quotation marks. You can use either single quotes (`<lie size='big'>`) or double quotes (`<lie size="massive">`), but you cannot mix the two in the same specification.

3

When you are working without a DTD (none of the XML code shown in today's chapter requires you to associate a DTD with the XML document), you can simply specify the attribute and its value when you use the element for the first time, as shown in Listing 3.1. When you specify attributes for the same element more than once (as in Lines 3 and 4 of Listing 3.1), the specifications are simply merged.

INPUT   LISTING 3.1   SPECIFYING ATTRIBUTES

```
1: <?xml version="1.0"?>
2: <home.page>
3:  <para number="first">This is the first paragraph.</para>
4:  <para number='second' color="red">This is
5:   the second paragraph.</para>
6:  </home.page>
```

ANALYSIS When the XML processor encounters line 3, it will record the fact that a para element has a number attribute. (Remember that this is in the absence of a DTD, which would explicitly declare what attributes a para element has.) Then, when it encounters line 4, it will record the fact that a para element also has a color attribute.

There is one attribute that is reserved for XML's own use—the xml:lang attribute. This attribute is reserved to identify the human language in which the element was written. The value of the attribute is one of the ISO 639 country codes; some of the most common language codes are shown in Table 3.4.

TABLE 3.4   COMMON ISO 639 LANGUAGE CODES

Code	Language
ar	Arabic
ch	Chinese
de	German
en	English
es	Spanish
fr	French
gr	Greek
it	Italian
ja	Japanese
nl	Dutch
pt	Portugese
ru	Russian

When there are several versions of a language, such as British and American English, the language code can be followed by a hyphen (-) and one of the ISO 3166 country codes. Some of the most common country codes are shown in Table 3.5. If you have spent much time on the Internet, you may well recognize these as the same codes that are used in email addresses and URLs. An element written in American English could be identified like this (note the cases; the language code is in lowercase and the country code is in uppercase):

```
<para xml:lang="en-US">My country 'tis of thee.</para>
```

TABLE 3.5   COMMON ISO 3166 COUNTRY CODES

Code	Country
AT	Austria
BE	Belgium
CA	Canada
CN	China
DE	Germany
DK	Denmark
EN	England
ES	Spain
FR	France
GR	Greece
IT	Italy
JA	Japan
NL	The Netherlands
PT	Portugal
RU	Russia
US	United States

The codes given in Tables 3.4 and 3.5 are not complete or exhaustive. There is another coding scheme registered by the Internet Assigned Numbers Authority (IANA), which is defined in RFC 1766. And if you really need to, you can devise your own language code. User-defined codes must be prefixed with the string x-, in which case you could declare an element as being in "computer geek" language like this:

```
<para xml:lang="x-cg">Do you grok this code?</para>
```

Naming Rules

So far you've learned about the markup used for elements and attributes, and all the descriptions mention that these markup objects have names. XML has certain specific rules governing which names you can use for its markup objects.

XML's naming rules are as follows:

- A name consists of at least one letter: a to z, or A to Z.
- If the name consists of more than one character, it may start with an underscore (_) or a colon (:). (Technically, there wouldn't be anything stopping you having an element called <_>, but that would not be very helpful.)
- The initial letter (or underscore) can be followed by one or more letters, digits, hyphens, underscores, full stops, and combining characters, extender characters, and ignorable characters. (These last three classes of characters are taken from the Unicode character set and include some of the special Unicode character symbols and accents. For a full list, refer to the XML recommendation online at http://www.w3.org/XML/REC-xml.)

Tip

> The World Wide Web Consortium (W3C) regularly reorganizes its Web site, and the URLs for recommendations, notes, and working drafts change quite often. When you visit their Web site, you will find a pointer to the URL Minder service. This free service is one of the many wonders of the Web. By registering a Web page—any Web page—you will automatically be sent an email message if anything on that page changes. This is an excellent way to keep track of any new developments.

Note that spaces and tabs are not allowed in element names (<one two> would be interpreted as two separate names), and the only punctuation signs allowed are the hyphen (-) and full stop (.).

Caution

> If you spend any time writing code in any other language (even Java or JavaScript), it's easy to get into the habit of using an underscore character (_) to separate long names into sensible chunks, as in: This_is_a_Long_Name. This use of underscores is illegal in XML. You would have to rewrite this as This.is.a.Long.Name.

There is no rule that says your choice of a name needs to make sense. As long as you obey the naming rules, you can call XML objects whatever you like and the names can be as long and meaningless as you like. However, one of the major benefits of using XML in the first place is that it is self-describing. If you have elements such as <thingy>, <whatever>, and <huh>, you're defeating the whole issue. Try to choose names that are at least slightly suggestive of the nature or purpose of the object. Don't forget that one of the XML's aims is to be readable by users. Being readable is one thing, but it also helps if they also make sense.

Comments

No self-respecting language, whether it's a programming language or a markup language, could hold its head up without allowing comments to be added to the code. From a maintenance point of view, it's also pretty important to have a lasting record of why you did particular things. The best way to document your code is to include the explanation with the code by using comments.

In keeping with the design constraint of keeping XML simple, its comment facilities are also simple. Comments have the form

```
<!-- this is comment text -->
```

Caution | The comment start tag (<!--) and end tag (-->) must be used exactly as they are shown here. Inserting spaces or any other characters into these strings can lead to the tags, or anything inside the comment, mistakenly being interpreted by the XML processor as markup.

Provided that you use the comment start tag and end tag correctly, everything in the comment text will be completely ignored by the XML processor. The following comment is therefore quite safe:

```
<!-- These are the declarations for the <title> and <body> -->
```

There is only one restriction on what you can place in your comment text: the string -- is not allowed. This keeps XML backward-compatible with SGML. (The string --> will obviously end the comment.)

Comments can be placed anywhere in an XML document *outside* other markup. The following is therefore allowed:

```
<para>This is simple <!-- So everyone tells me --> to do.</para>
```

while this is not allowed:

```
<para <!-- blatant lie --> >This is simple to do.</para>
```

Character References

Unlike SGML (and, as a result, unlike HTML), which is very much ASCII-based, XML was developed right from the start to support languages other than English. XML therefore has far better support for accented and foreign language characters than either SGML or HTML.

In HTML, you can always enter the code for the foreign language character you want (è would be è, i would be í, and û would be û). As you will see later in this chapter, these codes are in fact entity references. The abbreviations egrave, iacute, and ucirc are taken from the ISO 8859/1 character set (SGML's character set), which is derived from the ISO/IEC 646 version of the ASCII alphabet (the first 128 characters). ISO 8859/1 is also the basis for the Microsoft Windows fonts.

Although these character entity references will allow you to deal with most European and Scandinavian languages, things would come to a sudden stop if you tried to display or write in an Asian or Middle Eastern language such as Japanese, Hindi, or Arabic. However, XML is based on Unicode and the even more extensive ISO/IEC 10646 standards (which even allow the use of Chinese characters). You needn't concern yourself too much with these character sets now (or not at all if you are only interested in publishing Western languages on the Web), but we will return to this topic later on.

The most important thing you need to know about these exotic characters is that you can still enter them even if your keyboard doesn't support them. You do this by entering a character reference.

A character reference consists of the string &#, followed by the number of the character in the ISO/IEC 10646 alphabet and terminated by a semicolon (;). The character number may be either a decimal number, in which case you enter the number as-is, or in hexadecimal form, in which case you must precede the number with the letter x, such as x12ABC. For example, the character reference for the copyright symbol (©)—written in HTML as ©—is © (in decimal) or © (in hexadecimal).

Predefined Entities

Character references allow you to enter characters that you might not be able to enter from your keyboard. A variation on this theme is the set of *predefined entities*. These are characters that you can enter normally, but you shouldn't because they can easily be mistaken for markup characters. To refresh your memory, the set of predefined entities is shown in Table 3.6.

TABLE 3.6 THE PREDEFINED ENTITIES

Character	Replacement
&	& or &#38;
'	' or '
>	> or >
<	< or &#60;
"	" or "

You can enter a named entity to represent the character, such as ', or you can enter a character reference, such as '. The character references for the ampersand (&) and the less-than (<) character are special cases, however, so the character references are double-escaped. The reasons for this will be explained in the following section.

Entity References

As you remember from yesterday's discussion of the anatomy of an XML document, entities are normally external objects such as graphics files that are meant to be included in the document. To reference these external entities, you must have a DTD for your XML document. You will learn about these entities when you learn about DTDs, but there is one other type of entity that you can use already, called an *internal entity*. It can save you a lot of unnecessary typing.

Internal entities look very much like character references, but with one vitally important difference—you must declare an internal entity before you can use it.

Entity Declarations

The declaration of an internal entity has this form:

```
<!ENTITY name "replacement text">
```

Now, every time the string &name; appears in your XML code, the XML processor will automatically replace it with the replacement text (which can be just as long as you like). Judiciously used, entity references can save you a lot of typing.

The Benefits of Entities

You can almost think of an entity reference as a sort of macro. But whatever you call it, it can be a real time-saver when there is a piece of text that you want to use several times, or even if you want to use some kind of template text.

Consider the example shown in Listing 3.2, in which a copyright statement is used as an entity reference.

INPUT   LISTING 3.2   USING AN INTERNAL ENTITY

```
1:   <?xml version="1.0"?>
2:   <home.page>
3:     <head><title>Title Page</title></head>
4:     <body> <h1>The Title Page</h1>
5:       <para>(c) 1998, &rights;</para>
6:     </body>
7:   </home.page>
```

Given the following declaration for the rights entity:

```
<!ENTITY rights "All rights reserved. No part of this book, including
interior design, cover design, and icons, may be reproduced or transmitted
in any form, by any means (electronic, photocopying, recording, or
otherwise) without the prior permission of the publishers.">
```

This would result in the following substitution being made in line 5 of Listing 3.2:

OUTPUT
```
<para>(c) 1998, All rights reserved. No part of this book, including
interior design, cover design, and icons, may be reproduced or
transmitted in any form, by any means (electronic, photocopying,
recording, or otherwise) without the prior permission of the publishers.>
```

ANALYSIS   Using an entity reference in this way, you would only have to enter the text once, in the entity declaration, instead of having to search for and change every occurrence of the string in the text. Used in this way, entity references can simplify the task of creating and maintaining XML documents. On Day 8, "XML Objects: Exploiting Entities," you will learn how to expand this feature to use external entities as a sort of boilerplate text facility, enabling you to declare these text entities in a common document that can be accessed by any number of other documents.

Some of the Dangers of Using Entities

You've seen how handy internal entity references can be as a sort of shorthand for entering pieces of text, and as a means of dealing with variable content. Obviously, with a little thought and advance preparation, entity references can save you a lot of time and
effort later on.

Naturally, a feature this handy raises a very simple question: "Could I use this to insert
markup too?" It's an attractive idea and a natural thing to want to do. Can you put
markup inside the replacement text? Well, yes you can… but it's subject to a few restrictions, and you need to think it out quite carefully beforehand to avoid some unpleasant
surprises.

The first thing you must remember is that XML will process the contents of the entity
replacement text when it expands the entity reference. This means that you must not just
escape any markup characters in the replacement text; you must *double escape* the characters. Consider this simple example:

```
<!ENTITY dangerous "Black &#38; White">
```

When the XML processor sees the entity reference &dangerous; in the XML document,
it will immediately expand (dereference) the predefined entity before it inserts the
replacement text. This XML code seems harmless enough:

```
<text>This is not a &dangerous; choice.</text>
```

But let's look at what happens, step by step:

1. The XML processor sees the entity reference &dangerous; and looks for the
   replacement text.
2. Finding `Black &#38; White`, the XML processor dereferences this to `Black &
   White`.
3. The XML processor inserts the replacement text, and the resulting XML code is
   ```
   <text>This is not a Black & White choice.</text>
   ```
4. The XML processor then tries to parse the ampersand and reports an error because
   & has not been declared as an entity.

Avoiding the Pitfalls

You've seen some of the problems that entity references can create when their contents
are dereferenced. At worst, they can make a complete mess of your XML code. Of
course, there's a way to avoid these problems—double escape any markup contained in
the replacement text, like this:

```
<!ENTITY safe "Harry &#38;#38; Fred &amp;amp; Joe">
```

When the XML processor sees the entity reference &safe; in this XML document:

```
<text>The job was left to &safe; to fix.</text>
```

The expansion will still leave you with valid code. Let's see what happens as the XML processor dereferences the entity reference:

1. The XML processor sees the entity reference &safe; and looks for the replacement text.

2. Finding "Harry &#38; Fred &amp; Joe">, the XML processor dereferences this to Harry & Fred & Joe.

3. The XML processor inserts the replacement text, and the resulting XML code is

   ```
         <text>The job was left to Harry &#38; Fred &amp; Joe to
   ➥finish.</text>
   ```

4. The XML processor then parses the resulting code, sees the entity reference &, and dereferences that to produce

   ```
         <text>The job was left to Harry & Fred & Joe to
   ➥finish.</text>
   ```

As you can see from these examples, you can escape the markup by using either the entity reference form (in the example, &) or the character reference form (&) of the predefined entity.

Synchronous Structures

Other than these problems, there is one very important restriction on using markup in entities. On Day 2, "Anatomy of an XML Document," you learned that the logical and physical structures in the XML document must be synchronous.

At the time, the restriction might not have made too much sense because it's difficult to imagine the two structures *not* being synchronous. Well, here's an example of the two structures becoming asynchronous: The logical structure is composed of the elements in the XML document and in the replacement text. The physical structure is composed of the document entity (the root entity of the XML document containing the entity reference) and the internal entity (the replacement text). The two objects are discrete physical entities as far as XML is concerned, even though in this case they are actually in the same file. For the two structures to be synchronous, any element that is inside the replacement text must start and finish inside the replacement text (in other words, inside the entity).

The following would be allowed:

```
<!ENTITY safe "&#38#60;emph&#62;Harry&#38#60;/emph&#62; and Joe">
<text>The job was left to &safe; to finish.</text>
```

because the dereferenced entity reference would yield this:

```
<text>The job was left to <emph>Harry</emph> and Joe to finish.</text>
```

The following could create a lot of problems, however:

```
<!ENTITY unsafe ""&#38#60;emph&#62;Harry and Joe">
<text>The job was left to &safe;</emph> to finish.</text>
```

even though, when the entity reference has been dereferenced, the resulting markup would actually be quite legal:

```
<text>The job was left to <emph>Harry and Joe</emph> to finish.</text>
```

Although we are still talking about *internal* entities, which are completely within our control, the restriction is really pretty logical. The same dereferencing mechanism applies for external entities as well as internal entities and, bearing in mind that one of XML's design goals is to be used easily on the Web, we have absolutely no control over what is contained in external entities. XML's developers could have made a distinction between internal and external entities, but this would go against two more of XML's basic design goals—simplicity and clarity.

Where to Declare Entities

You have learned what an internal entity reference looks like, and you've seen some of the benefits and drawbacks of using entity references. Before we move on to something else, you still need to learn *where* to put the entity declarations.

Entity references are normally only allowed in the DTD that accompanies the XML document. The declarations of element structures and entities are in fact the only reason for having a DTD at all. You will learn all about DTDs in detail later on; for now, all you need to know is illustrated in Listing 3.3.

INPUT   **LISTING 3.3**   **DECLARING AN INTERNAL ENTITY**

```
1:  <?xml version="1.0"?>
2:  <!DOCTYPE home.page [
3:    <!ENTITY shortcut "This is the replacement text.">
4:  ]>
5:  <home.page>
```

ANALYSIS Line 1 of Listing 3.3 is the now-familiar XML declaration. Line 2 is a document type declaration. This is the line that will later be used to make the association between the XML document and the DTD that describes its structure.

NEW TERM The *document type declaration* is the XML statement that declares what type of XML document follows and identifies the document type definition (DTD), which contains the description of the allowed structure of this type of document. (It is quite easy to confuse these two terms.)

The document type declaration takes this form:

```
<!DOCTYPE name external.pointer [ internal.subset ]>
```

where `external.pointer` points to a separate file that contains the *external subset* of the DTD. Don't worry too much about this for now; the trick is that you can leave this out and concentrate on the *internal subset* of the DTD. The declaration you will need, then, looks like this:

```
<!DOCTYPE name [ internal.subset ]>
```

In this internal subset you can declare as many elements, attributes, and entities as you like without having an external DTD at all.

As you will discover later, there are all sorts of other tricks you can do with the internal DTD subset. Anything you put in the internal subset takes precedence over anything in an external subset. For example, you can declare a default set of global values for a whole suite of XML documents and then override the global values in an individual XML document when you want to, but that is another story.

Before we leave the subject of DTDs altogether, there is one last thing that you should get into the habit of doing, even if it doesn't make much sense at this point. Although you aren't using an external DTD yet, if and when you do, the name that you give to the document type must be the same as the name of the root element in the XML document. This is shown in Listing 3.3, where the document type name (`home.page` on line 2) is the same as the root (first) element name (line 5). This isn't a requirement when there isn't an external DTD, but it is still a good habit to get into.

CDATA Sections

You have learned how to escape markup characters by using the predefined entities and character references. Replacing every markup character in a piece of text could be a long and tedious process. Besides, there might be cases when you want to keep all those characters exactly as they are (like when you're sending the XML code on for further processing by a different application).

The way to do this is to use a CDATA (character data) section, like this:

```
<![CDATA[This is the text < 5 lines > that I want the &!%# XML processor
to leave alone!]]>
```

Nothing, absolutely nothing, that appears between the opening tag (`<![CDATA[`) and the closing tag (`]]>`) will be recognized as markup. You do not need to escape any markup characters in a CDATA section. (In fact, you can't anyway because the escape itself won't be recognized.) The only thing that will be recognized is the end-of-section tag (`]]>`), so obviously this string cannot be included in a CDATA section. As a logical consequence of this, you cannot put one CDATA section inside another.

Caution

Using markup characters in a CDATA section like this in an XML document, which is built around markup, rather goes against the grain. An XML processor is intended to prevent you from breaking this unwritten rule, and it's very unforgiving of any mistakes. The opening string and closing string of a CDATA section must be used exactly as it is shown here. The slightest deviation, a tab or a space character somewhere inside one of the strings, will be punished immediately. The content of the CDATA section will either be treated as markup, or the rest of your document (up to the next CDATA section that is closed properly) will be treated as part of the CDATA section and all the markup will be ignored. You have been warned!

3

CDATA sections are one of the recommended ways to embed application code (JavaScript, VBasic code, Perl code, and so on) in your XML code. You could place the embedded code in comments, as is often done in HTML documents, but the XML processor is not required to pass the comment text to an application. Therefore, there's always the risk that the contents of comments will be stripped out before the application sees them.

Even though it is quite legal to declare your own type of element to contain the embedded code (like the `<script>` element in HTML 4), you'd be implicitly breaking the spirit of generic markup. Nor would it prove to be much help if your embedded code contained characters that could be interpreted as markup, because the contents of these elements would be parsed in the normal way by the XML processor.

The other way to embed code, and probably the best way, is by using processing instructions.

Processing Instructions

Probably without even noticing it, you have already seen processing instructions. The XML declaration at the start of every XML document (or at least it *should* be there) is a processing instruction:

```
<?xml version="1.0"?>
```

XML markup is meant to be generic, and in a perfect world it would be. However, there will always be times when you need to enter instructions for specific applications. One of these applications could be a script interpreter, and so, like CDATA sections, processing instructions are good places to put embedded code. While CDATA sections are purely a way of avoiding characters being interpreted as markup, better still, processing instructions can be targeted to your application. For example, this would allow you to have two or more sets of embedded script code, intended for different processors or interpreters, and identify them separately, as shown in Listing 3.4.

LISTING 3.4   EMBEDDING CODE IN PROCESSING INSTRUCTIONS

```
1:   <para>This is text containing two
2:   processing instructions,
3:     <?javascript I can put whatever I like here?>
4:     <?perl And I can put whatever I like here too?>
5:   one for each interpreter.</para>
```

There are no restrictions on the content of the processing instructions (the XML processor doesn't even consider the content to be part of the document's character data), but the name that you choose must comply with XML's naming rules.

Summary

In this chapter you learned the details of XML's markup language. You also learned how to declare and use internal entities, as well as some of the benefits and dangers of using them. You were introduced to character references for entering characters not available on your keyboard, and you saw how you can use the characters that are normally reserved for markup in your character data by using character references and the predefined entities.

To conclude, you learned how to use comments and CDATA sections to hide text that could be interpreted as markup by the XML processor, and how you can extend this by using processing instructions to pass code through for processing by other applications.

Q&A

Q **Which of these element names is valid and which is not?**

a) `<para 1>`

b) `<para,1>`

c) `<para.1>`

d) `<Pa3A1>`

e) `<para!>`

A Only c and d are legal; a contains a space, b contains a comma, and e contains an exclamation mark.

Q **What is wrong with the following code fragment?**

```
<para size="12pt">'twas brillig and
the slithey toves <!-- I've no idea
 what these are --> did gyre and gymble
 in the wabe.</para>
```

A Comments may not be placed inside elements. They must be outside other markup.

Q **Where do you declare entities?**

A You can declare entities inside either the internal subset or the external subset of the DTD. If you have an external DTD, you will have to create a complete DTD. If you only need the entities and nothing else, you can get away with an internal DTD subset. Entity references in XML documents that have external DTD subsets are only replaced when the document is validated.

Q **Why do I need an XML declaration? It should be obvious that this is XML code.**

A Strictly speaking, you do not need an XML declaration. XML has also been approved as a MIME type, which means that if you add the correct MIME header (`xml/text` or `xml/application`), a Web server can explicitly identify the data that follows as being an XML document, regardless of what the document itself says. (MIME, or Multipurpose Internet Mail Extensions, is an Internet standard for the transmission of data of any type via electronic mail. It defines the way messages are formatted and constructed, can indicate the type and nature of the contents of a message, and preserves international character set information. MIME types are used by Web servers to identify the data contained in a response to a retrieval request.)

3

The XML declaration is not compulsory for practical reasons; SGML and HTML code can often be converted easily into perfect XML code (if it isn't already). If the XML declaration was compulsory, this wouldn't be possible.

Q Can I use entities in attribute values as well as in content? This would allow me to parameterize elements.

A Yes and no. You can use entity references in attribute values, but an entity cannot be the attribute value. There are strict rules on where entities can be used and when they are recognized. Sometimes they are only recognized when the XML document is validated. For details, see the XML recommendation itself (`http://www.w3.org/XML/REC-xml`).

Q Can I put binary data in a CDATA section?

A Technically there's nothing stopping you, even though it's really a character data section. Because the XML processor doesn't consider the contents of a CDATA section to be part of the document's character data, it will never know or care what you put in there. However, you would have to live with the increase in file size and all the transportation problems that would imply. Ultimately, it would be a shame to jeopardize the portability of your XML documents when there is a far more suitable feature of XML you can use for this purpose. Entities, which you learn about on Day 8, allow you to declare a format and a helper application for processing a binary file (possibly displaying it) and associate it with an XML document by reference.

Exercises

1. There are two mistakes in the following fragment of code. What are they?

   ```
   <![CDATA [This is the hidden &markup!] ]>
   ```

   You can check your answers by running the code through one of the XML parsers, as explained on Day 5, "Checking Well-formedness."

2. Yesterday you marked up an email message. Using the appropriate entities, change the markup to turn the XML code into a boilerplate for email messages to anyone.

DAY 4

Working with Elements and Attributes

Yesterday you learned the basics of XML specifications and how to use them to mark up elements and attributes in an XML document. Then, using the internal subset of the DTD without actually having to create an external DTD, you learned how to create internal entity declarations that you can then use in the XML document as a kind of macro.

Today you will extend this knowledge of markup by learning about the following:

- How to add element and attribute declarations to the internal DTD subset
- Element content models
- The basics of document modeling
- The principles of well-formedness

Armed with this knowledge, you'll take your first steps into the world of information modeling. There, using the element content models you declare in XML, you can control and check the contents of XML documents that conform to the DTDs that you will create.

By the end of today, you should be able to create quite complex XML documents and ensure that they are well-formed. You will then be ready to move on to Day 5, "Checking Well-formedness," where you will check whether you have put everything you've learned to good use and created well-formed XML documents.

Markup Declarations

Before we get into the details of actually declaring elements and attributes, let's quickly review where these declarations are made in the XML document. Listing 4.1 shows the basic skeleton for declaring an internal DTD subset in an XML document.

TYPE   **LISTING 4.1**   THE DECLARATION OF AN INTERNAL DTD SUBSET

```
1:  <?xml version="1.0"?>
2:  <!DOCTYPE page [
3:    <!-- this is where the internal DTD subset is located. -->
4:  ]>
5:  <page>
6:    <!-- this is the content of the (only) element -->
7:  </page>
```

ANALYSIS   As shown in Listing 4.1, the XML document begins with the XML declaration (line 1). At this stage you are still working without an external DTD, so the declaration as shown is sufficient.

Line 2 is the start of the DOCTYPE declaration, which ends on line 3. All the markup declarations for the XML document are therefore entered between the square brackets ([ ]).

Although the full syntax is somewhat more complex than described here (you will learn all about the full syntax when you need it), when it's used with an internal DTD subset only, the syntax takes this form:

```
<!DOCTYPE document.type.name [ internal.subset ]>
```

where the document type name is the same as the name of the XML document's root element (<page> in Listing 4.1).

Tip   At this stage it's not necessary for the document type name to be the same as the root element name, but it will become a requirement later on when you validate your XML documents. It's a good idea to get into the habit of using this naming scheme all the time because it can save some unnecessary reworking.

Element Declarations

The first kind of declaration that you will use inside a DTD, whether it's an internal or external subset, is the element declaration. This takes the following form:

```
<!ELEMENT name content>
```

The name is a standard XML name, constructed in accordance with the naming rules you learned yesterday.

The content part of the element declaration either describes a specific content in the form of the keyword EMPTY or ANY, or it consists of a content model that describes the sequence and repetition of elements that are contained inside (are children of) this element.

Before we take a look at these special sorts of element declarations, let's look at the very simple example of an email message, as shown in Listing 4.2.

TYPE   LISTING 4.2   A VERY SIMPLE EMAIL MESSAGE IN XML

```
 1:  <message>
 2:    <header>
 3:      <date>14 May 1998</date>
 4:      <From>Me</From>
 5:      <To>You</To>
 6:      <Subject>Test Message</Subject>
 7:    </header>
 8:    <Body> ...
 9:    </Body>
10:    <Sig>Some smart saying
11:    </Sig>
12: </message>
```

You haven't learned enough yet to declare the content of the elements right down to the level of the actual text. But given what you have learned, you should still be able to sketch out a skeleton set of content models, as shown in Listing 4.3.

LISTING 4.3   A PARTIAL DTD FOR THE EMAIL MESSAGE

```
1: <!ELEMENT message (Header, Body, Sig) >
2: <!ELEMENT Header (Date, From, To, Subject) >
```

4

Empty Elements

As you learned yesterday, empty elements have no content (they are forbidden to have any) and are marked up as either

```
<empty.element/>
```

or

```
<empty.element></empty.element>
```

An empty element is simply declared like this:

```
<!ELEMENT empty.element EMPTY>
```

You could use empty elements for things like external graphics (where, as you will learn later, you declare the name of the external file by using it as an attribute value).

Unrestricted Elements

The opposite of an empty element is an unrestricted element, which can contain any element that is declared elsewhere in the XML document's DTD (in either the internal or external DTD subset). You aren't using an external DTD subset at this point, so obviously there is no way the XML processor can know about any elements declared in one.

An unrestricted element's content is declared like this:

```
<!ELEMENT any.element ANY>
```

Obviously, you cannot declare that the contents should be in any order.

Element Content Models

Empty elements and unrestricted elements are special types of elements that are so straightforward that they more or less speak for themselves; they either allow everything or they allow nothing.

Of much more interest to you are elements that contain other elements. Using XML's element declarations, you can precisely specify which other elements are allowed inside an element, how often they may appear, and in what order. You do this by specifying an element content model.

> **Note**
>
> As you will learn later, you don't just *want* to be specific—you *must* be specific. One of the things that an XML processor (or an SGML parser, for that matter) cannot deal with is ambiguity. Your content models must be capable of being interpreted in only one way. This takes a bit of practice and can cause you a lot of head-scratching, especially in the beginning. You will learn all about ambiguous content models in due course.

An element content model consists of a very simple but very specific description of the elements that may appear in the current element, the order in which they may or must appear, and how often they may or must appear. More than this, though, you can arrange elements into groups and specify special container elements. In fact, you can organize the elements into a whole class of XML documents (the document type) to reflect the significance of and relationships between chunks of information.

Element Sequences

The simplest form of element content model consists of a list of the possible elements, enclosed in parentheses and separated by commas:

```
<!ELEMENT counting (first, second, third, fourth)>
```

This example says that a `counting` element must consist of a `first` element, followed by a `second` element, followed by a `third` element, and ending with a `fourth` element.

In this example, all four elements must be present in a `counting` element, and each one may only be present once. (You can specify how often an element may appear by using an occurrence indicator, which you will learn about later in this chapter.)

Element Choices

A choice of elements in an element content model is indicated by a vertical line (¦) between the alternatives:

INPUT   `<!ELEMENT choose (this.one ¦ that.one)>`

In this example, a `choose` element consists of either a `this.one` element or a `that.one` element. When use these elements in an XML document, you can write this:

```
<choose><this.one>I chose this one</this.one></choose> and
then <choose><that.one>I chose that one</that.one></choose>
```

ANALYSIS Notice once again that without an occurrence indicator, the chosen element can appear only once.

Also note that only one element can be selected, no matter how long the list of alternatives is:

```
<!ELEMENT choose (this.one ¦ that.one ¦ the.other.one ¦ another.one ¦
➥no.that.one.silly)>
```

Combined Sequences and Choices

You can combine content sequence and choices by grouping the element content into model groups. For example:

```
<!ELEMENT lots.of.choice (maybe ¦ could.be), (this.one, that.one)>
```

Here, a `lots.of.choice` element can consist of either a `maybe` element or a `could.be` element, followed by one `this.one` element and then one `that.one` element.

Ambiguous Content Models

You can combine sequences and choices in element content models, but be very careful. Although it is not an XML requirement (or at least not if you aren't going to validate your documents), you can create compatibility problems if your content models can be interpreted in more than one way.

INPUT Consider this possibility:

```
<!ELEMENT confused ((this.one, that.one) ¦ (this.one, the.other.one))>
```

ANALYSIS When the XML processor validates the XML document (checks its content to see if the elements are in an allowed order), it won't be able to decide what is allowed and what isn't. Having seen a `this.one` element, it's impossible for it to work out which element is supposed to come next.

Of course, the XML processor could read further and then check to see if what does occur is allowed, but XML processors are not meant to look ahead. They're meant to be simple and fast. For the processor to look ahead, it has to save what it has seen in memory, look ahead, read in the next part, save that in memory, compare the two memory contents, and then decide. All this takes extra processing time.

OUTPUT With careful consideration, you can avoid ambiguous content models with a little rewriting:

```
<!ELEMENT unconfused ( this.one, ( that.one ¦ the.other.one ) ) >
```

Generally, anytime you start combine these two operators, you should be on the lookout for ambiguities.

INPUT Consider another example:

```
<!ELEMENT confused.again ( this.one, that.one , the.other.one ¦
➥no.that.one ) >
```

ANALYSIS This could easily lead you (and the XML processor) to believe that the no.that.one element is an alternative to all of the other elements. Or is it just an alternative to the the.other.one element?

OUTPUT Again, some rewriting can resolve the ambiguity and make your intention a bit clearer:

```
<!ELEMENT explained ( this.one, that.one , ( the.other.one ¦ no.that.one )
➥) >
```

Note

You might have noticed that one of my ambiguous element content models wasn't really *completely* ambiguous; the XML processor would have been able to make sense of it. However, you may remember that one of XML's design goals is to be reasonably easy for human beings to understand without needing the assistance of software. It is an excellent idea to extend this same principle to XML DTDs as well. If you can, try to arrange your content models into groups so that it is easier to understand what they mean. After all, you have no idea how much time might pass before you will see the DTD again, but by which time you will probably have forgotten all of the wonderful reasoning that went into the design of your now-cryptic element content models!

4

Element Occurrence Indicators

By using an element occurrence indicator, you can specify how often an element or group of elements may appear in an element. There are three occurrence indicators (without an occurrence indicator, the element or group of elements must appear just once):

- The ? character indicates that the element or group of elements may be omitted or may occur just once. Consider this content model:

  ```
  <!ELEMENT testing (one, two?, three)>
  ```

  This would allow you to have

  ```
  <testing><one>tock</one><two>tock</two><three>tock</three></testing>
  ```

  or

  ```
  <testing><one>tock</one><three>tock</three></testing>
  ```

  in your XML document.

- The * character indicates that an element or group of elements may be omitted or may appear zero or more times. Consider this content model:

  ```
  <!ELEMENT nice (mmm, mmmm*)>
  ```

  This would allow you to have

  ```
  <nice><mmm>I can't complain.</mmm></nice>
  ```

  or

  ```
  <nice><mmm>I like this one.</mmm><mmmm>More, </mmmm><mmmm>more,
  </mmmm>
  <mmmm>more, </mmmm><mmmm>more, <mmmm>more.</mmmm></testing>
  ```

  in your XML document.

- The + character indicates that an element or group of elements must appear at least once and may appear one or more times. Consider this content model:

  ```
  <!ELEMENT funny (ha, haha+)>
  ```

  This would allow you to have

  ```
  <funny><ha>Who?</ha><haha>is he?</haha></funny>
  ```

  or

  ```
  <funny><ha>I laughed </ha><haha>until </haha><haha>I </haha>
  <haha>thought </haha><haha>I'd <haha>die!</haha></funny>
  ```

  in your XML document.

As you can see, occurrence indicators give you a little control over how often an element or group of elements occur—not at all, once, or an unlimited number of times. This "all or nothing" approach is a little too loose for a lot of possible XML applications.

One of the promises that XML has made is that it might finally be possible to seriously use it to model databases. (This was always a practically unachievable dream in SGML.) However, the syntax of XML element content models is not rich and precise enough to do this kind of modeling. Databases, for example, might need to specify an exact number of occurrences, rather than just 0, 1, or infinite.

Another example that programmers would probably welcome is some kind of conditional content model along the lines of "if element A and then B, choose between C and D; otherwise choose between E and F."

Complex content models like examples simply cannot be expressed in the syntax used in XML DTDs. To address this problem and fulfill the needs of a much wider range of users, a search has begun for alternative ways of describing and declaring XML content models (DCD, XML-Data, and RDF). You will learn about a few of the most important of these schemas on Day 17, "Using Meta-Data to Describe XML Data."

4

Character Content

There is one more type of element content, and I have been intentionally saving it because it is a little bit special.

When text—and only text—is allowed inside an element, this is identified by the keyword PCDATA (parseable character data) in the content model. To prevent you from confusing this keyword with a normal element name (and to make it impossible for you to use it as a name), the keyword is prefixed by a hash character (#), which is called the reserved name character (RNI).

Consider these element declarations:

```
<!ELEMENT para (title, text)>
<!ELEMENT title (#PCDATA)>
<!ELEMENT text (#PCDATA)>
```

These would allow you to write the following in your XML document:

```
<para><title>My Life</title><text>My life has been
very quiet of late.</text></para>
```

A parseable character data element cannot contain any further markup and the ends of the title and text element start tags is therefore where the markup stops and "normal" text takes over.

Note
Don't lose sight of the fact that XML's content models are only concerned with the structure of an XML document and make no attempt to control its content. An element that is totally devoid of data content will still match a #PCDATA content model.

Mixed Content Elements

Elements that can contain text (parseable character data), elements, or both are a real problem sometimes. They are called mixed content models, and they require extra care.

The important point is that it is difficult for an XML processor to distinguish between unintentional PCDATA (spaces, tabs, line endings, and so on) and element content. An accidental space between an end tag and the next start tag could lead to chaos.

To declare mixed content, you use the content model grammar you have learned so far, but you must use it in a particular way. The content model has to take the form of a single set of alternatives, starting with #PCDATA and followed by the element types that can occur in the mixed content, each declared only once. Except when #PCDATA is the only option (as you saw earlier), the * qualifier must follow the closing parenthesis:

```
<!ELEMENT pick (#PCDATA ¦ eeney ¦ meeney ¦ miney ¦ mo)*>
```

Attribute Declarations

In XML, you can declare only one element at a time. (In SGML, and by implication HTML, you can put whole groups of elements in one declaration and give them all the same content model at once.) However, elements can have lots of attributes, which are all declared at once in an attribute declaration list.

An attribute declaration list has the following form:

```
<!ATTLIST element.name attribute.definitions>
```

It is normal practice to keep an element's attribute declaration list close to the declaration of the element itself, but there is absolutely no requirement to do so. It just makes the DTD easier to understand and maintain.

An attribute declaration list consists of one or more attribute declarations. (For readability, they are often put on separate lines, but there is no requirement to do this.) It does the following for an element:

- It declares the names of allowed attributes.
- It states the type of each attribute.
- It may provide a default value for each attribute.

Each attribute declaration consists of a simple attribute name and an attribute type pair statement in the following form:

```
attribute.name attribute.type
```

Attribute Types

There are three types of attributes:

- A string attribute, whose value consists of any amount of character data.
- A tokenized attribute, whose value consists of one or more *tokens* that are significant to XML.
- An enumerated attribute, whose value is taken from a list of declared possible values.

String Attribute Types

The values of string types are simple strings of characters. Any attribute that is used in an XML document that does not have a DTD (either an internal or external DTD subset) is automatically treated as a string type attribute.

Here's an example of a string type attribute declaration:

```
<!ATTLIST owner CDATA>
```

You would use it like this:

```
<book owner="Hammersmith Public Library">
```

You can also use an internal entity (in this case it's given the more generic name *general entity*) in the value of a string type attribute:

```
<book owner="&my.local; Public Library">
```

Tokenized Attribute Types

Tokenized attributes are classified according to what their value, or values, can be:

- ID—This attribute serves as an identifier for the element. No two elements can have the same ID attribute value in the same document. An ID value must comply with the standard XML naming rules. An ID attribute type can be applied to any attribute, but it is standard practice to restrict its use to an attribute that is also called ID to make it easier to find.

  Here's an example of an ID type declaration:

  ```
  <!ATTLIST book
            id ID>
  ```

  You would use it like this:

  ```
  <book id="A51">
  ```

- IDREF—This attribute is a pointer to an ID (an ID reference). The value must match the value of an ID type attribute that is declared somewhere in the same document.

- IDREFS—The value of this attribute consists of one or more IDREF type values, separated by spaces.

  Here's an example of an IDREFS type declaration:

  ```
  <!ATTLIST book
            authors IDREFS>
  ```

  You would use it like this:

  ```
  <book authors="A51 A62 B87">
  ```

- ENTITY—This attribute is a pointer to an external entity that has been declared in the DTD, in either the external or internal DTD subset. The value of the attribute is the name of the entity, which must consist of name characters. The XML document can no longer be a standalone document if you use external entities. It is a little early to learn about external entities, but we will return to them on Day 8, "XML Objects: Exploiting Entities."

- ENTITIES—The value of this attribute consists of one or more ENTITY type values, separated by spaces.

  ENTITY and ENTITIES type attributes are normally used to refer to things like graphics files and other unparsed data:

  ```
  <!ELEMENT graphic  EMPTY >

  <!ATTLIST graphic   boardno   ENTITY >
  ```

- NMTOKEN—The value of this attribute is a name token string consisting of any mixture of name characters.
- NMTOKENS—The value of this attribute consists of one or more NMTOKEN type values, separated by spaces.

Enumerated Attribute Types

Enumerated attributes have values that are simply lists of possible values. Each value has to be a valid name token (NMTOKEN). Here is an example:

```
<!ATTLIST paint
        COLOR (RED ¦ YELLOW ¦ GREEN) "RED">
```

When a list of possible values is prefixed by the keyword NOTATION (which you will learn about on Day 8), the notations listed as possible values must all have been declared already:

```
<!ATTLIST image
        type NOTATION (GIF ¦ JPEG ¦ PNG) "GIF">
```

When matching an attribute value against the allowed values specified in the attribute definition, the XML processor carries out a non–case-sensitive match for all attributes, except those that are of the CDATA, IDREF, or IDREFS type.

4

Tip

> Strictly speaking, there is no such thing as an optional attribute in XML. However, there is a little-known trick using enumerated types that allows you to mimic the behavior of an optional attribute. Consider this attribute declaration list:
>
> ```
> <!ATTLIST clever.element
>         clever.att SORT ( A ¦ B ¦ C ) "" >
> ```
>
> Now, if you don't explicitly declare this attribute but simply leave it out, as shown here:
>
> ```
> <clever.element>This element has no declared
> attribute value.</clever.element>
> ```
>
> the default value would be assigned to the element, which in this case is empty.

Attribute Default Values

You can add a keyword to the end of an attribute specification to specify the action the XML processor should take when you leave out (or forget) the attribute in a particular start tag.

There are three possible keywords:

- #REQUIRED means that the attribute is required and should have been there. If it's missing, it makes the document invalid.

  Here's an example of a required declaration:

  ```
  <!ATTLIST book
           author ID #REQUIRED>
  ```

  Normally, ID type attribute values are specified as being required. You will learn later that they must be specified as required if the document is to be validated.

- #IMPLIED means that the XML processor must tell the application that no value was specified. It is then up to the application to decide what it is going to do.

  Here's an example of an implied declaration:

  ```
  <!ATTLIST section
           number #IMPLIED>
  ```

  Implied attribute values are often used for things like section and list item number-ing, where the application can calculate the value itself simply by counting. You would also use this implied value for attribute values that you want an element to inherit from its parent.

- If the default value is preceded by the keyword #FIXED, any value that is specified must match the default value or the document will be invalid.

  The following are examples of attribute declarations with default values:

  ```
  <!ATTLIST termdef
           id ID #REQUIRED
           name CDATA #IMPLIED>

  <!ATTLIST list
           type (roman ¦ arabic ¦ Roman ¦ Arabic) "roman">

  <!ATTLIST form
           method CDATA #FIXED "POST">
  ```

Well-Formed XML Documents

Elements, attributes, and entities are the three primary building blocks of XML docu-ments. Just having elements is already enough for you to be able to create true XML documents. Using all three objects, you can create quite complex XML documents and fulfil the needs of 90% of the applications for which you would use XML.

For such XML documents to be properly usable—in other words, for an XML processor to process these documents successfully—they must be well-formed. According to the XML standard, a data object is not officially an XML document until it is well-formed. You have already encountered most of the rules that an XML document must obey in order to be well-formed, but let's review them. A document that you can create now using just elements, attributes, and entities is well-formed if:

- It contains one or more elements.
- It has just one element (the document, or root element) that contains all the other elements.
- Its elements (if it contains more than one element) are properly nested inside each other (no element starts in one element and ends in another).
- The names used in its element start tags and end tags match exactly.
- The names of attributes do not appear more than once in the same element start tag.
- The values of its attributes are enclosed in either single or double quotes.
- The values of its attributes do not reference external entities, either directly or indirectly.
- The replacement text for any entity referenced in an attribute value does not contain a < character (it can contain the string <).
- Its entities are declared before they are used.
- None of its entity references contain the name of an unparsed entity.
- Its logical and physical structures are properly nested.

There are many ways to check whether an XML document is well-formed, and many tools to help you do it. At the very simplest, there are some public-domain Perl scripts and some very useful tools (you will learn about some of these tomorrow). Or you could even try loading your XML code into Mozilla, the development version of Netscape 5 (which you will learn more about on Days 13, "Viewing XML in Other Browsers," and 18, "Styling XML with CSS").

Summary

Today you learned the nuts-and-bolts details of element declarations and element content models. You have also learned how to declare and use element attributes. Put this together with what you have already learned about processing instructions, the internal DTD subset, and internal entities, and you have enough to get started using XML in applications.

In fact, if you're not at all interested in including external objects (graphics and referenced data) or validating your XML documents, you could probably skip the rest of this book! There's a lot more to come, though. Tomorrow you will learn how to use an XML parser to check that what you have created is well-formed, and after that we can really start to get technical with the next step: valid XML documents.

Q&A

Q Why is element grouping a useful tool in declaring element content models?

A They can be an important aid in avoiding ambiguous content models, and, when used intelligently, they can help to make DTDs easier to understand.

Q Why do mixed content models require special attention and care?

A It is essential for the XML processor to be able to distinguish between intentional whitespace, which it will treat as character data, and accidental characters. The order in which the content model is declared and the use of occurrence indicators is therefore very specific and must be followed exactly.

Q Is there any limit to the length of an element or attribute name?

A No. As long as you obey the restrictions on which characters you are allowed, a name can be as long as you want it to be. (In SGML, you have to make special arrangements to allow longer names.)

Q What is so different about an ID attribute value?

A An ID attribute value must be unique in an XML document.

Q What is the difference between a name and a name token?

A Name tokens are a little less restricted than names. Names have to begin with a letter, an underscore, or a colon; name tokens can start with any valid name character.

Q How can you tell if an XML document is well-formed?

A As well as using an XML processor, you can use one of many free utilities written in a variety of languages, including Perl, JavaScript, Java, and C, that can parse an XML document and point out any well-formedness errors.

Exercises

1. A hot topic for discussion in SGML circles (and it will become one in XML circles) is whether to use an element to describe information or to put the information in an attribute instead. Write down two reasons for each side of the argument.

2. The following fragment of XML code is taken from a simple parts catalog. Add an internal DTD subset to it.

```xml
<?xml version="1.0"?>
<parts>
  <part>
    <name>Widget</name>
    <catalog.number>11037</catalog.number>
    <price.code>4</price.code>
    <quantity>d</quantity>
  </part>
  <part>
    <name>Bolt</name>
    <catalog.number>11497</catalog.number>
    <thread>w</thread>
    <price.code>1</price.code>
    <quantity>100</quantity>
  </part>
  <part>
    <name>Screw</name>
    <catalog.number>10020</catalog.number>
    <type>countersunk</type>
    <price.code>7</price.code>
    <quantity>c</quantity>
  </part>
</parts>
```

3. The following content models are ambiguous. Rewrite them so they aren't.

a. (section?, section)

b. ((one, two) ¦ (one, three))

4

DAY 5

Checking Well-formedness

During the previous days, you have learned how to write well-formed XML. But how can you be sure that your XML files are indeed well-formed? Well, some help is at hand. There's now software whose main purpose is to check the syntax of your files according to the well-formedness rules specified in the XML recommendation. These programs are called non-validating parsers.

> **Note**
> Validating parsers are discussed on Day 9, "Checking Validity," when you have acquired knowledge about document type definitions.

> **Note**
> In addition to checking your XML files, XML processors give other applications access to the structure and content of your XML files.

In this chapter you will learn the following:

- Where you can find these XML parsers
- How to use the expat parser
- How to use the DXP parser from the DataChannel company
- How to check your XML files over the Web using RUWF
- How to check your XML files over the Web using other validation services

Where to Find Information on Available Parsers

Lists of available parsers can be found at the following URLs:

- Robin Cover manages the most complete reference site on SGML and XML. If you want to know anything about XML or SGML, start at `http://www.oasis-open.org/cover/`.
- Lars Marius Garshol maintains `http://www.stud.ifi.uio.no/~larsga/linker/XMLtools.html#C_Parsers`. Here you'll find a good overview of free XML tools, with lots of clarifying comments and all necessary pointers.
- Lisa Rein's `http://www.finetuning.com/parse.html` is another good resource page.
- James Tauber's `http://www.xmlsoftware.com/parsers/` offers the clearest overview. He lists the parsers according to the programming language used, the interfaces they offer, if they are validating or not, and so on.

Checking Your XML Files with expat

In this section you'll learn how to use the expat XML parser program to check your XML files. The expat program was written by James Clark, the technical lead of the W3C XML Working Group (WG) and author of other acclaimed free software for the SGML/XML community. The code is platform-independent C.

Mozilla 5, the next release of Netscape's browser, will use the expat parser. For more info, see `http:/www.mozilla.org/rdf/doc/xml.html`.

For Perl, there's an extension module named XML::Parser that is a Perl interface to expat. More information can be found at `http://www.netheaven.com/~coopercc/xmlparser/intro.html`.

Installing expat

expat is available for download from `ftp://ftp.jclark.com/pub/xml/expat.zip`. This ZIP file is 138KB large (version 19981122). Just unzip this distribution to your disk and you're ready to go.

Using expat

What's of interest to us is the xmlwf application. The executable is located inside the `bin` subdirectory of the expat distribution. This application takes as arguments one or more files to be checked for well-formedness.

The typical usage is as follows:

```
xmlwf file
```

For example:

```
xmlwf c:\xmlfiles\parse1.xml
```

Checking a File Error by Error

Let's go over a file step-by-step and see in detail which errors expat detects. We'll use the XML file shown in Listing 5.1.

LISTING 5.1   `wfq.xml`—CHECKING FOR SYNTAX ERRORS

```
1: <?xml version="1.0">
2: <?protext objid="I5678" ?>
3: <helptopic>
4: <title keyword="printing,network;printing,shared printer">How
➥to use a shared network printer?</title>
5: <procedure>
6: <step><action>In <icon>Network Neighborhood</icon>, locate and
➥double-click the computer where the printer you want to use is
➥located. </action>
7: <tip targetgroup="beginners">To see which computers have
➥shared printers attached, click the <menu>View</menu> menu,
8: click <menu>Details</menu>, & look for printer names or
➥descriptions in the Comment column of the Network
➥Neighborhood window.</tip>
9: </step>
10: <step>
11: <action>&doubleclick; the printer icon in the window that
➥appears.</action>
12: </step>
13: <step>
```

5

continues

LISTING 5.1   CONTINUED

```
14: <action>
15: To set up the printer, <xref linkend="id45">follow the
➡instructions</xref> on the screen.
16: </step>
17: </procedure>
18: <rule form=double>
19: <tip>
20: <P>After you have set up a network printer, you can use it as
➡if it were attached to your computer. For related topics, look up
➡&quot;printing&quot; in the Help Index.
21: </p>
22: </tip>
23: </helptopic>
```

Let's see what expat discovers.

INPUT   `xmlwf wfq.xml`

The first error message is

OUTPUT   `wfq.xml:1:19: syntax error`

ANALYSIS   This message shows four pieces of information:

- The name of the file where the error was encountered

- The line number with the error

- The position on that line where the error was detected

- A description of the error

In this file, there was a syntax error detected on line 1, character 19, which is in front of the > character. Indeed, the XML declaration needs to end with ?>, which wasn't the case in this file. Let's correct that:

```
1: <?xml version="1.0"?>
```

Run expat again and you'll receive a second error message:

OUTPUT   `wfq.xml:8:29: not well-formed`

ANALYSIS The problem seems to be with the ampersand character used. The XML specification says that "the ampersand character (&) may appear in its literal form only when used as a markup delimiter... If it is needed elsewhere, it must be escaped."

This escaping can be done by using the predefined entity &:

```
8: click <menu>Details</menu>, &amp; look for printer names
➥or descriptions in the Comment column of the Network
➥Neighborhood window.</tip>
```

The next error message is:

OUTPUT `wfq.xml:11:18: undefined entity`

ANALYSIS You have used an entity reference to the entity doubleclick, but this entity hasn't been declared.

Let's examine what the specification says: "A textual object is said to be a well-formed XML document... if, for each entity reference which appears in the document, either the entity has been declared in the document type declaration or the entity name is one of [the following]: amp, lt, gt, apos, quot."

So you need to add an entity declaration to your document, more specific to the document type declaration, which you don't have at the moment.

Let's start by adding one:

```
3: <!DOCTYPE helptopic []>
```

Now add the declaration of the entity doubleclick:

```
3: <!DOCTYPE helptopic [
4: <!ENTITY doubleclick "Double-click">
5: ]>
```

The XML file looks like Listing 5.2.

LISTING 5.2 wfq.xml—AN ENTITY DECLARED IN THE DOCUMENT TYPE DECLARATION INTERNAL SUBSET

```
1: <?xml version="1.0" ?>
2: <?protext objid="I5678" ?>
3: <!DOCTYPE helptopic [
4: <!ENTITY doubleclick "Double-click">
5: ]>
6: <helptopic>
```

continues

LISTING 5.2   CONTINUED

```
7: <title keyword="printing,network;printing,shared printer">How
➥to use a shared network printer?</title>
8: <procedure>
9: <step><action>In <icon>Network Neighborhood</icon>, locate and
➥double-click the computer where the printer you want to use is
➥located. </action>
10: <tip targetgroup="beginners">To see which computers have
➥shared printers attached, click the <menu>View</menu> menu,
11: click <menu>Details</menu>, &amp; look for printer names or
➥descriptions in the Comment column of the Network
➥Neighborhood window.</tip>
12: </step>
13: <step>
14: <action>&doubleclick; the printer icon in the window that
➥appears.</action>
15: </step>
16: <step>
17: <action>
18: To set up the printer, <xref linkend="id45">follow the
➥instructions</xref> on the screen.
19: </step>
20: </procedure>
21: <rule form=double>
22: <tip>
23: <P>After you have set up a network printer, you can use it as
➥if it were attached to your computer. For related topics, look up
➥&quot;printing&quot; in the Help Index.
24: </p>
25: </tip>
26: </helptopic>
```

Now, let's parse again:

 wfq.xml:19:2: mismatched tag

ANALYSIS   You encounter an end tag for the step element. Take a close look at what's happening inside the step element: an action element was encountered, but it isn't closed at the end of the step.

Let's examine the XML specification once more: "For all other elements (other than the root), if the start tag is in the content of another element, the end tag is in the content of the same element. More simply stated, the elements, delimited by start and end tags, nest within each other."

Therefore, line 19 needs to become

```
19: </action></step>
```

After this correction, the next parsing error you encounter is

OUTPUT `wfq.xml:21:11: not well-formed`

ANALYSIS The problem is in the line

```
21: <rule form=double>
```

Let's take a look at the attribute `form`. An attribute value needs to be inside quotes:

```
21: <rule form="double">
```

The next expat message is

OUTPUT `wfq.xml:24:2: mismatched tag`

ANALYSIS On line 24 there's an end tag for the element p, but there is no element p open. P is open. Both the start and end tag needs to be in the same case. Change the start tag to p:

```
23: <p>After you have set up a network printer, you can use it as
➥if it were attached to your computer. For related topics, look up
➥&quot;printing&quot; in the Help Index.
24: </p>
```

The next parse result we receive is:

OUTPUT `wfq.xml:26:2: mismatched tag`

ANALYSIS This is a tricky one. Do you see an error on line 26? Not immediately. The root element is being closed here. Remember that all other elements have to be nested inside this root element. Is this the case? Has every open element been closed?

No, the element rule is still open. But let's examine this element a little bit more closely. Does this element rule contain any content? No, it seems to be an empty element. And according to the specification, empty elements must take one of the following forms:

- `<tag></tag>`
- `<tag/>`

The following is what's needed:

```
21: <rule form="double"/>
```

5

After all these corrections, the file should look like Listing 5.3.

LISTING 5.3 wf.xml—THE CORRECTED XML FILE

```
1: <?xml version="1.0" ?>
2: <?protext objid="I5678" ?>
3: <!DOCTYPE helptopic [
4: <!ENTITY doubleclick "Double-click">
5: ]>
6: <helptopic>
7: <title keyword="printing,network;printing,shared printer">How
   to use a shared network printer?</title>
8: <procedure>
9: <step><action>In <icon>Network Neighborhood</icon>, locate and
   double-click the computer where the printer you want to use is
   located. </action>
10: <tip targetgroup="beginners">To see which computers have
   shared printers attached, click the <menu>View</menu> menu,
11: click <menu>Details</menu>, &amp; look for printer names or
   descriptions in the Comment column of the Network
   Neighborhood window.</tip>
12: </step>
13: <step>
14: <action>&doubleclick; the printer icon in the window that
   appears.</action>
15: </step>
16: <step>
17: <action>
18: To set up the printer, <xref linkend="id45">follow the
   instructions</xref> on the screen.
19: </action></step>
20: </procedure>
21: <rule form="double"/>
22: <tip>
23: <p>After you have set up a network printer, you can use it as
   if it were attached to your computer. For related topics, look up
   &quot;printing&quot; in the Help Index.
24: </p>
25: </tip>
26: </helptopic>
```

Let's run another parse. No messages appear: The file seems to be error-free.

Checking Your XML Files with DXP

DXP stands for DataChannel XML Parser and is based on NXP (Norbert Mikula's XML Parser), one of the first XML parsers. It is written in Java.

 Note

> Java is the most popular language for XML development. That's easy to understand. XML is SGML made easy and optimized for use on the Web. One of the design principles of SGML was to be independent of hardware, operating system, software, and so on. That's also exactly what Java does: it allows you to run your programs on different machines, on different operating systems, even on Web browsers. They make a perfect couple.
>
> So if you want to become involved in serious XML development, you need to learn Java.

You can use this parser not only to check the well-formedness of your files, but also to validate them, a subject treated during Day 9.

Installing DXP

You can download DXP from `http://www.DataChannel.com/xml.resources/dxp.shtml#download`. The actual file to download, `DXP.zip`, is 547KB. Next to the needed Java classes, you'll find a fair amount of documentation and examples.

How to install DXP:

1. Unzip the `DXP.zip` file.

2. Make sure you have Java Virtual Machine version 1.x running. You can use SUN's Java Development Kit or JDK (`http://java.sun.com/products/jdk/1.1/`), Sun's Java Runtime Environment or JRE (`http://java.sun.com/products/jdk/1.1/jre/index.html`), or Microsoft's SDK for Java (`http://www.microsoft.com/java/`).

   To install a Java Virtual Machine, see the book *Sams Teach Yourself Java 1.2 in 21 Days* or the documentation included with the preceding tools.

3. Make sure that your Java Virtual Machine can find the DXP classes by doing one of the following:

5

Adding to your classpath environment variable the packages directory of the DXP parser, `c:\DataChannel\dxp\classes`, or

In the case of JRE, setting the –cp parameter to the path on the command line: `jre –cp c:\DataChannel\dxp\classes`.

Using DXP

At the command line (DOS prompt), type

`jre -cp .;c:\DataChannel\dxp\classes dxpcl -s c:\xmlex\wfq.xml`

where

- `-cp` sets the classpath (where to find the classes used). In this case two paths are specified: the first (`.`), referring to the current working directory, and the second (`c:\DataChannel\dxp\classes`), both separated by `;`.

Note	The path separator on UNIX machines is a `:`.

- `dxpcl` is the name of the Java program (class).
- `-s` stands for silent mode.

Note	For the moment, we are only interested in the errors in this file. By asking for silent mode, the only output generated are the error messages.

- `c:\xmlex\wfq.xml` is the file to be checked.

Checking a File Error by Error

Let's go over this same file step-by-step and see in detail which errors DXP detects.

Checking the file `wfq.xml` results in the following error:

```
FATAL ERROR: encountered ">". Was expecting one of: <S> , "?"
Location: file:/c:/xmlex/wfq.xml:1:20

Found errors/warnings: 1 fatal error(s), 0 error(s) and 0 warning(s)
```

For every error message, you receive

- The kind of error with an explanation, and
- On a second line, the location of the error (line 1, character 20 in file wfq.xml)

> **Note** The XML specification makes a distinction between errors and fatal errors. Violations of well-formedness constraints are fatal errors. A XML processor must detect such errors and must not continue normal processing.

At the end you'll find a summary with the numbers of errors, fatal errors, and warnings.

You know already what the problems are with this XML file. The first error was the missing ? at the end of the XML declaration. We'll change that. Let's run the parser again:

```
FATAL ERROR: after the "&" there is no "entity-name" and ";"
➥following in the entity reference
Location: file:/c:/xmlex/wfq.xml:7:146

FATAL ERROR: reference to undefined entity "doubleclick"
Location: file:/c:/xmlex/wfq.xml:10:21

FATAL ERROR: name of the start-tag "action" doesn't match the
➥name of the end-tag "step"

Location: file:/c:/xmlex/wfq.xml:15:7

Found errors/warnings: 3 fatal error(s), 0 error(s) and 0 warning(s)
```

Now we're making some progress. There are three more errors, all familiar:

- The not-escaped &
- The undefined entity doubleclick
- The missing end tag of the element action

Correct them and run the parser again:

```
FATAL ERROR: encountered "double". Was expecting one of: "\"" , "\'"
Location: file:/c:/xmlex/wfq.xml:20:12

Found errors/warnings: 1 fatal error(s), 0 error(s) and 0 warning(s)
```

Attribute values need to be quoted. After this correction, you receive the following:

```
FATAL ERROR: name of the start-tag "P" doesn't match the name of
➥the end-tag "p"
```

5

```
Location: file:/c:/xmlex/wfq.xml:23:4
```

```
Found errors/warnings: 1 fatal error(s), 0 error(s) and 0 warning(s)
```

Get rid of this mismatch and parse once more:

```
FATAL ERROR: name of the start-tag "rule" doesn't match the name
➥of the end-tag "helptopic"
Location: file:/c:/xmlex/wfq.xml:25:12
```

```
Found errors/warnings: 1 fatal error(s), 0 error(s) and 0 warning(s)
```

Make the rule element empty. After this correction, you have a correct file. The parser doesn't generate any more messages.

Checking Your Files Over the Web Using RUWF

RUWF, the XML syntax checker, is a service provided by the Web site of XML.COM, a partnership between Seybold Publications and O'Reilly with the technical aid of Tim Bray, featuring the king of XML gossip, Xavier McLipps. You can reach this service at `http://www.xml.com/xml/pub/tools/ruwf/check.html`.

This service was built using Lark, the non-validating parser written by Tim Bray.

Using RUWF

1. Place your XML file on a Web server so it can be referenced by an HTTP address (such as `http://www.protext.be/wfq.xml`).

2. Go to `http://www.xml.com/xml/pub/tools/ruwf/check.html`.

3. Put your URL in the input field of the RUWF page and submit the page.

If you send `wfq.xml` to the URL, the HTML page shown in Figure 5.1 is returned.

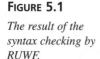

FIGURE 5.1

The result of the syntax checking by RUWF.

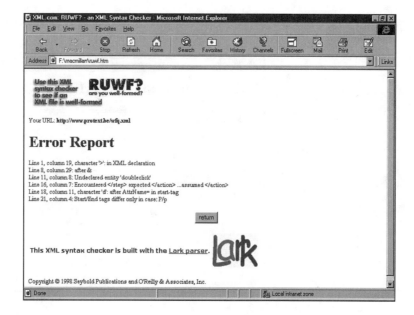

Checking Your Files Over the Web Using Other Online Validation Services

Here are some other online validation services:

- XML well-formedness checker from Richard Tobin at http://www.cogsci.ed.ac.uk/~richard/xml-check.html.

- XML Syntax Checker from Frontier at http://www.scripting.com/frontier5/xml/code/syntaxChecker.html. You can use the Frontier 5.1.3 built-in parser or the blox one, which is based on expat.

- The Koala XML Validation Service at http://koala.inria.fr:8080/XML/.

- The Techno 2000 Project XML Validation Service at http://xml.t2000.co.kr/xmlval/.

- WebTech's Validation Service at http://valsvc.webtechs.com/.

Using XML Well-formedness Checker

At http://www.cogsci.ed.ac.uk/~richard/xml-check.html, you'll find the page shown in Figure 5.2.

5

FIGURE 5.2

*The submit page of the
XML well-formedness
checker.*

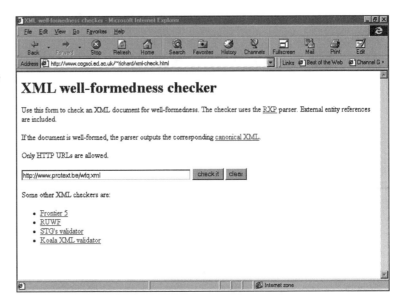

After supplying the URL of the file to be checked, you receive the results page shown in
Figure 5.3.

FIGURE 5.3

*The results page of the
XML well-formedness
checker.*

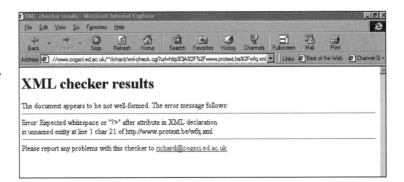

Using XML Syntax Checker from Frontier

Figure 5.4 shows you what the submit page looks like at
`http://www.scripting.com/frontier5/xml/code/syntaxChecker.html`.

INPUT

FIGURE 5.4

The submit page of the XML Syntax Checker of Frontier.

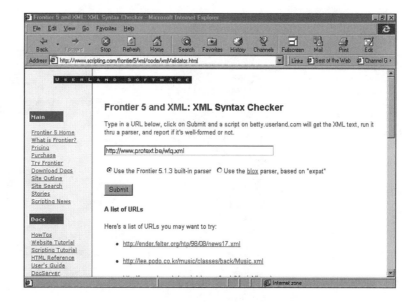

Depending on the parser chosen, you get what's shown in Figure 5.5...

INPUT

FIGURE 5.5

The results generated by the built-in parser of Frontier.

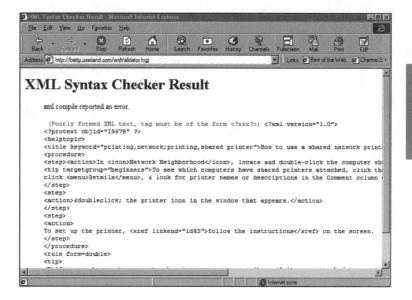

5

...or what's shown in Figure 5.6.

FIGURE 5.6

The results generated by Blox, using expat.

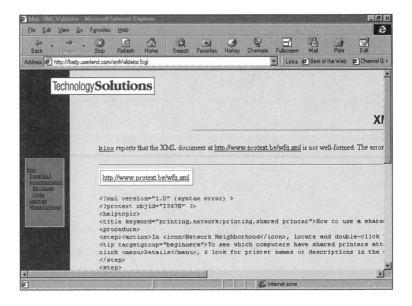

Summary

In an XML environment, you need to be sure that your documents are well-formed according to the XML recommendation. Non-validating parsers can help you meet this requirement.

A lot of these tools are available for free on the Web. We did our quality checks with the following:

- expat, a parser written by James Clark
- DXP, a parser written by DataChannel
- RUWF using Lark, written by Tim Bray
- Other online validation services

Do

Do check your XML files for well-formedness.

This is very important because when an XML file violates the specified well-formedness constraints, it contains fatal errors and the normal processing must be stopped.

Q&A

Q Why should I bother to have well-formed XML files?

A XML processors act as helpers for other applications, giving them access to the content and structure of the XML files. If an XML file contains violations against the specified well-formedness constraints, it has fatal errors. And in the case of fatal errors, the normal processing must be stopped.

This is indeed different from HTML, in which browsers try to make sense out of the rubbish they sometimes receive. Consequently, 75 percent of the code in Internet Explorer and Netscape Navigator is just for handling bad HTML.

Q I cannot make sense out of the error message I received. What can I do?

A If you have trouble understanding the message, use the annotated XML specification at `http://www.xml.com/axml/testaxml.htm`. This specification is heavily indexed and can help you find the relevant section.

Or submit the file to a different parser. Parsers vary substantially in the extent and clarity of their error messages.

Q What other well-formedness parsers are available?

A Other examples of non-validating parsers are Ælfred, developed by David Megginson (`http://www.microstar.com/XML/index.html`), and Microsoft XML Parser in C++, which is included Internet Explorer 4.0.

But for a complete overview, see the links at the beginning of the chapter.

5

Q Are HTML files well-formed?

A Not normally, but they can be made well-formed.

The most obvious violations against well-formedness in HTML files are

- Not all start and end tags are explicitly included
- The syntax of empty elements

Remember that in XML, empty elements need to encoded in one of two possible ways:

```
<name></name>
```

```
<name/>
```

Exercises

1. See the following XML file:

LISTING 5.4   function.xml—XML FILE TO CHECK FOR WELL-FORMEDNESS

```
1: <?xml version="1.0"?>
2: <!DOCTYPE functiondescription [
3: <!NOTATION GIF SYSTEM "" >
4: <!ENTITY idhelp782 SYSTEM "idhelp782.txt">
5: <!ENTITY idhelp785 SYSTEM "idhelp785.txt">
6: <!ENTITY idhelp645 SYSTEM "idhelp645.txt">
7: <!ENTITY buttonleft SYSTEM "http://www.protext.be/button.gif"
➥NDATA GIF>
8: ]>
9: <function>
10: <title>ctime</title>
11: <funcsynopsis>
12: <funcdef>
13: <function>ctime</function>
14: </funcdef>
15: <paramdef>
16: <parameter>time</parameter>
17: <parameter role="opt">gmt</parameter>
18: </paramdef>
19: </funcsynopsis>
20: <para>This function converts the value
21: <parameter>time</parameter>, as returned by <function>time()
➥</function>
22: or <function>file_mtime()</function>, into a string of the
➥form produced by <function>
23: time_date()</function>. If the optional argument <parameter>
➥gmt</parameter>
24: is specified and non-zero, the time is returned in <parameter>
➥gmt</parameter>.
```

```
25: Otherwise, the time is given in the local time zone.</para>
26: <para><emphasis role="strong" targetgroup="beginners role=
➥"strong">Related topics</emphasis></para>
27: <para>&doubleclick; the <mousebutton>
28: LEFT &buttonleft;</mousebutton> mouse button on a topic:
➥</para>
29: <itemizedlist>
30: <listitem><para><ulink url="&idhelp782;"><function>
➥file_mtime()</function>
31: built-in function</ulink></para>
32: </listitem>
33: <listitem><para><ulink url="&idhelp785;"><function>time()
➥</function> built-in
34: function</ulink></para>
35: </listitem>
36: </itemizedlist>
37:</function>
```

Using this XML file:

- Detect the errors and predict the error messages that the parser of your choice will generate

- Check the file with that parser

- Correct all problems discovered

2. Using an XML file you've made during the previous days:

- Introduce errors

| Tip | Use the W3C recommendation as your reference. |

- Parse the file with different parsers
- Study the differences between the results of different parsers

5

DAY 6

Creating Valid Documents

So far you have learned about XML tags, elements, and attributes, and you have seen how you can use simple tools to test whether an XML document is well formed. This chapter looks a little further and introduces the most obvious feature of XML that identifies it as being firmly on the side of SGML rather than next to HTML as just another set of tags. Today you will learn

- What a Document Type Definition (DTD) is
- The contents and purpose of the internal subset
- The contents and purpose of the external subset
- The basics of developing a DTD

This chapter is not intended to be a complete treatment of DTDs, but it should be enough to get you started. On Day 7, "Developing Advanced DTDs," we will look at the more advanced aspects of DTD development and cover some of the approaches to information modeling as it can be applied to DTD development.

XML and Structured Information

If you only wanted "proper tagging"—with all the text neatly wrapped inside elements—creating XML documents is quite possibly unnecessary. You could probably achieve just as much by using the standard HTML elements and inventing classes to do the work for you. For example, the HTML code shown in Listing 6.1 could do almost as much as the equivalent XML code.

LISTING 6.1   USING HTML TO MIMIC XML

```
 1: <HTML>
 2:   <HEAD>
 3:     <TITLE>HTML Mimicking XML</TITLE>
 4:   </HEAD>
 5:   <BODY>
 6:     <DIV ID="1" CLASS="CHAPTER">
 7:      <H1 CLASS="HEAD1">Chapter 1</H1>
 8:         <P CLASS="PARA">This actually comes quite close
 9:            to being acceptable as pseudo-XML.</P>
10:         <DIV ID="1.1" CLASS="SECTION">
11:           <H2 CLASS="HEAD2">Section 1.1</H2>
12:             <P CLASS="PARA">We can even bring in some
13:                kind of pseudo-structure by using
14:                attributes. </P>
15:          </DIV>
16:   </BODY>
17: </HTML>
```

ANALYSIS   Listing 6.1 shows an example of how HTML code can come quite close to being as rich as XML markup. By using HTML DIV elements (lines 6 and 10) and ID and CLASS attributes on as many elements as necessary, it is possible to build almost as much information into the markup as might be achieved with custom XML elements.

Now try comparing the HTML code shown in Listing 6.1 with the almost equivalent XML code shown in Listing 6.2.

LISTING 6.2   XML USING ELEMENTS TO MATCH HTML ATTRIBUTES

```
 1: <?xml version="1.0"?>
 2:   <DOCUMENT>
 3:     <TITLE>XML Being What it is</TITLE>
 4:   <CHAPTER>
 5:     <HEAD>Chapter 1</HEAD>
 6:         <PARA>This is quite
 7:            acceptable XML.</PARA>
 8:       <SECTION>
```

```
 9:            <HEAD>Section 1.1</HEAD>
10:                <PARA>The structure lies in the
11:                    elements themselves. </P>
12:            </SECTION>
13:        </CHAPTER>
14: </DOCUMENT>
```

ANALYSIS In Listing 6.2, the XML markup uses elements to achieve what HTML, which doesn't have the freedom to invent its own elements (or at least, not officially), is forced to use attributes for. On this small scale (or superficial level of complexity) you could use HTML just as readily as XML.

So what do you gain from using XML instead of HTML? The most obvious difference is that in HTML you are very limited in what attributes you can give an element (in most cases not much more than an ID and a CLASS), and not all elements can have these attributes. XML, in contrast, enables you to not only have as many attributes as you like, but to call them whatever you like (subject to the normal naming rules, of course). These attributes allow you to add a wealth of information to describe an element, as in the declaration of a graphic element shown in Listing 6.3.

Note The set of graphics attributes shown in Listing 6.3 is derived from a Department of Defense SGML DTD and is far more complex than anything you are ever likely to encounter. It is certainly far more complex than anything you will ever need to create yourself.

LISTING 6.3 A TYPICAL GRAPHIC ELEMENT DECLARATION

```
 1:<!ELEMENT graphic  EMPTY >
 2:<!ATTLIST graphic boardno    ENTITY        #REQUIRED
 3:                  graphsty   NMTOKEN       #IMPLIED
 4:                  llcordra   NMTOKEN       #IMPLIED
 5:                  rucordra   NMTOKEN       #IMPLIED
 6:                  reprowid   NMTOKEN       #IMPLIED
 7:                  reprodep   NMTOKEN       #IMPLIED
 8:                  hscale     NMTOKEN       #IMPLIED
 9:                  vscale     NMTOKEN       #IMPLIED
10:                  scalefit   %yesorno;     #IMPLIED
11:                  hplace     (left ¦ right ¦
12:                             center ¦ none) #IMPLIED
13:                  vplace     (top ¦ middle ¦
14:                             bottom ¦ none) #IMPLIED
15:                  coordst    NMTOKEN       #IMPLIED
16:                  coordend   NMTOKEN       #IMPLIED
17:                  rotation   NMTOKEN       #IMPLIED>
```

6

ANALYSIS The attributes in Listing 6.3 describe all the physical and placement properties for the image. This is information relevant to the processing of the element, but not information in the same way that the text in the XML document is. This meta information is rightly kept as attributes instead of being part of the normal element content of the document.

As you saw earlier, however, although HTML doesn't have the freedom to define new elements, it is perfectly legal to add as many attributes as you like.

So what about structure? XML is structured by its very nature; HTML has little or no structure. HTML, like any other SGML application, does have a DTD… it's just that unless you get involved with the technicalities of HTML you will probably hardly ever notice it and, depending on what software packages you use to create HTML code, you might never need to know that it's there. The HTML DTD is a fairly loose DTD, requiring very little and giving lots of room to choose the order of elements that suits you best. This is, however, purely a matter of usage. If you wanted to, you could apply a lot of self-discipline and turn out extremely well-structured results, as shown in Listing 6.4.

LISTING 6.4 STRUCTURED HTML

```
1:   <HTML>
2:    <HEAD>
3:      <TITLE>A Tale of Two Computers</TITLE>
4:    </HEAD>
5:    <BODY>
6:      <DIV CLASS="CHAPTER">
7:        <H1>CHAPTER ONE</H1>
8:        <P>It was a dark and stormy night.</P>
9:            <DIV CLASS="SECTION">
10:             <H2>At Home</H2>
11:             <P>The author huddled over his manuscript.</P>
12:           </DIV>
13:           <DIV CLASS="SECTION">
14:             <H2>At Work</H2>
15:             <P>The writer huddled over his draft.</P>
16:           </DIV>
17:      </DIV>
18:    </BODY>
19:  </HTML>
```

If you really want to do so, you can use HTML in a structured way. In contrast, it is quite possible to use just P tags and FONT attributes to make an HTML look like a very highly structured document when it's displayed in a Web browser. If you were to take a look at the raw HTML code, though, it would be almost impossible to find the actual text amongst the code, much less make sense of it.

Done carefully, you can encode almost as much information in HTML code as you can in XML. The problem is that you cannot count on any help from your tools. You certainly won't get any help from a Web browser; they have intentionally been built to accept any and all tags. If the Web browsers can't make sense of the tags, they will simply ignore them. The early Web browser developers were too worried about scaring people away from using HTML by enforcing rigid rules.

Yes, there are some HTML code verification packages (they even call themselves *validators*, but this is stretching the interpretation of the term just a little too far) and they are generally very good. The verifiers check that you have used the HTML tags properly and that your attributes are properly used, but they cannot help you by checking the structure of your document. If you use an H4 tag before an H2 tag, that's your problem. If you want to use <P><FONT SIZE="7"> instead of <H1>, it's all allowed by "the" HTML DTD (there are at least 19 different officially recognized HTML DTDs in circulation).

Why Have a DTD at All?

We've talked about DTDs and about how HTML has one too. Later in today's chapter you will discover that XML allows you to have many, but this begs the question of whether you need a DTD at all. Hasn't XML been touted as DTD-less SGML? True, as you have already learned, as long as it is well formed, there is no need to have a DTD. You will even learn later today that it is possible to derive a DTD just by looking at the XML document. There are, however, some important restrictions on an XML document that does not have a DTD.

If you want to be able to validate an XML document without a DTD:

- All the attribute values in the XML document must be specified; you cannot have default values for them.

- There can be no references to entities in the XML document (except of course amp, lt, gt, apos, and quot).

- There can be no attributes with values that are subject to normalization. (For example, when they contain entity references. We will return to entities on Day 9, "Checking Validity.")

- In elements with content consisting of only elements, there can be no whitespace (space, tab or other whitespace characters) between the starting tag of the container element and the starting tag of the first element contained in it. For example, this would be illegal:

```
<CHAPTER>  <SECTION>... </SECTION></CHAPTER>
```

6

This is a complicated point, but without the help of a DTD to tell the XML processor whether this whitespace is to be treated as meaningful (as PCDATA or as preserved whitespace), the XML processor has no way of knowing whether to delete it or not.

DTDs and Validation

The DTD describes a model of the structure of the content of an XML document. This model says what elements must be present, which ones are optional, what their attributes are, and how they can be structured with relation to each other. While HTML has only one DTD, XML allows you to create your own DTDs for your applications. This gives you complete control over the process of checking the content and structure of the XML documents created for that application. This checking process is called *validation*.

Of all the markup languages, SGML and XML are almost unique in that their documents can be truly validated. Yes, there are software packages that can "validate" HTML code, but this is validation of a completely different nature. HTML code validation is basically little more than tag syntax checking—looking for spelling mistakes and omissions. True validation in SGML and XML terms goes much farther than this. A valid XML document is one that isn't just syntactically correct, it's one with internal structure that complies with the model structure you declare in the DTD.

Depending on what you, as the DTD developer, want to achieve, you can exercise almost complete control over the structure and create a strict DTD. When you validate XML documents created using this strict DTD, you can insist that certain elements are present and you can enforce the set order you require. You can check that certain attribute values have been set and, to a limited degree, even check that these attribute values are the right general type.

On the other hand, you can also make almost everything optional and create a loose DTD. You could even have parallel versions of the same DTD, one that allows you to create draft versions of the XML that aren't complete and another that rigidly checks that everything is present. Going even further, and you will learn how to do this on Day 9, it is even possible to insert switches into a DTD that can be used to turn the strictness on and off again.

Based on what you have declared in the DTD, when the completed XML document is validated, what is allowed and what is not will be completely determined by the choices you made in designing the DTD. The author of the document can then be warned if required elements are missing, as shown in Figure 6.1, and warned when elements are not in the right place, as shown in Figure 6.2.

FIGURE 6.1

Missing element warning.

FIGURE 6.2

Faulty structure warning.

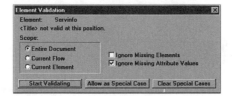

Document Type Declarations

So you've decided to use a DTD. How do you associate a DTD with an XML document? You use a document type declaration. Confusing? Even within established SGML circles there is a lot of confusion about the very similar terms *document type declaration* and *document type definition*. These are two completely different things, so it is good to know which is which. The document type definition (DTD) is an XML (and SGML) description of the content model of a type (or class) of documents. The document type declaration is a statement in an XML (or SGML) file that identifies the DTD that belongs to the document. If an external DTD file is used, the document type declaration identifies where the DTD entity (the file) can be found.

At its very simplest, the syntax of a document type declaration looks like this:

```
<!DOCTYPE DTD.name [ internal.subset ]>
```

`DTD.name` is the name of the DTD. When you read about validity later in this chapter you will discover that the DTD name should be the same as the root element of the document. So, a DTD designed for a document would be called book or something similar and the root element in the document would also be book. Don't forget that XML is case sensitive—if you call the DTD BooK then you should have a root element BooK.

`internal.subset` is the contents of the internal DTD subset, the part of the DTD that stays in the XML document itself. We will investigate the internal DTD subset shortly; it contains local element, attribute, and entity declarations. Without the internal DTD subset there wouldn't really be much point in including a document type declaration at all.

6

Internal DTD Subset

For an XML document to be well formed, all the external entities must be declared in the DTD. If you design your application carefully, it may be possible for you to put all the declarations in the internal DTD subset. With all the declarations in the internal DTD subset, the XML processor would not need to read and process external documents.

Note   The existence of an internal DTD subset does not affect the XML document's status as a standalone document. This can be a little confusing at first, since you might assume that being standalone means the document doesn't need to reference a DTD at all. As long as the declarations in the internal DTD subset follow a few basic rules, the XML document qualifies as a standalone document.

When you start off the XML document, the first line is the XML declaration, which can include a standalone document declaration:

```
<?xml version="1.0" standalone="yes"?>
```

The statement standalone="yes" means that there are no markup declarations external to the document entity (recalling our discussion of physical and logical structures on Day 2, "Anatomy of an XML Document"). In the XML document it is still perfectly acceptable to reference external entities (graphics files, included text, and so on) provided that the declarations of the external entities are contained inside the document entity (in other words, inside the internal DTD subset).

Standalone XML Documents

A document type declaration and the contents of an internal DTD subset are all you need to define the structure of an XML document. Without any external support and without referring to any other files, an XML document containing an internal DTD subset contains enough information to be used for quite complex applications.

Given what you have already learned about declaring elements and attributes, you should already be able to produce something like the basic catalog shown in Listing 6.5.

LISTING 6.5   A STANDALONE XML DOCUMENT WITH INTERNAL DTD SUBSET

```
1:  <?XML version="1.0" standalone="yes"?>
2:  <!DOCTYPE CATALOG [
3:
```

```
 4: <!ELEMENT CATALOG (PRODUCT+)>
 5:
 6: <!ELEMENT PRODUCT (SPECIFICATIONS+, PRICE+, NOTES?)>
 7: <!ATTLIST PRODUCT NAME CDATA #REQUIRED>
 8:
 9: <!ELEMENT SPECIFICATIONS (#PCDATA)>
10: <!ATTLIST SPECIFICATIONS SIZE CDATA #REQUIRED
11:                          COLOR CDATA #REQUIRED>
12:
13: <!ELEMENT PRICE (#PCDATA)>
14: <!ATTLIST PRICE WHOLESALE NMTOKEN #REQUIRED
15:         RETAIL NMTOKEN #REQUIRED
16:         SALES.TAX NMTOKEN #IMPLIED>
17:
18: <!ELEMENT NOTES (#PCDATA)>
19: ]>
20:
21: <CATALOG>
22:    <PRODUCT NAME="T-shirt">
23:      <SPECIFICATION SIZE="XL" COLOR="WHITE"/>
24:      <PRICE WHOLESALE="9.95" RETAIL="19.95" SALES.TAX="2.56"
➥SHIPPING="5.00"/>
25:      <NOTES>Dilbert</NOTES>
26:    </PRODUCT>
27:    <PRODUCT NAME="Shirt">
28:      <SPECIFICATION SIZE="38" COLOR="BLACK"/>
29:      <PRICE WHOLESALE="69.95" RETAIL="79.95" SALES.TAX="4.54"
➥SHIPPING="10.00">
30:      Euro</PRICE>
31:    </PRODUCT>
32: </CATALOG>
```

ANALYSIS   The XML markup shown in Listing 6.5 starts with the now familiar XML prolog that identifies what follows as being an XML version 1.0 document. I have added the STANDALONE statement to make it explicitly clear to the XML processor that it doesn't need to look for an external DTD.

Line 2 declares the document type to be a CATALOG and then we open the internal DTD subset.

The meat of the DTD is lines 4 to 18. We have a CATALOG element that contains one or more PRODUCT elements. A PRODUCT element (line 6) contains one or more SPECIFICATION elements, followed by one or more PRICE elements and then optional NOTES elements.

6

The SPECIFICATION and PRICE elements, as you can see in the markup (lines 21 to 31) are actually empty and their information is included in the form of attributes (lines 23, 24, 28, and 29).

I could have declared these elements as empty, but in this case I left them open. Just because an element isn't declared as empty, it doesn't stop someone leaving the element empty.

 Note

Validation can check the markup, but it actually does little or nothing to check what's between the markup (the content), other than looking for more markup. You can have perfectly structured garbage if you want, or even perfectly structured space and tab characters.

In this case I didn't really want to specify a currency attribute, so all the prices (the PRICE attribute values) are assumed to be in the local currency. This might not always be so, and I still have the option of adding this information as text inside the PRICE element (lines 29 and 30) without having to go back later and change everything.

Note that I have used elements to identify the main objects and properties of those objects in the DTD; a PRODUCT has SPECIFICATION elements inside it. Most of the real property data, however, is declared as the attribute values of the SIZE, COLOR, and PRICE elements.

It is difficult to decide when to use elements and when to use attributes. We will explore this problem a little further tomorrow. I have declared most of the attribute values as being #REQUIRED, which means that they must be given. There is one exception though; the SALES.TAX attribute, which is #IMPLIED. This means that if the value isn't specified to the computer system (actually the XML application running on the computer system), the system will still be able to calculate the value for me.

The XML document I have described can be validated. It contains enough of a DTD, the internal DTD subset, to allow the content and structure of the XML document to be checked. In this form the XML document is pretty portable and there are good arguments for leaving it at that. By adding some 14 lines to the XML markup (far less if you take out the line breaks and spaces added to make it easier to read) we've succeeded in making the document reasonably self-describing. The recipient can even perform a rough check that parts of it are complete. The fact that a complete product is missing could only be detected by the lack of a closing CATALOG tag (assuming the file was clipped in transit). You wouldn't be able to tell through validation how many products were missing (although you could easily modify the DTD—even on-the-fly—to allow this to be checked).

Getting Sophisticated, External DTDs

You have already learned that you can achieve quite a lot with a standalone XML document. While you have all the benefits of portability by keeping the DTD inside the XML document itself, you are only just touching the surface of what can be achieved when you take the next logical step and use an external DTD subset.

The fact that it's called a document *type* definition already gives us a clue that a DTD is intended for use with more than one XML document. Indeed, by not using an external DTD subset you miss out on many XML features as well as the ability to use the DTD as a sort of template for a limitless set of XML documents.

In XML contexts the external DTD subset is often called an *external* DTD, but in SGML contexts it's more often called *the* DTD. XML has one DTD, but it's a composite of both the internal DTD subset and the external DTD subset.

Tip

In XML, the internal DTD subset is read before the external DTD subset and so takes precedence. This allows you to use an external DTD subset to make global declarations and then override them on an individual basis by putting different declarations in the internal DTD subset.

You've already learned how to associate an internal DTD subset with an XML document. The association of an external DTD subset with an XML document is more complicated and uses either a system identifier (SYSTEM keyword) or a public identifier (PUBLIC keyword) and a system identifier:

```
<!DOCTYPE name public.identifier system.identifier [ internal.subset ]>
```

Both the system identifier and the public identifier are entity identifiers. We will return to these identifiers on Day 8, "XML Objects: Exploiting Entities." For now we will examine them in just enough detail for them to make sense when you use them to reference external DTDs.

6

System Identifier

A system identifier is a *URI* (Universal Resource Identifier), that can be used to retrieve the DTD. If you've ever opened a Web page in a browser or downloaded a file from an FTP site, you have already seen one form of a URI called a URL (Uniform Resource Locator). URLs are special forms of URIs intended for network (Internet) use. You will see the more technically precise name of URI used more often than URL, but for the majority of uses the two terms are virtually interchangeable.

A system identifier can reference an absolute location, as in:

```
<!DOCTYPE book SYSTEM "/mount/usr/home/dtds/book.dtd">
<!DOCTYPE book SYSTEM "http://wwwin.synopsys.com/~north/dtds/book.dtd">
```

or it can be a reference to a relative location:

```
<!DOCTYPE book SYSTEM "dtds/book.dtd">
<!DOCTYPE book SYSTEM "../../dtds/book.dtd">
```

Public Identifier

A public identifier is the officially recorded identifier for a DTD. Obviously it would be impossible to register every DTD (it was already impossible with SGML). Instead, the person or company who creates the DTD registers their own. The International Standards Organization (ISO) is responsible under the provisions of ISO 9070 for the registrations, but authority to issue identifiers and the associated record keeping is delegated to the American Graphic Communication Association (GCA).

A public identifier has the following form:

```
reg.type // owner //DTD description // language
```

reg.type is a plus (+) if the owner is registered according to the ISO 9070 standard. Normally, this will not be the case and so *reg.type* is simply a minus (-) sign.

- *owner* is the name of the owner; the name of you or your company.
- *description* is a simple text description. You can make this description as long as you like, but it's a good idea to keep it as short and informative as possible. Spaces are allowed in the description, so you could make it something really meaningful like "Simple Email Message."
- *language* is the two-character language code taken from the ISO 639 standard.

An example of the public identifier for a DTD developed by me could then be:

```
-//Simon North//DTD Simple Web Page//EN
```

An XML processor attempting to retrieve the DTD's content may use the public identifier to try to generate a location. For reasons that will be explained on Day 9, this is not always possible and so the public identifier must be followed by a so-called *system literal*, which is simply a URI. Using the public identifier and the system literal, the documentation type declaration would then look like this:

```
<!DOCTYPE home.page PUBLIC "-//Simon North//DTD Simple Web Page//EN"
➥"home.dtd">
```

Note | Note that before a match is attempted for a public identifier, all the strings of whitespace in it are normalized to single space characters, and any leading and trailing whitespace is removed.

Developing the DTD

There are many ways to describe information models, technically known as *schemas*. Indeed, there are several XML development activities devoted to defining schemas for describing XML data. One such schema is the XML DTD, which is inherited straight from SGML.

The task of developing a DTD can be as simple or as difficult as you make it. It all depends on what you want to do with the information you intend to model with the DTD, and what you intend to do with the information once it has been marked up. I cannot even hope to cover the subject of DTD development thoroughly here; to do so would require a book much thicker than the one before you now. In tomorrow's chapter I will try to address some of the major steps that you should go through while developing your DTD. For now, let's just look at some of the quick and easy methods.

There are two methods that may immediately spring to mind as possible shortcuts to creating a DTD:

1. Modify an existing SGML DTD
2. Create the DTD from the XML document, either automatically or manually

Modifying an SGML DTD

SGML and XML have DTDs. XML is a subset of SGML, so it would seem a logical step to simply take an SGML DTD (there are hundreds in circulation on the Internet) and modify it for use with XML document. Unfortunately, life is never that simple.

There are many differences between an SGML DTD and an XML DTD and, unlike SGML and XML documents, the two are a long way from being compatible with each other. The conversion of an XML DTD into an SGML DTD could be a relatively simple task (and will ultimately be a trivial task once the SGML has been amended to make XML SGML-compliant). On the other hand, it can be an extremely difficult task to convert an SGML DTD into an XML DTD.

6

The fact that there are so many SGML DTDs publicly available could tempt you to consider converting an SGML DTD into XML. I would advise you not to this, or at least not until you have learned enough about XML DTDs to appreciate and understand the differences. There are many features that SGML allows in a DTD that XML does not (and some of these features are so basic that they are used almost routinely) that you may at best be forced to remodel the structure in an XML approximation. At worst, you could even find it necessary to take a step backward (if you are lucky enough to have this option) and change the SGML model to make conversion possible. We will look at the problems of converting SGML DTDs into XML DTDs tomorrow.

Developing a DTD from XML Code

The easiest, quickest, and simplest method of creating an XML DTD is to create an XML document and work backward. Listing 6.6 shows a simple Web page with basic markup.

INPUT   LISTING 6.6   A BASIC WEB PAGE

```
 1:   <?xml version="1.0"?>
 2:   <page>
 3:     <head>
 4:       <title>My Home Page</title>
 5:     </head>
 6:     <body>
 7:       <title>Welcome to My Home Page</title>
 8:       <para>
 9:         Sorry, this home page is still
10:         under construction. Please come
11:         back soon!
12:       </para>
13:     </body>
14:   </page>
```

Given the XML document shown in Listing 6.6, we can already sketch out the rough hierarchy of the elements, where I have used spaces to show the hierarchy:

```
<page>
    <head>
        <title>
    <body>
        <title>
        <para>
```

If we now transpose this into DTD syntax, we arrive at an approximation like the following:

OUTPUT

```
<!DOCTYPE page [
    <!ELEMENT page (head, body)>
    <!ELEMENT head (title)>
    <!ELEMENT body (title, para)>
]
```

Tip

> Note that I have drafted this DTD as it would appear as an internal DTD sub-set at the start of the XML document. Keeping the DTD inside a document during its development can save you a lot of file swapping until you are sure that the DTD works. You can move the DTD to an external file once it has been finalized.

ANALYSIS   All I have said is this:

- The page is the root element.
- The page element consists of a head followed by a body.
- A head element contains a title element.
- A body element contains a title element followed by a para element.

This is the hierarchy of the elements. I now need to add occurrence indicators to specify any restrictions to the order of appearance of the elements and how many times they may appear (if at all). (Don't worry about the occurrence indicators—you will learn all about them tomorrow.)

Without leaping too far ahead into the details of DTD development, there are a few things we can already say about element modeling. In the beginning you should try to leave things as open as you can. Placing unnecessary restrictions will make the DTD harder to use and may force you to change it later on. It is better to go from an unre-stricted, open model to a tight, closed one than the other way around. The following might be what you'd want to aim at, for it ensures that there is a title inside a head, and at least one para inside the body:

```
<!ELEMENT page (head, body)>
<!ELEMENT head (title)>
<!ELEMENT body (title?, para)+>
```

6

You should keep things simple at first, and you might do well to leave the DTD like this:

```
<!ELEMENT page (head, body)>
<!ELEMENT head (title)>
<!ELEMENT body (title, para)*>
```

All I have done is add the '*' indicator to my content model for the body element. This is the *optional repeatable* indicator, which means that a body can be empty or it can contain an endless string of title and para elements in any order.

To complete the DTD, all we have to do is fill in the terminal (leaf) elements, those that contain the actual text or at least don't contain any more elements. The best thing to do is declare these as being text:

```
<!ELEMENT title (#PCDATA)>
<!ELEMENT para  (#PCDATA)>
```

Don't worry too much about the details of this right now—you'll see this in some detail tomorrow. All I'm trying to do now is give you a little feel for the major steps of DTD development.

Creating a DTD from an *instance* (a single XML document) like this goes completely against the grain for most SGML diehards, but SGML was primarily designed for longevity. The whole idea was that you could mark up your data in SGML and preserve it for a very long time, long beyond the lifetime of any one software package or any one computer system. XML is the other side of the coin—it's about information delivery right now, with a maximum lifetime that may be measured more in months than in years.

Granted, if you're intending to use XML as the back-end of a database, you have to think in terms of longer periods than a few months. In many ways, though, the database itself could probably give you most of the DTD design for free without you having to do much extra work (you'll learn about database modeling in DTDs tomorrow).

Creating the DTD by Hand

Although tools that will make the task of creating a DTD much simpler are starting to appear, there's little substitute for doing it with a pencil and a piece of paper.

My personal preference is to use a technique loosely based on the storyboarding techniques used in the film industry for planning a shooting sequence. The important thing is that you work visually, identifying the elements, arranging them into a structure, and then adding all the additional details such as the attributes. Once everything is in place you can simplify the structure, collecting common attributes and sub-element structures into parameter entities.

Tip

> The temptation to make a DTD as sophisticated as possible can be very strong. Bear in mind that a DTD isn't meant to be a showplace for your skill as a DTD developer. Think of the poor souls who have to try to understand what you created and why (this could also be you several years later). You should therefore resist the temptation to use advanced features such as parameter entities or, if you can justify their use (for example, on the grounds of ease of modification), you should document them clearly.

Whatever you decide to use to help you develop your DTDs (there are many different modeling and notation schemes in circulation), there's a good chance that you will eventually develop your own preferred method. The following sections describe the major steps and particular aspects of a DTD that I find help me.

Identifying Elements

For relatively simple Web pages, and some of the simple applications that we have discussed so far, simply typing out the intended XML document and then marking it up will most likely give you a flying start on developing your DTD. Before you do, though, make sure you have a clear idea of what you want to achieve with the DTD. You will learn about this in more detail tomorrow, but you need to be aware of what kind of markup you want to support. It can be

- **Content**—Here you are trying to describe what the information represents. You would then be looking for abstractions that represent real-world objects, such as part numbers and house addresses.

- **Structure**—Here you are more concerned with grouping elements such as lists, paragraphs, and tables. These are elements that break the information into units but do not really add anything informational.

- **Presentation**—Here you are concerned only with the way things look. You should think of line breaks, horizontal lines, and character attributes such as blinking and underlining. Avoid them.

Avoiding Presentation Markup

As far as generic markup is concerned (and the portability of your XML documents) presentation elements are the worst kind of element and should be avoided as much as possible.

6

Where you feel you need some kind of typographic embellishment in an XML document, like boldface, try to relate it to a function by asking yourself why you want it bold in the first place. Is it a keyword? Well, then, call it a KEYWORD element.

Compare this fragment that uses strictly presentational markup:

```
<para><bold>This is a <em>very</em> important aspect.</bold></para>
```

with this fragment that uses a more structural, semantic approach:

```
<note><para>This is a <emphasis>very</emphasis> important
aspect.</para></note>
```

Note

Note that by creating a separate note element I can actually increase the flexibility of the code. If I decide that the text isn't that important after all, I can simply "unwrap" the para element. I can let the note elements determine the appearance of the text, and identifying them as information units makes them much easier to find and deal with than seemingly arbitrary format instructions.

While you should be able to get rid of all the purely presentation elements, there will inevitably be some left. A line break element might be useful (although this should really be more properly solved by inserting a processing instruction addressed to the formatting or page layout application), but some of the more familiar candidates that you might think you'd need aren't worth it.

An example of this kind of presentation element is the horizontal line element, HR, in HTML. Yes, you can do some neat things with horizontal lines, but you should be asking yourself where you actually use them. If you can couple a presentation feature to an element, like putting a horizontal line before the start of a section, or you can link it to a context, like indenting paragraphs inside lists, you should think carefully about whether you could achieve the required effect by using a style sheet of some kind. For example, this XML code fragment

```
<section>
    <title>Section 4</title>
    <rule/>
</section>
```

could be much better written like this:

```
<section>
    <title type="rule under">Section 4</title>
</section>
```

but you could probably simply write this and let the style sheet handle all of the presentation-oriented aspects:

```
<section>
    <title>Section 4</title>
</section>
```

Structure the Elements

Having identified and named the elements in your XML document, the next step is to arrange the elements into some kind of hierarchical (tree) arrangement. The complexity of the tree that you make will largely depend on your application. If you're modeling a database, then you might want to keep the hierarchy fairly flat. At the very least, though, you must obey the rules for setting up well-formed elements and have just one root element that contains all the others. You will probably find that a pencil and lots of paper for sketching the structure will be a great help (you will learn some of the modeling techniques tomorrow). I prefer to scribble the name of each element on a yellow Post-It note and use a large surface like a wall to position them hierarchically. I find this allows me to shuffle elements around much more easily and if I do need to get a global picture I can literally take a few steps back and view the structure from an objective distance.

While structuring, look for group and container elements. Group elements are things like lists, definition lists, and glossaries that arrange sets of elements as units. Sometimes you will need to consciously create extra elements to collect elements so that it's easier for you to process them. For instance, a container list for a set of numbered paragraphs makes it easier to number the paragraphs and reset the number each time you start a new set of numbered paragraphs.

> **Tip**
>
> A useful clue that you need a container element is you find yourself thinking of a set, a list, or a group of elements. If that's the case you should automatically start thinking container.

Examples of container elements are the HEAD and BODY elements in HTML, or perhaps separate MESSAGE.HEADER and MESSAGE.TEXT elements for an email message DTD.

A rough general rule for containers is to look at the content model for the element. If you can't easily understand what it means (try reading it out loud) without having to stop and think, it's too complex and you should consider breaking it up with a container element. You will also find that these containers also give someone who's creating an XML using a DTD that implements containers a lot more flexibility in moving elements around. Consider Listing 6.7, which shows a fragment of an XML document that uses several containers to create a list.

LISTING 6.7   A TYPICAL XML FRAGMENT USING CONTAINER ELEMENTS

```
1:    <para>There are several techniques:</para>
2:    <list>
3:       <item>
4:          <body>
5:             <para>Blame someone else</para>
6:          </body>
7:       </item>
8:       <item>
9:          <body>
10:             <para>Pretend it wasn't you</para>
11:          </body>
12:       </item>
13:       <item>
14:          <body>
15:             <para>Be honest</para>
16:             <para>Not advisable!</para>
17:          </body>
18:       </item>
19:    </list>
```

Note how breaking an item into a body that contains para elements allows the author to move para elements between items without having to worry about constantly wrapping and unwrapping elements. This structure would also make it much easier to nest lists within lists and so on.

Enforce the Rules

So far, you should have been concentrating on simply getting everything identified and organized. Only when these stages have been completed should you start to think about enforcing your model, making elements optional and required. As I suggested earlier, think carefully about how strict you want to be and how much validation you need. If your XML code is to be computer-generated, perhaps from a database, there probably isn't much point in wasting time and energy in tightening up the DTD. After all, you then have complete control over the generation of the XML markup. On the other hand, if the XML markup is to be created by humans, you will probably want to make sure that certain elements aren't forgotten.

Be careful when you make elements optional that you don't make the content model ambiguous.

> **Note**
>
> Remember that XML processors aren't very complex and are unable to look ahead at what comes next in the XML document. At each point in the content model, it must be absolutely clear to the processor what element is allowed next based on what is visible at that point.

Sometimes, as you will learn tomorrow, you will have to use some pretty clever tricks to get round these ambiguities.

Assigning Attributes

Once you have arranged your elements into a hierarchical structure and grouped them as necessary, you can assign attributes to them (size, color, ID, and so on). You may find that you want to move some of the information into attributes, which is why it helps to keep the two tasks separate.

There are no real rules about when to use attributes and when to use elements, although there is a lot of discussion about it. You will learn more about it tomorrow, but for now you should simply go by feel and common sense. I, for example, have a head and a height. It's a pretty easy choice to say that my head should be an element, a physical part, and my height, which is not something I can hold in my hands, should be an attribute. You could therefore model this in the XML DTD something like the following:

```
<!ELEMENT me (head)>
<!ATTLIST me height CDATA " ">
```

The matching XML document code would then look something like the following:

```
<me height="6 feet">
   <head/>
</me>
```

Tool Assistance

6

There are already a number of very good XML editors available. Although some of them are still in the early stages of development and it's still unclear what features are actually required by users, a trend is apparent. In less than a year, along a path that very roughly parallels that followed by HTML tools, we have moved from markup-aware text editors to a sort of word processor package attuned to editing XML code.

The XML editors that are now appearing on the market are beginning to add in dedicated XML capabilities such as validation.

XML Pro (http://www.vervet.com) and Stilo WebWriter (http://www.stilo.com) are both excellent. XML Pro provides a superb and cheap editing environment that allows you to edit and validate XML documents. WebWriter goes one step further and allows you to actually generate a raw DTD straight from the XML document. I predict that more and more XML tools will incorporate this facility, as it's reasonably easy to extract at least the core of a DTD from the markup in an XML document.

A Home Page DTD

You have now learned the basics of XML DTDs and DTD modeling. It's time to put this knowledge to use and create a DTD for a very simple type of document, a beginner's Web home page. We'll reuse the example we used in Day 2, shown again in Listing 6.8.

INPUT   **LISTING 6.8**   A TYPICAL XML INSTANCE

```
 1:  <?xml version="1.0"?>
 2:  <home.page>
 3:    <head>
 4:      <title>
 5:        My Home Page
 6:      </title>
 7:      <banner source="topbanner.gif"/>
 8:    </head>
 9:    <body>
10:      <main.title>
11:        Welcome to My Home Page
12:      </main.title>
13:      <rule/>
14:      <text>
15:        <para>
16:          Sorry, this home page is still
17:          under construction. Please come
18:          back soon!
19:        </para>
20:      </text>
21:    </body>
22:    <footer source="foot.gif"/>
23:  </home.page>
```

If we pull this markup into the XML Pro editor, without a DTD (see Figure 6.3) we can then add elements, delete them, and move them around as much as we want. Once you've finished playing and are satisfied with the results, you can use the tree structure shown in the left window to see the way you have structured things. You can easily explore your tree by expanding and collapsing branches. The tree structure gives you a good head start on describing the structure you want in your DTD.

FIGURE 6.3

Exploring the structure in XML Pro editor.

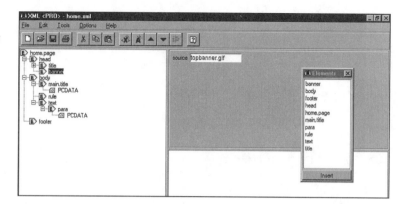

If you pull the same XML markup into Stilo WebWriter, it isn't quite as easy to navigate the structure as in XML Pro, but WebWriter compensates by allowing you to actually generate the DTD. See Figure 6.4.

FIGURE 6.4

Creating the DTD in Stilo WebWriter.

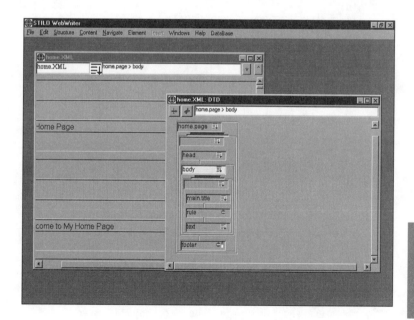

6

Let's see what WebWriter makes of our simple home page. Listing 6.9 shows the extracted DTD (I have added a few blank lines and spaces to make it a little more readable).

LISTING **6.9**   THE EXTRACTED DTD

```
 1: <?xml version = "1.0" ?>
 2: <!ELEMENT home.page  (#PCDATA ¦ head ¦ body ¦ footer)* >
 3:
 4:  <!ELEMENT head     (#PCDATA ¦ title ¦ banner)* >
 5:
 6:  <!ELEMENT title    (#PCDATA) >
 7:
 8:  <!ELEMENT banner     EMPTY >
 9:   <!ATTLIST banner     source CDATA "" >
10:
11:  <!ELEMENT body     (#PCDATA ¦ main.title ¦ rule ¦ text)* >
12:
13:  <!ELEMENT main.title (#PCDATA) >
14:
15:  <!ELEMENT rule     EMPTY >
16:
17:  <!ELEMENT text     (#PCDATA ¦ para)* >
18:
19:  <!ELEMENT para     (#PCDATA) >
20:
21:  <!ELEMENT footer     EMPTY >
22:  <!ATTLIST footer     source CDATA "" >
23:
24:  <!ENTITY lt "<">
25:  <!ENTITY gt ">">
26:  <!ENTITY apos "'">
27:  <!ENTITY quot """>
28:  <!ENTITY amp "&">
```

ANALYSIS   Obviously, WebWriter has sensibly played it a little safe in allowing every element to have mixed content (#PCDATA is allowed in all the content models), and
it was wise not to guess about the nature of the attributes, but what you have is a good
framework. All you need to do is tighten up the content models and fill in the attribute
declarations. One possible end result is shown in Listing 6.10.

LISTING **6.10**   THE FINALIZED DTD

```
1: <!ELEMENT home.page  (head ¦ body ¦ footer) >
2:
3:  <!ELEMENT head     (title ¦ banner?) >
4:
5:  <!ELEMENT title    (#PCDATA) >
6:
7:  <!ELEMENT banner     EMPTY >
8:  <!ATTLIST banner
```

```
 9:              src CDATA  #REQUIRED
10:              alt CDATA #IMPLIED
11:              align (top ¦ middle ¦ bottom) #IMPLIED >
12:
13:  <!ELEMENT body     (main.title ¦rule ¦ text) >
14:
15:  <!ELEMENT main.title (#PCDATA) >
16:
17:  <!ELEMENT rule       EMPTY >
18:  <!ATTLIST rule
19:             align (left¦right¦center) #IMPLIED
20:             size   NMTOKEN #IMPLIED
21:             width CDATA #IMPLIED >
22:
23:  <!ELEMENT text     (#PCDATA ¦ para)* >
24:
25:  <!ELEMENT para     (#PCDATA) >
26:
27:  <!ELEMENT footer      EMPTY >
28:  <!ATTLIST footer
29:              src CDATA  #REQUIRED
30:              alt CDATA #IMPLIED
31:              align (top¦middle¦bottom) #IMPLIED >
32:
33:  <!ENTITY lt "<">
34:  <!ENTITY gt ">">
35:  <!ENTITY apos "'">
36:  <!ENTITY quot """>
37:  <!ENTITY amp "&">
```

ANALYSIS Note that, in accordance with the XML specification, now that we are using a DTD, we have included the declarations of the default character entities (lt, gt, apos, quot, and amp).

Summary

You learned about the XML DTD and how it's divided into two subsets, an internal subset that is included in the XML document and an external subset that is contained in an external file. You have also learned how to reference the external DTD subset using a public identifier and a system identifier.

You have been introduced to some of the factors governing whether or not to use a DTD, and whether to include it externally or internally, and you are should be fairly familiar with the major content of a DTD.

6

You should now have an idea of the basics of DTD modeling and a few of the problems that you may encounter. Tomorrow we will pick up the DTD thread again and examine modeling and its problems in some detail. Don't let DTDs scare you off—they are complex, but they can also be very, very simple. If all else fails, this is still a perfectly acceptable, valid XML document with an internal DTD subset and it might be all you need:

```
<?xml version="1.0" standalone="yes"?>
<!DOCTYPE DOC [
<!ELEMENT DOC (#PCDATA)>
]>
<DOC>I can now put all this text in
my document and forget about any other
markup. </DOC>
```

Q&A

Q Is there any limit to the length of an element or attribute name?

A No, not in XML. As long as you obey the restrictions on what characters you are allowed, a name can be as long as you want it to be (in SGML you have to make special arrangements—you have to modify the SGML declaration—to allow longer names).

Q How many elements should you have in a DTD?

A It all depends on your application. HTML has about 77 elements, and some of the industrial DTDs have several hundred. It isn't always the number of elements that determines the complexity of the DTD. By using container elements in the DTD (which add to the element count), authoring software is able to limit the possible choices and automatically enter required elements. Working with one of the major industrial DTDs can actually be far easier than creating HTML! Because HTML offers you more free choice, you have to have a much better idea of the purpose of all the elements rather than just the ones you need.

Q Do you have to validate your XML documents?

A No, but unless you are certain that your documents are valid you cannot predict what will happen at the receiving end. Although the XML specification lays down rules of conduct for XML processors and specifies what they must do when certain invalid content is parsed, the requirements are often quite loose. Validation certainly won't do any harm—though it might create some extra work for you.

Q I can validate my XML documents, but how do I check that my DTD is correct?

A Simply validate an XML document that uses the DTD. There aren't as many tools specifically intended for checking DTDs as there are for validating documents. However, when an XML document is validated against the DTD, the DTD is checked and errors in the DTD are reported.

Exercises

1. Create a content-based XML DTD for a simple email message.

2. Create (part of a) DTD to deal with lists. Try creating two versions of the element structures, one using an attribute to describe the type of numbering (for example, bulleted or numbered), and one that uses separate item elements (such as `numberlist` and `bulletlist`). Now compare the two and consider the two versions and their advantages and disadvantages relating to ease of authoring and ease of formatting via a style sheet.

6

WEEK 1

DAY 7

Developing Advanced DTDs

Yesterday you learned about XML DTDs and mastered the basics of DTD development. Today's chapter will expand and deepen your knowledge of DTDs. You will do the following:

- Explore some of the issues concerning DTD development and information modeling raised yesterday.

- Look at some of the more technical aspects of DTDs.

- Learn some new features and tricks that will make creating a DTD much easier.

Caution

A word of warning: I added the word *advanced* to the title of this chapter with the express intention of scaring you off. So far in this book I have assumed you have far more knowledge of HTML than I would have liked. I've also made a lot more reference to SGML than I should have. But when it comes to DTDs, XML comes very close to SGML and it's hard to ignore it completely.

Although this chapter doesn't require you to know anything about SGML, it might make things clearer if you did.

Information Richness

Yesterday you learned that the content and complexity of a DTD is pretty much determined by the application. Essentially, the XML document and its markup follow what I call the Law of NINO: *Nothing In, Nothing Out*. This means that if you want to do something with a piece of information in an XML document, you must identify it. It doesn't matter whether you mark it up using elements or attributes. However, if you haven't marked it up, you either won't be able to find it all or, if you *do* find it, you won't be able to do anything with it.

Here's another acronym I invented to help bring the point home: YCEWIT, or You Can't Extract What Isn't Tagged. It's pronounced "you sow it," harkening back to the Biblical admonition that you shall reap what you sow.

Humor aside, a DTD that contains a lot of (informative) markup is called a *rich DTD*. As the DTD designer, you will always face a difficult compromise between the complexity of the DTD and the information-richness of XML documents that conform to that DTD. When humans are the authors of those documents, the complexity of the DTD can become a major obstacle. Always choose the richest information model you can:

- It is far easier to throw away information than it is to add it afterwards.

  Consider what happens when you go from XML, or even HTML, to plain text with no markup at all. It's a very simple conversion to make because you're moving from a higher level of information richness to a lower one. However, going the other way is not easy at all. The same applies for moving from SGML to XML, and from XML to HTML. At each conversion you throw information away, moving from an information-rich level (SGML) to a pretty information-poor level (HTML).

- You cannot always account for all media and all intended uses. No matter how carefully you research your application in advance, there will always be something you haven't thought of.

  With SGML, often it's only after you've got all your data marked up that you really start to appreciate what you can do with it. If you limit yourself to the minimum necessary for the current application, you may design yourself into a corner and have no room left for expansion.

  As in mechanical systems, information objects are subject to a sort of entropy law. In mechanical systems, the law of entropy says that a system will always tend to become more disorganized. Release some gas into a room, and after a while its molecules will be pretty evenly scattered. The chances of all the molecules magically finding their way back into the original container are very small (although it's actually possible at the quantum level). In the same way, the information-richness of an XML document will always have a tendency to slide down the slippery slope into garbage (high information entropy). The higher up the slope you start (the richer your start point), the longer you can fight off the decline.

- Remember the curse of legacy data.

  In SGML circles, data that either hasn't been marked up or has been marked up to an earlier version of a DTD is called *legacy data*. It's the stuff that's dumped on you, like the Biblical sins of the fathers being visited on the sons. It's also often a far greater problem than any of the new material you produce.

  Although you can achieve a lot by remapping attributes (as you will learn on Day 11, "Using XML's Advanced Addressing"), you are more or less stuck with the elements you started with.

Note

There is a proposal to implement a feature taken from HyTime called *architectural forms* for XML, but it is unlikely that the proposal will be adopted. Unfortunately, whereas SGML is now understood by quite a large number of people, even the eyes of SGML gurus have been known to glaze over at the very mention of HyTime. Architectural forms are not the easiest things to understand, and there is still very little software that can support them.

Don't underestimate the speed with which you will amass legacy data, and don't underestimate the longevity of your data. It's all too easy to start out with a DTD that works, thinking that it's only small-scale and will be superceded in a few months. If you do this, you're opening the door to a lifelong career as an editor.

7

You'll have to go back to modify every XML document you have created so far, and just when you think you've finished, something will change and you'll have to repeat the exercise all over again. This is the curse of legacy data.

Visual Modeling

Yesterday you learned that one of the basic DTD design process steps is to construct the hierarchy—use the content models in the DTD to arrange the elements in an XML document that uses the DTD into a hierarchical tree-like structure.

There are many information-modeling techniques, but detailed discussion of them falls outside the scope of this book. The important thing is that all of them recommend some kind of visual aid to help you. The same applies for DTD development, but each expert has his or her own set of symbols. Some prefer to model information using the blocks so familiar from flow diagrams, as shown in Figure 7.1.

FIGURE 7.1

Block diagram DTD modeling.

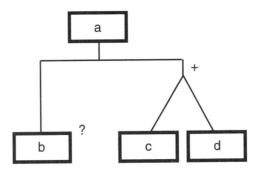

<!ELEMENT a (b?.(c | d)+>

An alternative is the somewhat sparser representation form shown in Figure 7.2.

ANALYSIS Note that both types of modeling graphics try to represent the sequence and OR models (a model in which there are two or more alternatives and one must be chosen) by using different kinds of connecting lines between the objects (diagonal line for an OR choice, straight line for a simple relationship, and rectangular connections for sequences). This type of graphics modeling is also incorporated into the top-of-the-line SGML DTD modeling package, Microstar's Near & Far (http://www.microstar.com), an example of which is shown in Figure 7.3.

FIGURE 7.2

Simplified diagram DTD modeling.

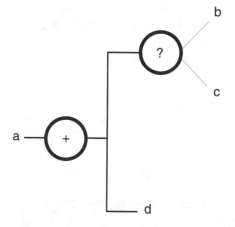

<!ELEMENT a ((b | c)? d)+>

FIGURE 7.3

Visual modeling in Near & Far.

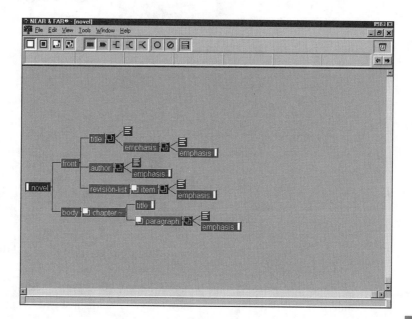

It is difficult to think of a better way of modeling DTDs visually than these kinds of models, especially in a software package where you can expand and collapse branches of the DTD tree as you work on them. However, as the DTD gets larger and larger, it becomes harder and harder to maintain a sensible overview. You shouldn't forget that

7

these are primarily SGML tools, and people using them are mostly working on a completely different scale than is probably useful in XML. Whereas an XML application might need a few dozen elements and a couple of hundred lines in a DTD, SGML applications routinely use several hundred elements and several thousand lines of declarations in a DTD.

It isn't just the number of elements that makes the DTD bulky, though. Often, elements that have a presentational function (like emphasized text) will be reused in almost every element. When you expand these models, even a well-designed visual presentation can simply become too cluttered to be much use unless you start finding other ways to manage DTDs of this scale or complexity (see Figure 7.4).

FIGURE 7.4

Reaching the limits of useful visual modeling.

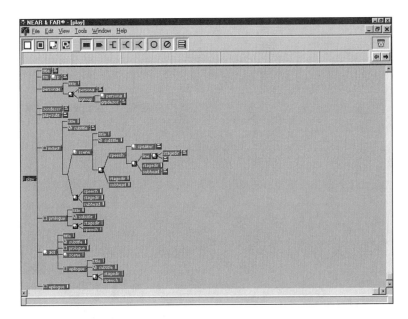

There are techniques for mastering DTDs of this scale, of course, such as breaking the DTD into modules of a more manageable size (as you will learn later in today's chapter). But there also comes a point where you must ask yourself whether it is really worth continuing in this way. Figure 7.5 shows a public-domain software package called EZDTD that gives a sort of tabular display of the elements in the DTD (go to `http://www.download.com` and search for "EZDTD").

FIGURE 7.5

Tabular modeling in EZDTD.

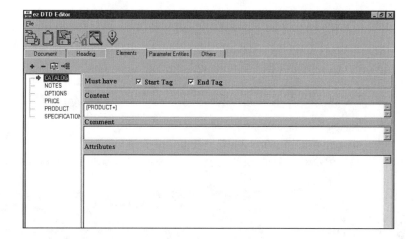

ANALYSIS All you have here is a list of elements, and you can display the content model for one model at a time. This kind of tool might be all you will ever need for simple XML applications and smaller DTDs, especially as you become more proficient in creating DTDs. Unfortunately, there is no way of displaying any kind of tree to show the relationships between elements. Again, once the scale of the DTD increases beyond a certain point, the usefulness starts to tail off (see Figure 7.6).

FIGURE 7.6

Reaching the limits of usefulness of a simplified form of visual modeling.

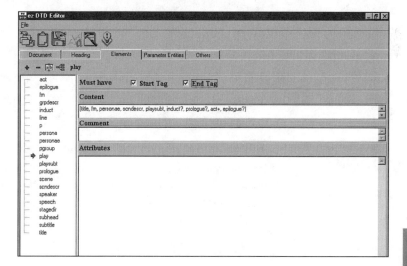

7

It may make more sense to give up on trying to visualize the DTD altogether, although I can highly recommend Earl Hood's public-domain DTD2HTML package for Perl (http://www.oac.uci.edu/indiv/ehood/perlSGML.html). This package converts a DTD into a set of interlinked HTML pages. The output isn't a great deal of help while you're actually developing the DTD, but it's extremely useful for checking the results of your work and is an excellent way to document the completed DTD.

Instead of visually modeling the DTD, you may ultimately find it easier to use a more conservative package, such as Innovation Partner's DTD Generator package (http://www.mondial-telecom.com/oddyssee), shown in Figure 7.7.

FIGURE 7.7

Creating a DTD with the XML DTD Generator package from Innovation Partners.

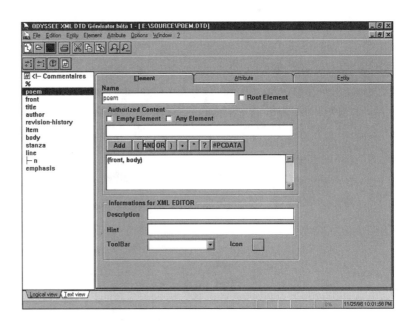

ANALYSIS This no-frills package is a sort of halfway point between the two camps. You have all the ease of dedicated buttons that allow you to add the parts of content models quickly, but there is no visual display. Instead, you can very quickly flip between the ease-of-use interface and the raw DTD code.

XML DTDs from Other Sources

As suggested earlier, one alternative to getting involved in the complexities of DTD design and development is to leave the DTD design to one side and simply work on a representative XML document. You must consider all the likely variations of the document, of course, and you will probably need several documents as your XML application becomes larger. However, once you have explored all the possibilities of the XML document, you can then use tools to create at least the core of the DTD. While this would be unthinkable, even heretical, to attempt with an SGML application, this approach is often a realistic choice for XML applications. As you can see from the real-life document loaded in XML Pro (http://www.vervet.com) in Figure 7.8, a good XML editor will allow you to browse through the structure of the document, adding elements and attributes wherever you need them. Although you may find yourself repeating some steps unnecessarily, it is easy enough to consolidate the multiple declarations afterwards.

FIGURE 7.8

Modeling the document before creating a DTD.

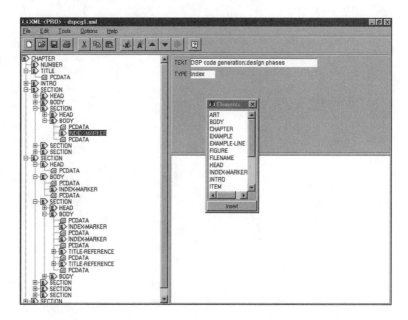

There is also one very significant benefit to this approach that no specialized DTD tool can give you: By exposing you to what amounts to a completed XML document using your (proposed) DTD, it gives you firsthand taste of what it would be like for a human author to work with your DTD.

Yet another way to leapfrog yourself into the middle of the DTD development process is to take a sort of "back door". Many of the mainstream software packages, such as Adobe's FrameMaker and even Microsoft's Office suite, will be supporting XML as an output format in the near future. This opens up all sorts of possibilities for perfecting the structure of an intended XML in one of those software packages and then creating the DTD from that document, or even skipping the DTD altogether.

7

An interesting development in this direction is the Majix software package from Tetrasix (`http://www.tetrasys.fr/ProduitsFrame.htm`). This software package (seen in Figure 7.9) allows you to create an XML document from a Microsoft RTF document. For example, if you use Microsoft Word and you can discipline yourself to use styles properly (remember, a DTD is just one way to describe the structure of an XML document), you can use these styles to drive the conversion into XML elements.

FIGURE 7.9

Converting RTF into XML with Majix from Tetrasix.

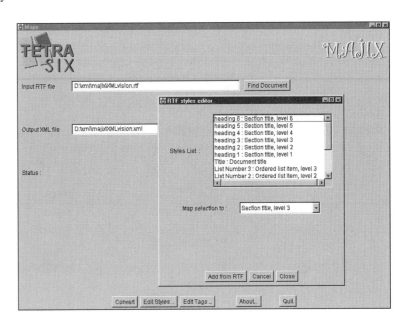

I'm not much of a fortune teller, but it's a safe bet that there will be a lot more of these conversion tools in the future, and they will make everyone's lives a lot easier.

Modeling Relational Databases

In all this discussion of developing DTDs, I have consistently talked of structuring the elements hierarchically. However, sometimes you may not want, or even need, to have too much of a hierarchy and want to keep the model "flat." For example, you might use XML to model a relational database, an application that XML is ideally suited for (subject to the planned XML data-typing initiatives bearing fruit).

Consider the very simple relational database description shown in Listing 7.1. Although the topic of database modeling in XML deserves far more extensive treatment than I can give it here (there are some excellent books devoted to the topic), even a quick appraisal shows that you don't really need that much depth at all. In fact, the simple database shown here needs only four levels:

- The database (the root element, `music`)
- The database tables (the `artists` and `disks` elements)
- The database records (the `artist` and `disk` elements)
- The database fields (the `name`, `label`, `title`, `date`, and `number` elements)

LISTING 7.1   A SIMPLE DATABASE IN XML

```
 1: <!DOCTYPE music SYSTEM "mymusic.dtd">
 2: <music>
 3:   <artists>
 4:     <artist>
 5:       <name>Cyndi Lauper</name>
 6:       <label>Sony</label>
 7:       <title>Twelve Deadly Guns</title>
 8:     </artist>
 9:     <artist>
10:       <name>Kate Bush</name>
11:       <label>EMI</label>
12:       <title>Hounds of Love</title>
13:     </artist>
14:   </artists>
15:   <disks>
16:     <disk>
17:       <title>Twelve Deadly Guns</title>
18:       <date>1994</date>
19:       <number>EPC 477363 2</number>
20:     </disk>
21:     <disk>
22:       <title>Hounds Of Love</title>
23:       <date>1985</date>
24:       <number>CDP 7 46164 2</number>
25:     </disk>
26:   </disks>
27: </music>
```

Once you have this structure, it's a simple matter to add table and record keys by assigning attributes. In this way you could create a forced division, using the elements to describe the content and structure of the database itself and reserving the attributes for the (internal) data that describes the relationships between the data.

7

Elements or Attributes?

Separating elements and attributes in an XML database description is just one of the many ways to make a distinction between elements and attributes. This question surfaces regularly in SGML circles and has never really been answered with any degree of conviction. The database example shows one possible answer, but it is just one of many. I have no quick answer either, but I can offer the following thoughts to help you decide which to choose:

- Elements can be remapped using architectural forms, and attributes can be remapped using XLink. From this perspective there is not a decisive reason to select either the element or the attribute (because both can be remapped).

- Historically, attributes have been reserved for intangible, abstract properties such as color and size, while elements are reserved for physical components. To deviate from this usage may confuse people, especially in an SGML context.

- It may be easier to edit elements than attributes with XML editing tools, and attribute values may not be as readily displayed as element content. This would favor elements when dealing with human authors.

- An XML processor can check the content of an attribute value more easily than it can check the content of an element. It can't check an attribute value for much, but it can barely check the content of an element at all.

- The attributes of elements from separate XML documents can be merged quite easily. It can be extremely hard to merge elements, so attributes may have the edge over elements in a distributed environment.

- In collaborative, multiple-author environments, it is reasonably easy to split XML documents into fragments based on the element structure rather than attribute values.

- Sensibly named elements can make authoring easier and less confusing. For example, when someone selects an element to contain a list, it's pretty obvious that she should choose a `list` element. However, the selection of the correct attribute can be less than obvious and not very visible (you will often see such cryptic attribute values as `ordered` and `unordered`, which come from HTML). Choosing container elements instead, like `list.numbered` and `list.bulleted`, may make the author's life much simpler.

You may notice a general trend here. Generally speaking, when human beings are expected to create or work with XML documents, it's better to use elements than attributes.

Saving Yourself Typing with Parameter Entities

You will learn a lot more about entities on Day 9, "Checking Validity." For the moment, we're concerned with one particular type of entity called the parameter entity, which can be extremely useful in XML DTDs.

Parameter entities are basically just like the character entities you learned about earlier. They too behave like macros and can be used as abbreviations for strings. However, whereas character entities serve as abbreviations for character strings, parameter entities serve as shortcuts for markup declarations and parts of declarations. Obviously, because they are concerned with markup declarations, they can be used only in DTDs. In fact, their use is even a little more restricted than this:

- In the internal DTD subset, parameter entities can be used only between other markup declarations.
- In the external DTD subset, parameter entities can be used both between and inside other markup declarations.

To make sure there's no confusion between parameter entities and character entities, the syntax for declaring and referring to parameter entities is quite different than the syntax for character entities. A parameter entity uses a percent sign (%), as in this example:

```
<!ENTITY % heading "H1 | H2 | H3 | H4 | H5 | H6" >
<!ENTITY % body.content "(%heading | %text | %block | ADDRESS)*">
<!ELEMENT BODY %body.content>
```

 The `heading` parameter entity saves a lot of typing (note that you can only use this particular trick in the external DTD subset).

You can also use a parameter entity to make your DTD declarations a little more comprehensible, as in Listing 7.2.

LISTING 7.2   SIMPLIFYING A DTD WITH A PARAMETER ENTITY

```
 1:<!ENTITY % color "CDATA" >
 2:
 3:<!ENTITY % body-color-attrs "
 4:      bgcolor %color #IMPLIED
 5:      text    %color #IMPLIED
 6:      link    %color #IMPLIED
 7:      vlink   %color #IMPLIED
 8:      alink   %color #IMPLIED
 9:      ">
10:
```

7

continues

LISTING 7.2   CONTINUED

```
11:<!ELEMENT BODY   %body.content>
12:<!ATTLIST BODY
13:           background %URL #IMPLIED
14:           %body-color-attrs; >
```

ANALYSIS Both examples shown here use internal parameter entities. No external file is required for the XML processor to determine the contents of the entities. It is also possible to have external parameters, as you will learn next, and these are used for quite different purposes.

Modular DTDs

When I talked about the size and complexity of DTDs earlier in this chapter, I mentioned the possibility of splitting up the DTD into modules. This is another use for external parameter entities. For example, the following DTD fragment declares and then immediately references a set of character entity declarations contained in an external file (this is such a common use for parameter entities that there is an extensive set of public identifiers that covers most of the less commonly used characters):

```
<!ENTITY % ISOnum PUBLIC "ISO 8879:1986//ENTITIES Numeric and Special
Graphic//EN">
%ISOnum;
```

External parameter entities really come in handy when you decide to reuse the results of work that you have invested in the development of other DTDs. For example, over the years the declarations of the elements in a table have become standardized around a model called the *CALS table* model (named after the American Department of Defense Computer Assisted Logistic Support initiative, under which a lot of early SGML developments were funded). It is hard to improve on this model (tables are pretty standard), so it is often provided as a common DTD fragment that all other DTDs can reference when they need it (it's also part of the official HTML DTDs):

```
<?xml version="1.0" standalone="no"?>
  <!DOCTYPE book SYSTEM "book.dtd" [
    <!ENTITY % calstable SYSTEM "cals.dtd">
    %calstable;
  ]>
```

ANALYSIS Note that this external parameter entity declaration, and the reference to it, are located in the internal DTD subset. Note, too, that I have explicitly stated that the XML document is *not* a standalone document.

> **Caution** If you're not going to validate an XML document, you must always be wary of what can go wrong with external parameter entities that contain markup declarations.

Listing 7.3 shows an external parameter entity being used in an internal DTD subset to include some declarations from an external file.

LISTING 7.3   A DANGEROUS EXTERNAL PARAMETER ENTITY

```
 1: <?xml version="1.0" standalone="yes"?>
 2: <!DOCTYPE menu [
 3:   <!ELEMENT menu (#PCDATA, front, meals+, back)* >
 4:   <!ATTLIST menu title CDATA "Carte Blanche">
 5:
 6:   <!ENTITY % entrees SYSTEM "entrees.xml">
 7:   %entrees;
 8:   <!ATTLIST menu desserts CDATA "Sweet Temptations">
 9: ]>
10: <menu><front>Sunday, July 11, 1998</front> ... </menu>
```

ANALYSIS   When this XML document is parsed, but not validated, the value of the menu element's title attribute will be Carte Blanche. The XML processor sees the declaration of the title attribute (line 4) even though it is inside the internal DTD subset (lines 2 to 9). Because it isn't validating (the document claims that it is a standalone document in line 1), the XML processor is not allowed to process any external entity references. The value of the desserts attribute has to remain unknown.

The default value (Sweet Temptations) has been declared, but the XML processor isn't allowed to use it. Maybe it seems odd, but what is contained in the entrees.xml file that is referenced by the entrees external parameter entity? I don't know, but it doesn't really matter because the XML processor is not allowed to know either. Suppose, though, that the entrees.xml file contained element declarations; the entity reference is inside the internal DTD subset, so it would be quite legal to do so. Suppose too that the file contained this attribute declaration:

```
<!ATTLIST menu desserts CDATA "Bitter Experiences">.
```

This would mean that the desserts attribute could not have the value Sweet Temptations.

7

So be careful with external parameter entities in the internal DTD subset, and consider the possible confusion they could cause when the recipient is not validating (something you have little or no control over). The only way you can protect yourself from this is to always use a standalone document declaration.

The purpose of this declaration is really to tell the recipient that the DTD could change the document, and that the DTD should be retrieved if the recipient wants to be certain that it's seeing the same thing as the application that created the document. Parsing the DTD would mean that external entity references would be dereferenced, so the external declaration would then be found. Although the declaration has no effect on the XML processor, changing the value of the standalone document declaration to `"no"` will inform the recipient that validation is needed if the document is to be seen as intended.

Conditional Markup

Yesterday, when you learned about the DTD design step of constraining the model, I said that you could always consider making two versions of the same DTD. You could use a loose DTD during authoring when, for example, not all the content has been filled in but you still want to validate the document, and another, tighter DTD for the finished XML document. There is a way to do this using *conditional sections* of the DTD and parameter entities. (You will learn more about conditional sections of a DTD on Day 9 when you learn about entity declarations.)

This trick involves wrapping the two variant declarations of the DTD inside blocks and starting each block with a reference to a parameter entity, as shown in this fragment:

```
<![%AuthoringSwitch;[
    <!ENTITY % body "chapter, intro?, section*">
]]>
<![%FinalSwitch;[
    <!ENTITY % body "chapter, intro, section+">
]]>
```

The parameter entities `AuthoringSwitch` and `FinalSwitch` can then be declared as the keyword `INCLUDE` or `IGNORE`, according to which version of this entity you want to use. For the first, loose version, you would insert the declarations like this, before the conditional sections:

```
<!ENTITY % AuthoringSwitch "INCLUDE">
<!ENTITY % FinalSwitch     "IGNORE">

<![%AuthoringSwitch; [
    <!ENTITY % body "chapter, intro?, section*">
]]>
<![%FinalSwitch; [
```

```
        <!ENTITY % body "chapter, intro, section+">
]]>
```

And for the second, tighter version, you would insert the declarations like this, before the conditional sections:

```
<!ENTITY % AuthoringSwitch "IGNORE">
<!ENTITY % FinalSwitch     "INCLUDE">

<![%AuthoringSwitch; [
    <!ENTITY % body "chapter, intro?, section*">
]]>
<![%FinalSwitch; [
    <!ENTITY % body "chapter, intro, section+">
]]>
```

ANALYSIS Conditional sections in DTDs might seem like a trivial feature with only a small section affected (as in the examples), but you can use pairs of parameter entities like this to control many separate sections of a DTD. By changing the values of just these two parameter entities, you could radically change the whole DTD.

Optional Content Models and Ambiguities

When you review a DTD you are working on, take a close look at the occurrence indicators. If there are a lot of optional elements in a content model, there may be something wrong with the model.

An example of this comes from the SGML world, where paper books are common items for markup. Consider the back part of a book. I am creating an XML DTD for a book, and I've created a container element BACK to make it easier to process the parts together. My BACK element consists, as books often do, of any number of appendices (including zero), followed by an optional glossary and then an optional index. When you can describe a content model in plain English like this, it is quite easy to model:

```
<!ELEMENT BACK (appendix*, glossary?, index?)
```

The content model might look good, but I now have a problem. Everything is now optional, making it possible for me to have an empty BACK element, which certainly wasn't the idea.

One way to get around this is to break up the content model into inner groups, where each group explicitly describes one of the possibilities:

```
<!ELEMENT BACK ( (appendix+, glossary?, index?) |
                 (appendix*, glossary, index?) |
                 (appendix*, glossary?, index) )>
```

7

That seems to cover it. Let's just check:

- Group 1: I can have one or more appendices, followed by an optional glossary and then an optional index.
- Group 2: I can have zero or more appendices, which must be followed by a glossary and then an optional index.
- Group 3: I can have zero or more appendices, followed by an optional glossary and then there must be an index.

Seems pretty complete—and no empty BACK elements allowed—except that I now have an even bigger problem. This markup won't work!

 Note
XML processors aren't very intelligent. They are not able to remember what they've seen, look ahead at what comes next, and then backtrack to confirm that your markup agrees with content model after all. All processors can do is read a piece of markup, check if it's valid, read the next piece, check that, and so on. Because of the limitations of processors, element content models have to be absolutely clear and capable of being interpreted in only one way.

When the XML processor sees an appendix element, it really cannot tell what's supposed to happen next—should there be a glossary element next or not? This content model is "ambiguous."

One way to get around this problem is to adopt what is called the waterfall approach, where you take each element in turn and work out only the new cases you need to cover. For the first element you'd have to consider a lot of possibilities, fewer for the second, and even fewer for the third until with the last element there are hardly any possibilities left. Let's adopt this approach here and follow the process step by step, re-examining the three groups I defined earlier as we go:

- Group 1: I can have one or more appendices, followed by an optional glossary and then an optional index. The first group seems OK.
- Group 2: I can have zero appendices (I've already covered the one or more possibility) which must be followed by a glossary and then an optional index.
- Group 3: I can have zero appendices and no glossary, but then there must be an index.

This is much better and once we write it out in the DTD it turns out to be the answer:

```
<!ELEMENT BACK ( (appendix*, glossary?, index?) ¦
                 (glossary, index?) ¦
                 (index) )>
```

Avoiding Conflicts with Namespaces

XML was designed with the Internet in mind, this is a given. XML also (as you will learn later) has extremely powerful mechanisms for linking documents that go much further than either HTML or even SGML. The linking features in XML actually allow you to go a step further than just "pointing" to another document: they allow you to pull the linked document (the link target) into the current document and include it as if it had been a physical part of the current document. This kind of linking is called *transclusion*.

NEW TERM *Transclusion* is a composite word, formed from *transversal* and *inclusion*. It means the activity of following a hypertext link from its source to its target and then copying the target to the point of reference as if it had been physically included at that point (much like the way graphics are included in HTML files by reference).

Now, suppose the link target is also an XML document. In itself, this needn't be a problem because XML has set rules for dealing with these conflicts:

- If the documents were created using the same DTD, with the same elements and the same element content models, this is probably not a problem at all.

- If they have the same elements but the elements have different attributes, the attributes are simply merged and the composite document elements have all the attributes.

- If they have different element declarations or the same attributes with different values, things start to get complicated. If you are validating an XML document, an element can only be declared once.

To get around this problem, under a proposal of the same name, each schema (this also applies for schemas other than DTDs) is considered to have a private "namespace" in which all the declarations are unique and have their own meanings. In between the XML declaration and the document type declaration, you then insert a declaration (an XML processing instruction) like the one shown in this fragment to identify the namespaces belonging to the schemas:

```
<?xml version="1.0" standalone="no">
<?xml:namespace name="http://www.synopsys.com/"

                 href="http://www.synopsys.com/~north/xml/version1.dtd"
                 as="v1"?>
```

7

The name attribute value locates the namespace owner, the href attribute value locates the schema itself, and the as attribute value declares a prefix that is used in front of every element and attribute that originates in this namespace. Now, when I have two attributes that mean different things in the different namespaces I don't have to discard one of them, and now I'm not going to get fatal validation errors because elements are declared twice. Instead I can keep them distinct by identifying them as coming from different namespaces and preserve the information they represent, as shown in this fragment:

```
<object v1.type:v2.sort="shirt">
<v1:size>10</size>
<v2:size>XXL</size>
</object>
```

 Note that the prefix used to identify the namespace occurs locally. This not only means that you can call it whatever you like, it also means there are none of the inevitable problems associated with trying to centralize the names used for the infinite number of namespaces.

> **Caution**
> The namespaces proposal is only a proposal and is still subject to change. Although it is already being adopted in various XML applications (including XSL), some of the implementations are non-standard and there may be some heated discussions before a suitable compromise is found.

A Test Case

So far, much of this chapter has been a bit theoretical. To complete what you have learned about DTD development so far, it might be useful to follow through with a practical demonstration.

> **Note**
> We can achieve only so much in such a short space and limited time (it isn't unusual for SGML DTDs to take several years and the involvement of hundreds of people to complete). But in a way, this is as it should be. After all, XML is much more suited to fast, lightweight applications.

Let's take something simple, like a set of address records. (I'm almost tempted to call it an "address database," which it isn't, but this kind of database-like information is perfect for XML-based applications.) A small fragment of the raw data is shown in Listing 7.4.

LISTING 7.4   THE RAW DATA FOR AN XML APPLICATION

```
 1:  Fred Bloggs MISTC
 2:  22 Chancery Lane
 3:  London SW17 4QP
 4:  England
 5:  44 1 800 3451
 6:  44 12 446 3382
 7:  fbloggs@hk.co.uk
 8:
 9:  Dr. Jon F. Spencer
10:  El Camino Real 44621
11:  Sunnyvale
12:  95144 California
13:  USA
14:  1 650 445 1273
15:  1 405 227 1877
16:  jdspencr@hiflier.com
```

Note

The raw data shown in Listing 7.4 consists of two different types of address details. This highlights some of the problems that you might encounter. For example, in the UK, designatory letters come after the name, although they can also come before, as shown in the US example. In a lot of European countries, they all appear before the name (like the Dutch example of "Prof. Mr. Dr. Ing. D.H.J. Heyden-Loods"). Also note the difference in the ZIP code formatting and position (no two countries have the same scheme) and in the telephone and fax numbers (again, no two countries have the same scheme).

Fortunately, the order in which these items appear in any rendered output is something that can be left to a style sheet. Our main concern is simply to identify information, not to specify how it will be rendered. However, this aspect cannot be ignored completely because inevitably there will be information that you want to identify in elements simply to apply some special rendering to it.

The first step is to abstract the information content out and identify it as elements. While you're doing this, you must look ahead and consider possibilities that might not actually occur in the test data, (such as addresses that consist of more lines than the number shown in Listing 7.4). Listing 7.5 shows my attempt to formalize the data as a hierarchy of elements.

7

LISTING 7.5   THE FORMAL ELEMENT STRUCTURE

```
1: People
2:     Person
3:        Name
4:             FirstName
5:             MiddleName
6:             FamilyName
7:             Title
8:        Address
9:           Street1
10:          Street2
11:          City
12:          State
13:          Country
14:          ZipCode
15:        PhoneNumber
16:        FaxNumber
17:        Email
18:        Notes
```

ANALYSIS   Notice how I've added an element for a middle name and one for a street address that can consist of two lines, even though neither of my two examples uses either. Also note that I haven't broken the telephone and fax numbers into separate numbers for the country code, area code, and so on. You might want to do this for your own records, especially if you want to select only people with a certain area code. For this application, we're only interested in the complete numbers, so there's nothing to be gained by adding extra elements.

Now that you have the basic element tree, you can start transcribing this into DTD syntax. Start with the top-level elements first:

```
1: <!DOCTYPE People [
2:
3:    <!ELEMENT People   (Person)>
4:
5:    <!ELEMENT Person   (Name, Address, PhoneNumber,
6:                        FaxNumber, Email, Notes)>
7:
8:    <!ELEMENT Name     (FirstName, MiddleName, FamilyName,
9:                        Title)>
10:
11:   <!ELEMENT Address (Street1, Street2, City, State,
12:                       Country, ZipCode)>
```

Once you've got the top-level elements sorted out, you can continue with the second level, and then the lower (leaf) elements:

```
13: <!ELEMENT FirstName    (#PCDATA)>
14: <!ELEMENT MiddleName   (#PCDATA)>
15: <!ELEMENT FamilyName   (#PCDATA)>
16: <!ELEMENT Title        (#PCDATA)>
17: <!ELEMENT Street1      (#PCDATA)>
18: <!ELEMENT Street2      (#PCDATA)>
19: <!ELEMENT City         (#PCDATA)>
20: <!ELEMENT State        (#PCDATA)>
21: <!ELEMENT Country      (#PCDATA)>
22: <!ELEMENT ZipCode      (#PCDATA)>
23: <!ELEMENT PhoneNumber  (#PCDATA)>
24: <!ELEMENT FaxNumber    (#PCDATA)>
25: <!ELEMENT Email        (#PCDATA)>
26: <!ELEMENT Notes        (#PCDATA)>
27: ]>
```

Tip

> Resist the temptation to specify the nature of element content unless it's really necessary, and even then, only do it when you're sure the data will always be of that type. Specifying a telephone number as being numerical data (NMTOKENS) can only create problems for you if you encounter numbers that include non-numeric data (such as dashes).

I have elected to play it safe in this DTD. All the leaf elements are simply PCDATA type (text) because either I cannot be sure what the contents of the elements will be, or I won't gain anything by adding a restriction on the data content.

Since this is such a simple DTD, I could safely leave it at this. However, there is one small optimization that almost demands implementation, and that's the long list of identical leaf element declarations. This is a perfect example of parameter entities saving you a lot of effort. The whole list can be collapsed like this:

```
1:  <!ENTITY % Data "(FirstName, FirstName, MiddleName,
2:                    FamilyName, Title, Street1, Street2,
3:                    City, State, Country, ZipCode,
4:                    PhoneNumber, FaxNumber, Email, Notes)">
5:
6:  <!ELEMENT %Data; (#PCDATA)>
```

7

Caution

> Note that there is a space on either side of the % symbol in the declaration of the Data parameter entity, but there is no space when the entity is actually used.

We aren't quite finished yet. You now need to go back and add the occurrence indicators, as shown in Listing 7.6.

LISTING 7.6   THE COMPLETED DTD

```
 1: <!DOCTYPE People [
 2:
 3:   <!ELEMENT People  (Person)+>
 4:
 5:   <!ELEMENT Person  (Name, Address?, PhoneNumber?,
 6:                      FaxNumber?, Email?, Notes?)>
 7:
 8:   <!ELEMENT Name    (FirstName?, MiddleName?, FamilyName,
 9:                      Title?)>
10:
11:   <!ELEMENT Address (Street1?, Street2?, City?, State?,
12:                      Country?, ZipCode?)>
13:
14:   <!ENTITY % Data "(FirstName, FirstName, MiddleName,
15:                      FamilyName, Title, Street1, Street2,
16:                      City, State, Country, ZipCode,
17:                      PhoneNumber, FaxNumber, Email, Notes)">
18:
19:   <!ELEMENT %Data; (#PCDATA)>
```

ANALYSIS   Almost every element in the complete DTD shown in Listing 7.6 can occur just once or can be omitted altogether. These elements are indicated with a ?. There are a few exceptions. For example, there must be at least one Person, and there can be as many as you like; the Person element is therefore marked with a +. A Person must have some kind of name or the record would be pretty pointless (although all the other data is optional). I therefore made the Name element a compulsory part of the Person element, and the FamilyName element must appear just once within the Name element (Name and FamilyName therefore don't have an occurrence indicator).

We're almost there. The very last step is to review the model and decide on any attributes. In this example, I've left a choice open. I added a Notes element that allows me to add descriptive information, but I won't be able to do much with anything that's inside the element because as far as the XML application is concerned, it simply contains text. You could consider adding an attribute to describe what kind of person this is. (This is an example where your choices can only be driven by what you want to do with the data.) For example, you could declare this:

```
 1:   <!ELEMENT Person  (Name, Address?, PhoneNumber?,
 2:                      FaxNumber?, Email?, Notes?)>
 3:
```

```
4:    <!ATTLIST Person Type (Business ¦ Personal) "Business">
5:
6:    <!ATTLIST Title Position (Before ¦ After) "Before">
```

ANALYSIS Here I've declared a Type attribute for a Person. Since the content of the attribute is a string, it's CDATA by default and I don't need to declare the attribute type. What I can do, though, is declare Business as the default value, which means I only need to specify a value in the XML data for all the people who are personal type entries.

Where the attributes come into their own is in solving presentation and rendering problems, like the title position problem that I mentioned earlier. Here I have specified a Position attribute for the title, with two options, Before and After. The Before value is the default, so I only need to explicitly specify the attribute when the title needs to appear after the name. The application and the style sheet control the rendered position.

So far I've been writing the DTD so that it can be used inside a test document as an internal DTD subset. All I have to do now is trim off the first line (<!DOCTYPE People [) and the last line (]>) and save the DTD in a separate file.

Tip

> If you're going to create more than just a few DTDs, you should be careful to choose filenames that describe the content. Generally, giving the file the same name as the root element will be enough, but you might want to be more specific (such as DOC_SHORT and DOC_FULL). Get this right first; going back to change all the references to a DTD in a lot of documents can be a real pain when all you want to do is change a filename.

You're now ready to mark up the XML and validate it against the DTD. Listing 7.7 shows my marked-up data.

LISTING 7.7 THE MARKED-UP DATA FOR AN XML APPLICATION

```
1:    <?xml version="1.0" ?>
2:    <!DOCTYPE People SYSTEM "People.DTD">
3:
4:    <People>
5:
6:      <Person Type="Personal">
7:        <Name>
8:          <FirstName>Fred</FirstName>
9:          <FamilyName>Bloggs</FamilyName>
10:         <Title Position="After">MISTC</Title>
```

7

continues

LISTING 7.7   CONTINUED

```
11:       </Name>
12:       <Address>
13:         <Street1>22 Chancery Lane</Street1>
14:         <City>London</City>
15:         <Country>England</Country>
16:         <ZipCode>SW17 4QP</ZipCode>
17:       </Address>
18:       <PhoneNumber>44 1 800 3451</PhoneNumber>
19:       <FaxNumber>44 12 446 3382</FaxNumber>
20:       <Email>fbloggs@hk.co.uk<Email>
21:     </Person>
22:
23:     <Person>
24:       <Name>
25:         <FirstName>Jon</FirstName>
26:         <MiddleName>Jefferson</MiddleName>
27:         <FamilyName>Spencer</FamilyName>
28:         <Title>Dr.</Title>
29:       </Name>
30:       <Address>
31:         <Street1>El Camino Real 44621</Street1>
32:         <City>Sunnyvale</City>
33:         <State>California</State>
34:         <Country>USA</Country>
35:         <ZipCode>915144</ZipCode>
36:       </Address>
37:       <PhoneNumber>1 650 445 1273</PhoneNumber>
38:       <FaxNumber>1 405 227 1877</FaxNumber>
39:       <Email>jdspencr@hiflier.com</Email>
40:     </Person>
41: </People>
```

There you have it—an XML instance, complete with its own DTD.

Summary

Today you have learned a lot more about DTDs and XML content modeling. You have also learned quite a few of the advanced tricks that can make things a lot simpler. You've seen for yourself some of the problems that can occur, and some of the ways to get yourself out of trouble. You should now be able to create complex XML DTDs, and you should have a pretty good idea of the best tools to use. On Days 8 and 9, we'll flesh out some of the more complex topics you learned yesterday and today.

Q&A

Q Why are ambiguities so important?

A Ambiguous content models are among the most common sources of problems for DTD developers, especially at the beginning. They're also some of the hardest problems to locate and fix. Anything you learn about them now can save you a lot of head-scratching later on.

Q At what point should I split up a DTD into pieces?

A There's no absolute value; it's simply a matter of how happy you are dealing with one unit. Size and complexity aren't the only criteria, though. You might want to split up a DTD earlier than strictly necessary in order to introduce some modularity.

Q I can have modular DTDs, so can I also have modular documents?

A Of course. To modularize a XML document, simply break it into text entities and combine them by using character entities in the main document. Don't forget the rules about parallel logical and physical structures. You can also use transclusions (inclusion by reference), which you'll learn about on Day 10, "Creating XML Links."

Exercises

1. Design a DTD for a basic Web home page (you can cheat and look at earlier examples).

2. Using your home page DTD as the basis, expand the DTD so it can be used to cover a complete Web site. Think in terms of internal DTD subsets and external parameter references.

3. Take any DTD you like and sketch it as a tree diagram (you can use whichever symbols you like). Now set the DTD elements in a table in which the first column contains the root element, the second column contains its children, and so on. Compare the two representations. This should convince you of the importance of modeling a DTD using a clear visual representation.

7

WEEK II

8 XML Objects: Exploiting
   Entities 151

9 Checking Validity 173

10 Creating XML Links 195

11 Using XML's Advanced
   Addressing 215

12 Viewing XML in Internet
   Explorer 227

13 Viewing XML in Other
   Browsers 267

14 Processing XML 291

8

9

10

11

12

13

14

DAY 8

XML Objects: Exploiting Entities

In yesterday's chapter, you learned much of what you need to know about markup. Now it's time to retrace some of these steps and go into greater technical detail about the real nuts and bolts of XML documents—the data you put into them. In this chapter, you will learn about

- XML entities
- Notations
- XML character sets
- Using (multiple) character encoding

Entities

Without getting too involved in the terminology (especially since this chapter takes a few liberties with some of the terms), XML brings markup a step closer to the world of object orientation, as in object-oriented programming. The basic object in XML is the entity, whether it's the XML document entity itself, the elements it contains, or the internal and external entities it references.

Of course, the DTD itself is an external entity that the document references (a special type of parameter entity, in fact), but the relationship is a little more complex than this. The DTD describes a class of XML document entities, of which the actual XML document is an instantiation.

The entities are divided into three types (excluding the XML document entity itself, which really isn't of any further interest in this context): character entities, general entities, and parameter entities. General entities can be further subdivided into internal entities and external entities. To confuse things a little more, external entities are subdivided into parsed entities (containing character data) and unparsed entities (usually containing binary data). Finally, common usage is that parsed general entities are usually referred to as internal and external text entities, and unparsed external general entities are often just called binary entities.

Personally, I find it easier to think in terms of text entities, which can be either internal or external, and binary entities, which have to be external. This minimal classification is actually helped by the way you declare the entities. An internal text entity declaration looks like this:

```
<!ENTITY name "replacement text">
```

An external text entity declaration looks like this (you will learn about the syntax of these declarations shortly):

```
<!ENTITY name SYSTEM "system.identifier">
<!ENTITY name PUBLIC public.identifier "system.identifier">
```

A character entity declaration (which is just a special case of an internal text entity) looks like this:

```
<!ENTITY name     "&#code;" >
```

When you refer to these entities, the text and character entity references look like this:

```
&name;
```

Now that you've been introduced to the basic types of entities, let's look at them in more detail.

Internal Entities

Internal entities are those whose definitions contain their values:

```
<!ENTITY intent "I am an internal entity, my declaration is self-
contained">
```

There is no separate physical storage object (file), and the content of the entity is given in the declaration. (It may be necessary for the XML processor to resolve any entity and character references in the entity value to produce the correct replacement text.)

Internal entities are parsed and must not contain references to themselves, either directly or indirectly.

In Chapter 4, you learned how to declare entities in a DTD so you can insert multiple occurrences of the text in a file without having to retype it every time. I won't recap the mechanism in any detail here, but let's look at a practical example.

INPUT I'm going to add the following code to my DTD:

```
<!ENTITY quick "a surprisingly long and boring piece
                of text that I haven't the slightest
                intention of entering more than once.">
```

Now I can reuse this text over and over again in my XML document by referencing it wherever I want it:

```
<p>The first part is &quick;,
the second part is &quick;, and
the third part is &quick;.</p>
```

When these references are displayed in an XML browser, they will be resolved and replaced with the entity text, as shown in Figure 8.1.

OUTPUT

FIGURE 8.1

How an entity is resolved in an XML browser.

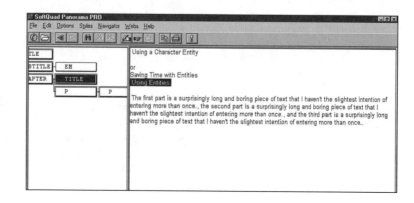

Note

> It would have been far more satisfying to have a true XML browser in Figure 8.1, but none of the current Web browsers can resolve entity references. Instead, the display shows SoftQuad's Panorama SGML browser. Fortunately, you can easily display XML code that doesn't differ too much from normal SGML code (and that has a DTD). An evaluation copy of Panorama can be downloaded at http://www.sq.com.

Binary Entities

Binary entities contain unparsed data (graphics, sound, and so on). When they are declared, they must be identified with a notation. The notation must also have been declared in the DTD:

```
<!NOTATION notation.name "public.identifier" "helper.application">
<!ENTITY entity.name NDATA notation.name>
```

Binary entities can only be referenced in the value of an attribute that has been declared to be of type ENTITY or ENTITIES in the DTD:

```
<!ELEMENT element.name EMPTY>
<!ATTLIST element.name
          attribute.name NDATA notation.name>
```

And this binary entity would then be referenced in the XML document, like this:

```
<element.name attribute.name="entity.name"/>
```

Listing 8.1 shows a typical example of a binary entity reference in an HTML file. An identical reference could also be used in an XML file.

INPUT   LISTING 8.1   A TYPICAL BINARY ENTITY REFERENCE

```
1:   <H4>
2:     <A HREF="http://www.w3.org/">
3:       <IMG alt="W3C" SRC="http://www.w3.org/
4:           pub/WWW/Icons/WWW/w3c_home.gif"
5:         WIDTH="72" HEIGHT=48>
6:     </A>Parsing Entities
7:   </H4>
```

When this code is displayed in a Web browser, you will see the graphic displayed at the place where the reference was made, as shown in Figure 8.2.

OUTPUT

FIGURE 8.2

How a binary entity (a graphics file) is resolved in a Web browser.

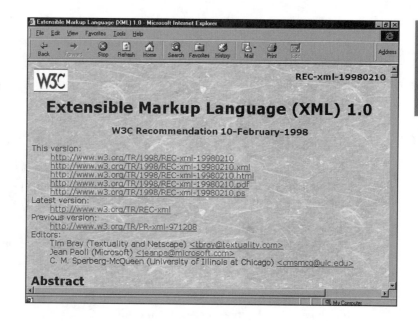

8

Note

Note that the reference to a binary entity appears as the value of an element attribute. Text entity references can appear in element content, but binary (unparsed) entity references can only appear inside attributes.

Notations

Notations identify by name the format of unparsed entities (binary files such as external graphics files), the format of elements that bear a notation attribute, or the helper application (capable of processing the data) to which a processing instruction is addressed.

A notation must be declared in the DTD before it is used. The absolute minimum acceptable form of a notation declaration is

```
<!NOTATION Name SYSTEM "">
```

where *Name* is something meaningful to you or the registered public identifier for a particular format.

If your system supports it (as Microsoft Windows will, provided that the extension is associated with an application), you may be able to get away with using a notation declaration like this:

```
<!NOTATION GIF SYSTEM "GIF">
```

This declaration takes advantage of the fact that as far as the XML processor is concerned, there doesn't have to be anything on the system that can interpret data in this notation. Interpreting the data, or handling the error when it can't handle the data, is entirely the application's problem.

If you know there's an application on the system that can handle data in a certain notation, you can help the application out by also pointing to the application:

```
<!NOTATION TIFF SYSTEM 'C:\PROGRAM FILES\PaintShop Pro 5\psp.exe'>
```

Obviously, this will only work if you know the name and location of the application that can handle a particular notation, and if no one moves it. This isn't a lot of use on the Internet.

It is also possible to use an existing SGML facility and a public identifier. There are a lot of registered public identifiers for notations, covering everything from the C programming language (ISO/IEC 9899:1990//NOTATION (Programming languages—C)) to time itself (ISO 8601:1988//NOTATION (Representation of dates and times)). Some of the best-known notations, and their SGML public identifiers as they would be used in an SGML notation declaration, are shown in Listing 8.2.

LISTING 8.2   SOME STANDARD SGML NOTATION DECLARATIONS

```
 1: <!NOTATION JPEG PUBLIC "ISO/IEC 10918:1993//NOTATION
 2:    Digital Compression and Coding of
 3:    Continuous-tone Still Images (JPEG)//EN">
 4:
 5: <!NOTATION BMP PUBLIC
 6:     "+//ISBN 0-7923-9432-1::Graphic Notation//NOTATION
 7:    Microsoft Windows bitmap//EN">
 8:
 9: <!NOTATION CGM-CHAR PUBLIC
10:    "ISO 8632/2//NOTATION Character encoding//EN">
11:
12:    <!NOTATION CGM-BINARY PUBLIC
13:    "ISO 8632/3//NOTATION Binary encoding//EN">
14:
15: <!NOTATION CGM-CLEAR PUBLIC
16:    "ISO 8632/4//NOTATION Clear text encoding//EN">
17:
18: <!NOTATION FAX PUBLIC "-//USA-DOD//NOTATION
19:    CCITT Group 4 Facsimile Type 1 Untiled Raster//EN">
20:
```

```
21: <!NOTATION GIF87a PUBLIC "-//CompuServe//NOTATION
22:   Graphics Interchange Format 87a//EN">
23:
24: <!NOTATION GIF89a PUBLIC "-//CompuServe//NOTATION
25:   Graphics Interchange Format 89a//EN">
26:
27: <!NOTATION PCX PUBLIC
28: "+//ISBN 0-7923-9432-1::Graphic Notation//NOTATION
29:   ZSoft PCX bitmap//EN">
30:
31: <!NOTATION WMF PUBLIC
32: "+//ISBN 0-7923-9432-1::Graphic Notation//NOTATION
33:   Microsoft Windows Metafile//EN">
```

There's no reason why you can't use these SGML declarations in XML documents, and there are some very good reasons why you should. But the SGML public identifiers have to be combined with system identifiers to allow you to do so, like this:

```
<!NOTATION GIF89a PUBLIC "-//CompuServe//NOTATION
    Graphics Interchange Format 89a//EN"
    'C:\Program Files\lviewpro.exe'>
```

Note that you use a system identifier, but you don't need the SYSTEM keyword.

After (and *only* after) you have declared the notation, you can use that notation by name in an entity declaration with the NDATA (notation data) keyword:

```
<!ENTITY figure1 SYSTEM 'figure1.gif' NDATA BMP>
```

You can also use the notation in one of the attribute declarations for an element by using the NOTATION keyword:

```
<!ELEMENT IMG  EMPTY >
<!ATTLIST IMG
        src      %URL      #REQUIRED
        alt      CDATA     #IMPLIED
        type     NOTATION (GIF ¦ JPEG ¦ BMP) "GIF" >
```

Note

Note that when you use enumerated notations in an attribute declaration, every notation you name must be declared in the DTD before the XML processor reaches that part of the DTD. For example, if you use notations in the internal DTD subset, you must declare the notation in the internal DTD subset too, and not in the external DTD subset. (As you may remember, the internal DTD subset is read before the external DTD subset.)

> **Note**
>
> Typing in the public identifiers for notations can very quickly become a tedious and error-prone business. There's also a good chance that you will use the same notations again and again. Therefore, it's a good idea to collect all your notation declarations into one file. Give the file an obvious name like `graphics.ent` so that when you reference it in an XML document, it will always be easy to trace back what is going on:
>
> ```
> <?xml version="1.0" standalone="no"?>
> <!DOCTYPE chapter SYSTEM "chapter.dtd" [
> <!ENTITY % myentities SYSTEM "mysymbols.ent">
> %myentities;
> ]>
> <chapter><number/> … </chapter>
> ```

ANALYSIS   By using an obvious filename and then referencing that file in all the DTDs you create by using an external entity declaration that points to it, you can save yourself a lot of unnecessary work. Why an obvious filename? Simple. You may return to a DTD after weeks, even months, and any extra clues about its content are bound to be welcome.

If for no other reason, keeping all your notation declarations in a separate file will mean that you'll only have to edit the file once if something changes, instead of having to edit every separate DTD. Also, there is less chance of you forgetting a declaration you need.

Identifying External Entities

Internal entities are self-contained, meaning that their definition is contained in their declaration. External entities are contained elsewhere, as their name suggests. There are two ways to identify the location of an external entity's content: through a system identifier or through a public identifier.

System Identifiers

A system identifier can be either a relative path to a filename (for example, `..\..\graphics\home.gif`) or an absolute path to a filename (for example, `c:\Program Files\LView\lview.exe`):

```
<!ENTITY my.file SYSTEM "c:\inetroot\filez\file1.xml">
```

A system identifier can also be a Universal Resource Identifier (URI). The URI is an enhancement of the Universal Resource Locator (URL) system used for World Wide Web addresses:

```
http://www.xs4all.nl/~sintac/books.htm
```

In this case, `www.xs4all.nl` is my service provider's Web server and `~sintac` is a pointer that the UNIX system translates into my login (home) directory. The Web server then directs the Web browser to the designated Web page directory coupled to my login name, and `books.htm` is obviously the name of the file. A URI is a type of Universal Resource Name (URN), which is a sort of superset. The two are more or less synonymous, so I will simply use "URL" and be done with it. (Old habits do die hard.) The syntax for a full URL looks like this:

```
scheme://login-name:password@host:port//path
```

In this URL, `scheme` is a protocol and most of the host information (`login-name`, `password,` and `port`) is only entered when it is really needed. The scheme could be `http` (Hypertext Transfer Protocol), `ftp` (File Transfer Protocol), `gopher` (the Gopher protocol), `news` (Usenet news—this one breaks the rule because the protocol is actually `nntp`, for Net News Transfer Protocol), `wais` (for Wide Area Information Servers), or `file` (for local file access). There are several more schemes, but many of them, like `mailto`, wouldn't make much sense for retrieving information.

Public Identifiers

A system identifier is reasonably straightforward; it simply points to a file. The public identifier is an inheritance from SGML. As far as entities are concerned, public identifiers result in the same things as system identifiers: somewhere, they are resolved into filenames. For notations, however, they represent a more formal method of identification. Using public identifiers allows the inclusion of such extra details as the language, the owner (or copyright holder), and the author.

Caution

There is still no *official* method for resolving public identifiers in XML. However, there is an SGML method that has been used for years. Most of the major XML tools come from SGML developers, so the same method has quietly been implemented in XML tools without any real discussion about whether it was needed or not.

SGML uses a public identifier resolution mechanism based on an industry agreement published as Technical Resolution 9401 in 1997 by the SGML Open Consortium (which recently changed its name to OASIS—the Organization for the Advancement of Structured Information Standards). More commonly known as the SGML Open Catalog (SOC), this mechanism uses a *catalog file* that is located in the same directory as the document (the application is free to change this location, of course). This file is usually called `catalog.soc` or, more frequently, just `catalog`. (A particular application will normally allow you to specify which file should be used as the catalog file.)

There is little point in going into all the technical details because the catalog file is really an SGML facility that in turn draws on some of the features of HyTime, and SGML and HyTime are well outside the scope of this book. As far as we are concerned, the catalog file is an ASCII file consisting of lines that couple a public identifier (officially a Formal System Identifier (FSI)) with a system object identifier. A *system object identifier* is basically a file, but it could also be some other kind of identifier that the system can convert into something meaningful. An example of a typical catalog file is shown in Listing 8.3.

LISTING 8.3   A TYPICAL CATALOG FILE

```
 1: -- catalog: SGML Open style entity catalog for HTML --
 2: -- $Id: catalog,v 1.3 1995/09/21 23:30:23 connolly Exp $ --
 3: -- Hacked by jjc --
 4: -- Ways to refer to Level 2: most general to most specific --
 5: PUBLIC     "-//IETF//DTD HTML//EN"                "html.dtd"
 6: PUBLIC     "-//IETF//DTD HTML 2.0//EN"            "html.dtd"
 7: PUBLIC     "-//IETF//DTD HTML Level 2//EN"        "html.dtd"
 8: PUBLIC     "-//IETF//DTD HTML 2.0 Level 2//EN"    "html.dtd"
 9:
10: -- Ways to refer to Level 1: most general to most specific --
11: PUBLIC     "-//IETF//DTD HTML Level 1//EN"        "html-1.dtd"
12: PUBLIC     "-//IETF//DTD HTML 2.0 Level 1//EN"    "html-1.dtd"
13:
14: -- Ways to refer to Strict Level 2: most general to most specific --
15: PUBLIC     "-//IETF//DTD HTML Strict//EN"         "html-s.dtd"
16: PUBLIC     "-//IETF//DTD HTML 2.0 Strict//EN"     "html-s.dtd"
17: PUBLIC     "-//IETF//DTD HTML Strict Level 2//EN" 'html-s.dtd"
18: PUBLIC     "-//IETF//DTD HTML 2.0 Strict Level 2//EN" "html-s.dtd"
19:
20: -- Ways to refer to Strict Level 1: most general to most specific --
21: PUBLIC     "-//IETF//DTD HTML Strict Level 1//EN" "html-1s.dtd"
22: PUBLIC     "-//IETF//DTD HTML 2.0 Strict Level 1//EN" "html-1s.dtd"
23:
24: -- ISO latin 1 entity set for HTML --
25: PUBLIC     "ISO 8879-1986//ENTITIES Added Latin 1//EN//HTML"
➥ISOlat1.sgm
```

> **Note**
>
> Note that the example shown in Listing 8.3 is a modified XML version of an SGML catalog file. In XML the filename has to be enclosed in quotes, while in SGML it doesn't.

There is nothing to prevent you from creating a catalog file with a text editor, but there are a few free catalog management packages (also called *entity management packages*) available on the Internet. Some software packages have their own built-in facility, often called an *entity manager*, for resolving entities. The only thing you need to know to make the mechanism work is that the left-hand part of a line (the FSI) in a catalog file must exactly match the declaration in the XML document.

Parameter Entities

A parameter entity is a completely separate sort of entity because of one major restriction: parameter entity references may only appear in a DTD.

To keep parameter entities distinct from general entities (and to prevent them from being used in a document), they're declared and referenced with a percent sign (%):

```
<!ENTITY % "front ¦ body ¦ back" >
```

Parameter entities are extremely useful as shortcuts for parts of declarations that occur often in a DTD. However, they can't contain markup (complete declarations). They can only contain parts of declarations:

```
<!ENTITY common "(para ¦ body ¦ text)">
<!ELEMENT chapter ((%common;)*, section+)>
<!ELEMENT section (%common;)>
```

When a parameter entity reference is resolved, one leading space and one trailing space is added to the replacement text to make sure that it contains an integral number of grammatical tokens.

Entity Resolution

The rules governing entity resolution—when entities are interpreted and when they are ignored—can be quite complicated. Table 8.1 shows what happens to entity references and character references. The leftmost column describes where the entity reference appears:

- **Inside an element**—The reference appears anywhere after the start tag and before the end tag of an element.

- **In an attribute value**—The entity reference occurs within the value of an attribute in a start tag, or in a default value in an attribute declaration.

- **As a name in attribute value**—The entity reference appears as a name, not as an entity reference, as the value of an attribute that has been declared as being of type ENTITY or ENTITIES:

```
<?xml version="1.0" standalone="yes"?>
<!DOCTYPE graphic SYSTEM "graphic.dtd" [
  <!ELEMENT graphic (icon)+>
  <!ELEMENT icon EMPTY>
  <!ATTLIST icon
          height   NMTOKEN #IMPLIED
          nsoffset NMTOKEN #REQUIRED
          width    NMTOKEN #IMPLIED >
  <!ENTITY icon8 SYSTEM "icon813.gif" NDATA gif>
]>
<graphic>
  <icon source="icon8"
        height="0.391in" nsoffset="0.000in"
        width="0.429in"/>
</graphic>
```

- **In an entity value**—The reference appears in a parameter or entity's value in the entity's declaration.

- **In the DTD**—The reference appears within either the internal or external subset of the DTD, but outside of an entity or attribute value.

TABLE 8.1   ENTITY RESOLUTION

Where Referenced	Entity Type			Character Reference
	Parameter	Internal	External	
Inside an element	Ignored	Replaced	Replaced if validating	Replaced
In an attribute value	Ignored	Replaced	Not allowed	Replaced
Name in Attribute value	Ignored	Not allowed	Passed to application	Ignored
In an entity value	Replaced*	Ignored	Not allowed	Replaced
In the DTD	Replaced if validating	Not allowed	Not allowed	Not allowed

*When the entity reference appears in an attribute value or a parameter reference appears in an entity value, single and double quotes are ignored so that the value isn't prematurely terminated.

8

An entity's replacement text may contain character references, parameter entity references, and general entity references. Character references and parameter entity references in the value of an entity are resolved when the entity is resolved. General entity references are ignored.

When an entity reference is replaced, the entity's replacement text is retrieved and processed, in place of the reference itself, as though it were part of the document at the location where the reference was recognized. The replacement text may contain both character data and markup (except for parameter entities). These are recognized in the usual way, except that the replacement text of the entities amp, lt, gt, apos, and quot is always treated as data.

Before a document can be validated, the replacement text for parsed entities also has to be parsed. If the entity is external and the document is not being validated, the replacement text doesn't have to be parsed. If the replacement text isn't parsed, it is up to the application to handle it.

When the name of an unparsed entity appears in the value of an attribute whose declared type is ENTITY or ENTITIES, the system and public (if any) identifiers for both the entity and its associated notation are simply passed to the application. The application is then responsible for any further processing (such as displaying the graphic in a window).

Getting the Most Out of Entities

As you may remember, there is a fixed order in which the external and internal DTD subsets are read and interpreted. First the internal DTD subset is read, and then the external DTD subset is read. If something is declared in the internal DTD subset, its declaration cannot be changed in the external DTD subset. However, some things (such as additional attributes) can be added to declarations.

With a little careful planning, you can use this hierarchical arrangement to construct your information collection, such as a Web site, to make the maximum use of shared data (see Figure 8.3):

- Global declarations can be placed in a central DTD that governs all the documents. As far as each document is concerned, this central DTD is the (common) external DTD subset.

    The central DTD references entities that contain common graphics (company logo graphics and letterhead material, special characters, and so on).

- Local declarations can be placed in the internal DTD subset of each document. This allows each document to override the global declarations and tailor them for its own purposes.

The internal DTD subset in each document references any graphics and text that the particular document needs.

FIGURE 8.3

Using local and global entities.

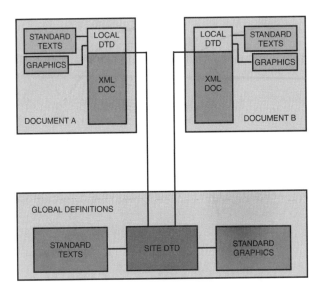

Breaking the documents into modules and exploiting the order in which the internal and external DTD subsets are parsed allows you to modularize a lot of documents, but you can go even further than this when you need to. You can even modularize the DTD itself and collect the parts that you need for a particular document type (although in this context you could almost call it a subtype).

There are many large industrial implementations of SGML that use this scheme. Some people call this the *pizza model*, where you build your DTD out of a core of essential elements and then add the toppings that you need for each particular document. Examples of major DTDs that use this model are the Text Encoding Initiative DTD and the DTDs that the American Department of Defense uses for Interactive Electronic Technical Manuals (IETM).

This same approach could be used just as easily in XML. In fact, it could probably be used a lot *more* easily because XML can include Internet URLs as the locators for fragments (which is being retrofitted to SGML). This makes it far easier to physically distribute data while still bringing it all together as a coherent set of information.

Character Data and Character Sets

As you have learned, XML entities contain data that can be either parsed (processed by the XML processor) or unparsed (this is normally non-XML data). Parsed data is made up of characters, some of which form character data and some of which form markup.

Taken at its most basic, an XML entity simply consists of a sequence of *characters*, each of which is an atomic unit of text—a unit of text that cannot be divided into anything smaller.

Internally, computers generally have used seven bits to store letters and characters in digital form. This representation was standardized as ISO/IEC 646, the now-familiar ASCII scheme in which each letter, number, and punctuation symbol is given a different seven-bit code. For example:

- The letter x is stored as `1111000`.
- The letter m is stored as `1101101`.
- The letter l is stored as `1101100`.

Rather than write out the binary representation in full, these bit patterns are commonly represented by a *hexadecimal number*, such as *6B* standing for the letter *k*.

The range of *legal characters*, the characters that can appear in an XML document, are those with the following hexadecimal values:

- `09` (the tab character)
- `0D` (the carriage return character)
- `0A` (the line feed character)
- `20` to `D7FF`, `E000` to `FFFD`, and `10000` to `10FFFF` (which are the legal graphics characters of Unicode and ISO 10646)

Unicode and ISO 10646 are standardized *character sets*, which you will learn about next.

Character Sets

There are only 128 different seven-bit patterns possible in the basic ASCII alphabet, so seven-bit ASCII can represent only 128 different characters. The eighth bit (there being eight bits in a byte, the basic unit of computer storage) is used as a *check bit* to make sure that the byte is stored or transmitted correctly. These 128 characters are known as the standard ASCII character set and have been the basis of computing for many years.

As computers have become more advanced and more of an international phenomenon, extra characters have become needed to cover things like the accented characters used in European languages. The eighth bit has been repurposed to give eight-bit character sets, thereby doubling the number of possible characters to 256. This is standardized as the ISO 8859 character set. In fact, there are many ISO 8859 variants, each tailored for a specific language. The version you'll probably see most often is 8859/1, which is the character set used for HTML and understood by Web browsers. This character set includes accented characters, drawing shapes, a selection of the most common Greek letters used in science and technology, and various other symbols. The first 128 characters of ISO 8859/1 are exactly the same as ISO 646, so it's backward compatible.

Eight bits are fine for most Western languages, but next to useless for languages such as Arabic, Chinese, Urdu, and so on. To cater to these languages, Unicode (with 16-bit encoding) and ISO 10646 took the next logical steps to support up to 32-bit patterns to represent characters. This allows more than two billion characters to be represented. ISO 10646 provides a standard definition for all the characters found in many European and Asian languages. Unicode is used in Microsoft Windows NT.

Unicode actually includes a number of different encoding schemes, which are named according to the number of bits they need. UCS-2 uses 16 bits (two bytes), which is identical to Unicode, and UCS-4 uses a full 32 bits (four bytes).

ISO 10646 is even more sophisticated. Using mapping schemes called UCS Transformation Formats (UTF), ISO 10646 allows a variable number of bits to be used. There's little point in using so many bits if you're only sending the basic 128 ASCII characters, so ISO 10646 allows you to claim extra bits as you need them.

XML supports two UTF formats: UTF-8 (eight-bit to 48-bit encoding), and UTF-16 (up to 32-bit encoding, but using a mapping that gives more than a million characters).

Entity Encoding

Every text entity in XML can use a different encoding for its characters. For example, you can declare separate text entities or elements to hold sections of an XML document that contain Chinese or Arabic characters, and assign the 16-bit UCS-2 encoding to these sections. The rest of the document can then use the more efficient eight-bit encoding.

By default, the ISO 10646 UTF-8 encoding is assumed. If the text entity uses some other encoding, you must declare what that encoding is at the beginning of the entity:

```
<?xml encoding="Encoding.Name" ?>
```

Where *Encoding.Name* is a character set name consisting of only the Roman alphabetic characters (A to Z and a to z), Arabic numerals, full stops, hyphens, and underscores. The XML processor has to recognize the following character set names:

- UTF-8
- UTF-16
- ISO-10646-UCS-2
- ISO-10646-UCS-4
- ISO-8859-1 to -9
- ISO-2022-JP
- Shift-JIS
- EUC-JP

Examples of encoding declarations are

```
<?xml version="1.0" encoding='UTF-16'?>
<?xml version="1.0" standalone="yes" encoding="EUC-JP"?>
```

The default (UTF-8) encoding is detected by the first four bytes of an XML text entity having the hexadecimal values 3C, 3F, 58, and 4D, which are the first characters of the encoding declaration. If there is no declaration, or if none of the other encoding schemes can be made to fit, the entity is simply assumed to be in UTF-8.

All XML processors can read entities in either UTF-8 or UTF-16. The standard ASCII alphabet is contained in the first part of the UTF-8 character set, so you do not need to declare the entity's character set if it is encoded in plain ASCII.

If an XML text entity is encoded in UCS-2, it must start with an appropriate encoding signature called the Byte Order Mark. This is FF FF for the standard byte order and FE FF for the byte-reversed order. These characters are not considered to be part of the markup or character data of the XML document.

Other than using the encoding declaration, the XML processor is allowed to assume that a certain encoding has been used based on the first few bytes it sees. In addition, the text/xml MIME type identification, which could be added by a Web server, can also be used to identify the character encoding used.

Entities and Entity Sets

Switching to a different encoding isn't the only way to represent characters that are not included in the UTF-8 character set. Don't forget that you can always reference any character by quoting its ISO 10646 character number in a character reference (such as &).

You can also declare an entity that represents the character you need, like this declaration of the degree sign (°) taken from the ISO 8859-1 character set:

```
<!ENTITY deg    "&#176;" >
```

You can then reference this entity in an XML document wherever you need it:

```
<para>The temperature today in the south will be 82 &deg;C.</para>
```

Not all computer systems and transfer media can handle the advanced character sets that you have learned about. The seven-bit ASCII character set is still the common denominator. These kinds of character entity declarations have been around since the early days of SGML and have been collected into *entity sets*.

These entity sets are included as part of the SGML standard (ISO 8879) and go under the somewhat cryptic names of ISOlat1 (Roman alphabet, accented characters), ISOnum (numeric and special characters), ISOcyr1 (Cyrillic characters used in Russian), and so on. They are really SGML facilities and cannot be used as they are in XML. (XML does not allow the use of an SDATA (system data) notation.) However, XML versions of the most important of these entity sets are being made publicly available, as you can see from the XML version of the ISOdia (diacritical marks) entity set shown in Listing 8.4.

LISTING 8.4   THE MODIFIED ISOdia ENTITY SET FOR XML

```
 1: <!-- (C) International Organization for Standardization 1986
 2:     Permission to copy in any form is granted for use with
 3:     conforming SGML systems and applications as defined in
 4:     ISO 8879, provided this notice is included in all copies.
 5: -->
 6: <!-- Character entity set. Typical invocation:
 7:     <!ENTITY % ISOdia PUBLIC
 8:         "ISO 8879:1986//ENTITIES Diacritical Marks//EN//XML">
 9:     %ISOdia;
10:
11: -->
12: <!-- This version of the entity set can
13:     be used with any SGML document
14:     which uses ISO 10646 as its document character set.
15:     This includes XML documents and ISO HTML documents.
16:     This entity set uses hexadecimal numeric character references.
17:
18:     Creator: Rick Jelliffe, Allette Systems
19:
20:     Version: 1997-07-07                -->
21:
```

```
22: <!ENTITY acute   "&#180;" ><!--=acute accent-->
23: <!ENTITY breve   "&#x2D8;" ><!--=breve-->
24: <!ENTITY caron   "&#x2C7;" ><!--=caron-->
25: <!ENTITY cedil   "&#184;" ><!--=cedilla-->
26: <!ENTITY circ    "^" ><!--=circumflex accent-->
27: <!ENTITY dblac   "&#x2DD;" ><!--=double acute accent-->
28: <!ENTITY die     "&#168;" ><!--=dieresis-->
29: <!ENTITY dot     "&#x2D9;" ><!--=dot above-->
30: <!ENTITY grave   "`" ><!--=grave accent-->
31: <!ENTITY macr    "&#175;" ><!--=macron-->
32: <!ENTITY ogon    "&#x2DB;" ><!--=ogonek-->
33: <!ENTITY ring    "&#x2DA;" ><!--=ring-->
34: <!ENTITY tilde   "&#x2DC;" ><!--=tilde-->
35: <!ENTITY uml     "&#168;" ><!--=umlaut mark-->
```

The entity sets are provided as separate files, one for each set. If you know that you're going to need a particular set of characters for an XML document, you can just include the necessary declaration in your XML DTD, as shown in Listing 8.5.

LISTING 8.5   TYPICAL NOTATION DECLARATIONS IN A DTD

```
 1: <?xml version="1.0" standalone="no"?>
 2: <!DOCTYPE chapter SYSTEM "chapter.dtd" [
 3:
 4: <!ENTITY % ISOlat1 PUBLIC "ISO 8879-1986//ENTITIES
 5:                    Added Latin 1//EN//XML" "isolat1.xml">
 6: %ISOlat1;
 7:
 8: <!ENTITY % ISOnum PUBLIC "ISO 8879:1986//ENTITIES
 9:            Numeric and Special Graphic//EN//XML" "isonum.xml">
10: %ISOnum;
11:
12: <!ENTITY % ISOpub PUBLIC "ISO 8879:1986//ENTITIES
13:            Publishing//EN//XML" "isopub.xml">
14: %ISOpub;
15: ]>
16: <chapter><number/> ... </chapter>
```

ANALYSIS   Note that the form of the entity declaration in the DTD differs slightly from that used in the entity file itself (Listing 8.4). A system identifier has to be used as well as the public identifier, but there is no SYSTEM keyword.

Summary

You've now learned several methods for getting characters into an XML text entity that aren't normally available from your keyboard. Not only have you learned about character encoding schemes, you've learned how to incorporate whole sets of special characters through entity sets.

You have also learned how to include external graphics files by declaring them with specific notations and then referencing them in the XML document, as well as how to declare a helper application that can be used to process the data.

Apart from the fact that you have to use external entities to include binaries such as graphics files in your formatted XML output (in the raw XML code, you just include entity references), entities can be a wonderful tool for breaking up a complex collection of many documents into manageable chunks. By using internal and external text entities, combined with the hierarchical ordering applied to interpreting the two DTD subsets, you can implement a staged hierarchy of template content. At the global level, you can safely set up default settings and then let individual XML documents implement local overriding changes when you need to.

As you will learn on Day 10, "Creating XML Links," XML's extremely powerful linking facilities make this task even easier. Tomorrow, you will put everything you've learned to the test by actually validating XML documents—the make-or-break evaluation of whether your XML code is going to work or not.

Q&A

Q How can you put unparsed (non-XML) text in an external entity?

A There are several ways. You could declare a TEXT notation, but this would not allow you to physically include the text in the XML document. (It would go the helper application you designated in the notation declaration.) The best way would probably be to declare the file containing the text as an external text entity and put the text in that file in a CDATA section.

Q You cannot use parameter entities in an XML document, but can you use general entities in a DTD?

A No. Parameter entities are exactly the same as general entities. They contain markup text (the only text you can have in a DTD, other than comments), so they perform exactly the same function.

8

Q Are there any limits on the size of entities?

A None that XML imposes. SGML does set some limitations on the size of certain objects (such as the lengths of names), but these have all been removed in XML. The only limits would be those imposed by your XML application or by the computer on which you're working.

Q Can you use an ANSI code for a character?

A No. Entering the ANSI code for a character was a feature available in some Microsoft Windows packages, and it has nothing to do with XML. There are fewer and fewer packages that support this shortcut, and a shortcut was all it was. All it did was give you another method of entering a character, in the current encoding scheme, that isn't available on the keyboard. If your editing package supports this and you want to use it, do. Don't confuse this with character encoding, however.

Q What happens if the software declared for a notation isn't there or can't be executed for some reason?

A As far as XML's concerned, nothing. All the XML processor will do is check that the declaration is correct. It's up to the XML application to process the contents of an entity that uses the notation. The application is also responsible for figuring out what to do if the helper application isn't there (it might have its own internal viewer, after all).

Exercises

1. Develop a simple DTD for a basic business letter. It needn't be complex—just enough for a letterhead, address blocks, and basic text.

2. Create a simple letter in XML using your letter DTD. Extend the XML code in the document and the DTD to include a standard letterhead that contains a GIF-format company logo.

3. Now set up your XML application so that you can quickly and easily put your name in the signature block.

DAY 9

Checking Validity

During the previous days you have learned how to write document type definitions (DTDs), the formal specifications of the structure of your XML files. Now you may have two questions:

- How can I check that my DTD is correct?
- How can I check that my documents comply with the rules defined in the DTD?

Validating parsers can do these jobs for you. In this chapter you will learn to:

- Check your DTD using DXP
- Check your DTD using XML for Java
- Check if your XML files comply with the rules of your DTD using the DXP parser
- Check if your XML files comply with the rules of your DTD using the XML for Java parser from IBM

Checking Your DTD with DXP

Finding and installing the DXP parser was discussed on Day 5. Now let's see how it can be used to check your DTDs.

At the DOS prompt, type

```
jre -cp .;c:\datachannel\dxp\classes dxpcl -s -v c:\xmlex\file.xml
```

where

- `jre` invokes the Java Runtime Engine.
- `-cp` sets the classpath (where to find the classes used). In this case two paths are specified: the first (`.`) refers to the current working directory, and the second is `c:\datachannel\dxp\classes`; they're separated by `;`.
- `dxpcl` is the name of the Java program (class).
- `-s` stands for silent mode.

- `-v` stands for validation on.
- `c:\xmlex\file.xml` is the file to be checked.

Walkthrough of a DTD Check with DXP

Now we're going to check the markup declarations shown in Listing 9.1.

INPUT   **LISTING 9.1**   dtdv.dtd—DECLARATIONS TO BE CHECKED USING DXP

```
 1: <!ENTITY % admonitions "(tip ¦ warning ¦ note)" >
 2: <!ENTITY % paracontent "(#PCDATA ¦ icon ¦ menu ¦ xref ¦
➥iconbmp)*" >
 3:
 4: <!ELEMENT helptopic (title, rule, procedure, rule?,
➥%admonitions;) >
 5: <!ATTLIST helptopic id ID #IMPLIED>
 6:
 7: <!ELEMENT title (#PCDATA) >
 8: <!ATTLIST title keyword CDATA>
 9:
10: <!ELEMENT procedure (step+)>
12: <!ELEMENT step (action, (%admonitions;)*) >
13:
14: <!ELEMENT action %paracontent; >
15: <!ELEMENT tip %paracontent; >
16: <!ATTLIST tip targetgroup (beginners ¦ specialists)
➥"beginners" >
17:
18: <!ELEMENT warning %paracontent; >
19: <!ELEMENT note %paracontent; >
20: <!ELEMENT icon (#PCDATA) >
21: <!ELEMENT menu (#PCDATA¦shortcut)+>
22:
23: <!ELEMENT xref (#PCDATA) >
24: <!ATTLIST xref linkend idref #REQUIRED>
25:
26: <!ELEMENT shortcut (#PCDATA)>
27: <!ELEMENT tip (#PCDATA) >
28:
29: <!ELEMENT iconbmp EMPTY>
30: <!ATTLIST iconbmp src ENTITY #REQUIRED
31:                   type NOTATION (bmp ¦ gif) "gif">
```

Note

This is a perfect opportunity to test your knowledge. Before letting the parser point out the errors to you, try to discover them by yourself: find how many there are, describe them, and figure out how you would solve them.

Markup declarations can appear in two places:

- In the external or
- In the internal subset of the document type declaration

When external, the markup declarations exist in an external file (a special kind of external entity), and the document type declaration in the XML file needs to point to this external file:

```
<!DOCTYPE helptopic SYSTEM "http://www.protext.be/help.dtd" []>
```

In our case, the XML file should be as shown in Listing 9.2.

LISTING 9.2   dtdv.xml—SIMPLE XML FILE TO PARSE USING DXP

```
1:   <?xml version="1.0" ?>
2:   <!DOCTYPE helptopic SYSTEM "dtdv.dtd" [
3:   ]>
```

You started your XML file with a document type declaration that refers to the external subset in file "dtdv.dtd".

 Note   Bear in mind that on the file system, your XML file (dtdv.xml) needs to be in the same location (subdirectory) as "dtdv.dtd".

Now let's run DXP to expose any errors:

```
jre -cp .;c:\datachannel\dxp\classes dxpcl -s -v c:\xmlex\dtdv.xml
```

The first error message appears:

 OUTPUT   FATAL ERROR: encountered ">". Was expecting one of: <EOF> , <S>
Location: file:///c:/xmlex/dtdv.dtd:8:30

Found errors/warnings: 1 fatal error(s), 0 error(s) and 0
warning(s)

ANALYSIS   For the structure of the error messages generated, see Day 5.

The problem has to do with this line:

```
"<!ATTLIST title keyword CDATA>"
```

Here you declare the attributes for the element title; in this case there's only one (keyword).

For each attribute, you need to have a definition with the following parts:

- The name of the attribute
- The type of the attribute
- A default

These are all separated by a space.

In this case, you have defined only the following:

- The name, keyword
- The type, CDATA or stringtype, which may take any literal string as value

You've forgotten to include the default. The missing default needs to be one of the following:

- #REQUIRED
- #IMPLIED
- An attribute value optionally preceded by #FIXED

And it needs to be preceded by a space.

You opt for #IMPLIED, so the line becomes

```
<!ATTLIST title keyword CDATA #IMPLIED>
```

Parse again and receive

OUTPUT
```
FATAL ERROR: encountered "+". Was expecting: "*"
Location: file:///c:/xmlex/dtdv.dtd:21:34

Found errors/warnings: 1 fatal error(s), 0 error(s) and 0
warning(s)
```

ANALYSIS It concerns <!ELEMENT menu (#PCDATA|shortcut)+>.

When you have mixed content—character data interspersed with child elements—the content model needs to have the * occurrence indicator. The line needs to become

```
<!ELEMENT menu (#PCDATA|shortcut)*>
```

The next error we receive is:

```
FATAL ERROR: encountered "idref". Was expecting one of:
➥"ID" , "IDREF" , "IDREFS" , "ENTITY" , "ENTITIES" , "NMTOKEN" ,
➥"NMTOKENS" , "NOTATION" , "CDATA" , "%", "("
```

```
Location: file:///c:/xmlex/dtdv.dtd:24:24
```

```
Found errors/warnings: 1 fatal error(s), 0 error(s) and 0
warning(s)
```

All keywords (including `"idref"`) need to be in uppercase in XML. After this correction we receive:

```
ERROR: element declared twice "tip"
Location: file:///c:/xmlex/dtdv.dtd:27:11
```

```
ERROR: notation not declared "bmp"
Location: file:///c:/xmlex/dtdv.dtd:31:41
```

```
ERROR: notation not declared "gif"
Location: file:///c:/xmlex/dtdv.dtd:31:44
```

```
FATAL ERROR: encountered end of file
Location: :3:4
```

```
Found errors/warnings: 1 fatal error(s), 3 error(s) and 0
warning(s)
```

Now this is interesting. You'll have three errors and one fatal error over here.

The element tip is declared twice. The specification clearly states that no element type may be declared more than once. This is a validity constraint. Violations against validity constraints are considered errors. Correct this by deleting the second element declaration of tip.

You receive errors on the notations, which is understandable because according to the specification, all notation names in the declaration must have been declared.

Add notation declaration for BMPs and GIFs at the start of your file:

```
1: <!NOTATION bmp SYSTEM "paint.exe">
2: <!NOTATION gif SYSTEM "">
```

Note

If you'd added those two notation declarations at the end of the file, the problems still wouldn't be resolved because notations (and entities) need to be declared before they are referenced.

After this, you are stuck with one more error:

```
FATAL ERROR: encountered end of file
Location: :3:4

Found errors/warnings: 1 fatal error(s), 0 error(s) and 0
warning(s)
```

Obviously, encountered end of file is the error message, because our file contains only a prolog and no element.

Because our interest is in simply checking the DTD, the missing element is not a concern for the moment.

You end up with no errors in your DTD, as shown in Listing 9.3.

LISTING 9.3 dtdv.dtd—THE DTD WITH NO ERRORS

```
1: <!NOTATION bmp SYSTEM "paint.exe">
2: <!NOTATION gif SYSTEM "">
3:
4: <!ENTITY % admonitions "(tip | warning | note)" >
5: <!ENTITY % paracontent "(#PCDATA | icon | menu | xref |
➥iconbmp)*" >
6:
7: <!ELEMENT helptopic (title, rule, procedure, rule?,
➥%admonitions;) >
8: <!ATTLIST helptopic id ID #IMPLIED>
9:
10: <!ELEMENT title (#PCDATA) >
11: <!ATTLIST title keyword CDATA #IMPLIED>
12:
13:<!ELEMENT procedure (step+)>
14:<!ELEMENT step (action, (%admonitions;)*) >
15:
16:<!ELEMENT action %paracontent; >
17:<!ELEMENT tip %paracontent; >
18:<!ATTLIST tip targetgroup (beginners | specialists)
➥"beginners" >
19:
20:<!ELEMENT warning %paracontent; >
21:<!ELEMENT note %paracontent; >
22:
23:<!ELEMENT icon (#PCDATA) >
24:<!ELEMENT menu (#PCDATA|shortcut)*>
25:
26:<!ELEMENT xref (#PCDATA) >
27:<!ATTLIST xref linkend IDREF #REQUIRED>
```

continues

LISTING 9.3   CONTINUED

```
28:
29: <!ELEMENT shortcut (#PCDATA)>
30:
31: <!ELEMENT iconbmp EMPTY>
32: <!ATTLIST iconbmp src ENTITY #REQUIRED
33:                    type NOTATION (bmp | gif) "gif">
```

When `internal`, the declarations appear between the brackets ([and]) of the document type declaration:

```
<!DOCTYPE helptopic [
<!ELEMENT helptopic (title, procedure)>
<!ATTLIST helptopic id ID #REQUIRED>
...
]
<helptopic>....
```

Note

Remember that the DTD of a document consists of both subsets, external and internal, taken together.

For the moment, all your declarations are in the external subset of your document type declaration.

What will happen if you copy the content of your file inside your internal subset and don't refer anymore to the external file with the declarations, as shown in Listing 9.4?

INPUT   LISTING 9.4   `dtdv.xml`—XML FILE WITH DECLARATIONS IN THE INTERNAL SUBSET

```
1: <?xml version="1.0" ?>
2: <!DOCTYPE helptopic [
3: <!NOTATION bmp SYSTEM "paint.exe">
4: <!NOTATION gif SYSTEM "">
5:
6: <!ENTITY % admonitions "(tip | warning | note)" >
7: <!ENTITY % paracontent "(#PCDATA | icon | menu | xref |
➥iconbmp)*" >
8:
9: <!ELEMENT helptopic (title, rule, procedure, rule?,
➥%admonitions;) >
10: <!ATTLIST helptopic id ID #IMPLIED>
11:
12: <!ELEMENT title (#PCDATA) >
13: <!ATTLIST title keyword CDATA #IMPLIED>
```

```
14:
15: <!ELEMENT procedure (step+)>
16: <!ELEMENT step (action, (%admonitions;)*) >
17:
18: <!ELEMENT action %paracontent; >
19: <!ELEMENT tip %paracontent; >
20: <!ATTLIST tip targetgroup (beginners ¦ specialists)
➦"beginners" >
21:
22: <!ELEMENT warning %paracontent; >
23: <!ELEMENT note %paracontent; >
24:
25: <!ELEMENT icon (#PCDATA) >
26: <!ELEMENT menu (#PCDATA¦shortcut)*>
27:
28: <!ELEMENT xref (#PCDATA) >
29: <!ATTLIST xref linkend IDREF #REQUIRED>
30:
31: <!ELEMENT shortcut (#PCDATA)>
32:
33: <!ELEMENT iconbmp EMPTY>
34: <!ATTLIST iconbmp src ENTITY #REQUIRED
35:                   type NOTATION (bmp ¦ gif) "gif">
36:
37: ]>
```

Parsing this file gives you the following:

```
FATAL ERROR: parameter entity reference in entity value in
➦internal subset for "admonitions"

Location: file:/c:/xmlex/dtdv.xml:9:65
```

ANALYSIS   In the internal subset, parameter-entity references (%admonitions; and %paracontent;) can occur only where markup declarations can occur, not within markup declarations such as the declaration of the element tip. This means that the following is allowed:

```
<!DOCTYPE helptopic [
<!ATTLIST helptopic a CDATA "A11">
<!ENTITY % buttons SYSTEM "button.ent">
%buttons;
]>
```

You can include the parameter entity reference %buttons; at that place because markup declarations could be entered also.

The following is *not* allowed:

```
<!DOCTYPE helptopic [
<!ENTITY % paracontent "(#PCDATA ¦ emphasis)*">
<!ELEMENT tip %paracontent; >
]>
```

This is because the parameter entity reference appears in a markup declaration. You can solve this by using either of these methods:

- Bring everything back to the external subset.

- Replace the parameter references with their declared content, as shown in Listing 9.5.

LISTING 9.5   dtdv.dtd—CORRECTED FILE WITH PARAMETER ENTITY REFERENCES REPLACED

```
 1: <?xml version="1.0" ?>
 2: <!DOCTYPE helptopic [
 3: <!NOTATION bmp SYSTEM "paint.exe">
 4: <!NOTATION gif SYSTEM "">
 5: <!ELEMENT helptopic (title, rule, procedure, rule?,
➥(tip ¦ warning ¦ note)) >
 6: <!ATTLIST helptopic id ID #IMPLIED>
 7:
 8: <!ELEMENT title (#PCDATA) >
 9: <!ATTLIST title keyword CDATA #IMPLIED>
10:
11: <!ELEMENT procedure (step+)>
12: <!ELEMENT step (action, ((tip ¦ warning ¦ note))*) >
13:
14: <!ELEMENT action (#PCDATA ¦ icon ¦ menu ¦ xref ¦
➥iconbmp)* >
15: <!ELEMENT tip (#PCDATA ¦ icon ¦ menu ¦ xref ¦ iconbmp)* >
16: <!ATTLIST tip targetgroup (beginners ¦ specialists)
➥"beginners" >
17:
18: <!ELEMENT warning (#PCDATA ¦ icon ¦ menu ¦ xref ¦
➥iconbmp)* >
19: <!ELEMENT note (#PCDATA ¦ icon ¦ menu ¦ xref ¦ iconbmp)* >
20:
21: <!ELEMENT icon (#PCDATA) >
22: <!ELEMENT menu (#PCDATA¦shortcut)*>
23:
24: <!ELEMENT xref (#PCDATA) >
25: <!ATTLIST xref linkend IDREF #REQUIRED>
26:
27: <!ELEMENT shortcut (#PCDATA)>
28:
```

```
29: <!ELEMENT iconbmp EMPTY>
30: <!ATTLIST iconbmp src ENTITY #REQUIRED
31:                    type NOTATION (bmp ¦ gif) "gif">
32:
33: ]>
```

Checking Your DTD with XML for Java

XML for Java is a validating XML parser written in 100% pure Java. The package (com.ibm.xml.parser) contains classes and methods for parsing, generating, manipulating, and validating XML documents. XML for Java is a robust XML processor and is very complete.

Installing XML for Java

- Download XML for Java from http://alphaworks.ibm.com/formula/xml. The file xml4j_1_1_9.zip is 1.288KB.

- Unzip xml4j_1_1_9.zip into a new directory, such as c:\xml4j.

 Note Because this is another Java implementation, make sure you have Java Virtual Machine version 1.x running. Refer to Day 5 for details.

Using XML for Java

At the DOS prompt, type

```
jre -cp c:\xml4j\xml4j.jar trlx c:\xmlex\dtdv.xml
```

where

- jre is used to invoke the Java Runtime Engine.
- -cp is used to set the classpath. In this case you refer to the jar (Java archive file) with the name xml4j.jar.
- trlx is the Java class that does the parsing.
- c:\xmlex\dtdv.xml is the file to be checked.

Walkthrough of a DTD Check with XML for Java

INPUT

You'll be using the same file as in Listing 9.1. Here are the error messages received:

OUTPUT

```
dtdv.dtd: 8, 30: Spaces are expected.
dtdv.dtd: 8, 30: '#REQUIRED' or '#IMPLIED' or '#FIXED' or
➥attribute value is expected.
dtdv.dtd: 21, 35: This content model is not matched with
➥the mixed model '(#PCDATA¦FOO¦BAR¦...¦BAZ)*':
'(#PCDATA¦shortcut)+'
dtdv.dtd: 24, 29: 'CDATA' or 'ID' or 'IDREF' or 'IDREFS'or
➥'ENTITY' or 'ENTITIES' or 'NMTOKEN' or 'NMTOKENS' or 'NOTATION'
➥or '(' is expected.
dtdv.dtd: 27, 24: Element 'tip' is already declared.
dtdv.dtd: 31, 27: NOTATION 'bmp' is not declared.
dtdv.dtd: 31, 33: NOTATION 'gif' is not declared.
c:\xmlex\dtdv.xml: 3, 3: The document has no element.
```

ANALYSIS

Every error message consists of the following:

- The file in which the error appears
- The line number
- The character position where the problem was detected
- A description

With XML for Java, you receive all errors in one run with very clear error messages.

The last error message has to do with not having a complete document, but only a pointer to the DTD.

With XML for Java, it is possible to check the DTD directly. You have to add the parameter –dtd to the command line and read the file with the external subset directly:

```
jre -cp c:\xml4j\xml4j.jar trlx -dtd c:\xmlex\dtdv.dtd
```

This is a much cleaner way of doing it. Of course, you will receive the same results except for the last error, The document has no element.

Checking Your XML Files with DXP

At the DOS prompt, type the following:

```
jre -cp .;c:\datachannel\dxp\classes dxpcl -s -v c:\xmlex\wfq.xml
```

where

- jre invokes the Java Runtime Engine.
- -cp sets the classpath (where to find the classes used). In this case you've specified two paths: the first (.) refers to the current working directory, and the second is c:\datachannel\dxp\classes; they're separated by ;.
- dxpcl is the name of the Java program (class).
- -s stands for silent mode.
- -v stands for validation on.
- c:\xmlex\wfq.xml is the file to be checked.

Walkthrough of an XML File Check with DXP

On Day 5, you made the file wfq.xml well-formed with the help of parsers. This file (shown in Listing 9.6) contains a description of a help topic.

LISTING 9.6   wfq.xml—THE WELL-FORMED HELP FILE

```
1: <?xml version="1.0" ?>
2: <?protext objid="I5678" ?>
3: <!DOCTYPE helptopic [
4: <!ENTITY doubleclick "Double-click">
5: ]>
6: <helptopic>
7: <title keyword="printing,network;printing,shared printer">How to
➥use a shared network printer?</title>
8: <procedure>
   <step><action>In <icon>Network Neighborhood</icon>, locate
➥and double-click the computer where the printer you want to
➥use is located. </action>
9: <tip targetgroup="beginners">To see which computers have shared
➥printers attached, click the <menu>View</menu> menu,
10: click <menu>Details</menu>, &amp; look for printer names or
➥descriptions in the Comment column of the Network
➥Neighborhood window.</tip>
11: </step>
12: <step>
13: <action>&doubleclick; the printer icon in the window
➥that appears.</action>
14: </step>
15: <step>
16: <action>
17: To set up the printer, <xref linkend="id45">follow the instructions
➥</xref> on the screen.
```

continues

LISTING 9.6 CONTINUED

```
18: </action></step>
19: </procedure>
20: <rule form="double"/>
21: <tip>
22: <p>After you have set up a network printer, you can use it as
➥if it were attached to your computer.
➥For related topics, look up &quot;printing&quot; in the Help Index.
23: </p>
24: </tip>
25: </helptopic>
```

Earlier in this chapter you corrected a DTD describing the structure of a help topic. (Refer to Listing 9.3.) Now you want to relate both. Do this by referring to the file dtdv.dtd in the DOCTYPE declaration of wfq.xml:

```
<!DOCTYPE helptopic SYSTEM "dtdv.dtd" []>
```

The change is shown in Listing 9.7.

INPUT LISTING 9.7 wfq.xml—THE DTD IS NOW REFERRED TO IN THE DOCTYPE DECLARATION

```
1: <?xml version="1.0" ?>
2: <?protext objid="I5678" ?>
3: <!DOCTYPE helptopic SYSTEM "dtdv.dtd" [
4: <!ENTITY doubleclick "Double-click">
5: ]>
6: <helptopic>
7: <title keyword="printing,network;printing,shared printer">How
➥to use a shared network printer?</title>
8: <procedure>
9: <step><action>In <icon>Network Neighborhood</icon>, locate and
➥double-click the computer where the printer you want to use is
➥located. </action>
10: <tip targetgroup="beginners">To see which computers have shared
➥printers attached, click the <menu>View</menu> menu,
11: click <menu>Details</menu>, &amp; look for printer names or
➥descriptions in the Comment column of the Network Neighborhood
➥window.</tip>
12: </step>
13: <step>
14: <action>&doubleclick; the printer icon in the window that
➥appears.</action>
15: </step>
16: <step>
```

```
17: <action>
18: To set up the printer, <xref linkend="id45">follow the
➥instructions</xref>   on the screen.
19: </action></step>
20: </procedure>
21: <rule form="double"/>
22: <tip>
23: <p>After you have set up a network printer, you can use it as
➥if it were attached to your computer. For related topics,
➥look up &quot;printing&quot; in the Help Index.
24: </p>
25: </tip>
26: </helptopic>
```

Let's start checking:

```
jre -cp .;c:\datachannel\dxp\classes dxpcl -s -v c:\xmlex\wfq.xml
```

The result is

OUTPUT

```
ERROR: Invalid content : procedure
Possible: rule
Location: file:/c:/xmlex/wfq.xml:8:2

ERROR: element not declared in DTD "rule"
Location: file:/c:/xmlex/wfq.xml:21:2

ERROR: attribute hasn't been declared in the DTD "form"
Location: file:/c:/xmlex/wfq.xml:21:7

FATAL ERROR: java.lang.NullPointerException:
Location: :0:0
```

ANALYSIS   What's the defined content of your help topic? Your help topic needs to start with a title, followed by a rule, and after that the procedure. This isn't the case in your document.

Let's start to add the rule to your document:

```
7: <title keyword="printing,network;printing,shared printer">How to
➥use a shared network printer?</title><rule/>
```

Note

> rule is an empty element. Remember this special syntax:
>
> ```
> ```
>
> Or
>
> ```
> ```

Let's run your parser again:

```
ERROR: element not declared in DTD "rule"
Location: file:/c:/xmlex/wfq.xml:8:2

ERROR: element not declared in DTD "rule"
Location: file:/c:/xmlex/wfq.xml:21:2

ERROR: attribute hasn't been declared in the DTD "form"
Location: file:/c:/xmlex/wfq.xml:21:7

FATAL ERROR: java.lang.NullPointerException:
Location: :0:0
```

The specification defines the following validity constraints:

- An element is valid if there is a declaration.

- An attribute must have been declared.

If this isn't the case, you have errors. So add declarations for the missing elements and attributes:

```
<!ELEMENT rule EMPTY>
<!ATTLIST rule form (single ¦ double ¦ dotted) "single">
```

When you parse again, you receive the following:

```
ERROR: Invalid content : p
Possible: iconbmp, icon, menu, #PCDATA, , xref
Location: file:/c:/xmlex/wfq.xml:23:2

ERROR: element not declared in DTD "p"
Location: file:/c:/xmlex/wfq.xml:23:2

ERROR: unknown ID referred "id45"
Location: file:/c:/xmlex/wfq.xml:26:14

Found errors/warnings: 0 fatal error(s), 3 error(s) and 0
warning(s)
```

The tip after the second rule contains a p, which isn't allowed by the DTD. Let's remove the start and end tag of p within element tip from wfq.xml.

```
ERROR: unknown ID referred "id45"
Location: file:/c:/xmlex/wfq.xml:25:14

Found errors/warnings: 0 fatal error(s), 1 error(s) and 0
warning(s)
```

ANALYSIS IDREF values must match the value of some ID attribute in the XML document, which isn't the case here. There's no element in your document with an attribute of type ID with the value `"id45"`.

Remove the `xref` element, which leads to a valid document.

Checking Your XML Files with XML for Java

9

At the DOS prompt, type the following:

```
jre -cp c:\xml4j\xml4j.jar trlx c:\xmlex\wfq.xml
```

where

- `jre` is used to invoke the Java Runtime Engine.
- `-cp` is used to set the classpath. In this case you refer to the `jar` (Java archive file) with the name `xml4j.jar`.
- `trlx` is the Java class that does the parsing.
- `c:\xmlex\wfq.xml` is the file to be checked.

Walkthrough of an XML File Check with XML for Java

INPUT Use the file in Listing 9.5. With XML for Java, you'll generate the following error messages:

OUTPUT
```
c:\xmlex\wfq.xml: 21, 22: Attribute 'form' of element 'rule'
➥is not declared.
c:\xmlex\wfq.xml: 21, 22: Can't find content model of '<rule>'.
c:\xmlex\wfq.xml: 24, 5: Can't find content model of '<p>'.
c:\xmlex\wfq.xml: 25, 7: Content mismatch in '<tip>'.  Content
model is ''(#PCDATA¦icon¦menu¦xref¦iconbmp)*'.
c:\xmlex\wfq.xml: 26, 13: Content mismatch in '<helptopic>'.
➥Content model is
'(title,rule,procedure,rule?,(tip¦warning¦note))'.
c:\xmlex\wfq.xml: 18, 45: ID 'id45' is not defined in the document.
```

The problems encountered are

- No element and attribute list declarations for the element `rule`.
- Using a p inside the element tip, which isn't allowed according to the DTD.
- The title needs to be followed by a `rule` element, according to the DTD.
- The `xref` element, through its attribute `linkend` of type IDREF, refers to a unique identifier ID, which doesn't exist in the XML document.

Summary

In this chapter you used two parsers written in Java, DXP from Datachannel and XML for Java from IBM, to do the following:

- Check the declarations in the DTD.

Note Remember that the treatment is different for declarations in the external subset compared to the internal subset.

- To check if XML documents comply with the rules defined in the Document Type Definition (DTD).

Q&A

Q Why should I bother to have valid XML files?

A Well, it is much easier to use valid XML files. If you know that the element tip may appear only in this or that context, you only need to worry about what to do with the element tip in your program or your style sheets for the contexts known. Whereas if a tip can appear everywhere, your program or style sheet will become much more complicated and elaborate.

In addition, it is much easier to exchange files when you know that they use the same grammar.

Q Does a browser care?

A No, a browser can work with a well-formed XML file. A well-formed file carries enough information for the browser to create a tree structure and render the file.

Note The quality of rendering depends on the styles co-delivered, of course.

Q Is there other software that cares?

A Authoring tools will care about validity. If you want to start editing a new XML file, the software will ask you which DTD to use. After that, the software will guide you through the editing process by only making available those tags that are allowed by the content model. In this way, you're sure to have well-formed and valid XML files.

Q Are there other validating parsers available?

A Yes. There's MSXML from Microsoft and Larval from Tim Bray at Textuality, both written in Java.

Exercises

1. This exercise involves the following XML file, `valq.xml`:

```
1: <!DOCTYPE references SYSTEM "docb.dtd" [
2: ]>
3: <refentry id="refentry.xref">
4:     <refmeta>
5:         <refentrytitle>delete_mark</refentrytitle>
6:     </refmeta>
7:     <refnamediv>
8:         <refname>delete_mark</refname>
9:         <refpurpose>Deletes the currently
selected region and puts it in the specified paste buffer
</refpurpose>
10:     </refnamediv>
11:     <refsynopsisdiv>
12:         <title>Synopsis</title>
13:         <cmdsynopsis>
14:             <command>delete_mark</command>
15:             <arg><option>-append</option></arg>
16:             <arg><replaceable>buffername</replaceable></arg>
17:         </cmdsynopsis>
18:         <cmdsynopsis>
19:             <command>delete_mark</command>
20:             <arg>null</arg>
21:         </cmdsynopsis>
22:     </refsynopsisdiv>
23:     <refsect>
24:         <title>Description</title>
25:             <para>This command deletes the currently selected
region and puts it in the paste buffer specified.
If no buffer name is supplied, the current paste buffer is
used (see <citerefentry><refentrytitle>set paste=buffername
</refentrytitle></citerefentry>).
26: If the <literal><replaceable>buffername</replaceable>
</literal>is <literal>null</literal>, the selection is
deleted without copying it to a paste buffer.
27: This command corresponds to the <interface>Delete</interface>
menu item on the default <interface>Edit</interface> menu.
28: If the <option>-append</option> option is selected, text
is inserted at the end of the buffer rather than
completely replacing its contents.</para>29 <command>dm
</command> is a synonym for <command>delete_mark</command>.
30: </para>
```

```
31: </refsect>
32: <refsect>
33:    <title>Examples</title>
34:    <screen>Command: <userinput>dm</userinput></screen>
35:    <screen>Command: <userinput>dm bufA</userinput></screen>
36:    <screen>Command: <userinput>dm -append buf2</userinput>
➥</screen>
37:</refsect>
38:</refentry>
```

And the following DTD file, `docb.dtd`, which is referred to in `valq.xml`:

```
1: <!ENTITY % in-line "option ¦ replaceable ¦ citerefentry
➥¦ refentrytitle ¦ literal ¦ userinput ¦ interface ¦
➥command ¦ arg" >
2: <!ENTITY % paracontent "(#PCDATA ¦ %in-line;)*">
3: <!ELEMENT refentry (refmeta?, refnamediv, refsynopsisdiv,
➥refsect+)>
4: <!ATTLIST  refentry id ID #REQUIRED>
5: <!ELEMENT refmeta (refentrytitle, refmiscinfo*) >
6:    <!ELEMENT refentrytitle (#PCDATA)>
7:    <!ELEMENT refmiscinfo (#PCDATA)>
8: <!ELEMENT refnamediv (refname, refpurpose)>
9:    <!ELEMENT refname (#PCDATA)>
10:    <!ELEMENT refpurpose %paracontent;>
11: <!ELEMENT refsynopsisdiv (title, cmdsynopsis+)>
12:      <!ELEMENT cmdsynopsis (command, arg+)>
13: <!ELEMENT refsect  (title, (para ¦ screen)+ )>
14:    <!ELEMENT title (#PCDATA)>
15:    <!ELEMENT para %paracontent; >
16:    <!ELEMENT screen %paracontent; >
17: <!ELEMENT option (#PCDATA)>
18: <!ELEMENT replaceable (#PCDATA)>
19: <!ELEMENT citerefentry (#PCDATA ¦ refentrytitle)*>
20: <!ELEMENT literal (#PCDATA)>
21: <!ELEMENT userinput (#PCDATA)>
22: <!ELEMENT interface (#PCDATA)>
23: <!ELEMENT command (#PCDATA)>
24: <!ELEMENT arg (#PCDATA ¦ option ¦ replaceable)*>
```

- Detect the errors and the error messages that the parser will generate.
- Check the file with the parser of your choice.
- Correct all problems discovered.

2. Using the XML file you made during the previous days.

- Introduce errors.

Tip

Use the W3C recommendation as your reference.

- Parse the file with different parsers.
- Study the differences between the results of different parsers.

9

DAY **10**

Creating XML Links

Amidst all the hype and speculation surrounding XML as a language, little attention has been paid to a pair of related proposals, XLink and XPointer, that are potentially far more exciting than the XML language itself. These two proposals, under the generic name of XML linking, represent a revolution in the way documents can be linked. (In the first proposal, they were combined as a common XML Linking Language (XLL) document.)

Today you will learn the following:

- The differences between HTML and XML hyperlinks
- The various types of hyperlinks in XML and how they can be used to link multiple points, link read-only documents, and describe links
- How to use the various attributes of link elements to control how and when links are activated
- How to remap the attributes of elements in existing XML documents to add hyperlink behavior that was not originally present

> Although XLink and HTML are constantly compared throughout this chapter, it is not at all necessary for you to understand any of the details of HTML hyperlinking. However, if you do understand at least a little of HTML, you will appreciate even more just how exciting the possibilities are that XLink opens up.

Hyperlinks

Anyone who has ever opened a Web page knows immediately what hypertext looks like. What distinguishes hypertext from normal text are hyperlinks, the characteristic blue underlined text that identifies hot spots that will move you to other pages when they're clicked with the mouse.

Arguably, it was the capability to link documents together that made the World Wide Web such a great success. It was certainly one of the design goals behind the original HTML. (At CERN—the European Laboratory for Particle Research—in Switzerland, the wide distribution of projects and their related documents prompted Tim Berners-Lee to look for some way to associate documents with each other regardless of their physical location on the computer network.)

A hyperlink (or link for short) is an association between two pieces of text, between a piece of text and an object (such as the graphics that are included on Web pages by placing a link to the image file), or even between an object and a piece of text (such as the image map mechanism in HTML that allows the link to point to a different document according to where you click on an image).

> In the official terminology of the XLink proposal, a link is "an explicit relationship between two or more data objects or portions of data objects." For the sake of simplicity, this chapter will just talk about links between XML elements, regardless of what they contain.
>
> The standards also talk about link resources, objects that participate in links. I prefer to use the rather less accurate but more manageable concept of a target, even though actuating a link in XML can result in far more than HTML's simple link transversal.

In the simple terms of HTML linking, a link is the association between a source and a target. The target may be a complete HTML page, in which case the description of the target (the locator) is a Universal Resource Identifier (URI), or it may be a named element within an HTML page, which is identified using the # symbol, called a fragment identifier, followed by the value of the NAME attribute of the target element. Tomorrow's discussion of the XPointer language gives more details about using fragment identifiers with XML documents.

The HTML code for the source of the link would look something like this:

```
<H3>Simple Linking</H3>
<P>This <A HREF="http://writer.xs4all.nl/simplelink.html#S15">link</A>
points to a specific section in the document. </P>
```

And the HTML code for the section in the target document would look something like this:

```
<H4><A NAME="S15">Target Section</A></H4>
<P>This section is the one I want to link to. </P>
```

HTML can safely talk about the sources and targets of links because its linking mechanisms are so simple. XML's linking language, XLink, is so much more powerful than HTML's that it is no longer possible to refer to sources and targets. XLink talks about *linking elements* instead of sources—links can be bidirectional, so the end of a link could be both a source and a target. And it talks about *resources* instead of targets—a resource could be a piece of data, the result of a database query, or an external link that acts as an intermediary en route to the final destination.

When you click on a link in an HTML page, a new page is invariably opened (although it might be in a new window or frame). In this simple scenario, it makes sense to talk about *following* a link because you do appear to travel from one document to another. As you will learn later, XLink's syntax allows you to specify multiple or grouped link locators, and the way in which they are processed can be more of an implementation issue (browser software) than a linguistic matter. For this reason, XLink talks about *traversing* a link.

Now that we've got some of the terminology sorted out, let's look at what it all actually means in practice.

10

Locators

XML links work with link elements. In turn, the link elements contain locators, in the form of attributes or other elements, that point to specific locations within a resource.

Generally, a locator is a URI, a fragment identifier, or a URI combined with a fragment identifier. Locators for XML documents are extended pointers (XPointers), which you will learn about tomorrow.

The syntax of locators allows you to use the following variations:

- `URI#fragment`—This fetches the whole of the resource identified by the URI and then extracts the part identified by the fragment identifier.
- `URI¦fragment`—The application can decide how it will process the URI in order to extract the resource. For example, this could be used to only retrieve a specific part of a document instead of the complete document.

If the fragment identifier is a character string that complies with XML's rules for a name, the string is treated as the value of the `id` attribute of an XML element. The locator `afile.html#ht7` would therefore point to the element in the file `afile.html`, whose `id` attribute value is `ht7` (for example, `<para id="ht7">`). This built-in interpretation is meant to encourage you to use ID addressing, which in itself is a good practice because it is completely unambiguous. This form of address does carry with it the risk of confusion, however, if your software does not ensure that all element ID values are unique within a document.

Link Elements

In HTML, there are only two elements that can act as links: `A` (anchor) and `IMG` (image). In XML, a link exists simply because the link element says it does. The existence of the link is identified by the element's attributes. This means that absolutely any XML element can act as a linking element if you ensure that it has the right attributes. Later today you will learn that you can actually redefine (remap) attributes as well. For now, we'll concentrate on the idea that a specific set of XLink attributes identify and describe a link.

The primary attribute that identifies an element as a link element is the `xlink:form` attribute, whose declaration in an XML DTD would look something like this (not forgetting that an element that is declared as a link element must also conform to the structure that you want to specify in the DTD):

```
<!ELEMENT CORRELATION ANY>
<!ATTLIST CORRELATION
     xlink:form CDATA #FIXED value >
```

Here, *value* is either `simple` or `extended`. (The value could also be `locator`, `group`, or `document`, but these are not linking elements in themselves but related elements.) The meanings of these values are explained in the following sections.

Note

> The current XLink working draft (March 3, 1998) describes the use of the `xml:link` attribute. Since publication of this draft, the XML Namespaces draft has made use of the `xml:` prefix inadvisable. In an email message on May 5, 1998, Eve Mailer, one of the editors of both the XLink and XPointer proposals, stated that this attribute was to be renamed `xlink:form` in the next version of the draft to avoid namespace problems. The publication of the next version has not been fixed, but I have already implemented the changed syntax in this description.

10

Simple Links

Simple links closely approximate the simple HTML linking mechanism described earlier today. Simple links have only one locator, and only work in one direction:

```
<simple.link xlink:form="simple"
href="http://me.com/title.xml">see also</simple.link>
```

This simple link element contains a piece of text that acts as a resource, one end of the link. This kind of link is called an inline link. You'll learn about inline and out-of-line linking later today.

Note

> Don't confuse the term *inline link* with links that are contained inside the current document—internal links—and those that point to other documents—external links. An inline link is simply a link with a piece of text that acts as one end of the link (like the A elements in HTML).

Extended Links

In simple links, XLink doesn't really offer that much more than the basic linking that you're accustomed to seeing in HTML documents (although even here there are a few substantial improvements). It is in extended links that XLink, and thus XML, really comes into its own. If nothing else can be considered special about extended links, it's exciting enough that they do not need to be physically contained in one of the XML files that the links go either to or from. It goes further than this, though. Extended links allow XML documents to do the following:

- Link together any number of resources, resulting in multiple targets instead of a simple one-to-one relationship as in HTML.

- Link to and from resources that cannot contain the links themselves. This includes such things as graphics files, sound files, read-only documents, and so on, whose coding doesn't allow you to modify them to embed links.

- Enable the (dynamic) filtering, addition, and modification of links. Imagine being able to modify the links at a certain point so experienced readers of a technical manual can take a different path than novice readers.

- Enable application software to process the links in many other ways according to its own needs.

Note

> Remember that the XLink and XPointer developments are still working drafts. Unfortunately, this means that the proposal has not been implemented in the major Web browsers (other than very basic support of XLink in Netscape's Mozilla source code), and it is highly unlikely that it will be implemented until the proposal has become more stable.
>
> Support is beginning to appear in other packages, however. The HyBrick software package (http://collie.fujitsu.com/hybrick) supports it, there's an experimental implementation of parts of XPointer in the public domain Jade DSSSL processor (http://www.jclark.com), and parts of it are being implemented in the IndelvIT viewer/editor package (http://www.indelv.com).

An extended link doesn't actually point to anything or link anything together. An extended link element identifies itself through its xlink:form attribute value and contains a set of locator elements that together form the extended link:

```
<comment xlink:form="extended">
    <opinion xlink:form="locator" href="note4"/>
    <reference href="#section2.1"/>
    <reference href="http://here.com/appB.html"/>
    <reference href="references.htm"/>
</comment>
```

As with the other link elements, the nature of the extended link element is specified by the xlink:form attribute. Here, a comment element declares itself to be an extended link and an opinion element declares itself to be a locator element. As you can see, this can be done in the element start tag without having to use a DTD. The declarations for these elements in a DTD could look something like this:

```
<!ELEMENT comment ANY>
<!ATTLIST comment
     xlink:form      CDATA      #FIXED "extended">

<!ELEMENT opinion ANY>
<!ATTLIST opinion
     xlink:form      CDATA #FIXED "locator">

<!ELEMENT reference ANY>
<!ATTLIST reference
     xlink:form      CDATA #FIXED "locator">
```

Note that I have used ANY as the content model for these elements, allowing any element to be contained inside one of these elements.

 Caution Don't forget that if you are going to validate the XML document, the elements used for linking must still comply with the structural rules declared in the DTD.

Where extended link elements contain locator elements that in turn contain elements themselves, only the locator elements themselves, and not the elements they contain, are considered to be link resources.

So how would this work in practice? Well, let's look at two paragraphs in an XML document that you want to cross-reference with each other. The easiest way to do this is to put a simple link in each paragraph that points to the other paragraph, as shown in Listing 10.1.

LISTING 10.1 CROSS-REFERENCING WITH SIMPLE LINKS

```
1: <para id="idea1"><xref href="idea2">A first
2:   impression of the subject matter
3:   would inevitably lead to the
4:   conclusion that ... </xref></para>
5: <para id="idea2"><xref href="idea1">Contrary
6: to our earlier conclusion, it
7: would appear that the evidence points
8: to a different ... </xref></para>
```

Listing 10.1 shows one direct solution to cross-referencing the two paragraphs, but what happens if you then expand the thesis by including a third point that you want to bring into the discussion? At best, you would have to do some annoyingly repetitious link editing; at worst, you might have to completely rethink all the affected markup code.

Extended links, and in particular a variety of extended link called an out-of-line link (which is covered later in this chapter) allow associative links like these to be created and maintained much more easily. Putting the links somewhere else in the document, perhaps at the start to make them easier to find, or even in a separate document, can make it much easier to make the links, find them, and keep them up to date, as shown in Listing 10.2.

 Note

> In an earlier chapter you learned how to place the DTD in an external file. Later on you learned how you can easily break up an XML document into parts that you can pull together using entities. Later in this chapter you will learn how to physically include pieces of text in the current document. Here, you are learning how the links themselves can be contained in an external document. The suggestion of modular document composition already should be dawning on you. These XML features open up possibilities for ease of document management and construction that go far beyond anything even remotely possible in HTML.

LISTING 10.2   CROSS-REFERENCING WITH EXTENDED LINKS

```
1: <argument xlink:form="extended">
2:     <theme xlink:form="locator" href="idea1">
3:     <theme xlink:form="locator" href="idea2">
4: </argument>
   .
   .
   .
5: <para id="idea1">A first impression of the subject matter
6: would inevitably lead to the conclusion that ... </para>
   .
   .
   .
7: <para id="idea2">Contrary to our earlier conclusion, it
8: would appear that the evidence points to a different ... </para>
```

How a viewer behaves when you click on one of the extended link resources shown in Listing 10.2, or even how it identifies the existence of an extended link, is an application issue and is not addressed by the XLink specification. However, a special icon might be displayed to show that there is associated material, or a menu could pop up from which you could choose one of the link ends. (There are other descriptive attributes for linking elements that would make this selection more purposeful; these are described later on.)

Figure 10.1 shows the menu list that is displayed in SoftQuad's Panorama SGML browser.

FIGURE 10.1

Picking a destination for a multiple-ended link.

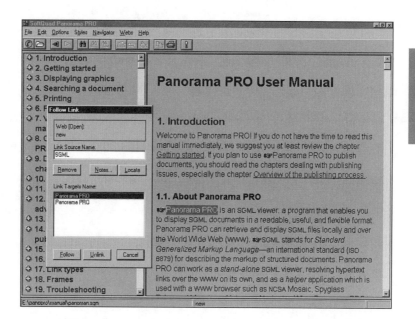

ANALYSIS In Figure 10.1, the two link ends next to the phrase "Panorama Pro" (indicated by the pointing hand icon) both reference the link end next to the word "SGML." Clicking on either of the Panorama Pro link ends will simply bring you to the SGML link end. When you click on the SGML link end (in Panorama all links are two-way), there are two possibilities, so Panorama displays a list of possible link ends so you can choose the one you want.

Note

It would have been more exciting to show you multiple links in a true XML package, but as yet there is no mainstream support for XML links (apart from the rudimentary support offered in Netscape's Mozilla).

SoftQuad's Panorama is an SGML browser with an embedded HyTime engine that supports a lot of the advanced HyTime linking facilities—some of the same facilities that were inherited from HyTime by XML. Despite the fact that it is meant to be used with SGML, Panorama will still do a reasonable job of rendering XML code, provided that the XML code you load into Panorama is valid and you do not drift too far from pure SGML code. (An evaluation version can be downloaded from http://www.sq.com.)

Interestingly, it would be a simple task to add links between elements long after the document has been completed without actually having to change any of the content (especially when the links aren't contained in the participating document). This will make a lot more sense tomorrow when you learn how to point to whole ranges of elements using extended pointers.

Note

The fact that you can add links to a document after it has been completed, without changing any of the content of the document, means that you can also link to and from parts of read-only documents, such as documents contained on CD-ROM.

Extended Link Groups

You've already learned that links can be located in external documents; this is achieved through the use of extended link groups. Like an extended link, an extended link group element doesn't point to anything or link to anything. Instead, it contains a set of document elements in which each document (identified by a URI) contains the link resources:

```
<xternal.refs>
    <ref.doc href="http://here.com/biblio.html"/>
    <ref.doc href="lists.htm"/>
</xternal.refs>
```

These element and attribute declarations could look something like this in the XML DTD:

```
<!ELEMENT xternal.refs (ref.doc*)>
<!ATTLIST xternal.refs
    xlink:form    CDATA    #FIXED "group"
    steps         CDATA    #IMPLIED>
```

```
<!ELEMENT ref.doc EMPTY>
<!ATTLIST ref.doc
    xlink:form      CDATA       #FIXED "document">
```

As with so many of the other XLink elements, no rules are given as to how a browser or viewer should behave when it encounters groups of links like this. However, with the additional descriptive attributes described later on, a viewer could display a pop-up list of all the associations of a particular type and allow you to pick one or more.

When using extended link groups, you are going to run the risk of one of the link document elements also containing an extended link group. What happens if that extended link group points back to the original document, or to a document containing yet another extended link group? It would take many linked extended link groups to land you in an impossible situation of infinite links and link loops. To prevent this from happening, you can declare a value for the steps attribute of the group element. This is a numerical value specifying how many layers of nesting you, as the author, will permit. (The application is not required by XLink to obey this attribute, but one can hope that the more user-friendly software packages will.)

10

Tip

If you are building a web around a central hub document, it would make a lot of sense to specify a value of 2 for the steps attribute of the base extended link group element (see Figure 10.2). This would prevent any extended link group elements in satellite documents from bouncing back through the original extended link group and getting viewers completely tied in knots.

Inline and Out-of-Line Links

In XLink, a link can be inline or out-of-line. By default, all link elements are inline (the value of the inline attribute is true), so you only need to declare the attribute if the link element is out-of-line (inline is false).

There is a lot of confusion about the meanings of these terms, especially when it is complicated by the idea of links being inside or outside a document. Whether a link is inline or out-of-line has absolutely nothing to do with whether it's located inside the document or not.

Simple links are essentially inline all the time. An out-of-line simple link is possible, but it is rather hard to imagine the actual use of such a thing. It would be a single-ended link, really, a pointer to a location without any other association… not much use to anyone.

Figure 10.2

Using steps to limit linking with a hub document.

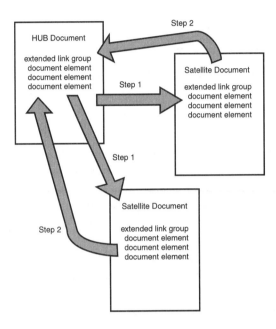

Where the distinction between inline and out-of-line links is relevant is in extended links. Listing 10.3 shows an example of an inline extended link in an XML document.

LISTING 10.3   AN EXAMPLE OF AN INLINE EXTENDED LINK

```
1: <para id="para4">This is a
2:    <xref.list>psychosomatic
3:       <see.also href="med1.xml"/>
4:       <see.also href="http://www.medical.com/defs.htm"/>
5:       <see.also href="para6"/>
6:    </xref.list> condition, brought on by ...
7: </para>
```

Here, the xref.list element contains character data that serves as part of the associative trail formed by the links. Therefore, the link element framed in the official terms of the XLink specification contains a local resource of the link.

If you look again at the same set of extended links, but rewritten as an out-of-line link, you should be able to see the difference straight away, as shown in Listing 10.4.

LISTING 10.4   USING AN OUT-OF-LINE EXTENDED LINK

```
1: <xref.list>
2:    <see.also href="para4"/>
3:    <see.also href="med1.xml"/>
4:    <see.also href="http://www.medical.com/defs.htm"/>
5:    <see.also href="para6"/>
6: </xref.list>
.
.
.
7: <para id="para4">This is a psychosomatic condition,
8:    brought on by ... </para>
```

When the extended link is rewritten as an out-of-line link, it is no longer located in the same place as the link resources and contains a *pointer* to the local link resource rather than the local link resource itself.

Link Behavior

Links in HTML documents are either passive, like the A (anchor) element links that do nothing until you actually click on them, or active, like the IMG (image) element that automatically inserts the graphics file that it references (you can normally suppress this behavior by changing the Web browser options so that images are not loaded automatically). The link behavior is tied to that particular element, and there is little you can do to affect it.

In XLink, not only can you control when a link is activated, or traversed, you can control what happens when a link is traversed. This link behavior is controlled by the show and actuate attributes.

Link Effects

In HTML, an image is always embedded at the point at which its anchor element (IMG) occurs. Other links are simple jumps to new documents, either in the same window, a new window, or a frame in either the current window or a new one.

In XLink, the show attribute allows you to formalize this behavior for all links—rather than relying on a link with a particular name—and allows you to do a little bit more:

- show="embed"—When the link is traversed, the designated resource is embedded at the point where the traversal started. This allows you to create virtual documents composed of fragments of other documents, for example. Or, more practically, you can create such things as dynamic tables of contents and indexes by picking up parts of other elements and (seemingly) physically copying them to the link location.

- `show="new"`—When the link is traversed, the designated resource is displayed (or processed) in a new context. This normally means that the resource is displayed in a new window. But the important point is that whatever is done to the target resource doesn't affect the display of the starting resource. This could be used to include a piece of text from an external document without its style declarations affecting the current document.

- `show="replace"`—When the link is traversed, the designated resource replaces the resource at which the traversal started. This is the equivalent of an HTML link in which the current HTML page is replaced with the new one.

When using extended links, it is possible for you to declare a default `show` attribute value for the extended link element that will then override any default values declared for the locator elements in the DTD. For example, in this fragment, the first `location` element has the default `show` attribute value of `replace`, but the second `location` element has a `show` attribute value of `new` that overrides the default definition:

```
<extended show="replace">
    <location href="mypage.html"/>
    <location href="hispage.htm" show="new"/>
</extended>
```

Link Timing

In HTML, an image is always automatically embedded at the point at which its anchor element (`IMG`) occurs. You don't have to do anything unless you have disabled automatic image loading in the Web browser itself. Other links are passive, meaning that absolutely nothing happens until you actually click on one.

In XLink, the `actuate` attribute allows you to formalize this behavior for all links rather than relying on a link with a particular name, and it allows you to do specify what happens when a link element is encountered:

- `actuate="auto"`—When any of the other resources of the same link are retrieved, this resource is to be retrieved automatically. Used together with the `show="replace"` attribute declaration, this link behavior can be used to automatically redirect a viewer to a new page, for example.

- `actuate="user"`—The resource is not to be retrieved until there is an explicit request to do so. This is the equivalent of an HTML link in which nothing happens until you click on the source of a link.

When using extended links, it is possible for you to declare a default `actuate` attribute value for the extended link element that will then override any default values declared for the locator elements in the DTD. For example, in the following fragment, the first `location` element has the default `actuate` attribute value of `user`, and the second `location` element has an `actuate` attribute value of `auto` that overrides the default value:

```
<extended actuate="user">
    <location href="mypage.html" show="embed"/>
    <location href="hispage.htm" actuate="auto" show="embed"/>
</extended>
```

With this code, you might not get the results you expected. The first resource (`mypage.html`) will be retrieved, as expected. However, while doing this, the second resource (`hispage.html`, which has `actuate=auto`) will be retrieved as well! Because they are both embedded, you will see them both, but with other values of the `show` attribute, you could end up with something completely different than what you thought would happen.

When there is more than one embedded link and the actuation is automatic, you might expect one resource to be actuated. It will be, but the actuation could be masked by a second actuation. The result will not be disastrous, but you should be alert to the problems that declaring this link behavior might cause.

The `behavior` Attribute

An application can do many things with links. It can display special icons, play sounds, change display characteristics... the possibilities are limitless.

In the latest beta release of Internet Explorer 5 (November 1998), Microsoft has implemented an extension to the CSS style sheet syntax that comes very close to the behavior attribute. This extension, called binary behaviors, allows a piece of executable code (such as a program) to be attached to an HTML or XML element.

XLink includes a behavior attribute that allows you to declare any other behavior associated with a link. The content and significance of any value that you give this attribute, and how the application reacts to that attribute value, is left for the application developer to decide.

Link Descriptions

One of the things that's sadly lacking in linking HTML documents is that it's an all-or-nothing situation. Either there's a link or there isn't, and all links are exactly the same. There is absolutely no way of describing the nature of the relationship between two link resources. You might follow an HTML link only to find out that the link between the source and the destination were rather more real in their creator's head than they are in the Web browser.

This lack of a way to provide a description of a link, the semantics, becomes even more critical when there are multiple resources participating in the link, as in extended links. Here, it becomes meaningless to offer multiple locators if there is no sensible way of either describing the relationship or, at the very least, distinguishing between two parallel resources.

XLink provides several attributes that allow you to describe links and link resources:

- A link can have a `role` attribute that identifies the meaning of the link to the application. For example:

    ```
    <extended role="bibliographies">
        <location href="myfile.htm"/>
        <location href="hisfile.html"/>
    </extended>
    ```

- When a link is inline, a local resource can have a `content-role` attribute and a `content-title` attribute. The `content-role` attribute identifies the part that the resource plays in the link (in addition to the link's own `role` attribute). The `content-title` attribute acts as a caption to explain to users the part that the resource plays in the link. For example:

    ```
    <mylink content-role="see also" content-title="Reference">
    as mentioned in my other book.</mylink>
    ```

- A remote resource can have a `role` attribute and a `title` attribute. The `role` attribute identifies the part that the resource plays in the link (in addition to the link's own `role` attribute). The `title` attribute acts as a caption to explain to users the part that the resource plays in the link. For example:

    ```
    <extended role="bibliographies">
     <location href="myfile.htm"
       role="reference" title="This Chapter"/>
     <location href="hisfile.html"
       role="reference" title="Whole Book"/>
    </extended>
    ```

Mozilla and the `role` Attribute

An example of the use of the role attribute can be found in the current (August 1998) release of Netscape's Mozilla code (which will most likely become Netscape Communicator 5 eventually). Mozilla uses `role="HTML"` to embed linked HTML documents into the current HTML document, as shown in Listing 10.5 (the base document) and Listing 10.6 (the "included" document). In technical terms, importing by linking like this is called transclusion.

10

INPUT   LISTING 10.5   MOZILLA CODE TO EMBED IN AN HTML DOCUMENT

```
1:  <?xml version="1.0"?>
2:    <page>
3:      <section>
4:        This text comes from the original (source) file.
5:      </section>
6:      <Foot XML-Link="LINK" Role="HTML"
7:        Show="EMBED" href="include.htm" />
8:      <section>
9:        This text also comes from the original file.
10:     </section>
11:   </page>
```

INPUT   LISTING 10.6   HTML CODE IN THE DOCUMENT TO BE EMBEDDED

```
1:  <!DOCTYPE HTML PUBLIC "-//W3C//DTD HTML 4.0 Transitional//EN">
2:  <HTML>
3:    <HEAD>
4:      <META HTTP-EQUIV="Content-Type"
5:        CONTENT="text/html; charset=iso-8859-1">
6:      <META NAME="GENERATOR" CONTENT="Mozilla/5.0 [en]
7:        (WinNT; N ;Nav) [Mozilla]">
8:      <TITLE>Included Text</TITLE>
9:    </HEAD>
10: <BODY>
11:     <HR>
```

continues

LISTING 10.6 CONTINUED

```
12:    <H1>
13:    <FONT COLOR="#FF6666">Included Text</FONT></H1>
14:    <DIV color="red">
15:      <FONT COLOR="#FF6666">
16:        This text comes from a second file
17:        and is automatically embedded
18:        via the XML-Link mechanism.
19:      </FONT>
20:    </DIV>
21:    <HR>
22:  </BODY>
23: </HTML>
```

The resulting display shows the two documents merged seamlessly (see Figure 10.3).

OUTPUT

FIGURE 10.3

Text inclusion by reference in Mozilla.

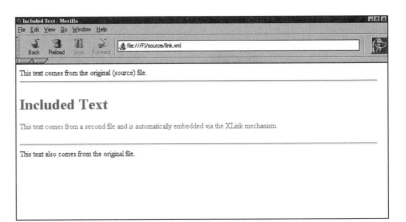

ANALYSIS Note that the current version of Mozilla supports an older version of the XLink proposal, when it was still known as XML-Link or XLL (XML Link Language). The combination of uppercase and lowercase characters (for example, "Role" and "Show"), also dating back to an earlier version of the proposal, has to be exactly as shown in Listing 10.5 or it won't work properly.

Attribute Remapping

Earlier today I suggested that it would be fairly easy to add links into an XML document after you had finished it.

As you will remember, any element can be a link. It is declared as being a link of a particular type through the xlink:form attribute. Although the names of the link elements can be freely chosen, the names of their attributes are fixed—actuate, behavior, content-role, content-title, href, inline, role, show, steps, and title.

Now, suppose that you want to use existing elements in an XML document as links. This very easy to do by using extended links located in an external document. The problems start when the elements in that document already have attributes with the same names as the XLink attributes. You can overcome this by using the xml:attributes attribute to remap existing attribute names onto new ones.

Consider this element declaration:

```
<!ELEMENT book (front, body, back) >
<!ATTLIST book
     title      CDATA              #REQUIRED
     role       (single¦volume)    #IMPLIED>
```

If you wanted to use this element as a link element, the title and role attributes would have to be remapped. You can do this by putting a declaration in an internal DTD subset. (Remember that a DTD can be split into an internal and an external DTD subset and that the internal DTD subset takes precedence.) The declaration you put in the internal DTD subset could look something like this:

```
<!ATTLIST book
   xlink:form      CDATA  #FIXED "simple"
   xml:attributes  CDATA  #FIXED "title mytitle role myrole">
```

This XML code in the document would be correctly recognized as a simple link:

```
<book title="Presenting XML" role="main" myrole="Reference"
mytitle="Other Books" href="http://www.amazon.com/search?Light+North"/>
```

Summary

This chapter looked at XLink, the linking part of XML's linking facilities. You've learned what the various types of links are, how they can be used, and their many attributes. Tomorrow you will learn about extended pointers (XPointers) and how they can be used to locate blocks of text, elements, groups of elements, and many other parts of an XML document.

10

Q&A

Q How would you define a link in XML to mimic HTML's behavior?

A A link element with `show="replace"` and `actuate="user"` would mimic HTML's behavior for a normal link to another HTML page.

Q What's the difference between an inline link and an out-of-line link?

A An inline link element contains one of its link resources. If it's a simple link, you could more or less say that the link element contains one end of the link.

Q Can a simple link be an out-of-line link?

A In theory, yes. In practice, it probably wouldn't be much use because such a one-ended link could do little more than associate certain semantics with a location.

Exercises

1. You have an XML document containing a `chapter` element divided into `section` elements. You knew you would want to make a table of contents, so each `section` element has been given an `id` attribute whose value is the number of the section. Draft the XML code (using an out-of-line extended link) to demonstrate how you would create an embedded table of contents.

2. You have a collection of XML documents, each representing the chapter of a book. You now want to create a brief table of contents that contains each chapter's `title` element from each of these documents. Draft the XML code (using an out-of-line extended link group) to accomplish this.

DAY 11

Using XML's Advanced Addressing

In yesterday's lesson you learned about linking in XML, but that's only half of the story. Today we'll learn about *locators*—the means of tying links to actual parts of XML files.

You have already learned one method of locating, using universal resource identifiers (URIs). In XML URIs can be used in much the same way that they are used in HTML—for navigating the World Wide Web. In this chapter I'm going to focus on a different kind of locator, the extended pointer (XPointer). In today's lesson you will:

- Learn a little about groves and XML's view of element trees
- Learn how to locate resources using absolute references (`root()`, `origin()`, `id`, `html`)
- Learn how to locate resources using relative terms (`child`, `descendant`, `ancestor`, `preceding`, `psibling`, `following`, `fsibling`)

- Learn how to locate link resources consisting of multiple elements and ranges of elements (spans)
- Learn how to select link resources by instance, element, attribute, and element content

Extended Pointers

As you may remember from yesterday's lesson, linking in XML is concerned with associating link resources with each other. (A link resource is really a pointer to one or more locations, or a means of resolving a pointer into a location.) You can use almost anything to resolve a location, such as a Web server CGI script or a database query. XML's extended pointers (XPointers) enable you to point into XML resources in a wide variety of ways. You can, as you will see, make full use of the structure of the document that is identified by means of the XML elements and attributes.

Extended pointers are described in a separate proposal called the *XML Pointer Language* (XPointer), which used to be part of the common XLL (XML Link Language) proposal.

 Note
> You can use an extended pointer with a URI to locate a link resource more precisely. If you point into an XML document, you must use an extended pointer. If you are pointing into something other than an XML document, the XPointer recommendation does not specify or restrict the syntax of the locator in any way, but you can still use some extended pointers.

Documents as Trees

Before you can understand how extended pointers work and how to use them properly, it's important for you to understand how an XML link processor (whatever software package is resolving a link to find the actual ends) "sees" the structure of an XML document.

As you have worked your way through this book, you have no doubt become used to the idea of thinking of an XML document as being composed of trees of elements; the "root" element is at the top or base (depending on how you want to visualize it), and all the other elements branch off from it.

FIGURE 11.1

A typical XML element tree.

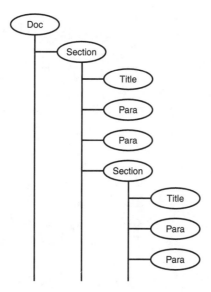

An ordinary tree structure is, however, too simple for discussing extended pointers. If I combine an absolute location with a relative link that begins somewhere deep inside the document, the resolution mechanism has to combine the tree that starts with the root element with the tree that starts with the element that acts as the start point for the relative location. From the viewpoint of an extended pointer, an XML document isn't just one element tree, it is hundreds.

A tree can be constructed for every possible entry point or reference point, so instead of talking about a tree we use the term *grove*. A grove is essentially a collection of trees; it is too small to be a forest but is more than just a super tree.

Each point in the tree is called a *node*. We've been talking about trees of elements, and so you'd suppose that nodes are just elements. Not so. A node can be an element, but it can just as easily be a piece of text (character data) within an element.

Note

> When you learn about DSSSL you'll see that a grove can be constructed using elements and attributes. This is not important for linking because you cannot use attributes as link resources.

Consider an element structure declared as follows:

```
<!ELEMENT section (#PCDATA ¦ title ¦ para )>
```

This is a typical mixed content element. It can contain both raw (untagged) character data and elements (title and para). Look at the following code fragment:

```
<section><title>Bert Goes to Bed</title>   <para>Hello, Bert.</para>
<para>Today is going to be a very special day.</para></section>
```

Let's now try and plot this fragment as a tree. It looks simple enough; we have a section element that includes one title element and two para elements. Or does it? Look at the fragment again, then look at what I make of it in Figure 11.2.

FIGURE 11.2

An element tree with hidden nodes.

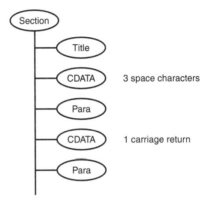

In Figure 11.2 I identified one section element containing a title element, a node of character data (3 whitespaces), a para element, an intervening character data node (a carriage return character or even, depending on the underlying operating system, a carriage return and a line feed character), and a last para element.

While this is a carefully chosen example of what can go wrong, these types of hidden nodes (not so much hidden as forgotten) can lead to some very unexpected results when you try to use extended pointers that employ node counting to find the link resource.

Location Terms

There are two types of location terms: absolute terms and relative terms.

Absolute terms are much like the location pointers that you may be more used to seeing in HTML. These terms more or less ignore any structural relationships and point directly to specific elements.

Relative terms are easier to appreciate, and much more powerful than absolute terms because they mimic the kind of route description you might give to a friend to find your office.

Absolute Terms

An extended pointer can use one of the following absolute location terms:

- root()—States that the location source for the location term is the root element of the current document. Note that the keyword root is followed by a pair of brackets (technically called an *empty argument*) to prevent it from being confused with IDs.

- origin()—States that the location source for the location term is the link resource at which traversal started, rather than the current root element. Note that the keyword origin is followed by a pair of brackets (technically called an empty argument) to prevent it from being confused with IDs.

- id(*name*)—States that the location source for the location term is the element (it has to be a unique element) that has an attribute declared as being an ID class. The value of that attribute is *name*. The actual name of the attribute could be absolutely anything, hence the importance of explicitly declaring attributes that you intend to use as IDs.

- html(*name-value*)—States that the location source for the first location term is the first element of type A that has a name attribute with a value of *name-value* (this is exactly the same as selecting a target in HTML using a # symbol).

11

> **Tip**
>
> If you do not specify the location source of the first location term in a traversal, the *root element* of the XML document that is the containing resource is used by default. This means that, officially at least, you shouldn't ever need to specify root(). However, including root() can't do any harm and it can make the intention of your extended pointer more clear to a human reader.

Relative Terms

In order to use a relative location term, you must already have a starting point (a location source). You can use relative location terms to move around the target XML document by describing a location in relation to where you are at that moment.

The ultimate goal of an extended pointer is to direct you to the correct location within an XML document. However, doing this is a bit like directing someone to a particular place in a city; it is difficult to give perfect directions on the first attempt. You might start with a known landmark (an absolute location), give a direction, count blocks or streets, and then describe buildings:

```
go to Central Station
go north on El Camino
take the third road on the left
go into the second building on the left
ask for Brian
```

Each step of these instructions depends on the previous step being followed correctly. After one mistake the rest of the instructions will only get you lost.

Extended pointers work in exactly the same way. They are a sequence of *location terms*, which are either absolute locations or a series of locations where each is relative to the previous one. Extended pointers describe elements and nodes within an XML document in terms of various properties, such as their type or attribute values, or simply by counting them.

Each relative location term consists of a *keyword*, followed by one or more *steps*. Each term is a hop along a path to the final location of the link resource. In the same way as you'd tell someone to: "take the third right, go three blocks, turn left and it's the second on the right," so with extended pointers you could say, for example, "take the third child of this element, find its oldest brother, and take the second child element of that one." This route description could then be rewritten using extended pointers to look something like this:

```
child(3,DIV).psibling(-2).descendant(4.para).string(5,"bottle",1,1)
```

The following are the relative term keywords that you can use:

- child—Selects the child elements of the location source.
- descendant—Selects the elements that appear within the content of the location source.
- ancestor—Selects the elements in whose content the location source is found.
- preceding—Selects elements that appear before the location source.
- following—Selects elements that appear after the location source.
- psibling—Selects the preceding sibling elements of the location source.
- fsibling—Selects the following sibling elements of the location source.

Figure 11.3 shows a sample grove. Let me now try to explain these keywords with reference to a point in this grove, element number 4.

FIGURE 11.3

Relative locations in an element tree.

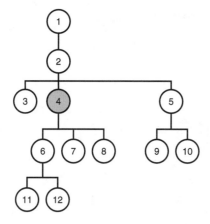

Using element number 4 as the location source, let's see what each of the absolute term keywords would select.

- child—Selects elements 6, 7, and 8 (the immediate children but not 11 and 12).
- descendant—Selects elements 6, 7, 8, 11, and 12 (the immediate children and their children).
- ancestor—Selects elements 1 and 2 (the elements that contain element 4).
- preceding—Selects elements 1, 2, and 3 (all the elements that appear before the location source).
- following—Selects elements 6, 7, 8, 11, 12, 5, 9, and 10 (all the elements that appear after the location source).
- psibling—Selects element 3 (the elements at the same level of hierarchy or generation that come before the location source).
- fsibling—Selects element 5 (the elements at the same level of hierarchy or generation that come after the location source).

Selection

So far you have learned to specify a type of location by using an absolute or relative term. These terms tell the processor what kind of element you're locating, but you still need to be able to specify which of those elements (or perhaps all of them) are of interest. Extended pointers offer several ways to select elements, as you will see.

11

Selecting by Instance Number

By specifying a number, you can pick out a particular element instance or range of element instances, for example:

```
child (2)
```

selects the second child element.

Specifying a negative number counts from the last instance backwards. For example:

```
(-1,PARA)
```

selects the last <PARA> element.

Selecting by Node Type

In addition to selecting a resource by number, you can specify a particular node type. To select a particular node type, the instance is followed by a comma and a node type, which can be one of the following values:

- A name value selects the elements that have a particular name.

  For example, child(2,para) selects the second para element that is a child of the current element.

- The keyword #element selects XML elements. This is also the default type if you do not specify a type, so you will probably never need to use this keyword.

- The #pi keyword selects XML processing instructions. Obviously, you can't go on to locate any attributes of a processing instruction, or any elements inside one (both are impossible), but you can locate text inside one (with string).

- The #comment keyword selects XML comments. Obviously, you cannot go on to locate any attributes of a comment, or any elements inside one (both are impossible), but you can locate text inside one (with string).

- The #text keyword selects text regions directly inside an element's character data (CDATA) sections. You cannot go on to specify any attributes, but you can locate specific parts of text inside a text region (with string).

- The #cdata keyword selects text regions inside character data (CDATA) sections. You cannot go on to specify any attributes, but you can locate specific parts of text inside a CDATA section (with string).

- The #all keyword selects all node types.

Selection by Attribute

The element type, if specified, can be qualified by an attribute name by using the `attr` keyword. You will get the value of the attribute you name.

Selecting Text

All of the absolute and relative location terms described so far select complete elements. The `string` location term actually allows you to look inside an element and select text located within it. String selectors are extremely useful when linking into non-XML data (such as text files) or into XML data that contains large blocks of text.

The `string` location term takes the following four arguments:

- A number that indicates which occurrence of the specified string is required. To select all the occurrences you can use the keyword `all`.

- The character string, enclosed in single or double quotes (for example, "this was not"), to be matched. Instead of a string, you can specify a number to identify a particular character.

- A position number that indicates how many characters to count forward from the start of the matched string to locate the actual string required. You may not specify 0 as a value. If you don't specify a value, 1 is assumed. A positive number (for example, +2) counts from the left end of the string to the right, a negative value (-4) counts backwards (to the left) from the right end of the string.

- A number that indicates the length of the string (the number of characters in the string) to be selected. If you specify 0, or don't specify a value, this is assumed to be the position immediately before the character indicated by the position number. You can specify an empty string (a pair of quotes: "") to specify the point just after the character string you're matching.

The following are examples of the use of `string`:

- `string(3,"the",1,2)` selects the characters "he" from the third occurrence of the word "the".

- Assuming that you've already selected the word, `string(2,"")` indicates the point between the character "t" and "h" in word "the".

- `string(all,"(",-2,1)` selects the last character of every word that appears before an opening bracket.

- `string(1,"amazing",-6,3)` selects the characters "maz" from the first occurrence of the word "amazing".

Selecting Groups and Ranges (spans)

A resource location can contain a single extended pointer or two extended pointers separated by a span keyword. If it has two extended pointers, the location is assumed to be everything from the start of the first extended pointer's target to the end of the second one.

Caution

> Spans are a major exception to the rest of the extended pointer language in that span locations are *not* trees. You cannot assume that a span is a meaningful chunk of an XML document. It is very unlikely to be a single element, or even a whole number of elements. This limits what an XML application can do with spans, but it is up to the XML software to find a sensible way of dealing with this.

Summary

This chapter looked at an XML document as an object constructed of various components. You've learned about markup and the distinction that XML makes between markup and character data. You have also seen how XML documents have both a logical and a physical structure and looked at the connection between these and XML's elements and entities.

Q&A

Q What is a grove?

A An XML document has a hierarchical tree-like structure. The view of an XML document that is used for linking is a collection of trees, called a grove. A leaf is called node and the branches are called children.

Q Why do you have to be careful with string and spans?

A Unlike the other extended pointers, which select whole elements or groups of elements, string and spans can select parts of elements. This could result in an XML document no longer being valid, or even no longer being well-formed.

Q Does the root() extended pointer serve any real function?

A Not really, but it can make your linking more readable for a human (remember that one of the design goals of both XML and XLL is that it should be reasonably readable for human beings).

Q Why are `root()` and `origin()` always written with brackets after them?

A The brackets are so-called empty arguments that prevent them from being confused with IDs.

Exercises

1. The following data is taken from a simple XML book catalog:

```
<catalog>
<title>Simon's XML Book Catalog</title>
<book>
<title>Presenting XML</title>
<author>Richard Light</author>
<author>Simon North</author>
<publisher>Sams.Net</publisher>
<date>1997</date>
<ISBN></ISBN>
<cd>no</cd>
</book>
<book>
<title>XML Complete</title>
<author>Steven Holzner</author>
<publisher>McGraw-Hill</publisher>
<date>1998</date>
<ISBN>0-07-913702-4</ISBN>
<cd>yes</cd>
</book>
<book>
<title>Designing XML Internet Applications</title>
<author>Michael Leventhal</author>
<author>David Lewis</author>
<author>Mathew Fuchs</author>
<publisher>Prentice Hall PTR</publisher>
<date>1998</date>
<ISBN>0-13-616882-1</ISBN>
<cd>yes</cd>
</book>
<book>
<title>Structuring XML Documents</title>
<author>David Megginson</author>
<publisher>Prentice Hall PTR</publisher>
<date>1998</date>
<ISBN>0-13-642299-3</ISBN>
<cd>yes</cd>
</book>
<book>
<title>The XML Companion</title>
<author>Neil Bradley</author>
<publisher>Addison-Wesley</publisher>
<date>1998</date>
```

11

```
<ISBN>0-201-34285-5</ISBN>
<cd>no</cd>
</book>
<book>
<title>XML: Extensible Markup Language</title>
<author>Elliotte Rusty Harold</author>
<publisher>IDG Books</publisher>
<date>1998</date>
<ISBN>0-7645-3199-9</ISBN>
<cd>yes</cd>
</book>
</catalog>
```

What extended pointer could you use to select the title of each book?

2. What extended pointer could you use to select the title of just the third book?

3. What extended pointer could you use to select the complete entry for the second and third books?

DAY 12

Viewing XML in Internet Explorer

Today we will discuss:

- Microsoft's vision for XML
- How to view XML data in Microsoft Internet Explorer 4
- How to view XML data in Microsoft Internet Explorer 5

Microsoft's Vision for XML

Let's start with a framework. XML can be used for marking up three different kinds of information:

- Data—Structured sets of information normally handled by relational databases
- Documents—Less structured sets of information with a specific characteristic— that the sequence of the information is important
- Meta-data—Data about other information, for instance who the author is, keywords, the target group, and so on

Previously, Microsoft's idea was that if you wanted to display documents to people, HTML was the markup language to use. They saw XML as the preferred vehicle for exchanging structured data between applications.

Here's an example of what they envisioned: A relational database is queried. The result of this query is that XML-tagged structured data is sent over the network to the client where the data can be queried, altered, displayed, computed, and so on.

Internet Explorer 4 already has those facilities for reading and displaying XML-tagged data.

Microsoft also uses XML for meta-data. Their Channel Definition Format is an XML application describing sites, which is meta-information (information about sites).

But the release of Internet Explorer 5 beta 2 brought us in addition direct XML document support.

Viewing XML in Internet Explorer 4

One can use XML with IE4 in different ways. We'll explore these ways more profoundly.

Overview of XML Support in Internet Explorer 4

Internet Explorer 4

- Performs CDF processing

    CDF stands for Channel Definition Format, which is an XML application

- Has two XML parsers: a non-validating parser in C and a validating parser written in Java

Those parsers weren't covered in Days 5 and 9 because at the time of this writing, they were not fully conformant to the W3C recommendation.

- Offers an XML Data Source object
- Offers an XML Object Model, and an interface (API) to let developers interact with XML data in the browser

It must be stressed that Internet Explorer 4 doesn't have facilities for natively displaying XML.

Viewing XML Using the XML Data Source Object

Data Source objects are used for what Microsoft calls *data binding*. Data binding is Microsoft's way of bringing data manipulation to the browser (client) and away from the server. Normally, if you want a new view on the data, you resubmit a query to the server. The server performs the necessary calculations and sends a new HTML page to the client. This doesn't happen with data binding. The server sends an HTML page together with the data to the client. They are stored locally and can be manipulated locally without reconnecting to the server.

Transferring processing from the server to the client is not a bad idea in a world where there is always a shortage of bandwidth.

12

To implement this data binding you need first to include a data source object in your page. The XML data source object is just one of the data source objects shipped with Internet Explorer 4.0.

Some of the other data source objects are as follows:

- The Tabular Data Control (TDC)
- The Remote Data Service (using OLE-DB or ODBC)
- The JDBC Applet

More information about data source objects can be found at the following Web site: `http://www.microsoft.com/workshop/c-frame.htm#/workshop/author/default.asp`.

After the insertion of the data source object, you need to define HTML elements that are able to read data from the data source: they are called "data consumers."

Let's make this concrete by using an example. First we need an XML file with structured data. See Listing 12.1.

LISTING 12.1   musicians.xml—AN XML FILE WITH STRUCTURED DATA

```
1:   <?xml version="1.0" ?>
2:   <musicians>
3:   <musician>
4:   <name>Joey Baron
5:   </name>
6:   <instrument>drums
7:   </instrument>
8:   <NrOfRecordings>1
9:   </NrOfRecordings>
10:  </musician>
11:  <musician>
12:  <name>Bill Frisell
13:  </name>
14:  <instrument>guitar
15:  </instrument>
16:  <NrOfRecordings>3
17:  </NrOfRecordings>
18:  </musician>
19:  <musician>
20:  <name>Don Byron
21:  </name>
22:  <instrument>clarinet
23:  </instrument>
24:  <NrOfRecordings>2
25:  </NrOfRecordings>
26:  </musician>
27:  <musician>
28:  <name>Dave Douglas
29:  </name>
30:  <instrument>trumpet
31:  </instrument>
32:  <NrOfRecordings>1
33:  </NrOfRecordings>
34:  </musician>
35:  </musicians>
```

An HTML file is needed as well. See Listing 12.2.

LISTING 12.2   HTML FILE TO ADD AN XML DATA SOURCE OBJECT

```
1:    <HTML>
2:    <HEAD>
3:    <TITLE>Overview of musicians</TITLE>
4:    </HEAD>
5:    <BODY>
6:    <H1>An overview of my favorite musicians</H1>
7:    <HR>
8:    <P>My favorite musicians are:</P>
9:    <!-- Things to come -- >
10:   <HR>
11:   <!-- some other stuff -- >
12:   </BODY>
13:   </HTML>
```

After that the XML Data Source object needs to be added. See Listing 12.3.

LISTING 12.3   AN XML DATA SOURCE OBJECT

```
1:    <APPLET
2:        code="com.ms.xml.dso.XMLDSO.class"
3:        id="xmldso"
4:        width="0"
5:        height="0"
6:        mayscript="true">
7:    <PARAM NAME="URL" VALUE="...">
8:    </APPLET>
```

... stands for the URL that points to an XML file.

Note   Normally, the XML data come from the same place as the HTML file containing the APPLET tag.

Listing 12.4 places the applet in our HTML file.

LISTING 12.4   HTML FILE WITH AN XML DATA SOURCE OBJECT ADDED

```
1:    <HTML>
2:    <HEAD>
3:    <TITLE>Overview of musicians</TITLE>
4:    </HEAD>
```

continues

12

LISTING 12.4   CONTINUED

```
 5:    <BODY>
 6:    <H1>An overview of my favorite musicians</H1>
 7:    <HR>
 8:    <P> My favorite musicians are: </P>
 9:    <APPLET
10:        code="com.ms.xml.dso.XMLDSO.class"
11:        id="xmldso"
12:        width="0"
13:        height="0"
14:        mayscript="true">
15:    <PARAM NAME="URL" VALUE="musicians.xml">
16:    </APPLET>
17:    <!-- More things to come -- >
18:    <HR>
19:    <!-- some other stuff -- >
20:    </BODY>
21:    </HTML>
```

The next step in our procedure is to include some HTML elements that are capable of rendering the data supplied by our XML data source object.

Not all HTML elements support data binding. The following lists the most important elements that do bind data:

- DIV
- SPAN
- TABLE

To bind information in the external data source to these elements, Microsoft added some attributes to these HTML elements. The most important of these are shown in Table 12.1.

TABLE 12.1   ATTRIBUTES FOR CONNECTING A DATA SOURCE OBJECT TO A DATA CONSUMER

Attribute	Function
DATASRC	Refers to the name of the data source object
DATAFLD	Specifies the data to which the element is bound

Let's make our example more complete by adding

```
<P><SPAN DATASRC="#xmldso" DATAFLD="name"></SPAN></P>
```

where the value of attribute DATASRC is referring to the ID of our applet, which is xmldso.

Note The # is used because it is a reference to a name inside the same document.

The value of the DATAFLD attribute refers to the name of an element used in our XML file.

Listing 12.5 shows how these data consumers are connected to the data source object.

INPUT **LISTING 12.5** DATA SOURCE OBJECT CONNECTED TO DATA CONSUMERS

```
 1:  <HTML>
 2:  <HEAD>
 3:  <TITLE>Overview of musicians</TITLE>
 4:  </HEAD>
 5:  <BODY>
 6:  <H1>An overview of my favorite musicians</H1>
 7:  <HR>
 8:  <P>My favorite musicians are:</P>
 9:  <APPLET
10:      code="com.ms.xml.dso.XMLDSO.class"
11:      id="xmldso"
12:      width="0"
13:      height="0"
14:      mayscript="true">
15:  <PARAM NAME="URL" VALUE="musicians.xml">
16:  </APPLET>
17:  <DL>
18:  <DT><B><SPAN DATASRC="#xmldso" DATAFLD="name"></SPAN></B></DT>
19:  <DD>on <SPAN DATASRC="#xmldso" DATAFLD="instrument"></SPAN></DD>
20:  </DL>
21:  <HR>
22:  <!-- some other stuff -- >
23:  </BODY>
24:  </HTML>
```

Figure 12.1 shows this HTML file loaded into Internet Explorer 4.0.

12

FIGURE 12.1

The result of data binding in IE4.

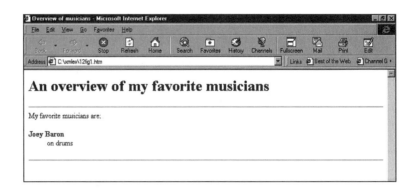

We now have the principle working. We were able to read information from our XML file, but the result is hardly exciting.

We just read information on the first musician that appears in our XML file.

When a data set (XML file) is loaded, the information is split into different records, only one of which is available. It is named the current record.

Note   After loading of the XML file, the first record is normally identified as the current record.

Of course we want information on all our musicians. We can use two techniques to obtain this information:

- We can add a facility for sequentially loading the data of each musician—in other words, to navigate through our data set.
- We could use an element that can handle more than one value, which is the HTML TABLE element.

Let's first investigate how we can navigate through the data set.

We'll use the code in Listing 12.6.

LISTING 12.6   ADDING BUTTONS TO NAVIGATE THROUGH THE DATA SET

```
1:  <input type=button value="<<"
2:      onclick='xmldso.recordset.movefirst();'>
3:  <input type=button value="<"
4:      onclick='xmldso.recordset.moveprevious();>
```

```
5:   <input type=button value=">"
6:       onclick='xmldso.recordset.movenext();'>
7:   <input type=button value=">>"
8:       onclick='xmldso.recordset.movelast();'>
```

Four buttons (INPUT type="button") have been added with semantics:

- Go to first (<<)
- Go to last (>>)
- Go to previous (<)
- Go to next (>)

The buttons are related to the four available methods to navigate the record set generated by our XML data source object.

But if you open this in your browser you'll see that it doesn't really work as intended.

For the next case some testing needs to be added to check if the end of file (EOF) is reached. And the same goes for previous for the beginning of the file (BOF), as done in Listing 12.7.

LISTING 12.7   CHECKING THE POSITION IN THE DATA SET

```
1:   <input type=button value="<<"
2:       onclick='xmldso.recordset.movefirst();'>
3:   <input type=button value="<"
4:       onclick='xmldso.recordset.moveprevious();
5:           if (xmldso.recordset.BOF)
6:           xmldso.recordset.movefirst();'>
7:   <input type=button value=">"
8:       onclick='xmldso.recordset.movenext();
9:           if (xmldso.recordset.EOF)
10:          xmldso.recordset.movelast();'>
11:  <input type=button value=">>"
12:      onclick='xmldso.recordset.movelast();'>
```

Figure 12.2 shows our HTML file with navigation buttons loaded into Internet Explorer 4.0.

12

OUTPUT

FIGURE 12.2

Navigation buttons added.

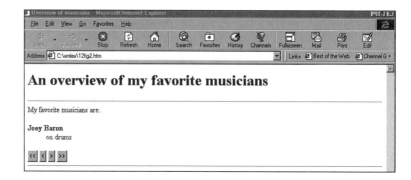

We can also use a second solution, the overview in tabular format. Let's bind a TABLE to the data. See Listing 12.8.

LISTING 12.8   USING A TABLE

```
 1:  <TABLE DATASRC="#xmldso">
 2:  <THEAD>
 3:  <TH>Musician</TH>
 4:  <TH>Instrument</TH>
 5:  </THEAD>
 6:  <TR>
 7:      <TD><SPAN DATAFLD="name"></SPAN></TD>
 8:      <TD><SPAN DATAFLD="instrument"></SPAN></TD>
 9:  </TR>
10:  </TABLE>
```

ANALYSIS The table is set bound to the data source. Inside the table are single-valued elements (SPAN) that refer to the different XML elements. See Listing 12.9.

INPUT   LISTING 12.9   THE COMPLETE HTML FILE

```
 1:  <HTML>
 2:  <HEAD>
 3:  <TITLE>Overview of musicians</TITLE>
 4:  </HEAD>
 5:  <BODY>
 6:  <H1>An overview of my favorite musicians</H1>
 7:  <HR>
```

```
8:    <P>My favorite musicians are:</P>
9:    <APPLET
10:       code="com.ms.xml.dso.XMLDSO.class"
11:       id="xmldso"
12:       width="0"
13:       height="0"
14:       mayscript="true">
15:   <PARAM NAME="URL" VALUE="musicians.xml">
16:   </APPLET>
17:   <TABLE BORDER="2" CELLPADDING="3" CELLSPACING="2" width="40%"
➥DATASRC="#xmldso">
18:   <THEAD>
19:   <TH>Musician</TH>
20:   <TH>Instrument</TH>
21:   </THEAD>
22:   <TR>
23:       <TD><SPAN DATAFLD="name"></SPAN></TD>
24:       <TD><SPAN DATAFLD="instrument"></SPAN></TD>
25:   </TR>
26:   </TABLE>
27:   <HR>
28:   <!-- some other stuff -- >
29:   </BODY>
30:   </HTML>
```

Figure 12.3 shows our musicians data in tabular format in Internet Explorer 4.0.

OUTPUT

FIGURE 12.3

Our data in tabular format in IE4.

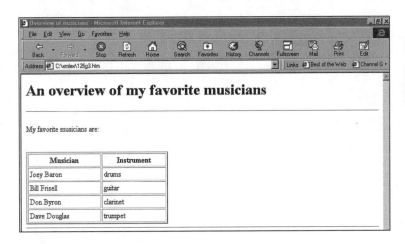

12

You have seen that the idea of bringing data from the server to the client is a very powerful one. A lot of filtering, sorting, and computation can be done on the client side without consuming bandwidth.

Caution Be careful, however. This data binding feature is part of Microsoft's implementation of Dynamic HTML, which is violently incompatible with Netscape's implementation.

In other words, this mechanism only works with Internet Explorer.

Viewing XML Using the XML Object API

This section shows you how to use JavaScript to access the XML Object Model (API) to transform the XML to HTML.

 Caution The object model used in IE4 has been superseded by the Document Object Model (DOM) defined by the W3 organization, which is implemented in IE5, beta 2.

An XML document is modeled as a tree structure. It starts with the top-level element (its root) and branches out to its descendants.

It uses three classes of objects:

- XML Document object
- XML Element object
- XML `Element Collection` object

Figure 12.4 gives a graphical representation of this model.

FIGURE 12.4

The XML Object Model in IE4.

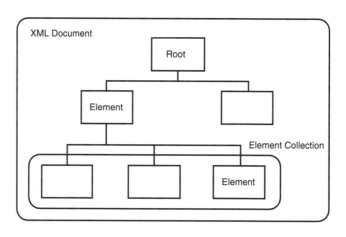

The Document object represents the XML source document. It holds the element tree and document information such as the character set used, the document type, the file size, and so on. Once this object is created you can access its information by calling its properties and manipulate it by calling its methods.

Examples of available XML Document object properties are shown in Table 12.2.

TABLE 12.2   XML DOCUMENT OBJECT PROPERTIES

Name	Returns
Root	The root element of the document
Charset	A string specifying the character set used by the input document
Version	The version of the XML specification being used
FileSize	The file size of the XML document

 Note   The full list of available properties and methods can be found at the following URL: http://www.microsoft.com/xml/articles/xmlmodel.asp

A document is modeled as a tree of nodes, where the root element contains other elements (nodes) containing other nodes... until you reach the leafs of the tree, which are empty elements, text, comments, and processing instructions.

In Internet Explorer 4 the XML Object Model distinguishes five types of element objects, of which three are important:

- ELEMENT type—If the node is a container or an empty element
- TEXT type—If the leaf node contains PCDATA or CDATA
- COMMENT type—For comments

Once an element object is created you can access its information by calling its properties and manipulate it by calling its methods.

The most useful XML Element object properties are shown in Table 12.3.

TABLE 12.3   XML ELEMENT OBJECT PROPERTIES

Name	Returns
Type	0 for type element, 1 for type text, and so on for the other types
Tag	Name, an uppercase string that is the name of the tag
Text	The text content of an element or comment
Children	An enumeration of the child elements of the specified element

12

Useful XML Element object methods are shown in Table 12.4.

TABLE 12.4   XML ELEMENT OBJECT METHODS

Name	Function
setAttribute()	Set an attribute value
removeAttribute()	Remove an attribute
addChild()	Add a child element
removeChild()	Remove a child element

The Element Collection object is used for manipulating the children of an element. Its main use is to iterate over the child elements.

The only XML Element Collection object property is explained in Table 12.5.

TABLE 12.5   XML Element Collection OBJECT PROPERTY

Name	Returns
length	The length of a collection (the number of nodes)

The only XML Element Collection object method is explained in Table 12.6.

TABLE 12.6   XML Element Collection OBJECT METHOD

Name	Function
item(index)	The requested item at the position (number) specified by the index parameter
	In other words, item(0) returns the first child element
item(elementname)	A collection of all elements with that specific name
item(elementname, index)	The element at the position (number) specified by the index parameter in the collection of the elements with that specific name
	In other words, item(ITEM, 3) returns the fourth ITEM element

We will be using a lot of those properties and methods in an example shortly.

This object model is language neutral and can be accessed from JavaScript, VBScript, C++, or Java.

Using a sample JavaScript, we will read our musicians.xml file and convert it to HTML by calling the properties and methods defined for the three different objects (Document object, Element object, Element Collection object).

The result will be a table for all the musicians. It will have a table row for each individual musician that will include the values for name, instrument, and number of recordings in separate cells.

The file musicians.xml is shown in Listing 12.1. We have our file with structured data. The next thing to do is to create a document object.

```
var xml = new ActiveXObject("msxml");
```

Then you need to specify the XML data file to be loaded by the XML document object

```
xml.URL = "file:///c¦/xmlex/musicians.xml";
```

Let's think for a minute what the rest of the program needs to do. Every node that's entered has to be checked to see if:

- It is an element
- It is text

If it is text, we simply want to output it. If it's an element, we need to know if the tag name is:

- musicians—We have to start the table.
- musician—For every musician, we have to start a new row.
- something else—The others (name, instrument, NrOfRecordings) start a table cell.

We implemented this logic into JavaScript as shown in Listing 12.10.

LISTING 12.10   JAVASCRIPT FUNCTION output_doc(elem)

```
 1:    function output_doc(elem)
 2:    {
 3:    if (elem.type == 0) //Check if the node type is an element
 4:          {
 5:                if (elem.tagName == "MUSICIANS") //tagnames are returned
➡in uppercase
 6:                {
 7:                      document.write("<TABLE BORDER='1' CELLPADDING='5'>");
➡//begin table
 8:                      traverse(elem); //to be defined yet; for traversing
➡the children
 9:                      document.write("</TABLE>");
10:                      }
11:                else if (elem.tagName == "MUSICIAN")
12:                {
13:                      document.write("<TR>"); //begin row
```

continues

12

LISTING **12.10** CONTINUED

```
14:                     traverse(elem); //to be defined yet; for traversing
➡the children
15:                     document.write("</TR>");
16:                         }
17:             else
18:             {
19:                     document.write("<TD>"); //begin cell
20:                     traverse(elem); //to be defined yet; for traversing
➡the children
21:                     document.write("</TD>");
22:                 }
23:
24:             }
25:   else if (elem.type==1) //Check if the node type is text
26:             document.write(elem.text);
27:         else
28:             alert("Unknown type encountered");
29:     }
```

The children for every element need to be processed in the same way: the same tests shown in Listing 12.10 have to be carried out—a clear case for recursion (a program/function that calls itself).

In Listing 12.11 we declare a function that iterates over all children elements, calling each time the already defined output_doc() function.

LISTING **12.11** JAVASCRIPT FUNCTION traverse(elem)

```
1:   function traverse(elem)
2:       {var i;
3:       if (elem.children != null)//if there are child elements
4:           {
5:           for (i=0; i < elem.children.length; i++) //repeat over all
➡children
6:               output_doc(elem.children.item(i)); //do the tests and the
➡output for every child
7:           }
8:       }
```

Now we want to start to traverse the tree. We need to define the root element to accomplish this:

```
var docroot = xml.root;
```

And for this root element we call our function output_doc.

```
output_doc(docroot);
```

The complete picture can be seen in Listing 12.12.

. INPUT LISTING 12.12 HTML FILE USING THE TWO JAVASCRIPT FUNCTIONS

```
1:    <HTML>
2:    <HEAD><TITLE>XML Object Model in Explorer 4.0</TITLE>
3:    </HEAD>
4:    <BODY>
5:    <SCRIPT LANGUAGE="JScript" FOR="window" EVENT="onload">
6:        document.write("<HTML><HEAD><TITLE>My favorite
➡musicians</TITLE></HEAD>\n");
7:        document.write("<BODY><H2>My favorite musicians</H2><HR>\n")     ;
8:        var xml = new ActiveXObject("msxml");
9:        xml.URL = "file:///c¦/xmlex/musicians.xml";
10:       var docroot = xml.root;
11:       output_doc(docroot);
12:
13:       function traverse(elem)
14:         {var i;
15:             if (elem.children != null)
16:                 {
17:                 for (i=0; i < elem.children.length; i++)
18:                 output_doc(elem.children.item(i));
19:                 }
20:         }
21:
22:       function output_doc(elem)
23:       {
24:             if (elem.type == 0)
25:                 {
26:                     if (elem.tagName == "MUSICIANS")
27:                         {
28:                             document.write("<TABLE BORDER='1'
➡CELLPADDING='5'>");
29:                             traverse(elem);
30:                             document.write("</TABLE>");
31:                         }
32:                     else if (elem.tagName == "MUSICIAN")
33:                         {
34:                             document.write("<TR>");
35:                             traverse(elem);
36:                             document.write("</TR>");
37:                         }
38:                     else
39:                         {
```

12

continues

LISTING 12.12   CONTINUED

```
40:                             document.write("<TD>");
41:                             traverse(elem);
42:                             document.write("</TD>");
43:                         }
44:
45:                     }
46:             else if (elem.type==1)
47:                     document.write(elem.text);
48:             else
49:                     alert("Unknown type encountered");
50:                 }
51: </SCRIPT>
52: </BODY>
53: </HTML>
```

The result of loading this page in Internet Explorer 4 is shown in Figure 12.5.

OUTPUT

FIGURE 12.5

*The result of our
JavaScript in IE4.*

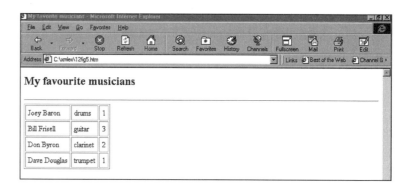

You can see that using this approach is a lot of hassle to simply make XML viewable by Internet Explorer 4.0. However, if you really need to do computing based on XML data, or need to execute transformations of XML data, this API is simple and powerful.

Viewing XML via MS XSL Processor

XSL stands for *Extensible Style sheet Language*. The first XSL proposal was jointly made by Microsoft, Inso Corporation, and ArborText. Microsoft has also made available an XSL processor for prototyping and testing. This processor allows XML data to be transformed into HTML.

> **Note**
>
> Please note that a conversion to HTML takes place. It is not the XML that is rendered directly.

The MS XSL Processor was available in two packages:

- The Microsoft XSL Command-line utility
- The Microsoft XSL ActiveX control

> **Caution**
>
> The XSL syntax to be used with the MS XSL Processor is completely outdated and superseded by a new XSL draft.
>
> The result of this is that the XSL Command-line utility has been withdrawn from Microsoft's Web site.

Let us explain the principle of working with an XSL style sheet.

On one hand we need an XML file, such as the `musicians.xml` file shown in Listing 12.1.

On the other hand we need an XSL style sheet. Let's name it `musicians.xsl`. The content is shown in Listing 12.13.

> **Caution**
>
> Don't spend too much time trying to understand the syntax because the XSL development work by the W3C is still ongoing and the syntax has gone through substantial changes already.

12

LISTING 12.13   `musicians.xsl`

```
1:    <xsl>
2:    <rule>
3:      <root/>
4:      <HTML>
5:        <HEAD>
6:            <TITLE>My favorite musicians</TITLE>
7:        </HEAD>
8:        <BODY>
9:            <H1>My favorite musicians</H1><HR/>
10:           <TABLE BORDER="2" CELLPADDING="5">
```

continues

LISTING 12.13   CONTINUED

```
11:                <children/>
12:                </TABLE>
13:          </BODY>
14:       </HTML>
15:    </rule>
16:    <rule>
17:       <target-element type="musician"/>
18:       <TR>
19:       <children/>
20:       </TR>
21:    </rule>
22:    <rule>
23:       <target-element type="name"/>
24:       <TD>
25:       <children/>
26:       </TD>
27:    </rule>
28:    <rule>
29:       <target-element type="instrument"/>
30:       <TD>
31:       <children/>
32:       </TD>
33:    </rule>
34:    <rule>
35:       <target-element type="NrOfRecordings"/>
36:       <TD>
37:       <children/>
38:       </TD>
39:    </rule>
40:    </xsl>
```

To use the XSL ActiveX control, place the following OBJECT element as shown in Listing 12.14 in your HTML page.

LISTING 12.14   OBJECT ELEMENT REFERRING TO THE XSL CONTROL

```
1:  <OBJECT ID="XSLControl"
2:  CLASSID="CLSID:2BD0D2F2-52EC-11D1-8C69-0E16BC000000"
3:  codebase="http://www.microsoft.com/xml/xsl/msxsl.cab"
4:  style="display:none">
5:  </OBJECT>
```

This object automatically downloads and installs the XSL ActiveX control.

Next, point the control to the XML document and XSL style sheet as shown in Listing 12.15.

LISTING 12.15   OBJECT ELEMENT REFERRING TO THE XML DOCUMENT AND XSL STYLE SHEET

```
1:  <OBJECT ID="XSLControl"
2:  CLASSID="CLSID:2BD0D2F2-52EC-11D1-8C69-0E16BC000000"
3:  codebase="http://www.microsoft.com/xml/xsl/msxsl.cab"
4:  style="display:none">
5:    <PARAM NAME="documentURL" VALUE="musicians.xml">
6:    <PARAM NAME="styleURL" VALUE="musicians.xsl">
7:  </OBJECT>
```

This object generates an HTML string from the XML document and the accompanying style sheet.

This HTML string has to be put somewhere in our page. See Listing 12.16.

LISTING 12.16   SCRIPT FOR LOADING THE GENERATED HTML

```
1:  <SCRIPT FOR=window EVENT=onload>
2:    var xslHTML = XSLControl.htmlText;
3:    document.all.item("xslTarget").innerHTML = xslHTML;
4:  </SCRIPT>
```

This script first captures the HTML in a variable and places it in the element with ID "xslTarget".

So we need to add an element with this ID on our page.

```
<DIV id=xslTarget></DIV>
```

The complete picture is shown in Listing 12.17.

INPUT   LISTING 12.17   LOADING GENERATED HTML

```
1:  <HTML>
2:    <HEAD>
3:      <TITLE>My favorite musicians</TITLE>
4:        <SCRIPT FOR=window EVENT=onload>
5:        var xslHTML = XSLControl.htmlText;
6:        document.all.item("xslTarget").innerHTML = xslHTML;
7:      </SCRIPT>
8:    </HEAD>
9:    <BODY>
10:        <OBJECT ID="XSLControl"
11:                CLASSID="CLSID:2BD0D2F2-52EC-11D1-8C69-0E16BC000000"
```

continues

12

LISTING **12.17**   CONTINUED

```
12:                         CODEBASE="http://www.microsoft.com/xml/xsl/msxsl.cab"
13:                    STYLE="display:none">
14:              <PARAM NAME="documentURL" VALUE="musicians.xml">
15:              <PARAM NAME="styleURL" VALUE="musicians.xsl">
16:       </OBJECT>
17:         <DIV id="xslTarget"></DIV>
18:   </BODY>
19:   </HTML>
```

Viewing XML in Internet Explorer 5

You can use XML with IE5 in different ways. We'll explore these ways more profoundly now.

 Caution | The information here is based on Internet Explorer Developer Release beta 2.

Overview of XML Support in Internet Explorer 5

In addition to the already existing XML support in Internet Explorer 4, expect to see the following in Release 5:

- Full conformance to the XML 1.0 specification
- Direct viewing of XML by using XSL or CSS (Cascading Style Sheets)
- A mechanism for embedding XML in HTML called "data islands"
- Namespace support
- Better performance
- Improved robustness

Viewing XML Using the XML Data Source Object

Internet Explorer 5 beta 2 ships with a new C++ Data Source object, giving you better performance and the ability to bind directly to an XML data island (see below) without the need to use an APPLET or OBJECT tag, as shown in Listing 12.18.

LISTING 12.18   USING THE XML DATA SOURCE OBJECT IN INTERNET EXPLORER 5 BETA 2

```
1:    <HTML>
2:    <HEAD>
3:    <TITLE>Overview of musicians</TITLE>
4:    </HEAD>
5:    <BODY>
6:    <H1>An overview of my favorite musicians</H1>
7:    <HR>
8:    <P>My favorite musicians are:</P>
9:    <XML ID="xmldso" src="musicians.xml"></XML>
10:   <TABLE BORDER="2" CELLPADDING="3" CELLSPACING="2" width="40%"
➥DATASRC="#xmldso">
11:   <THEAD>
12:   <TH>Musician</TH>
13:   <TH>Instrument</TH>
14:   </THEAD>
15:   <TR>
16:       <TD><SPAN DATAFLD="name"></SPAN></TD>
17:       <TD><SPAN DATAFLD="instrument"></SPAN></TD>
18:   </TR>
19:   </TABLE>
20:   <HR>
21:   <!-- some other stuff -- >
22:   </BODY>
23:   </HTML>
```

Viewing XML Using the XML Object API

A lot of thinking is going on in the W3C to define a standardized Document Object Model.

Note   See http://www.w3.org/DOM/.

Microsoft tries to keep in sync with these new developments. The result is that the Document Object Model used in Internet Explorer 5 has changed and been extended.

Microsoft's object model in IE5 uses four base classes of objects:

- Document object
- Node object
- NodeList object
- NamedNodeMap object

12

Figure 12.6 gives a graphical representation of this model.

FIGURE 12.6

*The XML Object
Model in Internet
Explorer 5.*

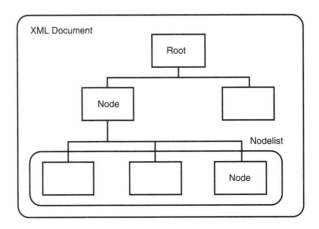

 Note   Note the difference in names used with the previous version: Node instead of
Element, and NodeList instead of Element Collection.

Each of these objects contains a number of properties and methods, enabling you to
access information about those objects and manipulate them.

The list of properties and methods has been extended compared to the previous version.

The Document object represents the top node of the tree.

Once this object is created you can access its information and manipulate it by calling its
properties and methods.

An example of a Document object property is shown in Table 12.7.

TABLE 12.7   IDOMDocument OBJECT PROPERTIES

Name	Returns
DocumentElement	The root element of the XML file

An example of a Document object method is shown in Table 12.8.

TABLE 12.8   IDOMDocument OBJECT METHOD

Name	Function
createElement(tagName)	Returns an Element with name tagName

The Node object represents a node in an XML document.

Internet Explorer 5's XML Object Model distinguishes 12 types of nodes:

- ELEMENT type
- ATTRIBUTE type
- TEXT type
- CDATA_SECTION type
- ENTITY_REFERENCE type
- ENTITY type
- PROCESSING_INSTRUCTION type
- COMMENT type
- DOCUMENT type
- DOCUMENT_TYPE type
- DOCUMENT_FRAGMENT type
- NOTATION type

Once this Node object is created you can access its information and manipulate it by calling its properties and methods.

The most useful Node object properties are shown in Table 12.9.

12

TABLE 12.9   IDOMNode OBJECT PROPERTIES

Name	Function
NodeType	Returns 0 for type element, 1 for type attribute, and so on for the other types.
NodeName	Returns or sets the name of a node.
NodeValue	Returns or sets the value (text) of a node.
ChildNodes	Returns an enumeration of the child nodes of the specified node.

Some Node object methods are shown in Table 12.10.

TABLE 12.10   IDOMNode Object Methods

Name	Function
insertBefore(newChild, refChild)	To insert a child node defined by parameter newChild to the left of the specified node refChild or at the end of the list
removeChild(oldChild)	To remove the specified childnode oldChild

The NodeList object is used for manipulating the children of a node, and its main use is to iterate over the child nodes.

The only NodeList object property is shown in Table 12.11.

TABLE 12.11   IDOMNodeList Object Property

Name	Returns
length	The length of a nodelist (the number of nodes)

You'll find an example of a NodeList object method in Table 12.12.

TABLE 12.12   IDOMNodeList Object Methods

Name	Function
item()	Returns the requested item from the enumerated nodes

We will be using a lot of those properties and methods in an example shortly.

This object model is language neutral and can be accessed equally well from JavaScript, VBScript, C++, or Java.

Due to the changes in the object model between versions 4.0 and 5.0, we need to rewrite the program listed in Listing 12.12. The new version is shown in Listing 12.19.

LISTING 12.19   USING THE DOCUMENT OBJECT MODEL IN INTERNET EXPLORER 5 BETA 2

```
1:    <HTML>
2:    <HEAD><TITLE>XML Object Model in Explorer 5.0</TITLE>
3:    </HEAD>
4:    <BODY>
5:    <SCRIPT LANGUAGE="JScript" FOR="window" EVENT="onload">
```

```
6:      document.write("<HTML><HEAD><TITLE>My favorite
➥musicians</TITLE></HEAD>\n");
7:      document.write("<BODY><H2>My favorite musicians</H2><HR>\n")    ;
8:      var xml = new ActiveXObject("microsoft.xmldom");
9:      xml.load(musicians.xml);
10:     var docroot = xml.documentElement;
11:     output_doc(docroot);
12:
13:     function traverse(node)
14:       {var i;
15:           if (node.childNodes != null)
16:               {
17:               for (i=0; i < node.childNodes.length; i++)
18:               output_doc(node.childNodes.item(i));
19:               }
20:         }
21:
22:     function output_doc(node)
23:       {
24:           if (node.nodeType == 0)
25:               {
26:                   if (node.nodeName == "musicians")
27:                       {
28:                           document.write("<TABLE BORDER='1'
➥CELLPADDING='5'>");
29:                           traverse(node);
30:                           document.write("</TABLE>");
31:                       }
32:                   else if (node.nodeName == "musician")
33:                       {
34:                           document.write("<TR>");
35:                           traverse(node);
36:                           document.write("</TR>");
37:                       }
38:                   else
39:                       {
40:                           document.write("<TD>");
41:                           traverse(node);
42:                           document.write("</TD>");
43:                       }
44:
45:               }
46:           else if (node.nodeType==1)
47:                   document.write(node.nodeValue);
48:           else
49:                   alert("Unknown type encountered");
50:           }
51: </SCRIPT>
52: </BODY>
53: </HTML>
```

12

Let's have a look at the differences in code between the new (for IE5) and the older version (for IE4):

- The ActiveX object that generates the XML document object has the progID of microsoft.xmldom

- To specify the XML data file to be loaded by the XML document object we need to call the load method and pass it the URL of the XML file to be loaded

- To identify the root element we use the documentElement property

- In the script itself we use the properties and methods of the node and the nodelist objects

- The tag names tested for musicians and musician are now in lowercase

Note

In the implementation of version 4 the tagName property of the Element object returned the name in uppercase. This isn't the case for the nodeName property of a Node object (version 5).

Viewing Embedded XML

With the newest release of Internet Explorer it will be possible to embed islands of data (called *data islands*) inside HTML pages. These data islands can be marked up using XML.

You'll do this by using the XML tag inside your HTML page. For getting in the XML data itself, you have two possibilities:

- Include your XML data inside the XML element.

- Use a URL to refer to the XML data.

Listing 12.20 shows an example of the XML data included inside the XML element.

LISTING **12.20** EMBEDDING XML IN AN HTML PAGE

```
 1:    <HTML>
 2:    <HEAD><TITLE>XML Object Model in Explorer 5.0</TITLE>
 3:    </HEAD>
 4:    <BODY>
 5:    <H2>My favorite musicians</H2>
 6:    <HR>
 7:    <XML id="myfavs">
 8:    <musicians>
 9:    <musician>
10:    <name>Joey Baron
```

```
11:    </name>
12:    <instrument>drums
13:    </instrument>
14:    <NrOfRecordings>1
15:    </NrOfRecordings>
16:    </musician>
17:    <musician>
18:    <name>Bill Frisell
19:    </name>
20:    <instrument>guitar
21:    </instrument>
22:    <NrOfRecordings>3
23:    </NrOfRecordings>
24:    </musician>
25:    <musician>
26:    <name>Don Byron
27:    </name>
28:    <instrument>clarinet
29:    </instrument>
30:    <NrOfRecordings>2
31:    </NrOfRecordings>
32:    </musician>
33:    <musician>
34:    <name>Dave Douglas
35:    </name>
36:    <instrument>trumpet
37:    </instrument>
38:    <NrOfRecordings>1
39:    </NrOfRecordings>
40:    </musician>
41:    </musicians>
42:    </XML>
43:    </BODY>
44:    </HTML>
```

12

Listing 12.21 shows an example of how to refer an XML file in an HTML page.

LISTING 12.21   REFERRING AN XML FILE IN AN HTML PAGE

```
1:    <HTML>
2:    <HEAD><TITLE>XML Object Model in Explorer 5.0</TITLE>
3:    </HEAD>
4:    <BODY>
5:    <H2>My favorite musicians</H2>
6:    <HR>
7:    <XML ID="myfavs" SRC="file:///C¦xmlex/musicians.xml">
8:    </XML>
9:    </BODY>
10:   </HTML>
```

If we open those files in our browser, nothing appears.

Once again, you need to use the Document Object API to access the XML data. First, though, you have to work with the HTML Document Object Model because the XML tag is in fact an HTML tag. You can easily refer to the XML element by using its id, which is `"myfavs"`.

Having found the XML tag, we need to find the root element of our XML data tree.

`myfavs.documentElement`

And from here on we can use the code we already know, as used in Listing 12.22.

LISTING 12.22   VIEWING 'REFERRED TO' XML IN A HTML PAGE

```
1:    <HTML>
2:    <HEAD><TITLE>XML Object Model in Explorer 5.0</TITLE>
3:    </HEAD>
4:    <SCRIPT>
5:     function traverse(node)
6:        {var i;
7:            if (node.childNodes != null)
8:                {
9:                for (i=0; i < node.childNodes.length; i++)
10:                 output_doc(node.childNodes.item(i));
11:                }
12:        }
13:
14:     function output_doc(node)
15:     {
16:            if (node.nodeType == 0)
17:                {
18:                    if (node.nodeName == "musicians")
19:                        {
20:                            document.write("<TABLE BORDER='1'
➥CELLPADDING='5'>");
21:                            traverse(node);
22:                            document.write("</TABLE>");
23:                        }
24:                    else if (node.nodeName == "musician")
25:                        {
26:                            document.write("<TR>");
27:                            traverse(node);
28:                            document.write("</TR>");
29:                        }
30:                    else
31:                        {
32:                            document.write("<TD>");
33:                            traverse(node);
```

```
34:                              document.write("</TD>");
35:                         }
36:
37:                  }
38:            else if (node.nodeType==1)
39:                  document.write(node.nodeValue);
40:            else
41:                  alert("Unknown type encountered");
42:            }
43:
44:  </SCRIPT>
45:  <BODY>
46:  <H2>My favorite musicians</H2>
47:  <XML ID="myfavs" src="musicians.xml"></xml>
48:  <SCRIPT>
49:  var root = myfavs.documentElement;
50:  output_doc(root);
51:  </SCRIPT>
52:  <HR>
53:  </BODY>
54:  </HTML>
```

Note

The following two lines are equivalent:

```
var root = myfavs.documentElement;

var root = document.all("myfavs").XMLDocument;
```

12

Viewing XML Directly

It is possible to open any XML file directly in IE5. A default XSL style sheet will be applied in this case.

For example, see the file shown in Listing 12.23.

INPUT   **LISTING 12.23**   `helptopic.xml`

```
1:  <?xml version="1.0" ?>
2:  <helptopic>
3:   <title keyword="printing,network;printing,shared printer">
4:   How to use a shared network printer?</title>
5:  <procedure>
6:   <step><action>In <icon>Network Neighborhood</icon>,
7:    locate and double-click the computer where the printer
8:    you want to use is located. </action>
```

continues

LISTING **12.23**   CONTINUED

```
 9:   <tip targetgroup="beginners">To see which computers have
10:   shared printers attached, click the <menu>View</menu> menu,
11:   click <menu>Details</menu>, and look for printer names or
12:   descriptions in the Comment column of the Network Neighborhood
➥window.</tip>
13:   </step>
14:   <step>
15:   <action>Double click the printer icon in the window that
➥appears.</action>
16:   </step>
17:   <step>
18:   <action>
19:   To set up the printer, follow the instructions on the screen.
20:   </action></step>
21:   </procedure>
22:   <tip>
23:    After you have set up a network printer, you can use it as if
24:    it were attached to your computer. For related topics,
25:    look up &quot;printing&quot; in the Help Index.
26:   </tip>
27:   </helptopic>
```

Figure 12.7 shows you the result of loading this XML file without a specific style sheet attached.

OUTPUT

FIGURE 12.7

Viewing an XML file directly in IE5.

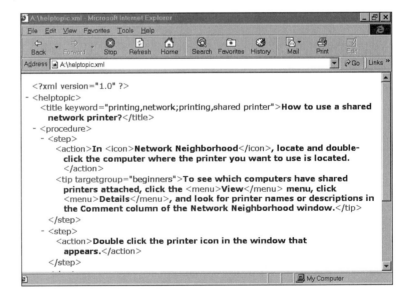

Of course if you want to present your XML file in a more exciting way, you need to supply a style sheet to render the XML data. This can be either an XSL or CSS style sheet.

Viewing XML with CSS

You specify the style sheet to be used by inserting a processing instruction of the following form:

```
<?xml:stylesheet type="text/css" href="helptopic.css" ?>
```

Note

The notation to be used is described in the W3C note, `http://www.w3.org/`
`TR/NOTE-xml-stylesheet`.

Let us use the XML file from Listing 12.22. The first lines are as in Listing 12.23.

LISTING 12.23   `helptopic.xml`

```
1:    <?xml version="1.0" ?>
2:    <?xml:stylesheet type="text/css" href="helptopic.css" ?>
3:    <helptopic>
4:    <title keyword="printing,network;printing,shared printer">
5:....
```

The content of our `heltopic.css` file could be as in Listing 12.24.

INPUT   **LISTING 12.24**   `helptopic.css`

```
1:    helptopic {     display: block;
2:         margin-top:3cm;
3:         margin-left:2cm;
4:         margin-right:2cm;
5:         margin-bottom:6cm;
6:         font-family:Verdana, Arial;
7:         font-size:11pt;
8:         padding:20pt; }
9:
10:   title {display: block;
11:        font-size:20pt;
12:        color:blue;
13:        font-weight:bold;
14:        text-align:center;
15:        margin-bottom:30pt;
16:        text-decoration:underline;}
17:
```

12

continues

LISTING 12.24 CONTINUED

```
18:  procedure {display:block;
19:      margin-bottom:30pt}
20:
21:   step {display:block;
22:      margin-bottom:18pt}
23:
24:  action {display:block;
25:      font-weight:bold;}
26:
27:  tip {display:block;
28:      font-size:10pt;
29:      margin-left:+1cm;
30:      margin-top:12pt;
31:      color:blue;}
32:
33:  icon {display:inline;
34:      font-size:12pt;}
35:
36:  todo {display:inline;
37:      color:red;}
38:
39:  menu {display:inline;
40:      font-style:italic;}
```

Figure 12.8 shows you the result of loading this XML file with a CSS style sheet attached.

OUTPUT

FIGURE 12.8

Viewing an XML file with a CSS style sheet in IE5.

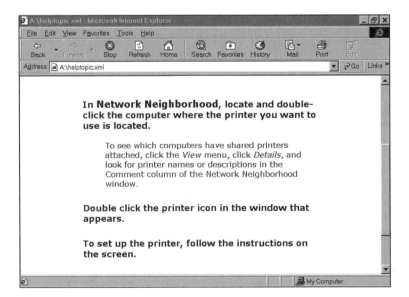

Viewing XML with XSL

You relate an XML document with an XSL style sheet by inserting a processing instruction of the following form:

```
<?xml:stylesheet type="text/xsl" href="helptopic.xsl" ?>
```

The first lines are as shown in Listing 12.25.

LISTING **12.25**   HELPTOPIC.XML

```
1:    <?xml version="1.0" ?>
2:    <?xml:stylesheet type="text/css" href="helptopic.css" ?>
3:    <helptopic>
4:    <title keyword="printing,network;printing,shared printer">
5:....
```

A sample `heltopic.xsl` file is shown in Listing 12.26.

 Caution | Please note that the XSL syntax for use with IE5 isn't completely in sync with the latest draft of the W3C, which is itself still a moving target.

LISTING **12.26**   `helptopic.xsl`

```
1:    <?xml version="1.0"?>
2:    <xsl:stylesheet xmlns:xsl="http://www.w3.org/TR/WD-xsl">
3:
4:    <!-- default behaviour, thanks to Ken Holman -->
5:
6:    <xsl:template><xsl:apply-templates/></xsl:template>
7:    <xsl:template match="textnode()"><xsl:value-of/></xsl:template>
8:
9:    <!-- specific behaviour -->
10:
11:     <xsl:template match="/">
12:       <html>
13:         <head>
14:           <title>Using an XSL stylesheet </title>
15:         </head>
16:         <body bgcolor="#FFFFFF">
17:           <xsl:apply-templates/>
18:          </body>
```

continues

12

LISTING **12.26**   CONTINUED

```
19:     </html>
20:  </xsl:template>
21:
22:  <xsl:template match="title">
23:   <H2>
24:     <xsl:apply-templates/>
25:   </H2>
26:  </xsl:template>
27:
28:  <xsl:template match="procedure">
29:    <OL>
30:      <xsl:apply-templates/>
31:    </OL>
32:  </xsl:template>
33:
34:  <xsl:template match="step">
35:   <LI>
36:     <xsl:apply-templates/>
37:   </LI>
38:  </xsl:template>
39:
40:  <xsl:template match="action">
41:  <B>
42:     <xsl:apply-templates/>
43:  </B><BR/>
44:  </xsl:template>
45:
46:  <xsl:template match="helptopic/tip">
47:   <H3>Tip!</H3>
48:     <xsl:apply-templates/>
49:  </xsl:template>
50:
51: </xsl:stylesheet>
```

Figure 12.9 shows you the result of loading this XML file with a XSL style sheet attached.

OUTPUT

FIGURE 12.9

Viewing an XML file with a XSL style sheet in IE5.

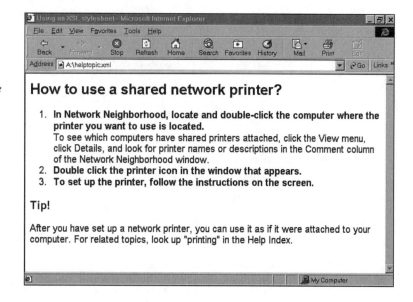

Summary

In this chapter we have seen how XML data can be used with:

- Internet Explorer 4
- Internet Explorer 5, beta 2

For each version we explored the different possibilities:

- The XML Data Source object
- The DOM API
- CSS style sheets
- XSL style sheets

12

Q&A

Q Should I use the DOM API, CSS, or XSL?

A From a standards view, both DOM and CSS are stable standards. This cannot be said of XSL, which is still on the drawing board. From an implementation point of view, the support of CSS in IE5, as it stands now, is far from perfect.

Q I receive white pages in IE5 when opening XML files.

A Chances are great that corruption was introduced during installation. Uninstall completely and then reinstall.

Exercises

Bring the following file into Internet Explorer 4.0 using the XML Data Source object. The data is restricted and should appear in the following order:

- Author
- Title
- ISBN number

Then, using the same XML file, bring it into Internet Explorer using the XML Object Model API to display only a list of authors.

```
1:    <?xml version="1.0"?>
2:    <books>
3:       <book>
4:          <title>Sam's Teach Yourself C++ in 21 Days, Second Edition
5:          </title>
6:          <author>Jesse Liberty
7:          </author>
8:          <description>This book teaches you the basics of object-
➥oriented programming with C++ and is completely revised to
➥ANSI standards. It can be used with any C++ compiler.
9:          </description>
10:          <ISBN>0-672-31070-8
11:          </ISBN>
12:          <pages>700
13:          </pages>
14:          <targetgroup>Beginning - Intermediate
15:          </targetgroup>
16:          <price unit="USA">29.99
17:          </price>
18:       </book>
19:       <book>
20:          <title>Maximum Java 1.1
21:          </title>
22:          <author>Glenn Vanderburg et al.
23:          </author>
24:          <description>Written by JAVA experts, this book explores
➥the JAVA 1.1 language, tools, and core JAVA API without
➥reviewing fundamentals or basic techniques.
25:          </description>
26:          <ISBN>1-57521-290-0
27:          </ISBN>
28:          <pages>900
29:          </pages>
30:          <targetgroup>Expert
31:          </targetgroup>
32:          <price unit="USA">49.99
33:          </price>
```

```
34:      </book>
35:      <book>
36:          <title>JavaScript Unleashed, Second Edition
37:          </title>
38:          <author>Richard Wagner et al.
39:          </author>
40:         <description>This book helps you thoroughly understand
➥and apply JavaScript.
41:          </description>
42:          <ISBN>1-57521-306-0
43:          </ISBN>
44:          <pages>1000
45:          </pages>
46:          <targetgroup>Casual - Experienced
47:          </targetgroup>
48:          <price>49.99
49:          </price>
50:      </book>
51:      <book>
52:          <title>Sam's Teach Yourself Visual C++ 5 in 21 Days, Fourth
➥Edition
53:          </title>
54:          <author>Nathan and Ori Gurewich
55:          </author>
56:          <description>This book merges the power of the best-selling
➥"Teach Yourself" series with the knowledge of Nathan and
➥Ori Gurewich, renowned experts in code, creating the most
➥efficient way to learn Visual C++.
57:          </description>
58:          <ISBN>0-672-31014-7
59:          </ISBN>
60:          <pages>832
61:          </pages>
62:          <targetgroup>New - Casual
63:          </targetgroup>
64:          <price>35.00
65:          </price>
66:      </book>
67: </books>
```

12

WEEK 2

DAY 13

Viewing XML in Other Browsers

On Day 12 we covered how XML can be used with Microsoft Internet Explorer version 4 and 5.

Today we will discuss how you can view XML in other browsers such as:

- Netscape Navigator/Mozilla/Gecko
- DocZilla
- Browsers based on the Inso/Synex Viewport engine

Viewing/Browsing XML in Netscape Navigator/Mozilla/Gecko

In this part we will discuss how XML is handled by Navigator/Mozilla/Gecko.

Netscape's Vision for XML

Netscape sees use of XML for three types of information: documents, data, and metadata.

For documents, Netscape uses XML with *CSS* (Cascading Style Sheets). As far as XSL is concerned, Netscape has adopted a wait and see approach, because XSL isn't a stable standard yet.

For data and metadata, Netscape favors the *RDF* (Resource Description Framework).

RDF is a framework for describing and interchanging metadata. It is a model for describing resources; resources that have properties that take certain values.

 A *resource* is any object that can have a URI (Uniform Resource Identifier).

 PropertyType is the name of the property.

 Value is the value of the property.

> **Note**   PropertyTypes and Values can be resources on their own.

An example of these concepts:

- Resource = `http://www.macmillan.com/history/history.htm`
- PropertyType = `lastupdated`
- Value = `2/12/1998`

The relationships between resources, PropertyTypes, and Values are represented by a directed labeled graph, as shown in Figure 13.1.

A *graph* is a collection of points in which some pair of points are connected by lines. In a *directed graph* the lines have arrowheads, indicating a travel direction.

FIGURE 13.1

Our example as a directed labeled graph.

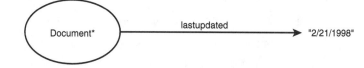

*http://www.macmillan.com/history/history.htm

XML is expected to become the preferred format for the interchange of these (meta)data.

 Note To learn more about RDF, visit `http://www.w3.org/TR/WD-rdf-syntax/`.

Viewing XML in Netscape Navigator 4

Netscape Navigator 4 does not support XML.

If you want to use XML with Netscape Navigator 4, you first need to convert (outside the Netscape environment) to HTML or another format that Navigator 4 can handle natively.

Viewing XML in Mozilla 5/Gecko

Netscape has put the source code of its browser in the public domain, where it is being developed further by the Free Software Community, under the name Mozilla.

Information on the Mozilla project can be found at the following Web sites:

- General information is at `http://www.mozilla.org/`.
- The FAQ about the Mozilla project is located at `http://junior.apk.net/~qc/dok/mozilla_faq`.
- The compiled binaries can be retrieved from `http://www.mozilla.org/binaries/html`.

13

`Gecko` is the name of just one part (module) of the Mozilla development effort: the new layout engine. It is aimed at being an embeddable object. It will be used by any application developer to add Web browsing functionality to their application.

You'll find the Gecko homepage at `http://developer.netscape.com/software/communicator/ngl/index.html`.

The XML support of Mozilla:

- Includes James Clark's expat parser
- Implements XML+CSS (Cascading Style Sheet) support at the document level
- Offers an API to the XML Document Object Model (DOM) via JavaScript and any plug-in
- Supports XLink
- Supports elements from the HTML namespace

From the standards viewpoint, Mozilla supports parts of CSS 2.0 and fully supports:

- The XML 1.0 recommendation
- The DOM 1.0 recommendation
- The CSS 1.0 recommendation

To view an XML file in Mozilla you need to define a CSS style sheet with formatting specifications. These are kept in a separate file. You relate your XML file to the CSS file by including a processing instruction inside your XML file.

Listing 13.1 is an XML file describing a help topic for an online help system.

LISTING **13.1** `helptopic.xml`

```
1:    <?xml version="1.0" ?>
2:    <?protext objid="I5678" ?>
3:    <!DOCTYPE helptopic SYSTEM "dtdv.dtd" [
4:    <!ENTITY doubleclick "<todo>Double-click</todo>">
5:    ]>
6:    <helptopic>
7:    <title keyword="printing,network;printing,shared printer">
➥How to use a shared network printer?</title>
8:    <procedure>
9:    <step><action>In <icon>Network Neighborhood</icon>,
➥locate and double-click the computer where the printer
➥you want to use is located. </action>
10:    <tip targetgroup="beginners">To see which computers
➥have shared printers attached, click the <menu>View</menu> menu,
➥click <menu>Details</menu>, and look for printer names or descriptions
➥in the Comment column of the Network Neighborhood window.</tip>
11:    </step>
12:    <step>
13:    <action>&doubleclick; the printer icon in the window that
➥appears.</action>
```

```
14:   </step>
15:   <step>
16:   <action>
17:   To set up the printer, <xref linkend="id45">follow the
➡instructions</xref> on the screen.
18:   </action></step>
19:   </procedure>
20:   <tip>
21:   After you have set up a network printer, you can use it as if it were
➡attached to your computer. For related topics, look up
➡&quot;printing&quot; in the Help Index.
22:   </tip>
23:   </helptopic>
```

We have to relate our XML file with a style sheet, `helptopic.css`. This is done by adding the following processing instruction (PI) to our XML file.

```
<?xml-stylesheet type="text/css2" href="helptopic.css"?>
```

Our XML file now looks as shown in Listing 13.2:

LISTING 13.2   `helptopic.xml` WITH PROCESSING INSTRUCTION ADDED

```
1:   <?xml version="1.0" ?>
2:   <?xml-stylesheet type="text/css2" href="helptopic.css"?>
3:   <?protext objid="I5678" ?>
4:   <!DOCTYPE helptopic SYSTEM "dtdv.dtd" [
5:   <!ENTITY doubleclick "<todo>Double-click</todo>">
6:   ]>
7:   <helptopic>
8:   ...
```

In this PI, we refer to a CSS file, `helptopic.css`.

Because there are no fixed semantics (how an element needs to be presented or how it needs to behave) associated with our XML elements, the first thing we need to indicate is whether an element is *inline-level* (does not cause line breaks) or *block-level* (causes line breaks).

An example of a block-level element is the `action` element that needs to be captured in CSS as follows:

```
action {display:block}
```

13

An example of an inline-level element is the todo element which, translated to CSS syntax, is:

```
todo [display:inline}
```

The rest of the style sheet is completed with traditional formatting specifications. See Listing 13.3.

LISTING 13.3   helptopic.css

```
 1:   helptopic {display: block;
 2:       margin-top:3cm;
 3:       margin-left:2cm;
 4:       margin-right:2cm;
 5:       margin-bottom:6cm;
 6:       font-family:Verdana, Arial;
 7:       font-size:11pt;
 8:       padding:20pt;}
 9:
10:   title {display: block;
11:       font-size:20pt;
12:       color:blue;
13:       font-weight:bold;
14:       text-align:center;
15:       margin-bottom:30pt;
16:       text-decoration:underline;}
17:
18:   procedure {display:block;
19:       margin-bottom:30pt}
20:
21:   step {display:block;
22:       margin-bottom:18pt}
23:
24:   action {display:block;
25:       font-weight:bold;}
26:
27:   tip {display:block;
28:       font-size:10pt;
29:       margin-left:+1cm;
30:       margin-top:12pt;
31:       color:blue;}
32:
33:   icon {display:inline;
34:       font-size:12pt;}
35:
36:   todo {display:inline;
37:       color:red;}
38:
39:   menu {display:inline;
```

```
40:       font-style:italic;}
41:
42:   xref {display:inline;
43:       text-decoration:underline;}
```

The result, in a Mozilla 5 browser, is shown in Figure 13.2.

FIGURE 13.2

*The XML file in
Mozilla 5 using CSS.*

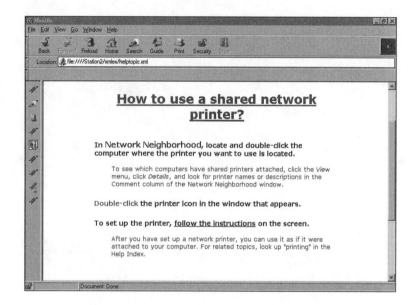

Figure 13.3 shows the source code.

This figure shows as source the XML file itself, not an HTML converted version of it.

At the time of writing, not much information was available about working with CSS and XML in Mozilla 5. It isn't clear, for example, which features of CSS Level 2 will or won't be implemented.

> **Note**   New documentation on the CSS support in Mozilla is announced at this
> address: `http://www.mozilla.org/rdf/doc/xml.html`.

Although documentation is lacking and all CSS Level 2 features may not be available in the near future, XML+CSS is the way to go for displaying XML documents.

13

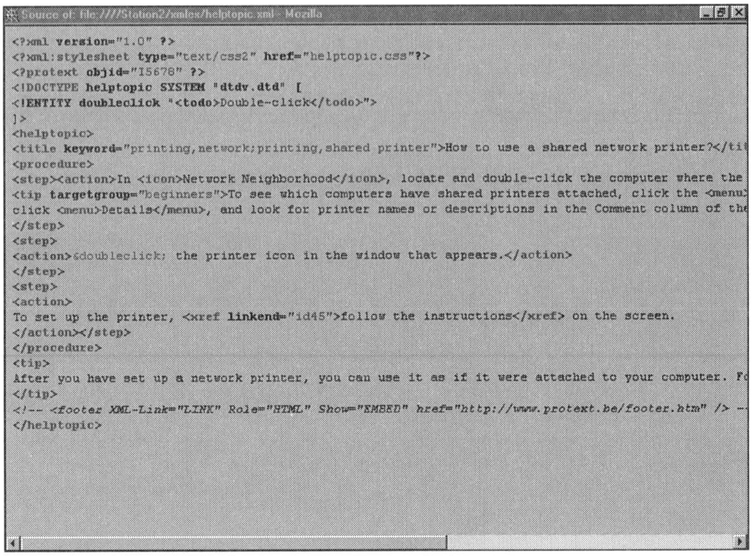

FIGURE 13.3

The source file of the Web page.

```
<?xml version="1.0" ?>
<?xml:stylesheet type="text/css2" href="helptopic.css"?>
<?protext objid="15678" ?>
<!DOCTYPE helptopic SYSTEM "dtdv.dtd" [
<!ENTITY doubleclick "<todo>Double-click</todo>">
]>
<helptopic>
<title keyword="printing,network;printing,shared printer">How to use a shared network printer</til
<procedure>
<step><action>In <icon>Network Neighborhood</icon>, locate and double-click the computer where the
<tip targetgroup="beginners">To see which computers have shared printers attached, click the <menu>
click <menu>Details</menu>, and look for printer names or descriptions in the Comment column of the
</step>
<step>
<action>&doubleclick; the printer icon in the window that appears.</action>
</step>
<step>
<action>
To set up the printer, <xref linkend="id45">follow the instructions</xref> on the screen.
</action></step>
</procedure>
<tip>
After you have set up a network printer, you can use it as if it were attached to your computer. Fo
</tip>
<!-- <footer XML-Link="LINK" Role="HTML" Show="EMBED" href="http://www.protext.be/footer.htm" /> --
</helptopic>
```

The XML data is directly rendered to HTML without any intermediate conversion or translation phase.

Mozilla 5 provides 100% support of the DOM 1.0 recommendation.

The following example is JavaScript source code. It uses the DOM API to replace a price in U.S. dollars with a price in Canadian dollars.

LISTING 13.4 books2.xml

```
1:   <?xml version="1.0"?>
2:   <?xml-stylesheet type="text/css" href="books.css"?>
3:   <books xmlns:html="http://www.w3.org/TR/REC-html40">
4:       <html:form>
5:           <html:h3>Convert to Canadian dollars:</html:h3>
6:           <html:input type="button" onclick="convert()" value="CAN"/>
7:       </html:form>
8:       <book>
9:           <title>Sam's Teach Yourself C++ in 21 Days, Second Edition
10:          </title>
11:          <author>Jesse Liberty
12:          </author>
13:          <description>This book teaches you the basics of
➥object-oriented programming with C++ and is completely revised to ANSI
➥standards. It can be used with any C++ compiler.
14:          </description>
15:          <ISBN>0-672-31070-8
```

```
16:            </ISBN>
17:            <pages>700
18:            </pages>
19:            <targetgroup>Beginning - Intermediate
20:            </targetgroup>
21:            <price unit="USA">29.99
22:            </price>
23:        </book>
24:        <book>
25:            <title>Maximum Java 1.1
26:            </title>
27:            <author>Glenn Vanderburg et al.
28:            </author>
29:            <description>Written by JAVA experts, this book explores
➥the JAVA 1.1 language, tools, and core JAVA API without reviewing
➥fundamentals or basic techniques.
30:            </description>
31:            <ISBN>1-57521-290-0
32:            </ISBN>
33:            <pages>900
34:            </pages>
35:            <targetgroup>Expert
36:            </targetgroup>
37:            <price unit="USA">49.99
38:            </price>
39:        </book>
40:        <book>
41:            <title>JavaScript Unleashed, Second Edition
42:            </title>
43:            <author>Richard Wagner et al.
44:            </author>
45:            <description>This book helps you thoroughly understand and
➥apply JavaScript.
46:            </description>
47:            <ISBN>1-57521-306-0
48:            </ISBN>
49:            <pages>1000
50:            </pages>
51:            <targetgroup>Casual - Experienced
52:            </targetgroup>
53:            <price>49.99
54:            </price>
55:        </book>
56:        <book>
57:            <title>Sam's Teach Yourself Visual C++ 5 in 21 Days,
➥Fourth Edition
58:            </title>
59:            <author>Nathan and Ori Gurewich
```

13

continues

LISTING **13.4**   CONTINUED

```
60:                </author>
61:                <description>This book merges the power of the best-
➥selling "Teach Yourself" series with the knowledge of Nathan and Ori
➥Gurewich, renowned experts in code, creating the most efficient way to
➥learn Visual C++.
62:                </description>
63:                <ISBN>0-672-31014-7
64:                </ISBN>
65:                <pages>832
66:                </pages>
67:                <targetgroup>New - Casual
68:                </targetgroup>
69:                <price>35.00
70:                </price>
71:        </book>
72:        <html:script src="convert.js" />
73:    </books>
```

ANALYSIS   Line 2 contains the processing instruction to use the style sheet defined in the books.css file.

On line 3 (the element books), the html namespace has been declared because HTML elements will be used within the file.

You'll find the HTML elements form, h3, and input on lines 4 through 7, and the script element on line 72.

By declaring this namespace the browser knows that the element h3 from namespace html receives the semantics (formatting and behavior) defined for this namespace.

The input element (line 6) refers to a JavaScript function defined in the convert.js file, referred to on line 72, and listed in Listing 13.5.

LISTING **13.5**   convert.js

```
1:  function convert() {
2:  var priceElements = document.getElementsByTagName("price");
3:  //returns a NodeList of all elements with the tag price
4:  var i;
5:  for (i=0;i < priceElements.length;i++) {
➥// looping over all those price elements
6:        var USAprice =
➥parseFloat(priceElements.item(i).firstChild.nodeValue);
7:        //the firstChild property returns the Text node
```

```
8:          //of this Text node we take the nodeValue, being the text itself
9:          //we convert this text to a number (floating)
10:         priceElements.item(i).setAttribute("unit","Canadian dollar");
11:         //we set the attribute "unit" to value "Canadian dollar"
12:         var convertedprice = USAprice * 1.4;
13:         //we convert the price to Canadian dollar
14:         var newprice = document.createTextNode(convertedprice);
15:         //we create a new Text node containing the new price
16:         priceElements.item(i).replaceChild(newprice,priceElements.
➥item(i).firstChild);
17:         //we replace the old Text node with the new one
18:         }
19:   }
```

ANALYSIS First we create a NodeList containing all the element nodes with name price (line 2).

We loop over all those element nodes (line 5).

For each price element we first use the firstChild property, which returns a node of type Text. We take the content from this text node by using the nodeValue property. This string needs to be converted to a number, hence the use of the parseFloat() function.

This number is converted on line 12.

With this value we create a new TextNode (line 14), which is then used to replace the old value (line 16).

Mozilla supports transclusions using Xlink syntax.

NEW TERM *Transclusions* are (portions of) other documents that are included at the place of reference as if they occurred locally.

In other words, you refer to another document and the contents of that document are placed at the point of reference.

The following is an example of a transclusion.

```
<footer xml:link="simple" role="HTML" show="embed" href="footer.htm"/>
```

The XML element footer is a link that retrieves the content of footer.htm and embeds it at its position in the XML file.

The content of footer.htm could be as shown in Listing 13.6.

13

LISTING 13.6   footer.htm

```
1:    <hr style="margin-top:2cm">
2:    <div class="footer" align="center">
3:    <small>
4:    Copyright ACME Company<BR>
5:    January 1997
6:    </small>
7:    </div>
```

This gives the result in the browser as shown in Figure 13.4.

FIGURE 13.4

*Transclusion in
Mozilla 5.*

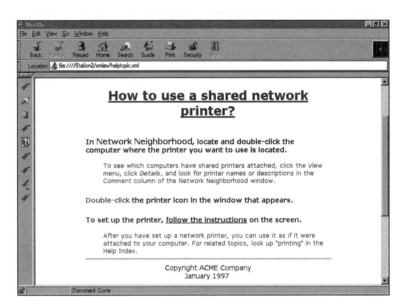

Using transclusions is a fine alternative for today's practice of server-specific server-side `include` statements. Now it is possible to define client-side inclusions.

> **Note**   Microsoft seems to be working on transclusion as well, but it's uncertain at the moment if their version will be compatible with other browsers.

Viewing XML with DocZilla

The Finnish company Citec Information Technologies is using the Mozilla 5 code to develop a high-end browser. This high-end browser will be a functional XML, SGML, and HTML browser with the following features:

- The ability to display documents with CSS
- Full DOM and ECMAscript support
- On-the-fly generation of TOCs
- A structured indexing and search mechanism

Note More information about Citec's browser can be found at
http://www.citec.fi/multidoczilla.

Viewing XML with Browsers Based on Inso's Viewport Engine

For years the Inso/Synex Viewport engine has been the market leader for browsing native SGML files.

The engine has been used in products such as

- Panorama (Interleaf, previously SoftQuad)
- SplitVision (Sörman Information)
- Multidoc Pro (Citec Information Technology)

The latest version of the engine is also able to render XML files.

Features of the Viewport Engine

Noteworthy features of the Viewport environment include the use of style sheets, navigators, webs, and other hypermedia support.

You can define one or more *style sheets* for every document. This can be done by using a graphical style sheet editor.

13

Note Unfortunately, the language used to define the style specification is Viewport specific. But in upcoming releases XSL will either complement or supersede the native style sheet format.

A *navigator* serves as an active and dynamic table of contents view.

Any document element can be extracted and assembled into a navigator. The elements maintain their original order and hierarchy in the document. This makes it possible to easily define a table of contents, a table of graphics, a table of tables, and so on.

A *web* is an independent file containing anchors and links.

Anchors can be attached to textual spans or to a region of a graphic. They can contain an annotation and can serve as a bookmark.

Links connect two anchors.

You can mount and unmount webs. If a web is mounted, anchors are attached to open documents and are displayed as clickable icons. This leads to very powerful possibilities. In one of our actual projects, we deliver the same document with two views: an "actual" view and a "change" view. In the actual view the user sees the information as it is now. In the change view another style sheet is opened, showing new information in red, changed information in blue with change bars, and deleted information as strikethrough. This change information is kept in the document in a revision attribute. Also in change view a web is opened containing a list of anchors referring to all the new and changed topics. This allows the user to go over all the changes very quickly. Furthermore, the reasons for the changes are explained in the associated annotation.

Note   The same concept of link information kept outside the document itself is also part of the XLink proposal.

How it Works

In addition to your XML file, you need accompanying style sheets and navigators. Both use specific markups defined in an SGML DTD. To create a style sheet, you need to create a file with an .ssh extension. The content of this file needs to be that shown in Listing 13.7.

LISTING **13.7**   A VIEWPORT STYLE SHEET DEFINITION

```
1:  <!doctype stylesheet PUBLIC "-//Synex Information AB//DTD stylesheet
➥V2.00//EN>
2:  <stylesheet>
3:  </stylesheet>
```

The additional content of the style specifications will be automatically supplied when you use the graphical style sheet editor.

To create a navigator you need to create a file with a .nav extension. The content of this
file needs to be that shown in Listing 13.8.

LISTING 13.8   A VIEWPORT NAVIGATOR DEFINITION

```
1:  <!doctype toc-def PUBLIC "-//SYNEX Information AB//DTD Navigator
➥v2.00//EN">
2:  <toc-def>
3:  </toc-def>
```

The additional content of this file is automatically supplied when you use
the browser to define navigators.

Now that we have our style sheet and navigator defined we need to establish a relationship between our XML file and these supporting files.

This can be accomplished in two ways:

- They can be related to the document itself.
- If a DTD having a public identifier is used, they can be related to this DTD.

In case of a relationship with the document itself, you have to add to the document the
following processing instruction:

```
<?stylespec "menuname" "filename"?>
```

for the style specification, where:

- menuname is the name that will be used on the View menu of the browser.
- filename is the name of the style sheet file (*.ssh).

and

```
<?navigator "menuname" "filename"?>
```

for the navigator, where:

- menuname is the name that will be used on the Navigator menu of the browser.
- filename is the name of the navigator file (*.nav).

13

If the DTD has a public identifier, you need to edit the ENTITYRSC file in the Viewport environment. In this ENTITYRSC file you can define a relationship between style sheets and navigators on one hand and public identifiers on the other. See Listing 13.9.

LISTING 13.9 DEFINING RELATIONSHIPS BETWEEN A DTD AND VIEWPORT STYLE SHEETS AND NAVIGATORS

```
1:  PUBLIC "-//Pro Text//DTD online help//EN"
2:      STYLESPEC "standard"     "standard.ssh"
3:      STYLESPEC "large"      "large.ssh"
4:      NAVIGATOR "topics"      "topics.nav"
5:      NAVIGATOR "figures"       "figures.nav"
```

Let's show an example starting with the XML file, as shown in Listing 13.10.

LISTING 13.10 musicians.xml

```
1:  <?xml version="1.0"?>
2:  <!DOCTYPE musicians [
3:  <!ELEMENT musicians  (musician)+ >
4:  <!ELEMENT musician  (name, instrument, NrOfRecordings)>
5:  <!ELEMENT (name, instrument, NrOfRecordings)  (#PCDATA)>
6:  ]>
7:  <musicians>
8:    <musician>
9:  <name>Joey Baron
10: </name>
11: <instrument>drums
12: </instrument>
13: <NrOfRecordings>1
14: </NrOfRecordings>
15:   </musician>
16:   <musician>
17: <name>Bill Frisell
18: </name>
19: <instrument>guitar
20: </instrument>
21: <NrOfRecordings>3
22: </NrOfRecordings>
23:   </musician>
24:   <musician>
25: <name>Don Byron
26: </name>
27: <instrument>clarinet
28: </instrument>
29: <NrOfRecordings>2
30: </NrOfRecordings>
```

```
31:    </musician>
32:    <musician>
33: <name>Dave Douglas
34: </name>
35: <instrument>trumpet
36: </instrument>
37: <NrOfRecordings>1
38: </NrOfRecordings>
39:    </musician>
40: </musicians>
```

Now add two style sheets and one navigator.

Files `musicians.ssh` and `musician2.ssh` contain the following:

```
<!doctype stylesheet PUBLIC "-//Synex Information AB//DTD stylesheet
V2.00//EN>
<stylesheet>
</stylesheet>
```

File `musician.nav` contains the following:

```
<!doctype toc-def PUBLIC "-//SYNEX Information AB//DTD Navigator
v2.00//EN">
<toc-def>
</toc-def>
```

Now let's bring the files together by including processing instructions in our XML file, shown in Listing 13.11.

LISTING 13.11   `musicians.xml` WITH PROCESSING INSTRUCTIONS

```
 1: <?xml version="1.0"?>
 2: <!DOCTYPE musicians [
 3: <!ELEMENT musicians  (musician)+ >
 4: <!ELEMENT musician   (name, instrument, NrOfRecordings)>
 5: <!ELEMENT name    (#PCDATA)>
 6: <!ELEMENT instrument   (#PCDATA)>
 7: <!ELEMENT NrOfRecordings (#PCDATA)>
 8: ]>
 9: <?stylespec "table" "musicians.ssh"?>
10: <?stylespec "indent" "musician2.ssh"?>
11: <?navigator "toc" "musicians.nav"?>
12: <musicians>
13: ...
14: </musicians>
```

13

`table` and `indent` will be added to the View menu now and `toc` to the Navigator menu.

Open the XML file with the Synex Viewport–based browser. See Figure 13.5.

FIGURE 13.5

The XML file opened for the first time.

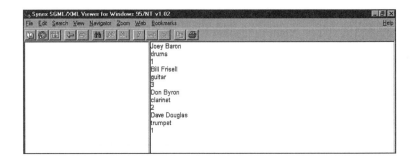

We don't see much for the moment, but that's because we didn't add information to our style sheets and navigators yet.

We change our view (using the View menu) to include tags and the tree structure of our document. See Figure 13.6.

FIGURE 13.6

Tag names and tree structure are visible.

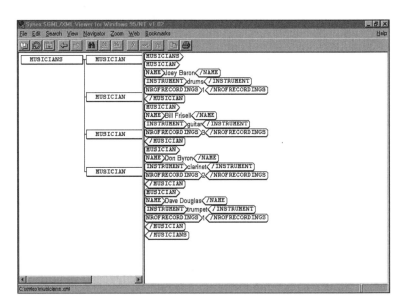

By clicking on a tag or a tree node with the right mouse button, you see the option to open the style sheet editor. See Figure 13.7.

FIGURE 13.7

The style sheet editor opened.

Figure 13.8 shows a possible result of our style sheet editing.

FIGURE 13.8

A finished style sheet applied.

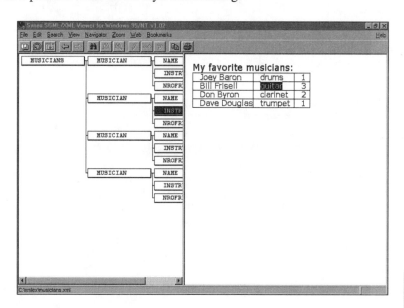

The next thing to do is to define a navigator. For this file it would be good to have an overview with the musicians' names.

To open the navigator editor, use the right mouse button to click on an element name that you want to include in your navigator. See Figure 13.9.

Clicking the mouse button displays the results shown in Figure 13.10.

13

FIGURE **13.9**

The navigator editor.

FIGURE **13.10**

The defined navigator.

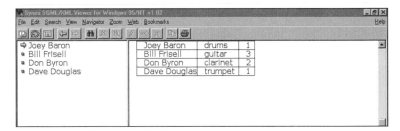

You'll see the same file but with another style sheet attached, as shown in Figure 13.11.

FIGURE **13.11**

Another style sheet attached.

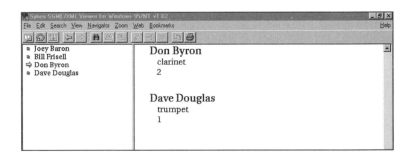

The style sheet used in this latest example is shown in Listing 13.12.

LISTING **13.12**   A SAMPLE STYLE SHEET

```
1:   <!DOCTYPE STYLESHEET PUBLIC "-//SYNEX INFORMATION AB//DTD STYLESHEET
➥V2.00//EN"[
2:   <!ELEMENT sheet (margins?)>
3:   <!ELEMENT margins EMPTY>
4:   <!ATTLIST margins
5:       left CDATA #IMPLIED
6:       right CDATA #IMPLIED
```

```
 7:        top CDATA #IMPLIED
 8:        bottom CDATA #IMPLIED>
 9:
10:   <!ELEMENT font-shadow EMPTY>
11:   <!ATTLIST font-shadow
12:        v NUMBER #REQUIRED>
13:
14:   <!ELEMENT shadow-color EMPTY>
15:   <!ATTLIST shadow-color
16:        v CDATA #REQUIRED>
17:
18:   ]>
19:
20:   <STYLESHEET>
21:
22:   <STYLE TAG="NROFRECORDINGS">
23:   <SPC-LEFT V="36">
24:   <BREAK-BEFORE>
25:   <BREAK-AFTER>
26:   </STYLE>
27:
28:   <STYLE TAG="MUSICIANS">
29:   <FONT-FAMILY V="Utopia">
30:   <FONT-SIZE V=14>
31:   <SPC-ABOVE V="12">
32:   <SPC-LEFT V="24">
33:   <SPC-BELOW V="12">
34:   <BREAK-BEFORE>
35:   <BREAK-AFTER>
36:   </STYLE>
37:
38:   <STYLE TAG="NAME">
39:   <FONT-WEIGHT V=Bold>
40:   <FONT-SCALE V="120">
41:   <SPC-ABOVE V="24">
42:   <BREAK-BEFORE>
43:   <BREAK-AFTER>
44:   </STYLE>
45:
46:   <STYLE TAG="INSTRUMENT">
47:   <SPC-LEFT V="36">
48:   <BREAK-BEFORE>
49:   <BREAK-AFTER>
50:   </STYLE>
51:
52:   </STYLESHEET>
```

13

The navigator used is shown in Listing 13.13.

LISTING **13.13** A SAMPLE NAVIGATOR

```
1:  <!DOCTYPE TOC-DEF PUBLIC "-//SYNEX INFORMATION AB//DTD NAVIGATOR
➥V2.00//EN">
2:
3:  <TOC-DEF SCALE=70>
4:  <TOC BODY="MUSICIAN" TITLE="NAME">
5:  </TOC-DEF>
```

The Synex Viewport engine is the state of the art for viewing native SGML files. That it also directly supports XML documents can only be applauded.

But there are also some drawbacks:

- The style sheet mechanism is proprietary.
- The browser doesn't come for free.
- The product is only known inside the SGML community, not in the much broader HTML community.

Summary

In this chapter we discussed other browsers you can use to browse/view XML. Although Mozilla 5 is still under development, it shows a lot of promise for directly displaying XML files with associated CSS style sheets.

Furthermore it attempts to consistently implement Web standards and recommendations. This alone needs to be heavily applauded.

The DocZilla and Synex Viewport were discussed as well.

Q&A

Q I downloaded Gecko and it doesn't seem to work well. What's happening?

A The Gecko development is continuously going on. Every day a new build of Gecko is made available. If the build of one day isn't stable enough, chances are great that the next build is already better.

Q I don't see formatted text in my Synex browser.

A Check if your XML file is in one way or another associated with a style sheet.

Exercises

Using Listing 13.14,

- Create a CSS (Cascading Style Sheet) file and relate the XML file

- Open the XML file with Mozilla/Gecko

LISTING 13.14 books.xml

```
 1:  <?xml version="1.0"?>
 2:  <books>
 3:      <book>
 4:          <title>Sam's Teach Yourself C++ in 21 Days, Second Edition
 5:          </title>
 6:          <author>Jesse Liberty
 7:          </author>
 8:          <description>This book teaches you the basics of
➥object-oriented programming with C++ and is completely revised
➥to ANSI standards. It can be used with any C++ compiler.
 9:          </description>
10:          <ISBN>0-672-31070-8
11:          </ISBN>
12:          <pages>700
13:          </pages>
14:          <targetgroup>Beginning - Intermediate
15:          </targetgroup>
16:          <price unit="USA">29.99
17:          </price>
18:      </book>
19:      <book>
20:          <title>Maximum Java 1.1
21:          </title>
22:          <author>Glenn Vanderburg et al.
23:          </author>
24:          <description>Written by JAVA experts, this book
➥explores the JAVA 1.1 language, tools, and core JAVA API without
➥reviewing fundamentals or basic techniques.
25:          </description>
26:          <ISBN>1-57521-290-0
27:          </ISBN>
28:          <pages>900
29:          </pages>
30:          <targetgroup>Expert
31:          </targetgroup>
32:          <price unit="USA">49.99
33:          </price>
34:      </book>
35:      <book>
```

13

continues

LISTING **13.14**   CONTINUED

```
36:          <title>JavaScript Unleashed, Second Edition
37:          </title>
38:          <author>Richard Wagner et al.
39:          </author>
40:          <description>This book helps you thoroughly understand and
➥apply JavaScript.
41:          </description>
42:          <ISBN>1-57521-306-0
43:          </ISBN>
44:          <pages>1000
45:          </pages>
46:          <targetgroup>Casual - Experienced
47:          </targetgroup>
48:          <price>49.99
49:          </price>
50:      </book>
51:      <book>
52:          <title>Sam's Teach Yourself Visual C++ 5 in 21 Days, Fourth
➥Edition
53:          </title>
54:          <author>Nathan and Ori Gurewich
55:          </author>
56:          <description>This book merges the power of the best-selling
➥"Teach Yourself" series with the knowledge of Nathan and Ori Gurewich,
➥renowned experts in code, creating the most efficient way to learn Visual
➥C++.
57:          </description>
58:          <ISBN>0-672-31014-7
59:          </ISBN>
60:          <pages>832
61:          </pages>
62:          <targetgroup>New - Casual
63:          </targetgroup>
64:          <price>35.00
65:          </price>
66:      </book>
67:  </books>
```

DAY **14**

Processing XML

Today you'll learn why and how XML data can be used for further processing. We will also discuss the two main programming paradigms used in XML processing:

- The event-driven approach
- The tree-based approach

Reasons for Processing XML

By using XML, you've already made the decision to mark up your data in the best possible way. You have also seen that some browsers can display your XML files natively. Why would you want to write programs to process your XML, then?

Well, the answer is limited only by your imagination, but let's enumerate some possible reasons:

- Delivery to multiple media
- Delivery to multiple target groups

- Adding, removing, and restructuring information
- Database loading
- Reporting

Delivery to Multiple Media

Information needs to be published via different media: on the Web, in hard copy, on CD-ROM, as help files, and so on.

For delivery on the Web, HTML will still be in place for awhile. But which type of HTML: version 3.2, version 4, DHTML Microsoft flavor or DHTML Netscape flavor?

Until now you had these choices:

- Use only those HTML tags that are supported by all browsers (the common denominator approach).
- Make browser-specific optimized HTML pages.
- Include scripts in your HTML pages to generate browser-specific code.

With XML, you can use another tactic. You can check which browser is asking for information and transform your XML data on-the-fly to the most appropriate version of HTML.

The big advantage of this approach is that you have to manage just one source file. All formatting and processing is kept separate from your data. This means that if a new flavor of HTML arrives, you need to write a new conversion but your data doesn't need to be modified.

For getting to hard copy, you can convert your XML data to RTF (Rich Text Format) for use with Microsoft Word, or to another markup language used in other text processing tools (for example, MIF for FrameMaker).

The XML file in Listing 14.1 can be used as source code for generating RTF output.

INPUT   **LISTING 14.1**   `musicians.xml`—YOUR XML FILE TO CONVERT

```
1: <?xml version="1.0"?>
2: <!DOCTYPE musicians [
3: <!ELEMENT musicians  (musician)+ >
4: <!ELEMENT musician  (name, instrument, NrOfRecordings)>
5: <!ELEMENT (name, instrument, NrOfRecordings)  (#PCDATA)>
6: ]>
7: <musicians>
8:   <musician>
9: <name>Joey Baron
```

```
10: </name>
11: <instrument>drums
12: </instrument>
13: <NrOfRecordings>1
14: </NrOfRecordings>
15:    </musician>
16:    <musician>
17: <name>Bill Frisell
18: </name>
19: <instrument>guitar
20: </instrument>
21: <NrOfRecordings>3
22: </NrOfRecordings>
23:    </musician>
24:    <musician>
25: <name>Don Byron
26: </name>
27: <instrument>clarinet
28: </instrument>
29: <NrOfRecordings>2
30: </NrOfRecordings>
31:    </musician>
32:    <musician>
33: <name>Dave Douglas
34: </name>
35: <instrument>trumpet
36: </instrument>
37: <NrOfRecordings>1
38: </NrOfRecordings>
39:    </musician>
40: </musicians>
```

This could become the RTF file in Listing 14.2.

Note

This is just one example of how XML can be converted to another markup language. How to do it will be discussed during the next few days.

OUTPUT **LISTING 14.2** `musicians.rtf`—THE RTF FILE AFTER CONVERSION

```
1: {\rtf1\ansi\ansicpg1252\uc1
2:
3: ... //lots of rtf code deleted
4:
5: \pard\plain \s18\li1440\sb320\widctlpar
6: \adjustright \b\f15\fs28\lang2057\cgrid {Joey Baron
```

14

continues

LISTING **14.2**   CONTINUED

```
 7: \par }\pard\plain \s19\li2880\sb120\widctlpar
 8: \adjustright \f15\fs20\lang2057\cgrid {drums
 9: \par }\pard\plain \s20\li3600\sb120\sa400\widctlpar
10: \adjustright \i\f15\fs20\lang2057\cgrid {1
11: \par }\pard\plain \s18\li1440\sb320\widctlpar
12: \adjustright \b\f15\fs28\lang2057\cgrid {Bill Frisell
13: \par }\pard\plain \s19\li2880\sb120\widctlpar
14: \adjustright \f15\fs20\lang2057\cgrid {guitar
15: \par }\pard\plain \s20\li3600\sb120\sa400\widctlpar
16: \adjustright \i\f15\fs20\lang2057\cgrid {3
17: \par }\pard\plain \s18\li1440\sb320\widctlpar
18: \adjustright \b\f15\fs28\lang2057\cgrid {Don Byron
19: \par }\pard\plain \s19\li2880\sb120\widctlpar
20: \adjustright \f15\fs20\lang2057\cgrid {clarinet
21: \par }\pard\plain \s20\li3600\sb120\sa400\widctlpar
22: \adjustright \i\f15\fs20\lang2057\cgrid {2
23: \par }\pard\plain \s18\li1440\sb320\widctlpar
24: \adjustright \b\f15\fs28\lang2057\cgrid {Dave Douglas
25: \par }\pard\plain \s19\li2880\sb120\widctlpar
26: \adjustright \f15\fs20\lang2057\cgrid {trumpet
27: \par }\pard\plain \s20\li3600\sb120\sa400\widctlpar
28: \adjustright \i\f15\fs20\lang2057\cgrid {1}{\f2\lang2067\cgrid0
29: \par }\pard\plain \widctlpar\adjustright \fs20\lang2057\cgrid {
30: \par }}
```

This file can be read by Microsoft Word and most other word processing software.

Delivery to Multiple Target Groups

Not only do you want to publish to different media, you probably also want to deliver different information to different types of groups. Some examples:

- Beginners, advanced users, experts
- Members, non-members
- Onshore, offshore

The XML file in Listing 14.3 could serve as source code for generating specific output according to user experience.

```
 1: <?xml version="1.0"?>
 2: <procedure type="disassemble">
 3:     <object>
 4: <type>Mismatcher</type>
 5: <seriesnr>21568</seriesnr>
 6:         </object>
 7:     <title>How to disassemble Mismatcher 21568</title>
 8:     <steps experience="firsttime">
 9:         <step>
10:             <action>Press ....
11:             </action>
12:             <result>The door ....
13:             </result>
14:         </step>
15:         <step>
16:             <action>Push ....
17:             </action>
18:             <result>The back ...
19:             </result>
20:         </step>
21:         <step>
22:             <action>Drill ....
23:             </action>
24:             <result>Part x123 ...
25:             </result>
26:         </step>
27:     </steps>
28:     <steps experience="donebefore">
29:         <step>
30:             <action>Throw it on the ground.
31:             </action>
32:         </step>
33:     </steps>
34:     <tip>Take a bottle of ....
35:     </tip>
36: </procedure>
```

This data allows you to customize the steps according to the experience of your reader. If your audience consists of first-time users, the element `steps`, with an attribute with the name `experience` and a value of `donebefore` (lines 28–33), can be stripped away.

You may also decide that the `tip` (lines 34 and 35) is only relevant for the first-timers and filter it for the target group `donebefore`.

14

Adding, Removing, and Restructuring Information

If you define the reports to be generated from your relational databases, you can arrange the data as you like: leave data out, compute new data based on existing ones (for example, an average), and so on.

The same goes for XML coded data. You can add, remove, and rearrange your data.

For example, take the data in Listing 14.4.

INPUT   LISTING 14.4   books.xml—AN XML FILE FOR RESTRUCTURING IDEAS

```
 1: <?xml version="1.0"?>
 2: <books>
 3:     <book>
 4:         <title>Sams Teach Yourself C++ in 21 Days, Second Edition
 5:         </title>
 6:         <author>Jesse Liberty
 7:         </author>
 8:         <description>This book teaches you the basics of
➥object-oriented programming with C++ and is completely revised
➥to ANSI standards. It can be used with any C++ compiler.
 9:         </description>
10:         <ISBN>0-672-31070-8
11:         </ISBN>
12:         <pages>700
13:         </pages>
14:         <targetgroup>Beginning - Intermediate
15:         </targetgroup>
16:         <price unit="USA">29.99
17:         </price>
18:     </book>
19:     <book>
20:         ...
21:     </book>
22: </books>
```

You can do the following things with this listing:

- Leave out the targetgroup information
- Add a second price element in "Canadian dollar"
- Add a list with all book titles or with all authors
- Put the ISBN number after the price

Database Loading

Refer to Listing 14.1. It would be a good idea to have this information in a database or a spreadsheet. In fact, this is how XML is mainly perceived by Microsoft: as a delivery and exchange format for structured data. And structured data normally resides in relational databases.

In the foreseeable future, you will have XML writers and XML readers for every database. However, you can write some code yourself to generate a comma-separated values file, as shown in Listing 14.5.

INPUT   LISTING 14.5   musicians.csv—A COMMA-SEPARATED VALUES FILE

```
1: Name,Instrument,NrOfRecordings
2: Joey Baron,drums,1
3: Bill Frisell,guitar,3
4: Don Byron,clarinet,2
5: Dave Douglas,trumpet,1
```

Or you can write some SQL code, as in Listing 14.6.

INPUT   LISTING 14.6   SOME SQL CODE

```
1: create table musicians (
2:     name text not null primary key,
3:     instrument text,
4:     nrofrecordings integer
5: );
6: insert into musicians values ('Joey Baron','drums',1);
7: insert into musicians values ('Bill Frisell','guitar',3);
8: insert into musicians values ('Don Byron','clarinet',2);
9: insert into musicians values ('Dave Douglas','trumpet',1);
```

Reporting

Processing the XML files can easily answer questions such as the following:

- How many musicians are there in the file?
- How many of them play guitar?
- What is the total number of recordings?

Now that you have turned your documents into real text databases, you can process them in many ways, generating output as needed.

14

Three Processing Paradigms

XML documents can be viewed as

- A special type of text file
- A sequence of events
- A hierarchy

An XML Document as a Text File

An XML file can be viewed as a text file, in which you find a mixture of the real data and markup language. You can find a lot of free tools on the market that excel in text manipulation using regular expressions: awk, grep, perl, and python.

If you want to know how many musicians you have in your musicians.xml file, you can use the following grep command:

```
grep -c "<musician>" musicians.xml
```

Here's a breakdown of this command:

- -c is the option to print only the number of lines matched.
- Within quotes, the text (or pattern) to be matched, in this case the start tag of element musician.
- The file to be searched, for example, musicians.xml.

This example will return 4.

An XML Document as a Series of Events

Everyone knows how to work with a graphical user interface such as Windows, Mac OS, or Motif. In these environments, the OS captures all kinds of events: mouse movements and clicks, keyboard input, and so on. Subsequently, the OS sends messages to the program indicating which event has occurred. It is the responsibility of the programmer of the application to code the responses to those events.

An analogy can be drawn for XML files. When you read an XML file in a sequential way, all kinds of events happen. You encounter the start of a document, you read start and end tags, you encounter comments and processing instructions, and so on. All of these can be looked at as data events.

It is the responsibility of the programmer to code the responses to these events. These responses are called *event handlers*.

NEW TERM   An *event handler* is the code that is executed when an event has occurred.

For the file `musicians.xml` (Listing 14.1), an event-based processor will generate the events listed in Listing 14.7.

OUTPUT   LISTING 14.7   EVENTS GENERATED BY THE `musicians.xml` FILE

```
 1: Start document
 2: Start element: musicians
 3: Start element: musician
 4: Start element: name
 5: Characters: Joey Baron
 6: End element: name
 7: Start element: instrument
 8: Characters: drums
 9: End element: instrument
10: Start element: NrOfRecordings
11: Characters: 1
12: End element: NrOfRecordings
13: End element: musician
14: ...
15: End element: musicians
16: End document
```

It is important to see that the traversal of the XML document happens in a hierarchically sequential, left-to-right fashion.

Consider the XML structure shown in Figure 14.1.

FIGURE 14.1

The XML tree.

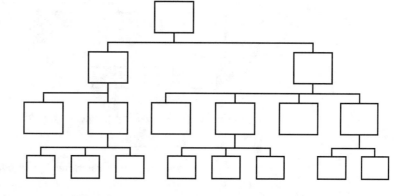

Figure 14.2 indicates the order in which the different nodes of the tree are traversed.

14

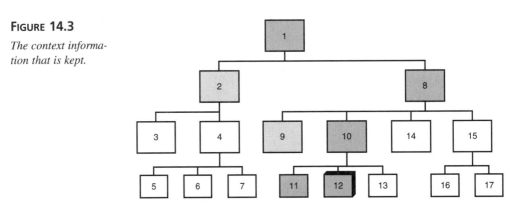

FIGURE **14.2**

The order of traversal.

During traversal, most of the event-based processors store information about already-traversed nodes.

In event-driven mode, Balise from the company AIS keeps track of element types and attributes for ancestor nodes up to the root and for the first-left siblings of these ancestor nodes as indicated in Figure 14.3.

FIGURE **14.3**

The context information that is kept.

Figure 14.3 shows which other nodes are being tracked for node number 12.

Note

The context information that is kept can differ from product to product. You can expect that at least the information on previous siblings within the same parent element and on all ancestors is stored.

Thanks to this cataloging of some context (however limited), you can write event handlers using this context:

- Start element: `para`, first after `title`.

  In this way, you can define a different response if your `para` element comes first after `title`.

- Start element: `li`, with an ancestor of `ol` and an attribute of `type` with a value of `i`.

  Here also, you can write a specific response if this condition occurs.

On the other hand, you cannot answer questions that require looking further in the data stream. For example:

- Is an element the last child element of its parent element?

  You can know this only after having processed the element, not when you receive the start element event.

- Does this element have an element in it that has an attribute with the name `experience` and the value `firsttime`?

  You can only know this after processing the element.

Note
> There are solutions, of course, but they require a second pass.

Advantages of this event-based processing are

- It's simple.
- It works fast.
- It doesn't consume a lot of memory.

Disadvantages are

- It's impossible to look ahead.

Two implementations are mentioned here:

- Omnimark
- SAX

Omnimark is the market leader for doing heavy conversions in the SGML community. Recently it has been XML-enabled, and a free (although restricted) version called Omnimark LE is available on the Web at `http://www.omnimark.com/develop/omle40/index.html`.

14

Omnimark will be covered in more depth in Day 15, "Event-Driven Programming."

SAX stands for a Simple API for XML. It came about after Peter Murray-Rust, one of the early adopters of XML, made a complaint on the XML developers' mailing list. He said that when he wanted to change the parser coupled to his XML browser, JUMBO, he had to rewrite code because the APIs of the different parsers differed. The question raised was, "While waiting for the API defined by the W3C (DOM), can we agree on a simple event-based API?"

This was publicly discussed on the XML-DEV list, and lots of people contributed. It was David Megginson who wrote the SAX proposal, together with its implementation in Java.

SAX can be found at `http://www.megginson.com/SAX/index.html`. It's also subject of the study on Day 15.

XML as a Hierarchy/Tree

A tree-based processor translates the XML document into an internal tree structure and allows an application to navigate that tree.

In the case of your `musicians.xml` file, a possible resulting tree structure is shown in Figure 14.4.

 Note   Trees can be more or less extensive depending on whether attributes, entities, and so on need to be stored as separate nodes.

Once the tree is constructed in memory, it can be navigated. Please note that you have two passes:

- Pass 1: Parsing and tree-building
- Pass 2: The data processing itself

In this way, it becomes possible to answer your questions that require a look ahead:

- Is an element the last child element of its parent element?
- Does this element have an element below it that has an attribute with the name `experience` and the value `firsttime`?

Because you have access to the full document (the complete tree), you have access to all information required.

FIGURE 14.4

A tree starting from
`musicians.xml`.

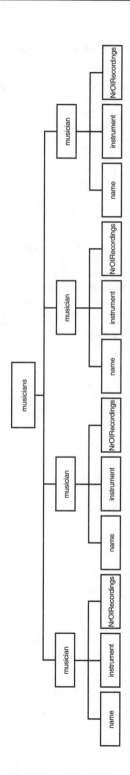

The advantage of this approach is that it gives access to the whole document, so it's easy to look ahead. The disadvantages are that it's more difficult to first build a tree and then navigate it, it requires more memory, and it's slower, requiring two passes.

The World Wide Web consortium (W3C) developed a standard tree-based API for XML and HTML. It is called the Document Object Model (DOM) and is a W3C recommendation as of October 1, 1998. The specification can be found at `http://www.w3.org/TR/ REC-DOM-Level-1/`.

The DOM will be implemented in version 5 of both Internet Explorer and Mozilla (Netscape). It's covered extensively on Day 16, "Programming with the Document Object Model."

Note

There is also software that brings you both worlds, mixing the event-driven approach and the tree-based approach. Balise, from the company AIS, is well known for this in the SGML community and includes a non-validating XML parser in its latest version. Unfortunately, no free version is available.

Summary

Today you saw many reasons why you would want to process your XML files. This processing can be done in different ways, depending on how you look at your XML data:

- Plain text files
- A series of events happening
- A tree that can be navigated and manipulated

In the next few days, you will explore these viewpoints and their implementations much more deeply.

Q&A

Q Is it easier to process XML than HTML?

A Yes, for two reasons.

The first is that you normally model your data better with XML than with HTML. You can better capture the hierarchical structure, the semantics, and the meta-data of your information without bothering too much with formatting.

The second reason is that XML files are well formed. You have a much better idea what comes in the data stream. HTML files, on the other hand, can take many forms and appearances.

Q Which processing approach do you recommend?

A It depends on the problem that you want to tackle.

For example, if you want to count the number of times the element `tool` is used in an XML document, it is not very efficient to first build a tree representation of your document and then traverse it. When you have to deal with complex structural objects such as tables that require a lot of look-ahead, the tree-based approach simplifies the processing task.

Also of importance is that the DOM, which is tree-based, is an official W3C recommendation now, and a lot of tools will support it as the standard API.

Exercise

See the following XML file:

```
 1: <?xml version="1.0"?>
 2: <memo>
 3:     <meta>
 4:         <from>P. Hermans</from>
 5:         <to>S. North</to>
 6:         <regarding>deadlines</regarding>
 7:     </meta>
 8:     <body>
 9:         <dear>Simon</dear>
10:         <p>I will <verystrong>not</verystrong> be able to finish
11: all chapters before leaving on 11..holidays.</p>
12:         <p>Please advise what to do.</p>
13:         <close>Paul</close>
14:     </body>
15: </memo>
```

Using this file:

- Write down the sequential list of events.
- Draw the tree structure.
- Indicate in which order the tree is navigated.
- For the last p element in the tree, indicate which other nodes still are accessible in the event-driven approach.
- For the body element in the tree, indicate which other nodes are still accessible in the tree-based approach.

14

WEEK III

15 Event-Driven Programming 309

16 Programming with the
    Document Object Model 343

17 Using Meta-Data to Describe
    XML Data 361

18 Styling XML with CSS 375

19 Converting XML with
    DSSSL 411

20 Rendering XML with XSL 453

21 Real World XML
    Applications 495

15

16

17

18

19

20

21

DAY 15

Event-Driven Programming

In the previous chapter we outlined the differences between event-driven and tree-based processing of XML files.

Today we will dig deeper into the subject of event driven processing by using two event-driven processing environments:

- Omnimark LE
- SAX

Omnimark LE

In this part we will cover the programming language Omnimark of Omnimark Technologies.

What Is Omnimark LE?

Omnimark LE is the light and free version of Omnimark, which is an event-driven programming language for processing data streams. The current version is 4.01 and is XML enabled.

 Caution

> The Omnimark XML parser is a validating parser that requires a valid XML DTD to process XML documents.

This free version has a limitation that you cannot compile and execute programs that contain more than 200 countable actions in the program source. A *countable action* is a statement that Omnimark executes.

Note

> What counts as a countable action is explained at the following URL:
> http://www.omnimark.com/develop/omle40/sampcode.html.

Most of the time the free version is perfectly suited for writing small to medium conversions.

 Tip

> If you are running against the countable action limit, consider splitting your script into different parts and running them sequentially or applying the tips and techniques mentioned at http://www.sesha.com/omlette/.

Finding and Installing Omnimark LE

Omnimark LE can be found at the following URL: http://www.omnimark.com/develop/omle40/index.html. The file omle40.exe is 1955 Kb large.

To install, double-click this file. An InstallShield wizard will take over to guide you through the installation.

How Omnimark Works

In the event-driven paradigm, pieces of code are executed when certain events occur during the processing of the input document.

15

Therefore we need to formulate rules. Rules define and associate both the actions to be executed and the events that cause these actions to be triggered.

This is reflected in the structure of a rule, which has two parts:

- A rule header
- A rule body

The rule header is used to define the event and has a structure of its own. It defines the event and, optionally, additional conditions that need to be satisfied before the actions are fired.

In the rule body are the actions that will be executed.

An Omnimark script/program is a collection of such rules.

Running Omnimark LE

You run Omnimark from the command line, which takes the following form:

```
Omle -s script.xom input.xml -of output.htm
```

Where:

- omle invokes the program
- The -s parameter refers to the script to use (such as script.xom)
- The input file comes next, which in our case is an XML file (such as input.xml)
- -of specifies the file toward which output is written (such as output.htm)

Basic Events in the Omnimark Language

The following are some of the basic events Omnimark detects:

- document-start
- document-end
- element
- processing-instruction

document-start allows you to do processing and produce output before the beginning of an XML file, as shown in Listing 15.1.

LISTING 15.1 A document-start RULE

```
1:  document-start   ;event
2:      output "<HTML>%n"        ;our action
3:      || "<HEAD>%n"
4:      || "<TITLE>Our first example</TITLE>%n"
5:      || "</HEAD>%n<BODY>"
```

ANALYSIS The rule header on line 1 defines the event, which is document-start.

The rule body (lines 2–5) lists the actions to be executed. When the document starts (event), we write a string with HTML tags to the output (action).

> **Note**
>
> %n stands for "end of line"
>
> || concatenates two strings
>
> ; starts a comment in your code

OUTPUT The result of this rule follows:

```
<HTML>
<HEAD>
<TITLE>Our first example</TITLE>
</HEAD>
<BODY>
```

document-end allows you to do processing and produce output after the end of an XML file, as shown in Listing 15.2.

LISTING 15.2 A document-end RULE

```
1:  document-end ;event
2:      output "</BODY>%n</HTML>%n"
```

ANALYSIS When the document ends (event), we write a string with HTML tags to the output (action).

OUTPUT The result of this rule follows:

```
</BODY>
</HTML>
```

ANALYSIS Line 3 being empty is the result of the %n end-of-line after the HTML end tag on line 2 of Listing 15.2.

When an element occurs you have to deal with three things:

- The start of the element
- Its content
- The end of the element

When dealing with the content of an element, parsing ceases in Omnimark to give you the ability to decide how and when to treat the content. You need explicitly get parsing going again. This can be done by using the following:

- The parse continuation operator %c as used in Listing 15.3.
- suppress, which continues parsing but suppresses the output of the parsed content as shown in Listing 15.4.

LISTING 15.3 USING THE PARSE CONTINUATION OPERATOR

```
1:   element musician   ; event, when the element musician is encountered
2:        output "<HR>%n" ; at the start of the element
3:        output "%c"     ; continue parsing
4:        output "<HR>%n" ; at the end of the element
```

or:

LISTING 15.4 USING THE SUPPRESS ACTION

```
1:   element meta    ; event, when the element meta is encountered
2:        suppress ; continue parsing but suppress output
```

Every rule must output the parsing continuation operator (%c) or suppress.

Note   Make sure that every element rule contains %c or suppress.

Different actions may be needed depending on element attribute information. Refer to Listing 14.3, which shows an example of delivering different information depending on the experience of the user.

```
<steps experience="firsttime">…</steps>
```

versus

```
<steps experience="donebefore">…</steps>
```

Omnimark allows you to add conditions based on this attribute information to your rule headers, as shown in Listing 15.5.

LISTING **15.5**   USING A CONDITION REFERRING TO AN ATTRIBUTE VALUE

```
1:   element steps when attribute experience = "firsttime"
2:      ;action
```

 This rule is only triggered if we encounter, in the XML document, the element steps that has the attribute named experience set to a value of firsttime.

> **Caution**   It is an error if more than one element rule applies to a single element in the document.

In the previous chapter we explained that event-driven systems keep some information about previously encountered nodes. This is also the case for Omnimark.

Omnimark gives access to:

- The parent element
- Ancestor elements
- Preparent elements
- Any open element

Or you can test for recently closed elements:

- The previous element
- The last subelement refers to the most recently closed subelement

Listings 15.6 through 15.9 show some examples of taking this context information into account.

LISTING **15.6**   CHECKING THE PARENT ELEMENT

```
1:      element li when parent is ol
2:      ;action
```

ANALYSIS This rule is triggered if we encounter, in the XML document, an element li with, as parent, the element ol.

LISTING 15.7 CHECKING THE ANCESTORS

```
1:  element p when ancestor is li
2:       ; action
```

ANALYSIS This rule is triggered if an element named p with an ancestor element named li is encountered in the XML document.

LISTING 15.8 CHECKING THE PREVIOUS ELEMENT

```
1:  element p when previous is title
2:       ; action
```

ANALYSIS This rule is triggered if we encounter a p element after an element title in the XML document.

It is possible of course to combine these context checks, as shown in Listing 15.9.

LISTING 15.9 USING A COMBINATION OF CONTEXT CONDITIONS

```
1:  element def when parent of parent is ol
2:       ; action
```

ANALYSIS This rule is triggered if we encounter a def element that has a grandfather named ol in the XML document.

You can also define and check context by counting elements:

- Using the occurrence—Returns the number of times the same element has been repeated, as used in Listing 15.10.
- Using the number of children—Counts the total number of children of the specified element seen so far, as shown in Listing 15.11.

LISTING 15.10 USING AN OCCURRENCE CONDITION

```
1:  element li when occurrence = 2
2:       ;action
```

ANALYSIS This rule is triggered if the element li is the second in a row of li elements.

Do	Don't
DO use "number of children" instead.	**DON'T** use occurrence to find the nth element in the parent element.

LISTING 15.11   USING THE NUMBER OF CHILDREN CONDITION

```
1:  element p when children of parent = 1
2:      ;action
```

ANALYSIS This rule is triggered if the element p is the first child element of its parent.

Normally `processing instructions` are ignored unless you specify an event handler for processing instructions.

Example:

```
processing-instruction "break"
    output "<BR>"
```

Looking Ahead

In the previous chapter (Day 14) we discussed the disadvantage of the event driven approach; it is not possible to make decisions based on information that comes later in the data stream.

Let's take following piece of XML.

LISTING 15.12   A PIECE OF XML TO BE CONVERTED

```
1: <cities id="L5">
2:      <city>Amsterdam</city>
3:      <city>Paris</city>
4:      <city>Toronto</city>
5:      <city>Vancouver</city>
6:      <city>Brussels</city>
7: </cities>
```

OUTPUT I would like to translate the previous XML fragment to the following piece of HTML:

```
<p>City 1 of 5<BR>
    Amsterdam</p>
```

```
<p>City 2 of 5<BR>
   Paris</p>
...
```

ANALYSIS In the data stream, when we arrive at the city Amsterdam we can test to know its position, but it is not possible to know at that point that there are 5 cities mentioned in total.

To solve this, Omnimark uses referents.

NEW TERM A *referent* outputs a value to be determined at some other point of processing, most of the time later on in the data stream.

By using referents you are able to stick placeholders in your output. Later on you can assign or change their values, as shown in Listing 15.13.

LISTING 15.13 nrofcities.xom—USING REFERENTS

```
1:  global counter nrofcities initial {0} ; a variable with
➥ name "nrofcities" and value "0"
2:
3:  element cities ;rule
4:      output "%c" ; continue parsing
5:
6:  element city
7:      increment nrofcities ; the variable "profcities"
➥is incremented (+1)
8:      output "<p>"
9:      output "City %d(nrofcities) of " ; the value of
➥variable "nrofcities" is sent to the output
10:     output referent "totalofcities"
11:             ; the referent is the placeholder for the
➥not known yet value of the total of cities
12:             ; the content of the placeholder is sent to
➥the output
13:     output "<BR>"
14:     output "%c"
15:     output "</p>"
16:     set referent "totalofcities" to "%d(nrofcities)"
17:             ; the value of "nrofcities" is placed in
➥the placeholder
18:             ; after the first its 1, then 2, and
➥finally for our example 5
```

ANALYSIS On line 1 we declare a variable named nrofcities. The initial value is set to 0.

On line 3 we have our element rule for the element `cities`. The action defined here is `continue parsing`.

On line 6 we define our element rule for the element `city`. First we increment our variable `nrofcities`. For Amsterdam the value will be 1, 2 for Paris, and so on. On line 8 we start writing to the output: `<p>City` followed by the current value of the variable `nrofcities`, followed by `of`, followed by the placeholder `totalofcities`, which we don't yet know the value for.

On line 16 the value of the placeholder `totalofcities` is set to the value of `nrofcities`. This means that after processing the file the value of `totalofcities` will be 5.

Because we have been using referents, a second pass/run of the file is needed. It is during this second pass that the placeholder is replaced by its final value.

> **Tip**
>
> The referent mechanism is also very useful for automatically generating all kinds of hypertext links.

Input and Output

Omnimark, besides being an event-driven processing language, is also a streaming language. Input and output streams are easily handled, which is very handy if you want to chunk a large XML-file into smaller pieces.

Other Features

Omnimark offers a complete environment with common programming language constructs, including conditional statements, loops, variables, functions (also external written in C, C++, Java), macros, arrays—including associative arrays.

A special mention goes to the featured pattern-matching language; patterns when captured also generate events.

An Example of an Omnimark Script

INPUT LISTING **15.14** `biblio.xml`—THE XML FILE TO CONVERT TO HTML

```
1:  <?xml version="1.0"?>
2:  <!DOCTYPE biblio [
3:  <!ELEMENT biblio (books, authors)>
4:  <!ELEMENT books (book)+ >
```

15

```
5:   <!ELEMENT book (title, author+, description, ISBN, pages,
➥targetgroup, price, related*) >
6:   <!ATTLIST book id ID #REQUIRED>
7:   <!ELEMENT title (#PCDATA) >
8:   <!ELEMENT author (#PCDATA) >
9:   <!ELEMENT description (#PCDATA) >
10:  <!ELEMENT ISBN (#PCDATA) >
11:  <!ELEMENT pages (#PCDATA) >
12:  <!ELEMENT targetgroup (#PCDATA) >
13:  <!ELEMENT price (#PCDATA) >
14:  <!ATTLIST price unit CDATA "USA">
15:  <!ELEMENT related (#PCDATA) >
16:  <!ATTLIST related linkend IDREF #REQUIRED>
17:  <!ELEMENT authors (authordesc)+ >
18:  <!ELEMENT authordesc (name, specialty+) >
19:  <!ELEMENT name (#PCDATA)>
20:  <!ELEMENT specialty (#PCDATA)>
21:  ]>
22:  <biblio>
23:  <books>
24:      <book id="TY1">
25:          <title>Sam's Teach Yourself C++ in 21 Days, Second Edition
26:          </title>
27:          <author>Jesse Liberty
28:          </author>
29:          <description>This book teaches you the basics of
➥object-oriented programming with C++ and is completely
➥revised to ANSI standards. It can be used with any
➥C++ compiler.
30:          </description>
31:          <ISBN>0-672-31070-8
32:          </ISBN>
33:          <pages>700
34:          </pages>
35:          <targetgroup>Beginning - Intermediate
36:          </targetgroup>
37:          <price unit="USA">29.99
38:          </price>
39:          <related linkend="TY2">Teach Yourself Visual C++ 5
➥</related>
40:      </book>
41:      <book id="MJ">
42:          <title>Maximum Java 1.1
43:          </title>
44:          <author>Glenn Vanderburg
45:          </author>
46:          <description>Written by JAVA experts, this book explores
➥the JAVA 1.1 language, tools, and core JAVA API without
➥reviewing fundamentals or basic techniques.
47:          </description>
```

continues

LISTING 15.14   CONTINUED

```
48:                <ISBN>1-57521-290-0
49:                </ISBN>
50:                <pages>900
51:                </pages>
52:                <targetgroup>Expert
53:                </targetgroup>
54:                <price unit="USA">49.99
55:                </price>
56:        </book>
57:        <book id="JS">
58:                <title>JavaScript Unleashed, Second Edition
59:                </title>
60:                <author>Richard Wagner
61:                </author>
62:                <description>This book helps you thoroughly understand
➥and apply JavaScript.
63:                </description>
64:                <ISBN>1-57521-306-0
65:                </ISBN>
66:                <pages>1000
67:                </pages>
68:                <targetgroup>Casual - Experienced
69:                </targetgroup>
70:                <price>49.99
71:                </price>
72:        </book>
73:        <book ID="TY2">
74:                <title>Sam's Teach Yourself Visual C++ 5 in 21 Days,
➥Fourth Edition
75:                </title>
76:                <author>Nathan Gurewich
77:                </author>
78:                <author>Ori Gurewich
79:                </author>
80:                <description>This book merges the power of the best-
➥selling "Teach Yourself" series with the knowledge of Nathan and
➥Ori Gurewich, renowned experts in code, creating the most
➥efficient way to learn Visual C++.
81:                </description>
82:                <ISBN>0-672-31014-7
83:                </ISBN>
84:                <pages>832
85:                </pages>
86:                <targetgroup>New - Casual
87:                </targetgroup>
88:                <price>35.00
89:                </price>
```

```
 90:        </book>
 91:    </books>
 92:    <authors>
 93:        <authordesc>
 94:            <name>Jesse Liberty
 95:            </name>
 96:            <specialty>C
 97:            </specialty>
 98:        </authordesc>
 99:        <authordesc>
100:            <name>Glenn Vanderburg
101:            </name>
102:            <specialty>Java
103:            </specialty>
104:        </authordesc>
105:        <authordesc>
106:            <name>Richard Wagner
107:            </name>
108:            <specialty>Opera
109:            </specialty>
110:        </authordesc>
111:        <authordesc>
112:            <name>Nathan Gurewich
113:            </name>
114:            <specialty>Visual Basic
115:            </specialty>
116:            <specialty>Visual C++
117:            </specialty>
118:        </authordesc>
119:    </authors>
120:    </biblio>
```

We name this file biblio.xml and will write a script to convert the XML into HTML.

We first write event handlers to convert every XML element to a HTML element, as shown in Listing 15.15.

LISTING 15.15   TOHTML.XML—OUR OMNIMARK SCRIPT TO CONVERT THE FILE BIBLIO.XML TO HTML

```
1:    DOWN-TRANSLATE with XML
2:
3:    element biblio
4:        output "<HTML>%n"
5:        || "<HEAD>%n"
6:        || "<TITLE>My bookshop</TITLE>%n"
7:        || "</HEAD>%n"
8:        || "<BODY>%n"
```

continues

Listing 15.15 CONTINUED

```
 9:         || "<H1>My bookshop</H1>%n<P> </P>%n"
10:         || "%c" ; continue parsing
11:
12: element books
13:     output "%c"
14:
15: element book
16:     output "%c"
17:     do when last subelement is related
18:             output "</P>"
19:     done
20:     output "<HR>%n"
21:
22: element title
23:     output "<H2 style='margin-top:40pt'>"
24:     using attribute id of parent
25:             do when attribute id is specified
26:             output "<A name='%v(id)'></A>"
27:             done
28:     output "%c</H2>%n"
29:
30: element author
31: do when previous is title
32:             output "<P><I>%c</I>"
33:     else
34:             output "<BR>%n"
35:             || "<I>%c</I>"
36:     done
37:
38: element description
39:     output "</P>%n" ; closing the p element started [cc]
with the first author
40:     || "<HR>%n"
41:     || "<P>%c</P>%n"
42:
43: element ISBN
44:     output "<P><CODE>ISBN-number: %c</CODE><BR>%n"
45:
46: element pages
47:     output "%c pages<BR>%n"
48:
49: element targetgroup
50:     output "Aimed at the '%c'<BR>%n"
51:
52: element price
53:     output "%c US$</P>%n"
54:
55: element related
56:     do when occurrence = 1
```

15

```
57:            output "<P><I>See also: </I><BR>"
58:        done
59:        output "<A HREF='#%v(linkend)'>%c</A><BR>"
60:
61:   element authors
62:        output "<H2 style='margin-top:40pt'>An overview of
➥our writers</H2>%n"
63:        output "<TABLE CELLPADDING='5'>"
64:        output "<TR><TH>Name</TH><TH>Specialty</TH></TR>%n"
65:        output "%c</TABLE>%n"
66:
67:   element authordesc
68:        output "<TR>%c</I></TD></TR>%n"
69:
70:   element name
71:        output "<TD>%c</TD>%n"
72:
73:   element specialty
74:        do when occurrence = 1
75:            output "<TD><I>%c"
76:        else
77:            output " - %c"
78:        done
79:
80:   document-end
81:        output "</BODY></HTML>"
```

We save this script as `tohtm.xom`.

ANALYSIS You see that we have defined an `element` rule for every XML element.

Previously we have only seen conditions as part of the rule header, but conditions can also be inserted in the rule body where the actions are defined. Refer to element `specialty` on line 73, where you find, starting on line 74, a `do when...`, `else...`, `done` construct, where a difference is made between an element specialty appearing first in a row of specialty elements and those specialty elements coming later.

Lines 24, 25, and 26 also deserve some explanation. For the element title, examine the attribute with name `id` of the parent of title, being `book` (line 24). If this attribute id has a value specified (line 25), write an HTML anchor to the output with an attribute name that has the value of this id (line 26).

Now we run from the command line:

```
omle -s tohtml.xom biblio.xml -of biblio.htm
```

Note

With this example, we're assuming that all files are in the same subdirectory as the `omle.exe` program.

This generates the file `biblio.htm`, as shown in Figure 15.1.

OUTPUT

FIGURE 15.1

The result of our first conversion.

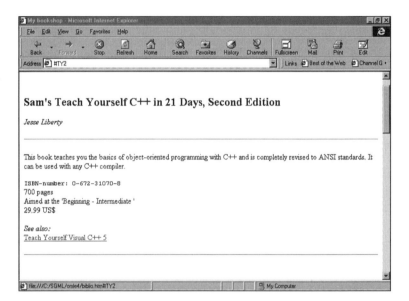

Let's try to split up the file and make a separate HTML file for each book and a separate file for the author's overview.

We need to change the code for two elements: `book` and `authors`, as shown in Listing 15.6.

LISTING 15.16 TOHTML.XML—CONVERSION TO MULTIPLE HTML FILES

```
1:  element book
2:        local stream bookhtm ;creating a variable with
➥name "bookhtm"" of type stream
3:        open bookhtm as file "%v(id).htm"
; this stream is written to a file,
➥based on the id of the book element
4:        using output as bookhtm ; now we write the output to
➥this stream (file)
5:        do ;everything between 'do' and 'done' needs to go to the stream
6:              output "<HTML>%n"
```

```
 7:                 || output "<HEAD>%n"
 8:                 || output "<TITLE>Book %v(id)</TITLE>"%n
 9:                 || output "</HEAD>%n"
10:                 || output "<BODY>%n"
11:                 output "%c"
12:                 do when last proper subelement is related
13:                         output "</P>"
14:                 done
15:                 output "<HR>%n"
16:                 output "</BODY></HTML>%n"
17:        done
18:
19:   element authors
20:        local stream authorshtm
21:        open authorshtm as file "authors.htm"
22:        using output as authorshtm
23:        output "<HTML>%n"
24:                 || output "<HEAD>%n"
25:                 || output "<TITLE>Authors</TITLE>"%n
26:                 || output "</HEAD>%n"
27:                 || output "<BODY>%n"
28:                 output "<H2 style='margin-top:40pt'>An overview of our
➥writers</H2>%n"
29:                 output "<TABLE CELLPADDING='5'>"
30:                 output "<TR><TH>Name</TH><TH>Specialty</TH></TR>%n"
31:                 output "%c</TABLE>%n"
32:                 output "</BODY></HTML>%n"
33:                 done
```

ANALYSIS For each book element we declare a local variable of type stream with the name bookhtm. On line 3 we open the stream as a file whose name is given by the string expression %v(id).htm, which is the value of the attribute id, or TY1 for the first book in our XML file. This is followed by .htm, resulting in TY1.htm. On line 4 we write our output to this file. Because we are writing to different files now we need to add the appropriate HTML start and closing information in each file, hence lines 6 to 10 and 16. The same principles have been applied to the element authors.

We run the program again, which results in the generation of 6 files.

The resulting files are

- biblio.htm
- TY1.htm
- MJ.htm
- JS.htm
- TY2.htm
- authors.htm

This is nice but we have two problems:

1. The link generated by the event handler of the `related` element doesn't work anymore. It was coded as a link to a place inside the same document. Now it must become a link to a different document.

2. We're missing navigation aids to move to the different files. Our wish is twofold:

   • To have a TOC inside the first `biblio.htm` file with an overview of all the books

   • Links on each page for going to the previous or next book

We first solve the broken link issue.

The link in the same file to this anchor

```
<A HREF="#TY2">.
```

needs to be changed to the following:

```
<A HREF="TY2.htm">
```

We change the Omnimark script:

```
55  element related
         . . .
59      output "<A HREF='%v(linkend).htm'>%c</A><BR>"
```

Remember that referents are just placeholders that have content defined later on.

For generating a TOC we first add a global stream variable, to be used as a referent to our script, as shown in Listing 15.17.

LISTING 15.17   TOHTML.XML—ADDING A TOC

```
 1:  global stream toc; to be used later on as a referent
 2:
 3:  element biblio
 4:      output  "<HTML>%n"
 5:      || "<HEAD>%n"
 6:      || "<TITLE>My bookshop</TITLE>%n"
 7:      || "</HEAD>%n"
 8:      || "<BODY>%n"
 9:      || "<H1>My bookshop</H1>%n<P></P>%n"
10:
11:      output referent "toc" ; here we will (out)put our toc
12:
13:      open toc as referent "toc" ; and we initialise it
14:      put toc "<HR><H3>Table of Contents</H3>%n<UL>"
```

```
15:      close toc
16:
17:      output "%c" ; continue parsing
```

If you try this out, you will receive the title "Table of Contents" in your `biblio.htm` file.

ANALYSIS In line 11 we asked to output the content of our placeholder with the name "toc". This placeholder has been filled in lines 13 to 15 with the title (line 14).

We need to add the titles of our books to the toc, so we need to write additional information in our placeholder toc every time we encounter a book title, as shown in Listing 15.18.

LISTING 15.18   TOHTML.XML—FILLING THE TOC

```
1:   element title
2:        ; putting the content into this variable since we
➥will use this content twice
3:        local stream titlecontent ; creating a variable of
➥type stream
4:        open titlecontent as buffer
5:        put titlecontent "%c"
6:        close titlecontent
7:
8:        ; existing code
9:        output "<H2 style='margin-top:40pt'>"
10:       using attribute id of parent
11:             do when attribute id is specified
12:             output "<A name='%v(id)'></A>"
13:             done
14:  output "%g(titlecontent)</H2>%n"
15:
16:  ; referent
17:  reopen toc as referent "toc"
18:      using attribute id of parent
19:      put toc "<LI><A HREF='%v(id).htm'>%g(titlecontent)</A></LI>"
20:      close toc
```

ANALYSIS First we put the content of our title inside a local variable with the name `title-content` (lines 3–7). This buffered content is used in line 15 and will be output into an H2 HTML element.

But the most important part starts at line 18, where our placeholder toc is reopened and the content on line 20 is added to the already existing content of our referent.

OUTPUT The result is shown in Figure 15.2.

Next comes the addition of next and previous navigation links at the bottom of each page.

Let's start with a link to the previous page. Because we have already passed this page, we were able to buffer this information and use it on our current page, as done in Listing 15.19.

LISTING 15.19   tohtml.xml—INCLUDING LINK TO PREVIOUS PAGE

```
1:   element book
2:        local stream bookhtm
3:        open bookhtm as file "%v(id).htm"
4:        using output as bookhtm
5:        do
6:               output "%c"
7:               do when last proper subelement is related
8:                      output "</P>"
9:               done
10:             output "<HR>%n"
11:             output "%g(prevpage)" ; here we add our previous link
12:             set prevpage to "<P><A
➥HREF='%v(id).htm'>Previous</A></P>"
13:               ; and we keep the information of this page for the next
➥one
14:        done
```

15

ANALYSIS On line 12 we set the content of the `prevpage` variable to a link containing the name of our actual HTML page. It is this content that will be used on line 11 for the next page.

Listing 15.20 shows how to create the link to the next page. This needs a referent.

LISTING 15.20 tohtml.xml—INCLUDING LINK TO NEXT PAGE

```
 1:    element book
 2:        local stream bookhtm
 3:        set referent "next-%v(id)" to ""
 4:    ; the next on this page is set to empty
 5:    ; this is done since we don't know yet if there is a next page
 6:        set referent "next-%g(previd)" to "<A
➥HREF='%v(id).htm'>Next</A>"
 7:        ; the next of previous page gets the info of this (being next)
➥page
 8:        open bookhtm with referents-allowed as file "%v(id).htm"
 9:        ; referents-allowed added since we put placeholders in this
➥stream now
10:        using output as bookhtm ; writing to the file
11:        do
12:            output "%c"
13:            do when last proper subelement is related
14:                output "</P>"
15:            done
16:            output "<HR>%n"
17:            output "%g(prevpage)"              ; the info of previous page
18:            output referent "next-%v(id)" ; our placeholder
19:            set prevpage to "<P><A
➥HREF='%v(id).htm'>Previous</A>   "
20:            set previd to "%v(id)" ; used in next page for filling in
➥placeholder
21:        done
```

ANALYSIS After the output of our previous link, we output a link to our next page, only we don't know its content, hence the referent used on line 18. The name of this referent refers to the id value of the book.

Because we also don't know at this level if there will be a next page, we initially set the content of our link to the next page to the empty string "" (line 3). If a next page exists, this content will be overwritten by the action on line 6. Notice that we capture the id of the book at the end of the rule body in the `previd` variable. This value is used in line 6 to fill in the placeholder on the previous page.

OUTPUT   The result is shown in Figure 15.3.

FIGURE **15.3**

Our generated HTML files with navigation links.

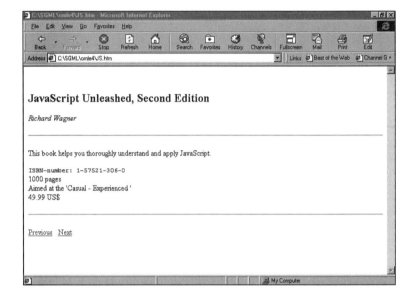

More Information

For more tips and techniques about converting XML to HTML, see the following URL:

`http://www.omnimark.com/magazine/tips/htmldown.html`

If you want to see more of Omnimark in action, download the Omnimark 4.0 Samples Viewer at `http://www.omnimark.com/magazine/tips/freeware.html`.

SAX

SAX stands for a *Simple API for XML*. It is a standard interface for event-based XML parsing and the result of a collaborative effort by members of the XML-DEV mailing list, coordinated and finalized by David Megginson.

SAX implementations are currently available in Java and Python.

The following are the current parsers that support the SAX interface:

- XML for Java (IBM)
- XP (James Clark)

15

- DXP (Datachannel)
- Ælfred (Microstar)
- SXP (Silfide)
- XML Library (Sun)

Thanks to third-party drivers two more parsers can be added to the list:

- Lark (Tim Bray)
- MSXML (Microsoft)

The following sections discuss the SAX Java distribution made available by David Megginson (`http://www.megginson.com`).

The Big Picture

To write a SAX application you'll need

- An XML parser that supports SAX.
- The SAX distribution, which is a collection of Java classes and interfaces. It can be found at `http://www.megginson.com/SAX/saxjava-1.0.zip`. This zip file is 118KB.
- Event handlers implemented by you based on those interfaces and classes.

Some Background on OO and Java Concepts

Classes are abstract blueprints from which individual objects can be made. They define properties and behaviors (methods).

 A *class* is a template for defining the behaviors and properties for a particular type of object.

In Table 15.1, we'll give an example of a class.

TABLE 15.1 AN EXAMPLE OF A CLASS

Concept	Example
Class	car
Property	speed
Behavior	change gear

Using the blueprint shown in Table 15.1, we can create a car (object) that has a specific speed and is able to change gear. Interfaces define a set of methods but don't implement them.

New Term An *interface* is a special kind of class that defines a set of methods.

A class can implement an interface, signing a kind of contract to provide (implement) the methods defined in the interface.

The Interfaces and Classes in the SAX Distribution

Part of these interfaces are aimed at *parser writers*. We will not cover these.

Others are aimed at *application writers*.

These interfaces are

- DocumentHandler
- ErrorHandler
- DTDHandler
- EntityResolver

Simple XML applications can already be developed by using only DocumentHandler and possibly ErrorHandler.

The following methods are the most important ones defined in the DocumentHandler interface:

- startDocument()—To receive notification of the beginning of a document
- endDocument()—To receive notification of the end of a document
- startElement(String name, AttributeList atts)—To receive notification of the beginning of an element, as shown in Table 15.2
- endElement(String name)—To receive notification of the end of an element, as shown in Table 15.3
- characters(char ch[], int start, int length)—to receive notification of character data, as shown in Table 15.4
- processingInstruction (String target, String data)—To receive notification of a processing instruction, as shown in Table 15.5

TABLE 15.3   PARAMETERS OF startElement

Name	Content	Type
name	The element name	String
atts	The attributes attached to the element	AttributeList

Note   AttributeList allows you to iterate an attribute list.

TABLE 15.4   PARAMETER OF endElement

Name	Content	Type
name	The element name	String

TABLE 15.5   PARAMETERS OF CHARACTERS

Name	Content	Type
ch	The characters from the XML doc	Array of char
start	The start position in the array	Integer
length	The number of characters to read from the array	Integer

TABLE 15.6   PARAMETERS OF processingInstruction

Name	Content	Type
target	The PI's target	String
data	The PI's data	String

Note   Note the similarity with the event handlers of Omnimark.

The SAX package also offers a HandlerBase class, which provides default implementations of the four interfaces mentioned in the preceding list.

Application writers have two possibilities now:

- They can define a class that implements the needed interfaces
- They can subclass the class HandlerBase—it already has default implementations of the interfaces

A subclass enables us to inherit variables (properties) and methods (behavior) from its superclass but also to override the methods.

NEW TERM   A *subclass* is a class that is a special case of another class.

Listing 15.21 shows our subclassing of the class HandlerBase.

LISTING 15.21   SUBCLASSING THE CLASS HandlerBase

```
1:   public class OurHandler extends HandlerBase { //subclassing
➥HandlerBase
2:
3:        public void startDocument ()
4:                  {
5:    //our implementation of the method, overriding  HandlerBase
6:    }
7:
8:    public void endDocument ()
9:                  {
10:                    //our implementation of the method, overriding
➥HandlerBase
11:               }
12:
13:        public void startElement (String name, AttributeList atts)
14:               {
15:                    //our implementation of the method, overriding
➥HandlerBase
16:               }
17:
18:        public void endElement (String name)
19:               {
20:                    //our implementation of the method, overriding
➥HandlerBase
21:               }
22:
23:        public void characters (char ch[], int start, int length)
24:               {
25:                    //our implementation of the method, overriding
➥HandlerBase
26:               }
27:  }
```

The main methods defined in the DocumentHandler interface are implemented on lines 3, 8, 13, 18, and 23.

An Example

The XML file of Listing 15.22 serves as input.

INPUT   **LISTING 15.22**   musicians.XML—INFO ABOUT MUSICIANS

```
 1:  <?xml version="1.0"?>
 2:  <musicians>
 3:      <musician>
 4:              <name>Joey Baron
 5:              </name>
 6:              <instrument>drums
 7:              </instrument>
 8:              <NrOfRecordings>1
 9:              </NrOfRecordings>
10:      </musician>
11:      <musician>
12:               <name>Bill Frisell
13:               </name>
14:              <instrument>guitar
15:              </instrument>
16:              <NrOfRecordings>3
17:              </NrOfRecordings>
18:      </musician>
19:      <musician>
20:              <name>Don Byron
21:              </name>
22:              <instrument>clarinet
23:              </instrument>
24:              <NrOfRecordings>2
25:              </NrOfRecordings>
26:      </musician>
27:      <musician>
28:              <name>Dave Douglas
29:              </name>
30:              <instrument>trumpet
31:              </instrument>
32:              <NrOfRecordings>1
33:              </NrOfRecordings>
34:      </musician>
35:  </musicians>
```

The OurHandler class is defined in Listing 15.23.

LISTING 15.23   OurHandler.java—CONCRETE IMPLEMENTATIONS OF EVENT HANDLERS

```
1:  import org.xml.sax.HandlerBase;
2:  import org.xml.sax.AttributeList;
3:  import java.io.*;
4:
5:  public class OurHandler extends HandlerBase { //subclassing
➥HandlerBase
6:
7:    private PrintWriter fout;
8:
9:      public OurHandler() throws IOException
10:          {
11:                  fout = new PrintWriter(new FileWriter("out.htm"));
12:                  //object created for writing to the file "out.htm"
13:          }
14:
15:      public void startDocument ()
16:          {
17:                  fout.println("<HTML>");
18:                  fout.println("<HEAD><TITLE>SAX
➥example</TITLE></HEAD>");
19:                  fout.println("<BODY>");
20:          }
21:
22:      public void endDocument ()
23:          {
24:                  fout.println("</BODY></HTML>");
25:                  fout.close();
26:          }
27:
28:      public void startElement (String name, AttributeList atts)
29:                      {
30:                  if (name == "musicians")
31:                      fout.println("<TABLE BORDER='1'
➥CELLPADDING='5'>");
32:                  else if (name == "musician")
33:                      fout.println("<TR>");
34:                  else
35:                      fout.println("<TD>");
36:          }
37:
38:      public void endElement  (String name)
39:                      {
40:                  if (name == "musicians")
41:                      fout.println("</TABLE>");
42:                  else if (name == "musician")
43:                      fout.println("</TR>");
44:                  else
45:                      fout.println("</TD>");
```

```
46:              }
47:
48:      public void characters (char ch[], int start, int length)
49:              {
50:                      for (int i=start; i < start+length; i++)
51:                              fout.print(ch[i]);
52:              }
53:      }
```

___

ANALYSIS First we import supporting classes and interfaces (lines 1–3). Then we start (line 5) our subclassing of the HandlerBase class.

On line 11 we create an object for writing to a file named out.htm.

Starting from line 15 you will see the different event handlers:

- At the event start of the musicians.xml document, the HTML content defined on lines 17, 18, and 19 is sent to the file out.htm

- At the event end of the musicians.xml document, the HTML content defined on line 24 is sent to the file out.htm

- At the event start of an element, additional testing is done (lines 30–35)

    - If the name of the element started is musicians, then output a table starttag

    - If the name of the element started is musician then output a table row <TR> starttag

    - If the name of the element started is something else then output a table cell <TD> starttag

- At the event end of an element the same testing is done

- At the event characters encountered, these are sent to the output

We also need to create an application (see Listing 15.24) to parse the document using our handler.

LISTING 15.24   convert.java—THE PROGRAM THAT USES OurHandler CLASS

```
1:   import org.xml.sax.Parser;
2:   import org.xml.sax.DocumentHandler;
3:   import org.xml.sax.helpers.ParserFactory;
4:
5:   public class convert {
6:        static final String parserClass = "com.ibm.xml.parser.SAXDriver";
7:        //using IBM's XML parser
```

continues

LISTING **15.24**   CONTINUED

```
8:        //static final String parserClass =
➥"com.datachannel.xml.sax.SAXDriver";
9:        //in case we want to use the DXP parser
10:       static final String xmlfile="c:\\xmlex\\musicians.xml";
11:
12:       public static void main (String args[]) throws Exception
13:          {
14:                  Parser parser;  //variable declaration
15:                  //the name parser will be used to refer to a
➥Parser object
16:                  DocumentHandler handler; //variable declaration
17:                  //the name handler will be used to refer to a
➥DocumentHandler object
18:                  parser = ParserFactory.makeParser(parserClass);
19:                  //A Parser object is created by supplying a class
➥name to the ParserFactory
20:                  handler = new OurHandler();
21:                  //The new object is created and initialized
22:
23:                  parser.setDocumentHandler(handler);
24:                  //handler is registered with the parser
25:                  parser.parse(xmlfile);
26:                  //our xml-file is parsed
27:
28:              }
29:       }
```

ANALYSIS   We declare a variable with the name parserClass and of type String. We assign a value to this variable—the full classname of the SAX driver of the parser we will be using: com.ibm.xml.parser.SAXdriver (line 6). This value can be replaced by com.datachannel.xml.sax.SAXdriver, for example (line 10), or com.microstar.xml.SAXdriver.

The rest of the code is about declaring variables and instantiating them (lines 14–21).

Finally (line 23) the handler OurHandler is registered with the parser and subsequently our XML file, musicians.xml, is being parsed.

In Figure 15.4 you'll see both files, OurHandler.java and convert.java, edited and compiled in the KAWA IDE (http://www.tek-tools.com/kawa/).

Getting Our Conversion Up and Running

Now that we know the content of the SAX distribution and how we can implement the SAX interfaces, we need to put all the pieces together.

FIGURE 15.4

*Our Java development
environment.*

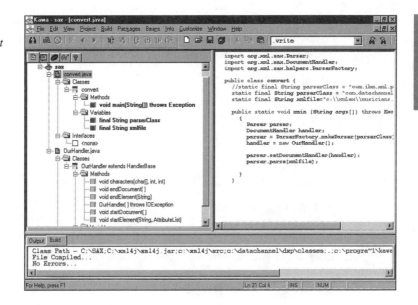

The needed components are as follows:

- A SAX enabled parser
- The SAX distribution
- The event handlers

We have two SAX enabled parsers installed on our system (see Day 5 "Checking Well-
formedness," and Day 9 "Checking Validity"):

- xml4j of IBM
- DXP of Datachannel

Note the full classname of their SAXdriver used in our convert class:

- `com.ibm.xml.parser.SAXDriver` for xml4j
- `com.datachannel.xml.sax.SAXDriver` for DXP

If needed, you can change your supporting parser by changing this classname. You don't
have to change anything else in your code.

> **Note**
>
> You'll recall from Day 14 that this was one of the main purposes of the SAX
> initiative: to be able to change parsers without changing code.

We need the SAX distribution (saxjava-1_0.zip) unzipped on our system, as well as the two compiled classes: `convert.class` (the main program) and `OurHandler.class` (which implements the event handlers).

Now we need to be sure that all the needed classes can be found by including their paths to the `CLASSPATH` variable.

In our case our `CLASSPATH` is:

```
C:\SAX;C:\xml4j\xml4j.jar;c:\datachannel\dxp\classes;.;
c:\progra~1\kawa30\classes.zip;c:\jdk1.1.5\lib\classes.zip
```

Once this is done the command to be run from the command-line is:

```
java.exe convert
```

`convert` is the name of our main program (class).

This generates the file `out.htm`, with our musicians in an HTML table.

Other Implementations

People with knowledge of the Python language should take a look at Lars Marius Garshol's implementation of SAX, at the following URL:
`http://www.stud.ifi.uio.no/~larsga/download/python/xml/saxlib.html`.

Building Further on SAX

SAXON is a JAVA class library built on SAX that provides additional services:

- It allows you to provide separate handlers for each element type
- It supplies context information (parent, preparent, and so on)
- It allows you to associate different output streams with individual elements or types

The standard element handlers allow you to do the following:

- Copy an element unchanged to the output
- Skip an element
- Replace start and end tags

It is clear that this class library is aimed at XML to XML or HTML conversions.

An overview of other SAX based applications can be found at the following URL:
`http://www.megginson.com/SAX/index.html`.

Summary

In this chapter we thoroughly studied two implementations of event driven processing, Omnimark and SAX. Omnimark is the longtime market leader for SGML conversions, and SAX is the result of the collaborative work on the XML-DEV mailing list.

15

Q&A

Q Which one (Omnimark or SAX) should I use?

A Longtime player Omnimark offers all the bells and whistles to suit all of your processing needs. It's fast, stable, and very reliable. On the other hand, it isn't a standard language and there is no guarantee that Omnimark Technologies will ever offer a free version.

SAX is young, doesn't offer the same functionality, but, as SAXON proves, can be a solid foundation for further development. Implementations are done in more general languages and the code is open and free.

Q Which programming style (event- or tree-driven) should I use?

A Event-driven programming is easy and fast, but tree-based programming is more powerful because the tree exists in memory and can be traversed in any way needed. Furthermore, the w3.org has standardized a tree-based API, called the Document Object Model. This model is expected to be implemented by all major players in the field. Our advice is to spend most of your time in studying this interface.

Exercises

1. For use in Omnimark, write the rule header for catching:

   - The element named note
   - The element tool that is a grandchild of the element procedure
   - The element result, which comes after action
   - The element listitem, which comes first in a sequence of listitems but isn't the first element in its parent

2. For SAX, write an event handler that outputs the following report taking the file musicians.xml as input:

```
1:  Start document
2:  Start element: musicians
3:  Start element: musician
4:  Start element: name
```

```
 5:  Characters: Joey Baron
 6:  End element: name
 7:  Start element: instrument
 8:  Characters: drums
 9:  End element: instrument
10:  Start element: NrOfRecordings
11:  Characters: 1
12:  End element: NrOfRecordings
13:  End element: musician
14:  ...
15:  End element: musicians
16:  End document
```

You can use the following template:

```
 1:  import org.xml.sax.HandlerBase;
 2:  import org.xml.sax.AttributeList;
 3:
 4:  public class YourHandler extends HandlerBase {
 5:
 6:      public void startDocument ()
 7:          {
 8:                  System.out.println("XXXXX");
 9:          }
10:
11:      public void endDocument ()
12:          {
13:                  System.out.println("XXXXX");
14:          }
15:
16:      public void startElement (String name, AttributeList atts)
17:          {
18:                  System.out.println("XXXXX");
19:          }
20:
21:      public void endElement (String name)
22:          {
23:                  System.out.println("XXXXX");
24:          }
25:
26:      public void characters (char ch[], int start, int length)
27:          {
28:                  System.out.println("XXXXX");
29:          }
30:  }
```

DAY **16**

Programming with the Document Object Model

In this chapter we will cover:

- The background of the Document Object Model (DOM)
- The W3C recommendation of October 1, 1998
- An example of using the DOM
- DOM implementations

Background

The Document Object Model is a model in which a document contains objects that have properties (attributes) and methods so that they can be manipulated.

This means that by accessing the DOM you are able to do the following:

- Add, delete, and change elements
- Change their contents
- Add, delete, and change attributes

Both Netscape and Microsoft offered the ability to dynamically change HTML pages in version 4 of their browsers. This functionality was based on an HTML document object model. Unfortunately, the respective implementations were highly incompatible.

Some standards work was clearly needed, and so a DOM working group was formed within the W3 Consortium. Their work resulted in a W3C recommendation, dated October 1, 1998. The Consortium's work can be found at http://www.w3.org/TR/WD-DOM/.

This DOM specification, named Level 1, only defines interfaces in a generic way, using *IDL* (Interface Definition Language). It is up to the developers to implement the DOM spec for a given language (JavaScript, VBScript, Java, C++, Python, Perl, and so on).

The Specification

We will take a closer look into the specification itself now. We'll see how it is organized, followed by a study of the most important objects/interfaces.

Structure

The W3C recommendation has two parts—the Core and HTML.

Note The HTML portion of the DOM is not relevant for our XML purposes and will not be discussed further.

The Core portion of W3C provides a set of fundamental interfaces that can represent any structured document (XML and HTML), and a set of extended interfaces needed for XML documents.

Note For a discussion of interfaces, refer to the OO concepts described on Day 15, "Event-Driven Programming."

The Interfaces

Since this model comes from object-oriented design, the interfaces are defined as objects.

The objects defined as fundamental follow:

- DOMException
- DOMImplementation
- DocumentFragment
- Document
- Node
- NodeList
- NamedNodeMap
- CharacterData
- Attr
- Element
- Text
- Comment

The extended interfaces, which are objects specific for XML documents are

- CDATASection
- DocumentType
- Notation
- Entity
- EntityReference
- ProcessingInstruction

Interface Relationships

These objects have relationships and some inherit properties and methods from other objects.

These relationships are shown in Figure 16.1. Objects lower in the tree inherit from the objects above.

16

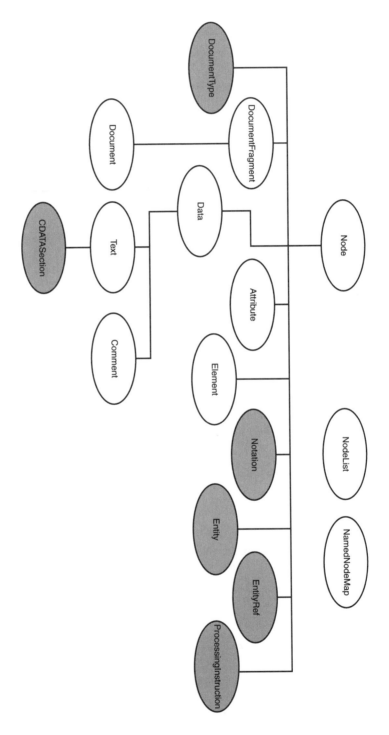

FIGURE 16.1

Inheritance relationships. The gray items belong to the extended interfaces.

In addition to this object-oriented approach using a hierarchy of inheritance, a more simplified way of working is possible. Simply make all manipulations via the Node Interface (see the next section).

Let's study the most important objects/interfaces in more detail.

The Node Object

The Node object is the primary datatype in the whole model. It represents a single node in the XML document tree. There are different types of nodes, as enumerated in Table 16.1.

TABLE 16.1 NodeTypes

Type	DOMCode
Element	1
Attribute	2
Text	3
CDATA Section	4
Entity Reference	5
Entity	6
Processing Instruction	7
Comment	8
Document	9
Document Type	10
Document Fragment	11
Notation	12

The Node object/interface provides you with generalized properties and methods for getting and setting node information. Other more specialized interfaces/objects (Element, Attribute, and so on) may contain additional and more convenient mechanisms for doing this.

Let's examine these general Node object properties first. See Table 16.2.

16

TABLE 16.2   Node Object Attributes/Properties

Name	Value
nodeName	Name (string) of the node (for example, tag, attributename)
nodeValue	Value (string) of the node (for example, attributevalue, text)
nodeType	The code representing the type of the object (1 for element, 2 for attribute, 3 for text, and so on for the other types)
parentNode	The parent (node) of the given node
childNodes	A NodeList object enumerating all children of this node
firstChild	The first child (node) of a node
lastChild	The last child (node) of a node
previousSibling	The node immediately preceding the node
nextSibling	The node immediately following the node
attributes	A NamedNodeMap containing the attributes

Listing 16.1 is a JavaScript example using nodeName, nodeValue, and nodeType.

LISTING 16.1   Using the nodeType, nodeValue, and nodeName Attributes of a Node Object

```
1:  //var node holds a Node Object
2:  if (node.nodeType == 2) //if an attribute
3:      return node.nodeValue;// return the attribute value
4:  if (node.nodeType == 1) // if an element
5:      return node.nodeName; // return the tag name
```

 If a specific node in the tree is of type attribute, then the value (attributevalue) is returned.

If that node is of type element, then the tag name is returned.

Listing 16.2 shows another JavaScript example using context.

LISTING 16.2   Using the previousSibling, nextSibling, and parentNode Attributes of a Node Object

```
1:  //var node holds a Node Object
2:  var previous = node.previousSibling;
3:  var next = node.nextSibling;
4:  var parent = node.parentNode;
5:
6:  return "Hi, I'm " + node.nodeName + " .";
```

```
7:
8:  if (parent != null)
9:       return "My father is " + parent.nodeName + " .";
10: if (previous != null)
11:       return "My older brother is " + previous.nodeName + " .";
12: if (next != null)
13:       return "My younger brother is " + next.nodeName + " .";
```

ANALYSIS The previous and next sibling and parent of a specific node are kept in 3 variables (lines 2–4). Then the name of the node is returned, followed by the name of the parent of the previous and the next sibling, if they exist.

16

Listing 16.3 is JavaScript example using the `childNodes` attribute of a Node object.

LISTING 16.3 USING THE `childNodes` ATTRIBUTE OF A Node OBJECT

```
1:  //var node holds a Node Object
2:  var children = node.childNodes; //returns a NodeList (cf.infra)
```

Table 16.3 is an overview of the Node object methods.

TABLE 16.3 Node OBJECT METHODS

Name	Returns
insertBefore(newChild,refChild)	The node being inserted, where newChild is the node to insert and refChild is the node before which the node will be inserted
replaceChild(newChild,oldChild)	The node being replaced, where newChild is the node that replaces the node oldChild
removeChild(oldChild)	The node removed
appendChild(newChild)	A node, where newChild is the node added to the end of the list of children
hasChildNodes()	true or false, depending on whether the node has children or not
cloneNode(deep)	A duplicate of the node. If the deep parameter is set to true, the cloning is done recursively for all the nodes in the subtree.

Listing 16.4 shows another JavaScript example.

LISTING 16.4   USING THE METHODS OF A NODE OBJECT

```
1:   //var node holding a Node Object
2:   //the node newElement has been created by the createElement method
3:   //of the Document Object (cf. infra)
4:   node.insertBefore(newElement,node.lastChild);
5:   //inserting the new element before the last child element
6:   node.replaceChild(newElement,node.firstChild);
7:   //replacing the first child element with the new element
```

ANALYSIS   In this piece of code we assume that we already have a variable named node holding a Node object and that we have created a new node named newElement using the createElement method of the Document object, to be discussed later.

Line 4 inserts the newElement node before the last child of the node with name node.

Line 6 replaces the first child element of node node with the newElement.

The NodeList Object/Interface

The NodeList object/interface is an ordered collection of nodes. Ordered means that they have a numbered place in a sequence.

The childNodes property of the Node object returns a NodeList, as shown in Listing 16.4.

LISTING 16.4   A PROPERTY OF AN OBJECT RETURNING A NodeList OBJECT

```
1:   //var docroot holds the root element of the document
2:   var children = docRoot.childNodes;
```

Table 16.5 gives an overview of the NodeList object properties.

TABLE 16.5   NodeList ATTRIBUTES/PROPERTIES

Name	Value
length	The number of nodes in the NodeList

Listing 16.6 shows a JavaScript example using this property.

LISTING 16.6 GETTING THE LENGTH OF A NodeList

```
1:  //children holds the NodeList Object with the child nodes
2:  var nrofchildren = children.length;
```

Table 16.6 gives an overview of the NodeList object methods.

TABLE 16.6 NodeList METHODS

Name	Returns
item(n)	The nth item (node) of the collection

Listing 16.7 shows a JavaScript example using this method.

LISTING 16.7 USING THE NTH ITEM OF A NodeList

```
1:  //children holds the NodeList Object with the child nodes
2:  var i;
3:  for (i=0, i < children.length, i++) //loop over all child nodes
4:      return children.item(i).nodeName; //return the names
```

ANALYSIS We use a variable, I, for iterating over all the items of a NodeList containing the list of children.

In line 4 we return the name for every child (the tag name if the child is an element, the attributename if an attribute, and so on.

The NamedNodeMap Object

The NamedNodeMap object is another collection of nodes, the difference being that this collection is accessible by name.

Table 16.7 shows the NamedNodeMap object properties.

TABLE 16.7 NamedNodeMap ATTRIBUTES/PROPERTIES

Name	Value
length	The number of nodes in the NamedNodeMap

Listing 16.8 shows a JavaScript example using this property.

16

LISTING 16.8 GETTING THE LENGTH OF A NamedNodeMap

```
1:  //var node holding a Node Object
2:  if (node.attributes != null)
3:  //testing if the node has attributes
4:      return node.attributes.length;
5:  //returns the number of attributes
```

Table 16.8 shows the methods of the NamedNodeMap object.

TABLE 16.8 NamedNodeMap METHODS

Name	Returns
getNamedItem(name)	A node with the specified name (string) or null
setNamedItem(arg)	Nothing, but adds a node specified in arg to the NamedNodeMap
removeNamedItem(name)	The removed node with the specified name (string)
item(n)	The nth item of the collection

Listing 16.9 shows a JavaScript example using the getNamedItem() method.

LISTING 16.9 USING THE getNamedItem() METHOD OF A NamedNodeMap
OBJECT/INTERFACE

```
1:  //var node holds a Node Object
2:  return node.attributes.getNamedItem("unit");
3:  //returns the node of type attribute with name "unit"
```

A DocumentFragment is an object that can contain pieces of documents (document fragments) for copying and pasting, rearranging, and so on. It inherits from the Node object class.

The Document Object

The Document object represents the complete XML document. It inherits from the Node object class. This is the only interface that allows you to create the other objects that can be found only inside documents.

Table 16.9 shows the properties of the Document object.

TABLE 16.9 DOCUMENT OBJECT ATTRIBUTES/PROPERTIES

Name	Value
documentElement	The root Element object of the document
doctype	DocumentType object (defined in the extended interfaces)

Listing 16.10 shows a JavaScript example for getting the root element of an XML document.

LISTING 16.10 GETTING THE ROOT ELEMENT OF AN XML DOCUMENT

```
1:  //var xml holds the xml document
2:  var docRoot = xml.documentElement;
3:  return "The root element is " + docRoot.nodeName + " element.";
4:  //the nodeName property returns the tag name of the element
```

Table 16.10 shows the methods of the Document object.

TABLE 16.10 DOCUMENT OBJECT METHODS

Name	Returns
createElement(tagName)	A new Element object named tagname (string)
createTextNode(data)	A new text node with the specified data (string)
createComment(data)	A new comment with the specified data (string)
getElementsByTagName(tagname)	A NodeList of all descendant elements with the given tagname (string)

Listing 16.11 shows a JavaScript example for creating a new element in an XML document.

LISTING 16.11 CREATING AN ELEMENT

```
1:  //var xml holds the XML document object
2:  var newElement = xml.createElement("remark");
```

Caution

This method does not make the node part of the document tree. The insertBefore or appendChild methods of the Node object can be used for that purpose.

The Data Object

The CharacterData interface gives you a set of properties and methods to access and manipulate character data. It extends the Node object. No document objects correspond directly with the Data object. The Text object, Comment object, and CDATASection object inherit from it.

Table 16.12 shows the properties of the CharacterData object.

TABLE 16.12   CharacterData OBJECT ATTRIBUTES/PROPERTIES

Name	Value
data	The character data (string) of the node
length	The number of characters

Its methods are shown in Table 16.13.

TABLE 16.13   CharacterData OBJECT METHODS

Name	Returns
substringData(offset,count)	The specified substring, where start specifies the start offset, and count specifies the number of characters
appendData(arg)	Nothing, but appends the string arg to the end of the data in the object
insertData(offset,arg)	Nothing, but inserts the string arg at the specified offset
deleteData(offset,count)	Nothing, but removes a range of characters, specified by offset and count
replaceData(offset,count,arg)	Nothing, but replaces the characters starting at offset and count along with the string specified in arg

You'll see an example of using the appendData method in listing 16.12.

LISTING 16.12   GETTING AND CHANGING TEXT

```
1:    //var node holds a Node Object
2:    if (node.nodeType == 3) //if text
3:        var content = node.nodeValue;
4:        content.appendData("  !");
```

 ANALYSIS   If the variable node is of type text node, then its content is placed inside the content variable. An exclamation point is appended to this content.

The Other Objects

The main interfaces were covered in the previous section. The more specialized interfaces, such as the Element object just extend the more general Node object and add some more specific properties and methods that allow you to access and manipulate the object in a more convenient and specific way.

The Element object offers the facilities (properties and methods) to access and manipulate tag names, attribute names, and attribute values.

For a deeper understanding, access the following URL: http://www.w3.org/TR/WD-DOM/.

An Example of Using the DOM

We would like to convert the prices in the XML file shown in Listing 16.13 to Canadian dollars.

LISTING 16.13 PRICES TO BE CONVERTED

```
 1:   <?xml version="1.0"?>
 2:   <books>
 3:       <book id="TY1">
 4:               <title>Sams Teach Yourself C++ in 21 Days, Second Edition
 5:               </title>
 6:               <author>Jesse Liberty
 7:               </author>
 8:               <price unit="USA">29.99
 9:               </price>
10:       </book>
11:        <book id="MJ">
12:               <title>Maximum Java 1.1
13:               </title>
14:               <author>Glenn Vanderburg
15:               </author>
16:               <price unit="USA">49.99
17:               </price>
18:       </book>
19:       <book id="JS">
20:               <title>JavaScript Unleashed, Second Edition
21:               </title>
22:               <author>Richard Wagner
23:               </author>
24:               <price unit="USA">49.99
25:               </price>
26:       </book>
```

continues

LISTING **16.13**   CONTINUED

```
27:        <book ID="TY2">
28:            <title>Sams Teach Yourself Visual C++ 5 in 21 Days, Fourth
➥Edition
29:            </title>
30:            <author>Nathan Gurewich
31:            </author>
32:            <author>Ori Gurewich
33:            </author>
34:            <price unit="USA">35.00
35:            </price>
36:        </book>
37:    </books>
```

Listing 16.14 shows a piece of JavaScript using the DOM to convert the U.S. prices to
Canadian dollars.

LISTING **16.14**   JAVASCRIPT FOR CONVERSION TO CANADIAN DOLLARS

```
 1:   //var xml holds the Document Object
 2:   var priceElements = xml.getElementsByTagName("price");
 3:   //returns a NodeList of all elements with the tag price
 4:   var i;
 5:   for (i=0;i < priceElements.size;i++) { // looping over all those price
➥elements
 6:        var USAprice = parseFloat(priceElements.item(i)
➥.firstChild.nodeValue);
 7:        //the firstChild property returns the Text node
 8:        //of this Text node we take the nodeValue, being the text itself
 9:        //we convert this text to a number (floating)
10:        priceElements.item(i).setAttribute("unit","Canadian dollar");
11:        //we set the attribute "unit" to value "Canadian dollar"
12:        var convertedprice = USAprice * 1.4;
13:        //we convert the price to Canadian dollar
14:        var newprice = xml.createTextNode(convertedprice);
15:        //we create a new Text node containing the new price
16:        priceElements.item(i).replaceChild(newprice,
➥priceElements.item(i).firstChild);
17:        //we replace the old Text node with the new one
18:        }
19:
```

 On line 2 of Listing 16.14 we make a Nodelist object containing all the
elements in our XML document with the tag name price.

For each of those elements (loop on line 5), we take the first child (firstChild property), a text node. From this text node we take the value (nodeValue property), the content. This content is converted to a number by the ParseFloat() function in JavaScript. The resulting number is used to calculate the price in Canadian dollars (line 12).

On line 14 we create a new text node, using the createTextnode() method of the document object.

This Text node is used (line 16) to replace the old text node.

Implementations of the DOM

Microsoft Internet Explorer 5 beta 2 has full DOM support in compliance with the W3C DOM recommendation.

The same is the case for Mozilla/Gecko. Expectation is also high that vendors of editing tools such as SoftQuad will implement the DOM API in their editing tools, and the same is true for the vendors of repositories such as POET, Chrystal, Oracle, Texcel, and so on.

On the parser side, DataChannel, IBM, and Sun implemented the DOM API in their Java XML parsers.

The Future of the DOM

For the moment, the DOM level 1 spec is limited to those methods that are needed for representing and manipulating structure and content.

Missing pieces that will be addressed in future levels of the DOM are as follows:

- The interfaces for internal and external subsets
- The ability to validate
- The ability to control rendering via style sheets
- The ability to control access

A lot of tool vendors will probably implement this API. Although the concrete language to be used (EcmaScript, VBScript, Java, and so on) can differ, you will always deal with the same objects with the same well-known properties and methods. This makes knowledge of the DOM a necessity.

Summary

In this chapter we covered level 1 of the DOM:

- What the DOM is
- What you can do with the DOM
- Why the DOM was developed
- The interfaces (objects) defined in the DOM
- A short example
- Implementations of the DOM
- What the future will bring

Q&A

Q I'm not sure if my code selects the right node. Is there a utility I can use?

A On Microsoft's Web site you'll find in the Site Builder Workshop in the XML demos area the XML Tree viewer. This is a Web page for use with IE5 in which you can display a tree view of your XML files. An input field allows you to enter JavaScript code to select the node(s) you are after. The result of your input is shown in the tree view itself.

Q I'm not succeeding in capturing the text content of a node.

A Be sure to first capture the text node itself. If found, you'll use the `nodeValue` property of this text node to get at the content (text) itself.

Q I have created a new element in my document but it doesn't appear.

A Remember that in addition to creating a new element you have to add it to your document explicitly. Refer to the `"insertBefore"` or `"appendChild"` methods.

Exercises

We'll use the JavaScript that was used in Internet Explorer 4 for transforming an XML file.

The script seen below in Listing 16.15 has been written in an outdated syntax of the DOM. Rewrite the script so it conforms to the recommended spec of the DOM.

LISTING 16.15   A SCRIPT TO UPDATE

```
1:   <SCRIPT LANGUAGE="JScript" FOR="window" EVENT="onload">
2:      document.write("<HTML><HEAD><TITLE>My favorite
➡musicians</TITLE></HEAD>\n");
3:      document.write("<BODY><H2>My favorite musicians</H2><HR>\n")    ;
4:      var xml = new ActiveXObject("msxml");
5:      xml.URL = "file:///c¦/xmlex/musicians.xml";
6:      var docroot = xml.root;
7:      output_doc(docroot);
8:
9:      function traverse(elem)
10:         {var i;
11:             if (elem.children != null)
12:                 {
13:                 for (i=0; i < elem.children.length; i++)
14:                 output_doc(elem.children.item(i));
15:                 }
16:         }
17:
18:      function output_doc(elem)
19:      {
20:                 if (elem.type == 0)
21:                     {
22:                         if (elem.tagName == "MUSICIANS")
23:                             {
24:                                     document.write("<TABLE
➡BORDER='1' CELLPADDING='5'>");
25:                                     traverse(elem);
26:                                     document.write("</TABLE>");
27:                             }
28:                         else if (elem.tagName == "MUSICIAN")
29:                             {
30:                                     document.write("<TR>");
31:                                     traverse(elem);
32:                                     document.write("</TR>");
33:                             }
34:                         else
35:                             {
36:                                     document.write("<TD>");
37:                                     traverse(elem);
38:                                     document.write("</TD>");
39:                             }
40:
41:                     }
42:                 else if (elem.type==1)
43:                         document.write(elem.text);
44:                 else
45:                         alert("Unknown type encountered");
46:                 }
47:   </SCRIPT>
```

16

DAY **17**

Using Meta-Data to Describe XML Data

One of XML's most anticipated features is its ability to use the markup for data, such as for encoding the contents of databases (this was always an unfulfilled dream of the SGML community).

The XML DTD is only one way of describing the data model (the schema) of an XML document. Given the inadequacies of the DTD, there are many initiatives under way to find other alternatives. According to the experts we're probably several years away from having an accepted replacement schema for XML documents. Fortunately, there are already several excellent candidates and probably more on the way.

In this chapter you will:

- Learn why the XML DTD is inadequate for data applications
- Learn the basics of three of the major candidates that could become the future XML schema

What's Wrong with DTDs?

Remember that the XML DTD describes the structure of the elements in an XML document and that the document can be validated against the DTD to check that it conforms to the structure. This ability to validate the contents of a document gives XML an edge over other methods of marking up text. There is, for example, no way to check the markup of TeX code (a computer typesetting language still popular with mathematics and scientific academics) or TROFF code (the primitive markup language used to format online help information with the UNIX man utility).

The DTD also provides a certain amount of control over attributes, but offers very little ability to check the actual data inside the elements. It can check that there is a DATE element, but it has no way of confirming that what is inside that DATE element isn't absolute nonsense that couldn't be turned into data no matter how much imagination you applied to the task.

If you want to use XML to encode the contents of a database or use it to transfer credit card transaction data across the Internet, which is a much more commercially viable proposition, there are ways of enforcing tighter control over the data. Most of these systems work on the age-old principle of "garbage in—garbage out" (*gigo*) and the only way to avoid a lot of manual cleaning up is to ensure the data that goes in is clean. You want to be able to ensure that a numerical value doesn't contain any text, that a currency value only has two digits on the right of the decimal point (or comma, depending on what currency), and so on. Perhaps because XML is a derivative of SGML, which is very document-oriented and considers data rather than documents, the DTD fails dismally.

To add to this already major problem, there is a general feeling that it is already asking a lot for people to learn the syntax of the XML language. The XML DTD, however, isn't really an XML document, and it isn't even an SGML document—the DTD has a syntax all its own. Apart from the fact that this increases the burden of learning even further, it takes away one of the major potential strengths of XML—automation.

Although there aren't that many XML tools yet, there probably will be soon. The situation will probably prove comparable to the way HTML developed. In the beginning there were very few tools and most people used whatever tools they had. They were often reduced to writing HTML code by hand. It didn't take long for sophisticated tools to arrive and we have now reached the point where it is quite easy to produce HTML documents without having a clue what HTML looks like.

The story of XML's development has been driven by a desire to automate—a desire to make machine-generation of XML a genuine possibility. XSL went from being a sophisticated variant of the LISP programming language to a more simplified style language that shares XML's syntax. XLink and XPointer have followed a similar path from being a blend of SGML and HyTime to a simplified language that also shares XML's syntax. The end result is that it becomes realistically possible to consider machine-generating the XML code and the code for its appearance and its linking to other documents.

The general trend in the initiatives aimed at developing an alternative to DTDs is towards an XML schema that provides the tighter content control that data applications require, while sharing XML's syntax in order to implement a complete machine-generation environment.

One weakness of XML that has been increasingly drawing attention is XML's data model—the last nail in the DTD's coffin. The relationship between elements in an XML document is purely hierarchical; there's no way to express relationships in a richer fashion. (There is an SGML application called Topic Map Navigation that offers a solution, but this hasn't had much impact yet.) If you consider the problems of transferring massive amounts of data across an already overburdened Internet, matters of scale and economy become crucial. Many believe what XML needs is an object-oriented hierarchy; it must be possible to work with classes of objects, like `purchases` and `sales`. These classes would be subclasses of a wider class, such as a `transaction` from which the classes could inherit properties like `value`, `date`, `credit card number`, and so on, but could also add "local" properties such as `sales discount`. None of this could possibly be achieved with a DTD, but all of this is inherent in the design of some of the possible replacements.

The XML DTD isn't dead yet—but it can only be a matter of time before it becomes obsolete. There's no single replacement, but many are waiting in the wings. It has been claimed that they are contending candidates, especially since Microsoft is one originator (XML-Data) and Netscape is another (RDF). It isn't a genuine contest, though, because these two schemas don't necessarily address the same problems. A third schema you will encounter (DCD) manages to combine them both. All we can do is let the interested parties sort out exactly which one is going to be the replacement or (more likely) come up with the ultimate replacement.

XML-Data

XML-Data was the first XML schema and is very definitely a programmer's solution, using schemas that define the characteristics of classes of objects.

Schemas are composed of declarations for concepts and classes of objects with class hierarchies, properties, constraints, and relationships.

Like all of the XML data (small d this time!) proposals, XML-Data uses elements and, to identify the significance of the elements, namespaces. The syntax of a typical XML-Data schema looks like this:

```
XML version='1.0' ?>
<?xml:namespace name="urn:uuid:BDC6E3F0-6DA3-11d1-A2A3-00AA110C14882/"
   as="msschema"/?>
<msschema:schema id='ExampleofSchemaSyntax'>
  <!-- schema goes here. -->
</msschema:schema>
```

ANALYSIS We have already talked a little about namespaces. Normally, namespace declarations point to Web sites that (supposedly) contain vocabularies describing the elements used in the schema; their names, purpose, and content. In this case the pointer is a URN and the address is very similar to a Microsoft Windows Registry entry (just as the Windows Registry entry value is given for the Microsoft Data Source object used to map XML elements onto HTML elements for display in Internet Explorer, as described in Day 12, "Viewing XML in Internet Explorer").

XML-Data is, as its name suggests, highly adapted for data. It has datatypes like string and integer; it has constraints, such as maximum and minimum values; it allows multipart keys, which allows data to be assembled from multiple locations. Perhaps most important of all is the fact that XML-Data allows other schemas, such as database schemas, to be mapped onto the XML-Data schema.

Resource Description Framework

The Resource Description Framework (RDF) is intended to offer a solution to the problem that although everything on the Web is *machine-readable*, it is not *machine-understandable*. RDF proposes a scheme of metadata, data about data, to describe the data on the Web.

Drawing on previous work from the PICS initiative and the Dublin Core (two other important metadata initiatives), RDF emphasizes facilities to enable the automated processing of Web resources. RDF is intended for use in a variety of application areas, and so the distinction between what is data and what is metadata is left open for the application itself to decide. The authors of the RDF working draft see the following areas as their prime targets:

- Facilitating "resource discovery" to provide better search engine capabilities
- Cataloging the content and content relationships available at a particular Web site, page, or digital library

- Enabling intelligent software agents for knowledge sharing and exchange
- Providing content ratings to describe collections of pages that represent a single logical document
- Guarding the intellectual property rights of Web pages
- Specifying user privacy preferences and the privacy policies of a Web site
- Implementing digital signatures for electronic commerce

NEW TERM The *Platform for Internet Content Selection (PICS)* was originally developed for the more down-to-earth task of providing a means for "adult" Web sites to implement a form of screening so that filter software could shield "unsuitable" content from accidental access.

NEW TERM Named after Dublin, Ohio, the home of the Online Computer Library Center, the *Dublin Core* is a set of elements developed by librarians, digital library researchers, and text-markup specialists that identify certain basic atoms of information. These elements include, for example, DATE, TITLE, SUBJECT, and LANGUAGE.

In practice (although I am simplifying a great deal), the mechanism of RDF is extremely simple. The model consists of just three parts: a resource (a URI), a property type, and a value. All three of these items of information are straightforward XML elements and so, to identify them, the XML code uses the RDF namespace. Listing 17.1 shows the RDF code (in XML of course) for a book. According to the Dublin Core, a book has a title and the author is called the creator.

INPUT **LISTING 17.1** A SIMPLE RDF EXAMPLE FOR A BOOK

```
1: <?xml version="1.0"?>
2:   <rdf:RDF
3:     xmlns:rdf="http://www.w3.org/TR/WD-rdf-syntax#"
4:     xmlns:books="http://www.booksRus.com/schemas/books/">
5:     <rdf:Description about="http://www.xs4all.nl/~sintac">
6:       <books:Creator>Simon North</books:Creator>
7:     </rdf:Description>
8:   </rdf:RDF>
```

ANALYSIS The RDF namespace (you don't have to use the string rdf as the namespace identifier—you can use whatever you like), refers back to the W3C Web page that describes RDF (http://www.w3.org/TR/WD-rdf-syntax). The books namespace points, supposedly, to a location on the Books'R'Us site where there would be a vocabulary of what these elements mean. By using namespaces and Web sites in this way, you aren't limited as to what element names you use; by referring back to the vocabulary, any application can find the significance or purpose of the information contained inside the element.

In addition to using simple elements, RDF also allows you to assemble collections of resources called bags and sequences. They are basically the same; the difference is that in a bag the order doesn't matter while in a sequence the order does matter. Listing 17.2 shows the use of a bag where the book has more than one author.

INPUT   **LISTING 17.2**   A SIMPLE RDF EXAMPLE FOR A BOOK

```
1:  <?xml version="1.0"?>
2:  <rdf:RDF
3:    xmlns:rdf="http://www.w3.org/TR/WD-rdf-syntax#"
4:    xmlns:books="http://www.booksRus.com/schemas/books/">
5:    <rdf:Description about="http://www.xs4all.nl/~sintac">
6:      <books:Creator>
7:        <RDF:Seq>
8:          <books:LI>Simon North</books:LI>
9:          <books:LI>Paul Hermans</books:LI>
10:       </RDF:Seq>
11:     </books:Creator>
12:   </rdf:Description>
13: </rdf:RDF>
```

ANALYSIS   I used a Seq element to group the two authors because the order of their listing does matter; if it didn't I'd have used the Bag element instead.

There is, obviously, a lot more to RDF than what I have described so far, but that lies beyond the scope of this book because it is all rather theoretical. One practical side of RDF that you will notice, though, is that Netscape is already implementing RDF in Mozilla (its testbed for future Netscape Communicator versions) for describing bookmarks. RDF is, in this sense, Netscape's counterpart of Microsoft's Active Desktop and channels (which are based of CDF, another XML application). Listing 17.3 shows a typical Mozilla RDF file.

LISTING 17.3—A MOZILLA RDF RESOURCE FILE

```
1:  <RDF:RDF>
2:  <Topic id="NC:Toolbar">
3:  <child>
4:  <Topic id="NC:CommandToolBar" name="Command Toolbar"
5:       toolbarBitmapPosition="top"
6:  toolbarButtonsFixedSize="yes"  >
7:  <child href="command:back" name="Back"/>
8:  <child buttonTooltipText="Reload this page from the server"
9:     buttonStatusbarText="Reload the current page"
10:     href="command:reload" name="Reload"/>
11: <child href="command:stop" name="Stop"/>
```

```
12: <child href="command:forward" name="Forward"/>
13: <child name="separator0" href="nc:separator0"/>
14: <child href="command:urlbar" name=" "
15:     buttonStatusBarText="Location/Search Bar"
16:    buttonTooltipText="Location/Search Bar"
17: urlBar="Yes" urlBarWidth="*"/>
18: <child name="separator2" href="nc:separator2"/>
19: </Topic>
20: </child>
21:
22: <child>
23: <Topic id="NC:InfoToolbar" name="Info Toolbar">
24:     <child>
25:     <Topic id="NC:Bookmarks" name="Bookmarks"></Topic>
26:     </child>
27:     <child>
28:     <Topic id="NC:History"
29:    largeIcon="icon/large:workspace,history" name="History">
30:          <child href="NC:HistoryMostVisited"
31:        name="Most Frequented Pages"/>
32:      <child href="NC:HistoryBySite" name="History By Site"/>
33:     <child href="NC:HistoryByDate" name="History By Date"/>
34:          </Topic>
35:          </child>
36:     <child href="NC:Sitemaps" name="Related"
37:      htmlURL="http://rdf.netscape.com/rdf/navcntradvert.html"/>
38: </Topic>
39: </child>
40:
41: <child>
42: <Topic id="NC:PersonalToolbar" name="Personal Toolbar">
43: </Topic>
44: </child>
45: </Topic>
46:
47: <Topic id="NC:NavCenter">
48: <child href="NC:Bookmarks" name="Bookmarks"/>
49: <child href="NC:Search"
50:     largeIcon="icon/large:workspace,search" name="Search"/>
51: <child href="NC:History" name="History"/>
52: <child id="NC:Sitemaps" name="Site Tools"
53:   htmlURL="http://rdf.netscape.com/rdf/navcntradvert.html" />
54: <child id="NC:LocalFiles" name="Files"
55:    largeIcon="http://rdf.netscape.com/rdf/heabou.gif"/>
56: </Topic>
57:
58: <Topic id="NC:SmartBrowsingProviders">
59:   <child href="http://altavista.digital.com/
60:          cgi-bin/query?q=link%3A"
```

17

continues

LISTING 17.3   CONTINUED

```
61:              name="Who points to me?"
62:              resultType="TEXT/HTML"/>
63:      <child href="http://www-rl1.netscape.com/wtgn?"
64:        name="Related Links"
65:              resultType="TEXT/RDF" />
66:  </Topic>
67:
68:  </RDF:RDF>
```

Document Content Description

XML-Data and RDF were submitted to the W3C for consideration within months of each other. Immediately, whether rightly or wrongly, the players involved (Microsoft: XML-Data and Netscape: RDF) were accused of proposing proprietary solutions that would lock people into their solution.

The Document Content Description (DCD) proposal attempts to find the best compromise between the two proposals, taking a subset of the XML-Data proposal and expressing it in a way that is consistent with RDF (in technical terms, DCD is an RDF vocabulary).

Put most simply, the heart of DCD is an `ElementDef` element that has either the `Type`, `Model`, `Occurs`, `RDF:Order`, `Content`, `Root`, `Fixed`, and `Datatype` attributes, or that contains these elements. The `ElementDef` element, in fact, describes an element contained in an XML document. As well as these "special" elements (or attributes), the `ElementDef` element also contains details of the elements that it may contain and the definitions of their attributes. A typical DCD declaration in an XML DTD could look like the following:

```
<ElementDef Type="shape" Model="Elements">
  <AttributeDef Name="n" Occurs="Optional"/>
  <AttributeDef Name="Sides"/>
</ElementDef>

<ElementDef Type="squareshape" Model="Element">
  <AttributeDef Name="Sides" Occurs="Optional">
     <Default>3</Default>
  </AttributeDef>
  <Element>side</Element>
  <Extends Type="shape"/>
</ElementDef>
```

And in the associated XML document, a typical element could look something like this:

```
<squareshape n="4">
  <side><dimension unit='in'>5<dimension></;side>
</squareshape>
```

Just as in RDF, child elements can be grouped and, if required, you can declare whether the order of the child elements is important or not, as shown in Listing 17.4.

LISTING 17.4   TYPICAL DCD ELEMENT DEFINITIONS

```
 1:  <ElementDef Type="Candidate" Model="Elements" >
 2:    <Description>Personal Details</Description>
 3:    <Group RDF:Order="Seq">
 4:      <Element>GivenName</Element>
 5:      <Group Occurs="Optional">
 6:         <Element>Initial</Element>
 7:      </Group>
 8:      <Element>FamilyName</Element>
 9:      <Element>common:Address</Element>
10:      <ElementDef Type="Telephone" Datatype="string"/>
11:    </Group>
12: </ElementDef>
13:
14: <ElementDef Type="Loan">
15:    <Description>Morgage Loan</Description>
16:    <Group RDF:Order="Seq">
17:      <Element>InterestRate</Element>
18:      <Element>Amount</Element>
19:      <Element>Maturity</Element>
20:    </Group>
21: </ElementDef>
```

Because DCD is a product of both XML-Data and RDF, all the strong points of both are present, such as XML-Data's data typing and RDF's flexibility.

XSchema

While XML-Data, RDF, and DCD have some big names behind them (Microsoft, Netscape, and IBM), XSchema is the result of extended discussions on the XML-DEV Internet mailing list. Although its contributor list sounds a bit like the roll call for the XML Hall of Fame, XSchema has had no major commercial development support and is simply the result of the hard work of a few dedicated individuals; not least among them Simon St. Laurent, who acts as coordinator, motivator, contributor, and editor.

The XML-Data, RDF, and DCD proposals all require you to include the schema information in the DTD. XSchema is different. It *has* a DTD, which in a sense is a good way of formalizing its syntax, but it uses a schema document that is in standard XML syntax rather than a separate DTD syntax. The first software that can be used to convert an XML DTD into an XSchema document is already becoming available. Other tools—including one to do the reverse conversion—should follow in due course.

17

As with the other proposals, the heart of XSchema is an element declaration. XSchema uses an element declaration whose own declaration (from the XSchema DTD) looks like this:

```
<!ELEMENT ElementDecl (Doc?, More?, Model, AttGroup?)>
<!ATTLIST ElementDecl
          Name    NMTOKEN  #REQUIRED
          id      ID       #REQUIRED
          prefix  NMTOKEN  #REQUIRED
          ns      CDATA    #IMPLIED
          Root    (Recommended ¦ Possible ¦ Unlikely) "Possible">
```

ANALYSIS Most of these child elements and attributes speak for themselves, but one isn't quite so obvious and deserves special attention. The More element allows anyone to extend XSchema by adding their own supplements. You could, for example, add to XSchema to more tightly control the possible content of element models.

The latest draft of XSchema is, at the time of writing, less than a week old. As a result, there's not too much more to be said about it other than to go into more technical detail, which is outside the scope of this book. Although XSchema is very definitely still in the experimental stage, the skill, knowledge, and enthusiasm of the people involved in it has ensured that XSchema has a lot of potential and holds a lot of promise.

Architectural Forms

It is an unfortunate fact of life that the best technical solution doesn't always win. In this case, the best technical solution is HyTime, or rather a part of HyTime called the architectural form. I won't try to explain HyTime, but architectural forms have been proposed as a possibility for XML and I believe they deserve a mention here. They are, by far, the most powerful and most perfect mechanism, but they suffer from being extremely difficult to comprehend and being almost impossible to actually implement. Where XML applications will be numbered, at the least, in thousands, SGML applications are numbered, possibly, in hundreds and HyTime applications are numbered, hopefully, in tens.

NEW TERM The *Hypermedia/Time-based Structuring Language (HyTime)* is an application of SGML that provides facilities for representing static and dynamic information that is processed and interchanged by hypertext and multimedia applications.

HyTime provides standardized mechanisms for specifying the interconnections (hyperlinks) within and between documents and other information objects, and for scheduling multimedia information in time and space. In essence, HyTime makes it possible to represent links to anything, anywhere, at any time.

An XML DTD describes document architecture. It contains rules that govern every aspect of how conforming (valid) documents are to be represented and processed (or at least as far as you can do so in SGML).

Instead of specifying complete document types, it is possible to define rules, known as *architectural forms*, for creating and processing elements (just as document architectures are rules for creating and processing documents).

Architectural forms are specified principally by attribute definitions. However, an architectural form can also include rules for constructing the content models of element types conforming to the form.

The set of architectural forms and related declarations for an architecture act as a sort of meta-DTD. Applications can create their own architecture forms, which means that how an application looks at the information is a matter that it can decide for itself, or in common with another application. The architectural form therefore provides a very powerful and extremely rich and sophisticated mechanism for describing, and exchanging, information about information and data about data.

The essence of the architectural form is that it allows the set of attributes for an element to be extended without changing the basic processing, parsing, and integrity of the DTD or associated document. By extending the set of attributes, information that would otherwise require the use of external files can be expressed and preserved.

The attraction of this approach is that it does not require the use of new structures and processes; it uses the SGML parser and an extended, but perfectly standard, form of the DTD to convey the information. The architectural form directly encodes the relationship between the elements and target application's semantics in the DTD.

To take a practical example of the importance of this, consider the now famous advantage of XML—that it will make searching on the Web much simpler. Will it really? Well, I suppose it would if you could persuade everyone to use the same standard element names, or to comply with namespace vocabularies. That way you could not only easily find all the books with a certain title, you could easily find all the books by the same author. But there lies the problem. Making information easy to find also makes it easy to compare, and there are already hints of packages that will automatically perform price comparisons and return you the address of the best offer. It can hardly be in the retailers' best interests to open up their information to this sort of activity. Architectural forms offer a sort of compromise, and a sort of workaround. Suppose you want to find all the prices for a certain book, but you don't know how the price has been tagged. By defining an architectural form, the search engine could look for the architectural forms instead of the tag names. Architectural forms are a wonderful mechanism; for a more extensive, and much deeper, discussion, read David Megginson's book (*Structuring XML Documents*, Prentice Hall Computer Books, ISBN: 0136422993). Architectural forms make namespaces largely irrelevant and they are future-proof. However, to return to my original theme, the best technical solution doesn't always win, and this one probably won't either. It would take a long time and a lot of work to implement architectural forms and the Web won't wait. The Web requires instant, working solutions.

Summary

XML schemas are a very dry, very technical subject. They are, however, crucial to the success or failure of XML and will play an increasingly visible role in its future. This lesson has tried to minimize the technical detail and show you the fundamentals of most of the current schema proposals.

Q&A

Q Why aren't DTDs sufficient for data?

A DTDs do not constrain the content of elements, and where they do constrain content (in attributes) the constraints are far too loose. The relationships between elements are too simplistic and DTDs have a different syntax to XML documents, which makes machine generation difficult.

Q Why did XML-Data and RDF seem to face so much criticism?

A Both were, rightly or wrongly, viewed with some suspicion as being proprietary solutions that broke the open policy established by XML.

Q What makes XSchema so different from the other proposals?

A Unlike the other proposals, which use the differing DTD syntax, XSchema uses the same syntax as normal XML documents.

Q What makes architectural forms so radically different from all the other proposals?

A Apart from the fact that architectural forms pre-date XML by several years, the radical difference is that they do not rely on namespaces.

Exercises

1. Most of the XML schema proposals rely on a namespace pointer that is a URL. In theory at least, the pointer should identify a vocabulary that describes the elements that belong to that namespace. URLs—as you will have noticed if you've spent

more than a few hours on the Web—change, often with no notice and no forwarding mechanism. This would be unacceptable for a namespace and so a lot of the URLs are being converted into PURLs (persistent URLs). Go to a good Web search engine, find out what PURLs are, and see if you can register for one.

2. Join the XML-DEV mailing list. You might not have much to say, and the discussions may get pretty technical at times, but it can't do any harm to know that someone is listening who might act as a sanity check. Besides, provided you behave, contributions are always welcome—beware, though, this is not a list for beginners' questions.

17

DAY **18**

Styling XML with CSS

Throughout the previous lessons you have seen ways to make your XML code more readable. There are various ways to convert XML code into HTML or otherwise process it in order to display it inside a Web browser.

The two leading browsers (Netscape's and Microsoft's) have completely different ideas about how to do this. If your code accommodates one browser, it can't be displayed sensibly in the other. To make matters worse, there is no standardization in their approaches and no consistency across different versions of the same product. Internet Explorer versions 4 and 5, for example, currently have different expectations and requirements.

What, you might ask, is the point of having a standardized markup language if there are no standards for rendering it? The same thought must have passed through hundreds, even thousands of heads, as it crops up in mine every time I need to build an application to display XML code in yet another proprietary implementation of SGML and XML software.

To solve this, and many other related problems, a large number of attempts have been made to develop a standardized rendering (style) language. In this and the next two chapters, several of these style languages are reviewed. Fortunately, XML is able to leverage many of the fruits of these efforts. You can process it using the *Document Style Semantics and Specification Language* (*DSSSL*, pronounced dissle), which it inherits from SGML because XML still has a lot of its roots in SGML. You can also use *Cascading Style Sheets* (*CSS*) from HTML, reflecting that XML and HTML have a common parent in SGML and a common environment in the World Wide Web.

Today you will

- Briefly review the history of some of the major style languages of importance
- Learn the basics of the Cascading Style Sheet language and how it can be applied to XML code

The Rise and Fall of the Style Language

Throughout the history of SGML there have been various attempts to define a style language as a means of rendering marked up text on paper or on a screen.

The first style specification language was *FOSI* (*Formatting Output Specification Instance*, pronounced fosey), which met with some limited success in American defense circles, but never had much mass impact due to its complexity. (ArborText was the only software company I know of that came close to having a commercially available working implementation.) In parallel with the FOSI initiative came *DSSSL*, the *Document Style Semantics and Specification Language*, which provides a full-scale programming language for specifying the style of an SGML document. DSSSL can also be applied to XML documents and on Day 19, "Converting XML with DSSSL," you'll learn a lot more about it.

DSSSL is extremely powerful and complex, and for use on the Web it was perhaps a little too much. A stripped down version called *DSSSL-Lite* was therefore proposed. DSSSL-Lite was refined into an Internet variation called DSSSL-o (short for *DSSSL-online*). DSSSL-o was published in December 1995 and reissued in August 1996 to include a few corrections resulting from changes in the final version of the DSSSL standard. DSSSL-o became the basis for the first version of XSL (called *XS*, short for *xml-style*).

In May 1997, Jon Bosak, the co-editor of the XML language specification, made a personal draft of a projected style section for the XML specification publicly available on the Internet. (At the time the XML specification was split into three parts, one for the language—what has now become the XML Language Recommendation—one for linking, and one for style.) The thought-provoking title of this document, "XML Part 3: Style [NOT YET]," was intended to warn that the contents should be viewed with suspicion because they were very likely to change. This didn't deter some courageous souls, and it wasn't long before the first software appeared.

In August 1997, a radically improved version of XS, now called *XSL* (*extensible style language*), appeared. This was the first version of XSL. I call this version *XSL1* to distinguish it from its previous version. XSL1 incorporated all of DSSSL-o, but added new objects and characteristics to support all of the functionality of CSS.

One major difference between DSSSL-o to XSL1 was the complete change in syntax. DSSSL-o was clearly a LISP derivative; recognizable by the rows of brackets that are so familiar to LISP programmers. XSL1, on the other hand, had the same syntax as XML. The implications of this change were quite exciting. For example, it made the style language part of XML as accessible to computer processing (or even generation) as the XML language itself.

While the syntax of the style language changed, a lot of the original DSSSL concepts survived (things like flow objects) almost intact. This incarnation of the XML style language was, however, quite short-lived (less than a year), even though a lot of the software available still supports this version of the language.

On August 18, 1998, a new version of XSL was submitted to the *W3C* (*World Wide Web Consortium*). This was actually the first working draft document to be submitted; the other documents were just notes, which didn't convey much official status. This version of XSL still isn't the definitive version of the XML style language, but it gives the development community a reasonable basis on which to move forward.

You will learn about this new version of XSL in detail on Day 20, "Rendering XML with XSL." I call this version of XSL *XSL2* here to distinguish it from the earlier version.

While development proceeds on a dedicated XML style language, it shouldn't be forgotten that HTML also has its own style language, CSS. CSS can also be applied to XML code and, because CSS is firmly directed toward the display of markup inside a Web browser, it is extremely useful for basic display purposes. In the rest of this chapter we'll examine how you can exploit Web browser support of CSS and HTML to display XML code with the minimum amount of effort.

18

Cascading Style Sheets

I mentioned earlier that XSL1 improved on XS by adding features from CSS. XSL1 adopted some of the CSS properties as flow objects (you will learn all about these on Day 19). This was intended to make it easier for people to convert CSS style sheets into XSL style sheets, not just by converting code but also by being able to keep to the same concepts.

> **Note**
>
> There are two versions of CSS: *CSS level 1* (*CSS1*), which is a W3C recommendation dating from December 1996, and *CSS level 2* (*CSS2*), which was published as a proposal in November 1997 and currently exists in the form of a working draft dating from January 1998. As yet, few Web browsers actually support the latest version of CSS (quite a few have problems supporting the older version) and so I will only deal with CSS1 here. CSS2 adds a lot of extra features, but it is backward compatible with CSS1.

I'm not going to teach you CSS here. There are plenty of excellent books covering CSS, but there are also literally hundreds of tutorials available on the Web and thousands of sample pages for you to learn from.

> **Tip**
>
> Using other peoples' HTML and CSS code is theft. However, no one can really blame you for examining code in order to learn from it.
>
> An easy way to download the CSS code is to use an old version of a Web browser. Netscape 2 or even Mosaic is a good choice, but you want to make sure that it's a version that doesn't support CSS style sheets. When you see a style sheet that looks interesting in your regular Web browser, check the HTML source code (use View > Page Source in Netscape, or View > Source in Internet Explorer) for the address of the style sheet (look in the META tags at the start of the document). Cut the address of the style sheet, fire up the old version of the browser, and paste that address into the URL box (don't forget to add the path to the original document and resolve any relative paths). You should see the contents of the style sheet displayed as plain ASCII text and you can save the file to your hard disk.

Caution

When you use a second browser you must be careful to avoid DLL or other conflicts. You can destroy your bookmarks or favorites and even seriously damage your preference settings. If you use a really old version you probably won't have any problems, but you should consider setting up separate profiles for the two versions.

XML, CSS, and Web Browsers

Instead of teaching you CSS, I am going to show you how to use CSS with XML code.

Note

Everything that I explain here will, of course, change because the three browsers I use (Microsoft Internet Explorer 5 beta preview 2, Netscape Communicator 4.5 preview 2, and Netscape Mozilla, September 1998 build) are not official products but test versions.

Unfortunately, as you will see, trying to display XML sensibly (with some kind of useful layout) is a pretty hit-and-miss affair; you will probably end up spending a lot of time modifying code, loading it, and modifying it again, until you either achieve what you want or, more likely, you give up trying. Don't give up hope—there are some cheats you can adopt that will allow you to use the browsers' built-in HTML interpretations, and later in this chapter I will show you how to use these. Sadly, just as the "proper" ways of displaying XML differ, so do the "illegal" ones!

18

XML, CSS, and Internet Explorer

Microsoft is currently putting a lot of effort into XML (you will learn a bit more about what they have planned for us on Day 21, "Real World XML Applications"). However, Microsoft is committing itself to supporting Dynamic HTML as the basis of displayable code. This means that the support for XML in Internet Explorer 5 is somewhat limited. Although it does allow you to view XML code, Microsoft's policy is centered on dynamically converting XML elements into HTML elements (XML data source objects were described earlier on Day 12, "Viewing XML in Internet Explorer"). XML becomes little more than a glorified data transmission scheme, part of what Microsoft calls "islands of data."

Whatever Microsoft's plans with XML, it is still interesting to note that Internet Explorer version 5 (IE5, which is currently available as a preview from the Microsoft Web site, `http://www.microsoft.com/msdownload/iebuild/`) is currently the only Web browser with any real support for XML. (Netscape's Mozilla code has some support, as you will see later in this chapter, but this browser is only available as source code and compilation is no small task.) Unfortunately, IE5 supports XML in a pretty unconventional, non-standard way. No one can really blame Microsoft for this; when the standards aren't really standard, and when they keep changing, it's quite hard to conform.

Before we look at how to display XML code in IE5, let's have a look at the perfect end result of what we're trying to achieve. Figure 18.1 shows a simple Web page written in HTML and using a separate CSS style sheet to give the visual layout. The HTML code is shown in Listing 18.1 and the CSS code is shown in Listing 18.2.

INPUT   **LISTING 18.1**   THE HTML CODE FOR THE TARGET DOCUMENT

```
 1: <!DOCTYPE HTML PUBLIC "-//W3C//DTD HTML 4.0 Transitional//EN">
 2: <HTML>
 3: <HEAD>
 4:    <LINK rel="stylesheet" href="SAMPLEXML.css">
 5:    <TITLE>Sample XML Home Page</TITLE>
 6: </HEAD>
 7: <BODY>
 8: <DIV CLASS="CHAPTER">
 9: <H1>SAMPLE WEB PAGE</H1>
10: <P>Welcome to one of the world's first WWW Home pages
11: written entirely in XML. This web page has been
12: constructed using:</p>
13: <UL>
14: <LI>basic XML code (derived from HTML)</LI>
15: <LI>a CSS stylesheet to get the page to display
16: in Microsoft Internet Explorer</LI>
17: <LI>a separate CSS stylesheet to get the page
18: to display in Netscape Communicator</LI>
19: <LI>another CSS stylesheet to get the page to display
20: in Netscape Mozilla (a September 1998 build)</LI>
21: <LI>variations of the XML code embedded as pseudo-HTML
22: code inside a standard HTML web page</LI>
23: </UL>
24: <P>Explore to your heart's content.</P>
25: <P CLASS="WARNING">Note that all of this code is experimental so don't
➥be disappointed
26: if something doesn't quite work the way you think it should.</P>
27: <CENTER>
28: <ADDRESS>
29: <HR NOSHADE WIDTH="100%">This page last updated: 21 August
➥1998</ADDRESS>
```

```
30: </CENTER>
31: </DIV>
32: </BODY>
33: </HTML>
```

OUTPUT

FIGURE 18.1

The styled HTML target document in IE5.

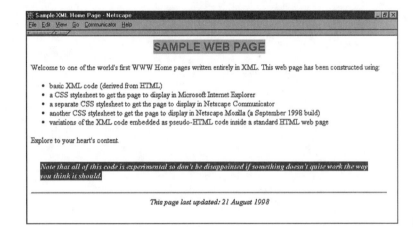

Tip

If you examine Listing 18.1 closely, you will note that even though it is HTML code, it also (with the exception of the empty HR, horizontal rule, element) perfectly acceptable XML code. It contains a document type declaration, all of the elements are nested properly, the attribute values are enclosed in quotes (""), and all the elements have closing tags. This is a good way to practice the right habits for hand-coding XML documents, should you ever feel inclined to do that. (Note, however, that unless the HTML 4 DTD was a legal XML DTD, which it isn't, you cannot hope to validate any documents against the DTD.)

18

LISTING 18.2 THE HTML CODE FOR THE TARGET DOCUMENT

```
1:  BODY {
2:      color: #000000;
3:  }
4:
5:  H1 {
6:      font-family: Arial;
7:      font-size: 18pt;
8:      font-weight: bold;
9:      color: #FF0000;
10:     background-color: #C0C0C0;
```

continues

LISTING 18.2   CONTINUED

```
11:      text-align: center;
12:      border-top: solid;
13:      border-bottom: solid;
14:      border-left: solid;
15:      border-right: solid;
16:    }
17:
18: A:LINK {
19:      color: #0000FF;
20:      }
21:
22: A:VISITED {
23:      color: #990099;
24:      }
25:
26: .WARNING {
27:      font-style: italic;
28:      font-size: 12pt;
29:      font-weight: bold;
30:      color: #FFFFFF;
31:      background-color: #0000FF;
32:      text-decoration: blink;
33:      margin-top: 8pt;
34:      margin-bottom: 8pt;
35:      margin-left: 10pt;
36:      margin-right: 10pt;
37:      padding-top: 1%;
38:      padding-bottom: 1%;
39:      padding-left: 1%;
40:      padding-right: 1%;
41:      border-top: dashed #000000;
42:      border-bottom: dashed #000000;
43:      border-left: dashed #000000;
44:      border-right: dashed #000000;
45: }
```

ANALYSIS Note that the CSS code shown in Listing 18.2 could have been made a lot shorter by combining some of the properties. Note also that I haven't bothered to declare the properties for a lot of the elements. I can safely leave the Web browser to apply its own default properties. As you will see shortly, once you switch over to XML you will have to explicitly specify properties for every element.

The sample HTML code is nearly XML code. Because this is about the display mechanisms, let's not be too adventurous. To convert the HTML code into XML code, I will simply rename some of the elements. The document becomes a PAGE element, a UL becomes a LIST element, and so on. The end result is shown in Listing 18.3. (Note that I cheated a little by dropping the HR element. A horizontal rule could easily be added to the style for the element above or below where you want it to appear, but I didn't want to complicate the style sheet unnecessarily.)

INPUT   **LISTING 18.3**   THE TARGET DOCUMENT REWRITTEN AS XML CODE

```
 1:  <PAGE>
 2:  <TITLE>SAMPLE WEB PAGE</IE5:TITLE>
 3:  <PARA>Welcome to one of the world's first WWW Home pages
 4:  written entirely in XML. This web page has been
 5:  constructed using:</PARA>
 6:  <LIST>
 7:  <ITEM>basic XML code (derived from HTML)</ITEM>
 8:  <ITEM>a CSS stylesheet to get the page to display in
 9:  Microsoft Internet Explorer</ITEM>
10:  <ITEM>a separate CSS stylesheet to get the page to display
11:  in Netscape Communicator</ITEM>
12:  <ITEM>another CSS stylesheet to get the page to display
13:  in Netscape Mozilla (a September 1998 build)</ITEM>
14:  <ITEM>variations of the XML code embedded as pseudo-HTML
15:  code inside a standard HTML web page</ITEM>
16:  </LIST>
17:  <PARA>Explore to your heart's content.</PARA>
18:  <WARNING>Note that all of this code is experimental so
19:  don't be disappointed if something doesn't quite work the
20:  way you think it should.</WARNING>
21:  <UPDATE>This page last updated: 21 August 1998</UPDATE>
22:  </PAGE>
```

18

When you display this code as it is, you will see something like the display shown in Figure 18.2. Internet Explorer will display a navigable rendering of the structure of the elements in the document.

ANALYSIS   As you can see from Figure 18.2, the results could actually have been worse. While IE5 shows the markup, this raw content display gives you easy access to the structure of the information in the document. By clicking on the minus (-) and plus (+) symbols you can expand and collapse the element structures as you want. Obviously, there are no styles applied because no link was made to a style sheet and to have properly rendered XML elements you would have to provide an XSL style sheet.

FIGURE 18.2

The raw XML document displayed in IE5.

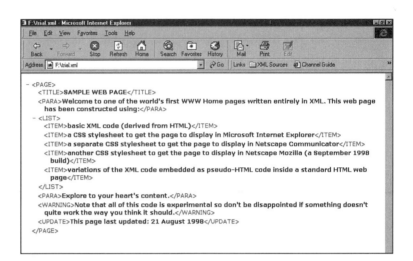

As well as handling XML code, IE5 is of course hardwired to understand HTML. So, instead of going to all the effort of creating a full XSL style sheet, what we can do is create a CSS style sheet and attach it to the XML code. While IE5 doesn't know what to do with XML code, it does know that it exists. To mix the XML elements with the HMTL elements you need to declare a namespace and say that the XML elements belong to this namespace. The modified XML code, complete with the HTML wrapper, is shown in Listing 18.4.

INPUT   **LISTING 18.4**   THE XML DOCUMENT WITH A CSS LINK

```
 1:  <?xml:stylesheet href="css.css" type="text/css"?>
 2:  <PAGE>
 3:  <TITLE>SAMPLE WEB PAGE</TITLE>
 4:  <html:IMG xmlns:html="htmluri" SRC="logo.gif" ALIGN="middle"/>
 5:  <PARA>Welcome to one of the world's first WWW Home
 6:  pages written entirely in XML. This web page has been
 7:  constructed using:</PARA>
 8:  <LIST>
 9:  <ITEM>basic XML code (derived from HTML)</ITEM>
10:  <ITEM>a CSS stylesheet to get the page to display in
11:  Microsoft Internet Explorer</ITEM>
12:  <ITEM>a separate CSS stylesheet to get the page to
13:  display in Netscape Communicator</ITEM>
14:  <ITEM STYLE="color:green;>another CSS stylesheet to get the page to
15:  display in Netscape Mozilla (a September 1998 build)</ITEM>
16:  <ITEM>variations of the XML code embedded as
17:  pseudo-HTML code inside a standard HTML web page</ITEM>
18:  </LIST>
```

```
19: <PARA>Explore to your heart's content.</PARA>
20: <WARNING>Note that all of this code is experimental so
21: don't be disappointed if something doesn't quite work the way you
22: think it should.</WARNING>
23: <UPDATE>This page last updated: 21 August 1998</UPDATE>
24: </PAGE>
```

ANALYSIS In Listing 18.4, I reference the CSS style sheet using an XML processing instruction. If you look carefully you will see that my syntax is actually incorrect; according to the XML specification I should write xml-stylesheet, but Internet Explorer 5 doesn't complain about my use of xml-stylesheet (it doesn't mind if you use XML either). This is a little surprising because IE5 thoroughly checks all the other aspects of an XML file.

I modified the XML code to add a reference to a graphic in line 4. This syntax is somewhat non-standard because the namespace I'm using (html) isn't declared anywhere. There is, however, no disputing the fact that it works.

Tip

> Another way to add a style to your XML code is to inline the style specification by placing it in the element start tag (also demonstrated in line 14 of Listing 18.4):
>
> ```
>             <ITEM STYLE="color:green;">another CSS stylesheet to get
> ➥the page to
> >
> ```

18

The CSS style sheet is shown in Listing 18.5.

INPUT **LISTING 18.5** THE CSS STYLE SHEET

```
1: PAGE {display: block; font-family:arial,sans-serif;}
2: TITLE { font-size: 24pt; font-weight: bold;}
3: PARA { display: block; padding-top: 6pt; }
4: LIST { display: block; list-style-type: lower-roman; padding-top: 6pt;}
5: ITEM { display: block; padding-top: 6pt;text-indent: 10pt;}
6: UPDATE { display: block; text-align: center;  font-style: italic;
7:         border-top: 2pt solid black; padding-top: 6pt; padding-bottom:
➥6pt; }
8: WARNING { display: block; margin-left:24pt; color: red; padding-top:
➥6pt; }
```

Note that there should be a format specification for every element in the document you want to see. If you leave one out, or forget an element, it won't be displayed at all.

You will also see (in the next to last line of Listing 18.5) that I added a border-top specification to the UPDATE element to compensate for having removed the HTML HR element.

Once the completed XML file, along with its CSS style sheet, has been loaded into IE5, the result looks something like Figure 18.3.

FIGURE 18.3

The XML document displayed in IE5, using CSS.

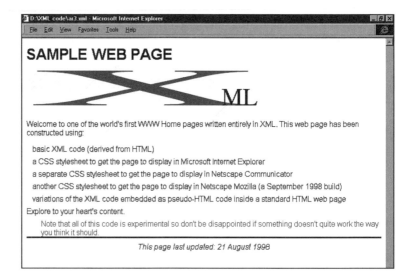

The layout of this XML document can actually come close to the HTML layout shown in Figure 18.1 (I left out the border and shading for the title to keep the code simple). It isn't perfect, but it does come close. Unfortunately, this version of IE5 doesn't fully support CSS (yet) and so the browser doesn't interpret the display: list-item specification for the ITEM element. I am therefore unable to get the list items to be displayed using bullets.

Of course, the modifications lock the XML and CSS code into this browser, and even lock them into this version of the browser, since IE5 behaves slightly differently. Load this code into the Netscape Communicator browser and you will see absolutely nothing. As seen in Figure 18.4, when you load the code into Mozilla you will see display results that are very similar to the IE5 display. Mozilla doesn't support some of the CSS properties yet and so the horizontal line near the bottom of the page isn't displayed.

FIGURE 18.4

The IE5 XML document displayed in Mozilla.

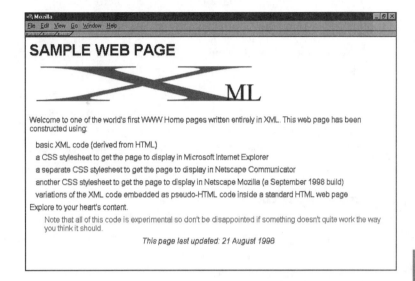

Despite the fact that we have now had to create XML code that drifts dangerously far from being acceptable, this is a reasonable way to render XML without writing any code to map it onto HTML elements (as described on Day 12). Once CSS is fully supported, this could be a feasible solution. Now let's look at the other side of the story: XML code in Mozilla.

XML, CSS, and Mozilla

While Internet Explorer 5 is only a preview (the version used here is preview 2, and rumor has it that there will be another beta test version before the package is officially released sometime in 1999), it still enjoys a more official status than Mozilla. Furthermore, IE5 is pretty stable and fairly complete. Mozilla is another story. Netscape's open source policy for Mozilla, by which anyone is welcome to contribute to the code, means that the end results are less visible and less predictable. However, the compiled versions available on the Internet and gossip among the developers indicate that Mozilla's support for XML will be more solid than Microsoft's.

I personally doubt there was a battle of the browsers between Microsoft and Netscape. To the best of my knowledge, Netscape makes far more money selling Web servers and supporting software than it could ever have made from selling browsers. Microsoft did start giving away Internet Explorer for nothing, but it wasn't the browser market they were interested in so much as trying to protect Windows' position as an Internet platform. Besides, there are other (and even better) browsers such as Opera, Amaya, Mosaic, Likse, and Lynx, to name just a few of the better known ones. However, even if it isn't true it does make a good story and there is little doubt that Microsoft is slowly gaining more and more ground (an amazing feat considering the very late and very mistaken start they made).

Development of the Netscape Communicator continues in parallel (4.5 is the current official release) and it is anyone's guess when, or even if, Mozilla will become an official product. Netscape's policy is to take the best parts of this public browser and incorporate them back into the mainstream product. Meanwhile, although the package is extremely unstable, it can be exciting and extremely educational to experiment with it.

Getting Mozilla

Sadly, the Mozilla program is a major download and you need a lot of your own software to do anything with the source code (a compiler for a start). Worse, with all the program libraries you need and all the modifications you need to make to adapt the code for your local situation, compiling the code isn't a simple task. It requires a fair bit of programming experience, a lot of patience, an amazing amount of time, and a heroic amount of determination. Fear not; there are places where you can download fully compiled ready-to-run executables (although only for Windows 95 or Windows NT). Four places I can recommend are `http://www.wynholds.com/mike/mozilla/`, `http://www.mozilla.org`, `http://www.mozillaZine.org`, and `http://mozilla.hypermart.net/`. (The generosity and open-heartedness of quite a few people on the Internet continues to amaze me, even after 12 years of being online.)

Installing the program is very easy and, with a small modification to your Netscape Communicator profiles, it happily coexists with any other browser (unlike IE5, which replaces a lot of files that are essential for running IE4).

Displaying XML Code in Mozilla

It isn't really my intention to compare IE5 with Mozilla. As you have already seen on Day 12 (when you learned to use data source objects to map XML elements onto HTML elements) and Day 10, "Creating XML Links," (when you learned about XML linking and Mozilla's support for transclusions), the two packages have different approaches and support different features. Nevertheless, it still makes sense to follow the same route to display XML in Mozilla as we did with IE5; we will start with an HTML file that has a styled appearance and try to re-create it in Mozilla.

The first step is to take an HTML file and a CSS style sheet and load them into Mozilla. The resulting display will be our baseline (it would be a bit unreasonable to expect better from the XML code than the HTML code). I used the same code that I did for the IE5 exercise (Listing 18.1 and 18.2). The end result is shown in Figure 18.5.

OUTPUT

FIGURE 18.5

The HTML target file displayed in Mozilla.

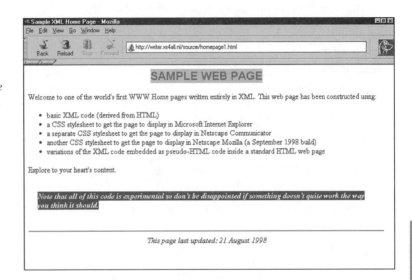

ANALYSIS As you can see, the same HTML and CSS code looks different in Mozilla compared to IE5, but because neither of them is 100% "correct" we'll settle for what we see.

The next step is to convert the HTML code into XML code by changing the names of the elements, just as we did before. We'll then load this XML code into Mozilla, as shown in Figure 18.6.

OUTPUT

FIGURE 18.6

The raw XML target file in Mozilla.

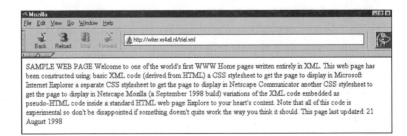

18

ANALYSIS The next step is to couple some styling to the XML code. With Mozilla, you don't have to go to nearly as much effort you did with IE5. As far as Mozilla is concerned (other than the parsing that the file goes through when it's loaded), an element is an element and you can add the format specifications for the XML elements in exactly the same way as you would if they were HTML elements. Let's look again at the input XML, shown in Listing 18.6.

INPUT   **LISTING 18.6**   THE RAW XML FILE

```
1:  <PAGE>
2:  <TITLE>SAMPLE WEB PAGE</TITLE>
3:  <PARA>Welcome to one of the world's first WWW Home pages
4:  written entirely in XML. This web page has been
5:  constructed using:</PARA>
6:  <LIST>
7:  <ITEM>basic XML code (derived from HTML)</ITEM>
8:  <ITEM>a CSS stylesheet to get the page to display in
9:  Microsoft Internet Explorer</ITEM>
10: <ITEM>a separate CSS stylesheet to get the page to display
11: in Netscape Communicator</ITEM>
12: <ITEM>another CSS stylesheet to get the page to display
13: in Netscape Mozilla (a September 1998 build)</ITEM>
14: <ITEM>variations of the XML code embedded as pseudo-HTML
15: code inside a standard HTML web page</ITEM>
16: </LIST>
17: <PARA>Explore to your heart's content.</PARA>
18: <WARNING>Note that all of this code is experimental so
19: don't be disappointed if something doesn't quite work the
20: way you think it should.</WARNING>
21: <UPDATE>This page last updated: 21 August 1998</UPDATE>
22: </PAGE>
```

ANALYSIS You probably didn't even notice there was something missing from the raw XML file (a round of applause if you did!). There is no XML declaration. This isn't a problem when you're wrapping the XML code inside HTML code, and the chances are that Mozilla won't even mind if you omit it. Strictly speaking it isn't compulsory, and you don't really need it unless you aren't using the default character set, but it's a good idea to include it. In an HTML context, the XML declaration would be treated as if it were a standard SGML processing instruction and would be ignored. Keeping one in can't do any harm.

So let's add the XML declaration and another processing instruction to link the CSS style sheet to the XML code. Note that the syntax for doing this is quite different from the way you do it in HTML, as shown in Listing 18.7.

INPUT   **LISTING 18.7**   THE COMPLETED XML FILE

```
 1:  <?xml version="1.0"?>
 2:  <?xml:stylesheet type="text/css2" href="xmlmoz.css"?>
 3:  <PAGE>
 4:  <TITLE>SAMPLE WEB PAGE</TITLE>
 5:  <PARA>Welcome to one of the world's first WWW Home
 6:  pages written entirely in XML. This web page has been
 7:  constructed using:</PARA>
 8:  <ITEMST>
 9:  <ITEM>basic XML code (derived from HTML)</ITEM>
10:  <ITEM>a CSS stylesheet to get the page to display in
11:  Microsoft Internet Explorer</ITEM>
12:  <ITEM>a separate CSS stylesheet to get the page to
13:  display in Netscape Communicator</ITEM>
14:  <ITEM>another CSS stylesheet to get the page to
15:  display in Netscape Mozilla (a September 1998 build)</ITEM>
16:  <ITEM>variations of the XML code embedded as
17:  pseudo-HTML code inside a standard HTML web page</ITEM>
18:  </LIST>
19:  <PARA>Explore to your heart's content.</PARA>
20:  <WARNING>Note that all of this code is experimental so
21:  don't be disappointed if something doesn't quite work the way you
22:  think it should.</WARNING>
23:  <UPDATE>This page last updated: 21 August 1998</UPDATE>
24:  </PAGE>
```

18

When this code is loaded into Mozilla, the result should be similar to that shown in Figure 18.7.

OUTPUT

FIGURE 18.7

The final XML file in Mozilla.

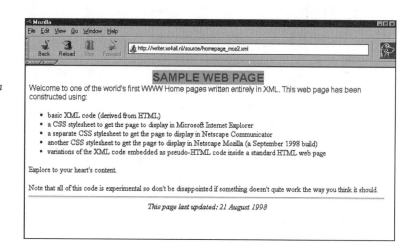

ANALYSIS As you can see, Mozilla's support for CSS is somewhat poorer than IE5's. However, I think that there is a very good chance that Mozilla will fully support CSS in due time (there's every reason to believe so, because Netscape Communicator supports CSS). Considering the few changes that have to be made to the XML code (and all of them perfectly legal XML), it would seem that by using CSS we could be just a small step away from displaying XML in a Netscape browser almost as if it were HTML.

Cheating

So far I've shown you one way to more or less alter your XML code to get it to display in one browser, and another way to keep your XML code but display it in an altered manner in another browser. It's a difficult choice!

Before I leave the topic of CSS styling and move on to "real" style languages, there's a trick that could come in handy if you have enough freedom in choosing the names of your elements. I call this technique cheating because it really is; it's exploiting a browser's weakness for HTML to make it believe that it's not seeing XML, but HTML.

There's no secret coding, nothing even very complicated—the trick is to exploit existing HTML element names. Let's face it, a list is a list is a list, no matter how you want to look at it. It might be a parts list or a price list, but by carefully thinking about what you call the elements and how you nest them (and don't forget you can also use attributes to add information about elements), it's quite possible to use HTML elements. Compare this:

```
<price.list>
<item>shoe, black</item>
<item>shoe, brown</item>
</price.list>
```

with this:

```
<price.list>
<ul>
<li> shoe, black</item>
<item>shoe, brown</item>
</ul>
</price.list>
```

Big deal? Well, not really. All I'm suggesting is that instead of wrapping XML code inside HTML code, you mix the two together. Any browser that understands HTML will automatically pick out, recognize, and render the HTML elements. All you have to worry about is the remaining XML elements.

Does this work? Well, no—not really, but then again it doesn't work any worse than "pure" XML, and sometimes it works a lot better. Take a look at an example of such a mix, shown in Listing 18.8.

> **Note**
>
> The beta preview version 1 of Internet Explorer 5 also supported hybrids but, with the introduction of better XSL support, it disappeared in preview version 2.

INPUT   **LISTING 18.8**   A HYBRID XML FILE FOR MOZILLA

```
 1:  <?xml version="1.0"?>
 2:  <?xml:stylesheet type="text/css2" href="samplexmlmoz1.css"?>
 3:  <page>
 4:  <maintitle>SAMPLE WEB PAGE</maintitle>
 5:  <p>Welcome to one of the world's first WWW Home pages
 6:  written entirely in XML. This web page has been
 7:  constructed using:</p>
 8:  <UL>
 9:  <LI>basic XML code (derived from HTML)</LI>
10:  <LI>a CSS stylesheet to get the page to display in
11:  Microsoft Internet Explorer</LI>
12:  <LI>a separate CSS stylesheet to get the page to
13:  display in Netscape Communicator</LI>
14:  <LI>another CSS stylesheet to get the page to
15:  display in Netscape Mozilla (a September 1998 build)</LI>
16:  <LI>variations of the XML code embedded as
17:  pseudo-HTML code inside a standard HTML web page</LI>
18:  </UL>
19:  <P>Explore to your heart's content.</P>
20:  <warning>Note that all of this code is
21:  experimental so don't be disappointed if something doesn't quite
22:  work the way you think it should.</warning>
23:  <UPDATE>This page last updated: 21 August 1998</UPDATE>
24:  </page>
```

The code isn't radically different. You make major gains because in the CSS style sheets you only need to specify the format for the XML elements and those HTML elements for which the default layout is unacceptable. You can simply rely on the browser to properly render those HTML elements that look fine as they are.

> **Tip**
>
> Mixing HTML elements like this is a very useful workaround when the browser doesn't support a particular CSS property, as with Mozilla.

18

So much for the code—show me the pictures! Figure 18.8 is the Mozilla hybrid file rendered in Mozilla. Judge for yourself, and compare the results with Figure 18.3 (pure XML in IE5) and Figure 18.7 (pure XML in Mozilla).

OUTPUT

FIGURE 18.8

The hybrid XML file in Mozilla.

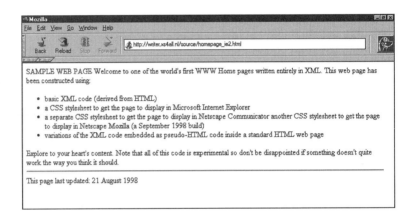

ANALYSIS When you compare the outputs, you can see that how faithfully you keep to pure XML when your main concern is display in a Web browser is largely determined by the power of the browser and your determination to get a nice looking display.

I sometimes feel that a lot more could have been achieved using HTML without even having to go as far as XML. HTML (and certainly the latest version, 4) has features like DIV elements, element classes, and attributes that allow you to add almost as much descriptive information as XML can do with elements. Consider the pure (semantic) HTML variant of the XML file we have been working toward throughout this chapter, shown in Listing 18.9.

LISTING 18.9 SEMANTIC HTML CODE

```
 1:  <!DOCTYPE HTML PUBLIC "-//W3C//DTD HTML 4.0 Transitional//EN">
 2:  <HTML>
 3:  <HEAD>
 4:     <LINK rel="stylesheet" href="SAMPLEXML.css">
 5:     <TITLE>Sample XML Home Page</TITLE>
 6:  </HEAD>
 7:  <BODY>
 8:  <DIV CLASS="PAGE">
 9:  <H1 CLASS="PageTitle">SAMPLE WEB PAGE</H1>
10:  <P CLASS="first">Welcome to one of the world's first
11:  WWW Home pages written entirely in XML. This web page has
12:  been constructed using:</p>
13:  <UL CLASS="list">
```

```
14: <LI CLASS="item1">basic XML code (derived from HTML)</LI>
15: <LI CLASS="item2">a CSS stylesheet to get the page to display
16: in Microsoft Internet Explorer</LI>
17: <LI CLASS="item3">a separate CSS stylesheet to get the page to
18: display in Netscape Communicator</LI>
19: <LI CLASS="item4">another CSS stylesheet to get the page to
20: display in Netscape Mozilla (a September 1998 build)</LI>
21: <LI CLASS="last">variations of the XML code embedded as
22: pseudo-HTML code inside a standard HTML web page</LI>
23: </UL>
24: <P>Explore to your heart's content.</P>
25: <P CLASS="WARNING">Note that all of this code is experimental
26: so don't be disappointed if something doesn't quite work the
27: way you think it should.</P>
28: <HR NOSHADE WIDTH="100%">
29: <P CLASS="update">This page last updated: 21 August 1998</P>
30: </DIV>
31: </BODY>
32: </HTML>
```

OK, so it isn't really a fair comparison. If nothing else, the CSS style sheet to render this is going to be enormous and, of course, I'd be throwing away all the additional features of XML like linking, addressing, and validation. However, if all you want is semantic information, HTML can be almost as useful as XML.

Embedding CSS in XSL

On Day 20 you will learn all about XSL. Before you get that far though, I'm going to jump the gun a little and demonstrate how, with the absolute minimum of XSL knowledge, you can embed CSS properties in an XSL style sheet.

Although there is a W3C note (http://www.w3.org/TR/NOTE-XSL-and-CSS.html) suggesting how CSS and XSL code should be combined, a different method is already implemented in Internet Explorer 5, beta preview 2.

Listing 18.10 shows the later example XML code modified to use an XSL style sheet. Essentially all that changes is the name of the style sheet file and the type declaration.

LISTING 18.10 THE XML CODE MODIFIED TO INCLUDE AN XSL STYLE SHEET

```
1:  <?XML:stylesheet href="css.xsl" type="text/xsl"?>
2:  <PAGE>
3:  <TITLE>SAMPLE WEB PAGE</TITLE>
4:  <html:IMG xmlns:html="htmluri" SRC="logo.gif" ALIGN="middle"/>
```

continues

LISTING **18.10**   CONTINUED

```
5:   <PARA>Welcome to one of the world's first WWW Home
6:   pages written entirely in XML. This web page has been
7:   constructed using:</PARA>
8:   <LIST>
9:   <ITEM>basic XML code (derived from HTML)</ITEM>
10:  <ITEM>a CSS stylesheet to get the page to display in
11:  Microsoft Internet Explorer</ITEM>
12:  <ITEM>a separate CSS stylesheet to get the page to
13:  display in Netscape Communicator</ITEM>
14:  <ITEM>another CSS stylesheet to get the page to
15:  display in Netscape Mozilla (a September 1998 build)</ITEM>
16:  <ITEM>variations of the XML code embedded as
17:  pseudo-HTML code inside a standard HTML web page</ITEM>
18:  </LIST>
19:  <PARA>Explore to your heart's content.</PARA>
20:  <WARNING>Note that all of this code is experimental so
21:  don't be disappointed if something doesn't quite work the way you
22:  think it should.</WARNING>
23:  <UPDATE>This page last updated: 21 August 1998</UPDATE>
24:  </PAGE>
```

All the changes occur in the style sheet, as shown in Listing 18.11.

INPUT   LISTING **18.11**   THE XSL STYLE SHEET CONTAINING THE CSS CODE

```
1:  <?xml version="1.0"?>
2:  <xsl:stylesheet xmlns:xsl="http://www.w3.org/TR/WD-xsl">
3:
4:    <xsl:template>
5:      <xsl:value-of/>
6:    </xsl:template>
7:
8:    <xsl:template match="/">
9:      <HTML>
10:       <HEAD>
11:         <TITLE>
12:           Sample Web Page
13:         </TITLE>
14:         <STYLE>
15:           <![CDATA[
16:             LI  { margin-left:  24pt; margin-right: 24pt }
17:           ]]>
18:         </STYLE>
19:       </HEAD>
20:       <BODY BGCOLOR="#FFFFFF" TEXT="#000000">
21:         <xsl:for-each select="PAGE">
22:           <xsl:apply-templates/>
```

```
23:          </xsl:for-each>
24:        </BODY>
25:      </HTML>
26:  </xsl:template>
27:
28:  <xsl:template match="PAGE/TITLE">
29:    <H1>
30:       <xsl:apply-templates/>
31:    </H1>
32:  </xsl:template>
33:
34:  <xsl:template match="PARA">
35:    <P>
36:       <xsl:apply-templates/>
37:    </P>
38:  </xsl:template>
39:
40:  <xsl:template match="LIST">
41:    <UL>
42:       <xsl:for-each select="ITEM">
43:         <LI>
44:            <xsl:apply-templates/>
45:         </LI>
46:       </xsl:for-each>
47:    </UL>
48:  </xsl:template>
49:
50:  <xsl:template match="WARNING">
51:    <P STYLE="margin-left:24pt; color: red;">
52:       <xsl:apply-templates/>
53:    </P>
54:  </xsl:template>
55:
56:  <xsl:template match="UPDATE">
57:    <HR/>
58:       <ADDRESS STYLE="text-align: center">
59:         <xsl:apply-templates/>
60:       </ADDRESS>
61:  </xsl:template>
62:
63:</xsl:stylesheet>
```

Note

Note that the XSL is an XML document; it must therefore be well-formed or the browser won't accept it.

You will learn all about the syntax of XSL in due course. For now all you need to know is that you need a set of XSL statements for each XML element that you want to display that maps the XML element onto the appropriate HTML element:

```
<xsl:template match="PARA">
  <P>
    <xsl:apply-templates/>
  </P>
</xsl:template>
```

If you want to explicitly select an element inside an element, use the parent/child method form so that LIST/ITEM only applies to ITEM elements that appear inside LIST elements. XSL always chooses the most specific match it can find so that none of the other ITEM elements will be affected by this.

If you want to add some style properties to the element you can, as you would in "normal" CSS code, put them inside the element start tag, as shown in lines 51 and 58.

If you want to apply global styles, put them inside a CDATA section, where the code is hidden from the XML processor, as shown in lines 14 to 18.

The end result, shown in Figure 18.9, is almost perfect. Because we're mapping each XML element onto an HTML element, the browser enables you to access as many of the CSS properties as it supports.

FIGURE 18.9

The XML file in IE5 using CSS inside XSL.

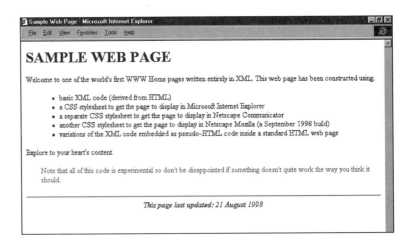

Caution The XSL code shown in Listing 18.11 isn't the same as that shown in the draft XSL proposal. Apparently, Microsoft has already implemented changes in the XSL syntax that have not yet been made public. While this is the syntax as currently supported in IE5, beta preview 2, there is absolutely no guarantee that this is what the XSL syntax will actually be changed to, or that it will be supported in IE5 or any other Web browser.

CSS Style Sheet Properties

You've now learned how to *use* CSS style sheets with XML, but I haven't told you much about CSS itself. Well, sorry, I'm not going to do so. There are plenty of good books on the subject, the Web is awash with tutorials, and the Internet abounds with examples to learn from (especially if you use the tip I gave you near the beginning of this chapter). No matter how much you read about CSS, it won't take you long to realize that no two browsers interpret it in exactly the same way. You have to employ a little trial and error to find the best compromise. To conclude this chapter, the following sections give you a brief overview of the CSS1 properties and I'd say loudly: Go out and experiment with them!

18

Units

Distance and size units can be specified as absolute values that will be consistent regardless of their context:

```
Width: 50px;
margin-left: 2em;
```

You can use any of the following absolute units. Note that there is no space between the value and the unit:

- cm (centimeter; 1cm = 10mm)
- in (inch; 1in = 2.54cm)
- mm (millimeter)
- pc (pica; 1pc = 12pt)
- pt (point; 1pt= 1/72 in)

These units can be specified as percentages to define sizes in relative terms that are calculated with respect to their context (the size of the browser window, the size of the table, and so on):

```
width: 80%;
```

You can use any of the following relative units. Note, again, that there's no space between the value and the unit:

- em (em, the height of the element's font)
- ex (x-height, the height of the letter x)
- px (pixel, relative to the screen resolution; 72 dpi is an average EGA/VGA screen resolution, giving 72 pixels to the inch)

Color units are used by various properties to define colors. You can specify the colors using the same hexadecimal code system as HTML uses. This consists of a hash symbol (#) followed by a pair of hexadecimal characters (00 to FF) for red (#FF0000), green (#00FF00), and blue (#0000FF), where 00 is nothing and FF is the maximum of that color. You also can specify percentages of red, green, and blue, although the simplest way is to name the color you want:

```
color: #FF0000;
color: rgb(100%,0%,0%);
```

Specifying CSS Properties

You specify a property you want by naming the element whose properties you want to set, followed by pairs of property names and values:

```
Element {property1: value1; property2: value2; }
```

For example:

```
BODY { margin: 0;
       font-family: arial, helvetica, sans-serif;
       font-size: 14px;
       color: black; }
```

If you want to set the same properties for more than one element at the same time, you group them into a single style declaration:

```
H1, H2, H3, H5 {color: red;}
```

Going a step further, if you only want properties to apply to an element when it's inside another element, group the elements into a single style declaration but omit the separating comma. For example, with this style declaration:

```
H1 B { color: red; }
```

the text inside a B element will only be red if the B element is enclosed in an H1 element:

```
<DOC>
<H1>This part will be <B>very red</B></H1>
<P>But this part will be <B>totally unaffected</B>
by the declaration.</P>
</DOC>
```

Classes

Class selectors can be used to define types of elements rather than named elements. A class selector is a string preceded by a period, and is called using the STYLE attribute.

```
.warning {color: red;}
    <H1 class="warning">WARNING!</H1>
    <P class="warning">Danger, Will Robinson!</P>
```

ID Attributes

An ID selector can be used to pick out a specific element according to the value of its ID attribute. An ID selector is the ID attribute string value preceded by a hash mark (#). The hash mark doesn't appear in the value of ID attribute itself.

```
#i5 {color: brown;}
    <P ID="i5">This is text with an ID of 'i5'.</P>
```

CSS1 Property Summary

The following is a brief overview of all the CSS1 properties that can be applied to elements.

- background—This is a shorthand property for all the other background properties. The values can be written in any order:

  ```
  BODY {background: white url(bg41.gif) fixed center;}
  ```

- background-attachment—This property specifies whether or not the background image is to scroll with the element. It is generally only applied to the root element (or the BODY element in an HTML document) as it makes little sense with most other elements. Allowed values are scroll and fixed.

  ```
  BODY {background-attachment: scroll;}
  ```

- background-color—This property sets the background color of an element. This background color extends out to the edge of the element's border.

  ```
  H4 {background-color: white;}
  ```

- background-image—This property sets an image to be the background pattern. In conjunction with the other background properties, the image may be tiled or might repeat in one direction only.

  ```
  BODY {background-image: url(../grafix/steel1.gif);}
  ```

- background-position—This property sets the starting position of the background color or image. If the property value is a color, the color fill continues from the set position. If the property value is an image, the first image is placed at the set position and its frequency of repetition is determined by background-repeat. Possible

18

values are `top`, `center`, `bottom` for the vertical position and `left`, `center`, `right` for the horizontal position, a length or a percentage.

        BODY {background-position: top center;}

- `background-repeat`—This property specifies how a background image is to be repeated. Allowed values are `repeat`, `repeat-x`, `repeat-y`, and `no-repeat`.

        BODY {background-repeat: no-repeat;}

- `border`—This is a shorthand property that defines the width (see `border-width`), color (see `border-color`), and style (see `border-style`) of the border on all sides of an element.

        H1 {border: 2px dashed tan;}

- `border-bottom`—This is a shorthand property that defines the width, the color, and the style of the bottom border of an element.

        UL {border-bottom: 0.5in grooved green;}

- `border-bottom-width`—This property sets the width of the bottom border of an element. The border inherits the element's background but it may have a foreground of its own (see `border-style`). Negative values are not allowed. Allowed values are `thin`, `medium`, `thick`, or a length.

        UL {border-bottom-width: 1in;}

- `border-color`—This property sets the foreground color of the border on all sides of an element (see `border-style`). The border inherits the element's background.

        H1 {border-color: blue; border-style: solid;}

- `border-left`—This is a shorthand property that defines the width, the color, and the style of the left border of an element.

        P {border-left: 3em solid gray;}

- `border-left-width`—This property sets the width of the left border of an element. The border inherits the element's background, but it may have a foreground of its own (see `border-style`). Negative values are not allowed. Allowed values are `thin`, `medium`, `thick`, or a length.

        P {border-left-width: 3em;}

- `border-right`—This is a shorthand property that defines the width, the color, and the style of the right border of an element.

        IMG {border-right: 30px dotted blue;}

- `border-right-width`—This property sets the width of the right border of an element. The border inherits the element's background, but it may have a foreground of its own (see `border-style`). Negative values aren't allowed. Allowed values are `thin`, `medium`, `thick`, or a length.

        IMG {border-right-width: .5in;}

- `border-style`—This property sets the style of the border on all sides of an element. Allowed values are `none`, `dotted`, `dashed`, `solid`, `double`, `groove`, `ridge`, `inset`, and `outset`. The color is set by `border-color`.

      H1 {border-style: solid; border-color: red;}

- `border-top`—This is a shorthand property that defines the width, the color, and the style of the top border of an element.

      UL {border-top: 0.5in solid black;}

- `border-top-width`—This property sets the width of the top border of an element. The border inherits the element's background, but it may have a foreground of its own (see `border-style`). Negative values are not allowed. Allowed values are `thin`, `medium`, `thick`, or a length.

      UL {border-top-width: 0.5in;}

- `border-width`—This property sets the width of the border on all sides of an element. The border inherits the element's background, but it may have a foreground of its own (see `border-style`). Negative values are not allowed. Allowed values are `thin`, `medium`, `thick`, or a length.

      H1 {border-width: 2ex;}

- `clear`—This property specifies which floating elements (if any) can be positioned on each side of the element (see also `float`). Possible values are `left`, `right`, `both`, and `none`.

      H1 {clear: both;}

- `color`—This property sets the color of a given element. For text, this sets the text color; for other elements, such as a horizontal line (`HR`), it sets the foreground color.

      STRONG {color: red;}

- `display`—This property classifies elements into broad categories. The most common value is `none`, but is useful when it's set to `list-item` (see the '`list-style-`' properties). Allowed values are `block`, `inline`, `list-item`, and `none`.

      .hide {display: none;}

- `first-letter`—This pseudo-element applies to the first letter in an element. This property can be used to generate such things as drop cap effects and should only be applied to block-level elements.

      P:first-letter {color: red;}
      <P>The letter 'T' at the beginning of this element is
    ➥red.</P>

18

- first-line—This is a pseudo-element that applies to the first displayed line of text in an element. If you resize the window and the first line is wrapped onto a second line, the line's properties will stay as you set them. This property should only be applied to block-level elements.

```
P:first-line {color: red;}
<P>The first line of this element will be red.
The second and other lines will be unaffected.</P>
```

- float—This property sets the float characteristics for an element (see also clear). This property is often applied to images to allow text to flow around them, but it can be specified for any element. Possible values are left, right, and none.

```
IMG {float: left;}
```

- font—This is a shorthand property for all the other font properties. The order of the values is important, and must be as follows:

```
font {font-style font-variant font-weight font-size/
➥line-height font-family;}
```

Any of these properties can be omitted. As well as naming a specific font, you can specify a generic family, which is either serif (Times), sans-serif (Arial or Helvetica), cursive (Zapf-Chancery), fantasy (Western), or monospace (Courier).

```
P {font: bold 12pt/14pt Helvetica,sans-serif;}
```

- font-family—This property declares a specific font to be used, or a generic font family, or both. To cover systems where a font may not be present, you can specify more than one font in order of priority from left to right.

```
P {font-family: Arial,Helvetica,sans-serif;}
```

- font-size—This property sets the size of the font. The size can be an absolute size (xx-small, x-small, small, medium, large, x-large, or xx-large), a relative size (larger or smaller), a length, or a percentage.

```
H2 {font-size: 200%;}
H3 {font-size: 36pt;}
```

- font-style—This property selects the character style. Possible values are italic, oblique, and normal.

```
EM {font-style: italic;}
```

- font-variant—In CSS1 this property has two values: small-caps and normal.

```
H3 {font-variant: small-caps;}
```

- font-weight—This property sets the weight of a font, making it heavier or lighter. Possible values are normal, bold, bolder, lighter, 100, 200, 300, 400, 500, 600, 700, 800, and 900. The names are relative; the numerical values are absolute, but because not all fonts have nine weights, the closest weight may be chosen.

  ```
  B {font-weight: 500;}
  ```

- height—This property sets the height of an element. This is generally applied to images, but can be used on any block-level or replaced element. Negative values are not allowed. The height can be a length, a percentage, or the keyword auto (which is the default).

  ```
  IMG.icon {height: 50px;}
  ```

- important—This property declares that a style specification is important. Important specifications override any other declarations, regardless of their origin or specificity.

  ```
  H1 {color: red ! important;}
  ```

- letter-spacing—This property sets the amount of whitespace between letters (any displayed characters). Possible values are normal or a length.

  ```
  P {letter-spacing: 0.5em;}
  ```

- line-height—This property sets the vertical distance between baselines in an element. Negative values are not permitted. Possible values are normal, a number (which is multiplied by the font's number size, see font-size), a length, or a percentage.

  ```
  P {line-height: 18pt;}
  H2 {line-height: 200%;}
  ```

- list-style—This is a shorthand property for all the other list-style properties. The values apply to all elements with a display value of list-item (see display).

  ```
  UL {list-style: square url(sqbullet.gif) outer;}
  ```

- list-style-image—This property specifies an image to be used as the bullet in an unordered or ordered list. The value applies to elements with a display value of list-item.

  ```
  UL {list-style-image: url(bullet3.gif);}
  ```

- list-style-position—This property specifies the position of the bullet or number in an unordered or ordered list with respect to the content of the list item. The value applies to elements with a display value of list-item. Possible values are inside or outside, with outside being the default. If the value inside is used, the lines wrap under the marker instead of being indented.

  ```
  LI {list-style-position: outside;}
  ```

18

- list-style-type—This property specifies the type of bullet or numbering system to be used in an unordered or ordered list. The value applies to elements with a display value of list-item. Possible values are disc, circle, square, decimal (1,2,3), lower-roman (i,ii,iii) upper-roman (I,II,III), lower-alpha (a,b,c), upper-alpha (A,B,C), and none.

      UL {list-style-type: square;}
      OL {list-style-type: lower-roman;}

- margin—This property sets the size of the overall margin around an element. Negative values are allowed, but the contents of the element may then be obscured.

      H1 {margin: 2ex;}

- margin-bottom—This property sets the size of the margin below an element. Negative values are allowed, but the contents of the element may then be obscured.

      UL {margin-bottom: 0.5in;}

- margin-left—This property sets the size of the margin on the left of an element. Negative values are permitted, but be careful not to position the element beyond the edge of the window.

      P {margin-left: 3em;}

- margin-right—This property sets the size of the margin on the right of an element. Negative values are permitted, but be careful not to position the element beyond the edge of the window.

      IMG {margin-right: 30px;}

- margin-top—This property sets the size of the margin above an element. Negative values are allowed, but the contents of the element may then be obscured.

      UL {margin-top: 0.5in;}

- padding—This property sets the size of the padding on all sides of an element. The padding inherits the element's background. Negative values are not allowed.

      H1 {padding: 2ex;}

- padding-bottom—This property sets the size of the padding below an element. The padding inherits the element's background. Negative values are not allowed.

      UL {padding-bottom: 0.5in;}

- padding-left—This property sets the size of the padding on the left of an element. The padding inherits the element's background. Negative values are not allowed.

      P {padding-left: 3em;}

- padding-right—This property sets the size of the padding on the right of an element. The padding inherits the element's background. Negative values are not allowed.

    ```
    IMG {padding-right: 30px;}
    ```

- padding-top—This property sets the size of the padding below an element. The padding inherits the element's background. Negative values are not allowed.

    ```
    UL {padding-top: 0.5in;}
    ```

- text-align—This property sets the horizontal alignment of the text in an element. Possible values are left, right, center, and justify. The property can only be applied to block-level elements.

    ```
    P {text-align: justify;}
    H4 {text-align: center;}
    ```

- text-decoration—This property sets certain effects for the text, such as underline and blink. Possible values are none, underline, overline, line-through, and blink. You can combine values.

    ```
    STRONG {text-decoration: underline;}
    .old {text-decoration: line-through;}
    ```

- text-indent—This property sets the indentation of the first line in an element. The property only applies to block-level elements. Negative values are allowed.

    ```
    P {text-indent: 5em;}
    H2 {text-indent: -25px;}
    ```

- text-transform—This property changes the case of the letters in an element, regardless of how the original text was typed. Possible values are none, capitalize, uppercase, and lowercase.

    ```
    H1 {text-transform: lowercase;}
    .title {text-transform: capitalize;}
    ```

- vertical-align—This property sets the vertical alignment of an element's baseline with respect to its parent element's line-height. This property can only be applied to inline elements (such as table cells). Negative values are allowed. Possible values are baseline, sub, super, top, text-top, middle, bottom, text-bottom, or a percentage.

    ```
    SUP {vertical-align: super;}
    .fnote {vertical-align: 50%;}
    ```

18

- white-space—This property defines how whitespace (spaces, tabs, and so on) within an element is to be treated. Possible values are normal (collapse multiple spaces into one), pre (don't collapse multiple spaces), nowrap (don't allow line wrapping without a <BR> tag).

```
DL {white-space: nowrap;}
DD {white-space: pre;}
```

- width—This property sets the width of an element. The property is normally only applied to images, but it can be used on any block-level or replaced element. Negative values are not allowed. The width can be a length, a percentage, or the keyword auto (which is the default).

```
TABLE {width: 80%;}
```

- word-spacing—This property sets the amount of whitespace between words (strings of characters surrounded by whitespace). Possible values are normal or a length.

```
P {word-spacing: 0.5em;}
```

Summary

This lesson has shown you how to modify your XML and attach CSS style sheets to it so it can be displayed in current Web browsers. Although the modifications are rather rough and ready, so are the browsers themselves. To prepare you for things to come, you have also seen how, with a little cut-and-paste work on the sample code given here, you can easily put an XSL style sheet together that will allow you to convert your XML elements into HTML elements and attach CSS style properties to the resulting HTML elements.

It is to be expected that more rugged, more conforming versions of these browsers will become available soon, and that their support for XML and XSL will be more complete. In the meantime, however, this chapter has given you enough information to experiment for yourself.

Q&A

Q With DSSSL and XSL around, why bother with CSS at all?

A DSSSL is more of a processing language than a style language. XSL has not yet been fully specified and will not be supported for quite a while. CSS is the lowest common denominator of all style languages, but it is also the best supported. In the short term, rendering XML using CSS can be a viable alternative to waiting.

Q Why XSL *and* CSS? Surely one style language is enough.

A CSS is designed for use with HTML. XSL is designed for use with XML. XML is not intended to replace HTML (although it might), and XSL is not intended to replace CSS (although it probably will). XML needs to be backward compatible and so it also has to support CSS properties, but CSS still provides a quicker and much simpler way of attaching style to HTML elements. However, possible Microsoft extensions to CSS (such as CSS behaviors) may lead to CSS continuing in a niche of its own.

Q What is to be gained from mixing XML elements with HTML elements in the same document?

A Web browsers are hardwired to recognize HTML tags and render the text that follows accordingly. You can trick a browser into applying its default formatting to XML elements by using the names of HTML elements. This saves you from having to explicitly specify the style.

Exercises

1. Pick a simple XML document of your own. Make sure it is simple; it's very easy to underestimate the amount of time you'll waste in experimenting. Create a style sheet for displaying it in IE5.

2. Now take the same document and create a style sheet for displaying the file in Mozilla.

3. Look again at your XML document and think about whether it could more easily have been coded in a semantic HTML (using attributes to identify elements). Limiting yourself to just the display aspects, which would have been easier to work with, the XML code or the HTML code? What effect would your choice have on the portability of your code?

18

DAY 19

Converting XML with DSSSL

In yesterday's lesson I traced the path of the development of XML style languages from CSS (the most simple), through DSSSL (the most complex) and on through DSSSL-o, XS, XSL1, and XSL2. You learned how to use CSS style sheets to render XML code so that it can be displayed in a Web browser, either as real XML code, wrapped in HTML code, or a hybrid mix of both XML elements and HTML tags. Today we will continue journeying through the style languages. Today you will learn

- The basics of DSSSL as supported by jade, the public domain DSSSL engine created by James Clark

- How to put together a simple, free, development environment to run jade and process XML code

- How to write basic DSSSL stylesheets to convert XML code into HTML, RTF (Microsoft Word), and MIF (FrameMaker interchange format)

Where DSSSL Fits In

It is no exaggeration to say that DSSSL (pronounced *dissle*) is complex. To do anything serious with DSSSL you need a fair familiarity with not just the programming language LISP, but a specific dialect of LISP called Scheme. You could probably cram the world's supply of Scheme programmers into one small room.

It isn't easy to learn DSSSL because there's next to no documentation other than the drafts of the ISO standard. In June 1997 a volunteer project to create a DSSSL handbook was begun on the DSSSL Internet mailing list, the address of which is given in Appendix B, but it hasn't produced much so far (volunteers are welcome).

The complexity of DSSSL (compounded by the fact that it describes two languages and not just one—the transformation language and the style language) very quickly led to an attempt to create a simplified version called *DSSSL-Lite*. DSSSL-Lite, in its turn, gave rise to an Internet variation of DSSSL called DSSSL-o (short for DSSSL-online).

The very first version of the XML style language (then called XS) was based very heavily on DSSSL-o, and the available DSSSL-o software was slowly being adapted to accommodate XS, which made migration very simple.

XS was adapted, HTML additions were brought in to make it more compatible with existing CSS styles, and a lot of the DSSSL-o features were removed. The syntax was radically different, but the conceptual model was still the one inherited from DSSSL. This all resulted in the first version of XSL.

In August 1998, a revised and very incomplete revision of the language was released as a Working Draft. This version of XSL still uses the same processing model as DSSSL but, again, the syntax is radically different. New software tools are already starting to appear (you will learn to use the first of them on Day 20, "Rendering XML with XSL"), but it is clear that it will be quite some time before XSL has stabilized and even longer before it is widely supported by tools and browsers.

XSL is still in a state of flux. Meantime, DSSSL hasn't gone away and the jade package is just as good as it ever was. If anything, it just goes from strength to strength because the latest release (1.2) includes a `mif` backend that can convert SGML and XML code (and therefore, by definition, HTML code too) into the Maker Interchange Format. The Maker Interchange Format that can be read directly by Adobe's FrameMaker and Frame+SGML high-end DTP software packages.

A DSSSL Development Environment

I have already mentioned jade, James Clark's DSSSL engine. If you are using Microsoft Windows, you can build yourself an almost perfect free development environment using the following software packages (for other platforms you may need to compile the jade source code, which is also freely available):

- jade—This package can be downloaded from James Clark's Web site at `http://www.jclark.com/jade`.

- PFE (programmers' file editor)—This package can be downloaded from the author Alan Philips' site at Lancaster University in England at `http://www.lancs.ac.uk/people/cpaap/pfe/pfefiles.htm`.

  PFE is much more than a text editor (although it excels at that too). It can do a lot of extremely useful things like recording key strokes, matching brackets, executing a DOS command and capturing the result in a window, and a lot more.

When I am experimenting with DSSSL code (the only way to learn!), I load the source code (XML, SGML, or even HTML) into one text window. I load the DSSSL style sheet into a second window and then I load the jade error output file into a third window. I then use a command line window to enter the jade commands (see Figure 19.1). I use 4NT because it is far more powerful than any of its competitors (you can find 4NT via `http://www.jpsoft.com`), but you can just as easily use a standard MS-DOS command prompt window. Note that for technical reasons this screen capture is made at a resolution of only 800×600; at my normal 1152×864 you see a lot more of the file contents.

PFE is able to recognize when the jade error log file changes. I keep to a standard `error.log` name for this file to make it easier to clean up afterwards. After running a jade command, switching back to PFE prompts you to reload the error log file. You can easily track down any errors by toggling the PFE file display to show the line numbers in the problem file.

Of course, this isn't the only environment. If you're prepared to spend some time getting it all set up, EMACS has a DSSSL mode but its use, while extremely powerful in skilled hands, is not something for the faint hearted.

Installing jade

There isn't much to installing jade. The first step is simply to unpack the ZIP archive (assuming that you download an executable; if you are downloading source code you will have to consult the jade documentation for build instructions) into its own directory and make sure that `jade.exe` is added to your path.

19

FIGURE 19.1

*A DSSSL development
environment using
jade, PFE, and 4NT.*

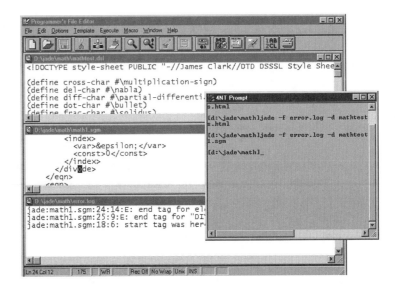

Running jade

jade is, as you probably gathered from Figure 19.1, a command-line program; it doesn't
have any user interface with menus and dialog boxes to enter all the parameters.

Before running jade, you should copy the `catalog` file (supplied in the jade distribution)
and edit the entries to reflect the location of the jade support files on your computer.

If any of the SGML or XML files that you will be processing reference a DTD by means
of a PUBLIC identifier, you will also have to add an entry for each of them. An example
of a modified catalog file is shown in Listing 19.1.

LISTING 19.1   A SAMPLE catalog FILE FOR JADE

```
 1: PUBLIC "-//James Clark//DTD DSSSL Flow Object Tree//EN"
 2:      "d:\jade\fot.dtd"
 3: PUBLIC "ISO/IEC 10179:1996//DTD DSSSL Architecture//EN"
 4:      "d:\jade\dsssl.dtd"
 5: PUBLIC "-//James Clark//DTD DSSSL Style Sheet//EN"
 6:      "d:\jade\style-sheet.dtd"
 7: PUBLIC "-//IETF//DTD HTML Strict//EN" "d:\jade\html-s.dtd"
 8: PUBLIC "-//W3C//DTD HTML 3.2//EN" "d:\jade\html32.dtd"
 9: PUBLIC "ISO 8879-1986//ENTITIES Added Latin 1//EN//HTML"
10:      "d:\jade\ISOLat1.sgm"
11: PUBLIC "-//Free Text Project//DTD Play//EN"
12:      "d:\jade\work\play.dtd"
```

ANALYSIS The first three lines of the catalog file are essential; without these lines jade simply won't output anything but a long list of errors. The other lines are all optional—one for each PUBLIC DTD declaration you will encounter (this saves you the trouble of having to edit every file to change the document type declaration into a SYSTEM identifier).

> **Tip** The easiest way to ensure that you put the correct entry in the catalog file is to open the XML file in question, copy the part of the document type declaration starting with the keyword PUBLIC, and paste it directly into the catalog file. You can then add the path to the file containing the DTD.

The following are some typical commands you will need for running jade:

This command converts an HTML file into RTF (Microsoft Word 97):

```
jade -f error.log -t rtf -d html32hc.dsl -o simon.rtf simon.html
```

The DSSSL style sheet html32hc.dsl is distributed with jade, and is a good style sheet for general purpose HTML to RTF conversion. It even adds a table of contents to the RTF file (to update the page number entries, press Control + End, press Control + A, and then press F9).

This command converts an XML file into MIF (FrameMaker Interchange Format):

```
jade -f error.log -t mif -wxml -d simon.dsl -o simon.rtf simon.xml
```

Note the additional -wxml parameter. Jade is really designed to work with SGML files and it will complain about the missing tag minimization characters in the XML DTD if you don't use this parameter. Generally, these errors are just a nuisance and can be ignored but it is better to be safe than sorry. This parameter only applies if the XML document is valid (there is an SGML parser hidden inside jade). If your XML document is only well-formed and not necessarily valid, or if you just want to skip the validation step, use the -wno-valid parameter instead.

This command converts an XML file into HTML:

```
jade -f error.log -t sgml -wno-valid -d simon.dsl
simon.xml > simon.html
```

Note that this time you will have to pipe the output (using the > character) to the output file.

19

This command converts an HTML file into XML:

```
jade -f error.log -t xml -d simon.dsl simon.html > simon.xml
```

Now that you've got the basics of the jade command line, let's look at the official meanings of these command-line parameters (these are also explained in the jade documentation):

- -c *catalog_file*—An alternative to copying the catalog file (described earlier) to the directory in which you are going to run jade is to specify the path to the catalog file with this parameter.

- -d *dsssl_spec*—This parameter gives the path to the DSSSL style specification (style sheet) to be used.

NEW TERM   Officially the file that contains the DSSSL formatting instructions is a *style sheet* that contains one or more DSSSL style specifications. In jade the style sheet is actually an SGML document that conforms to the style sheet DTD.

To avoid confusing you with too many terms, I'm simply going to use the term DSSSL style sheet throughout the rest of this chapter. Our style sheets will only contain one style specification and, because the DTD allows all of the element start and end tags in a style sheet to be omitted, you won't ever have to worry about the difference.

- -f *log_file*—This parameter gives the name of the file to which error messages are to be written.

- -G—This switch enables debug mode. When an error occurs in the evaluation of an expression, jade displays a stack trace. You will probably find this doesn't help much until you've gained quite a bit of experience using jade. (There are also some more powerful DSSSL debugging functions on the Web that will give you much more useful information.)

- -t *output_type*—This parameter specifies the type of output to be created, where *output_type* is one of the following keywords:

    fot—An XML representation of the flow object tree.

    Rtf or rtf-95: Microsoft's Rich Text Format—rtf-95 produces output optimized for Word 95 rather than Word 97.

    tex—TeX.

    sgml—SGML (used for SGML-SGML transformations).

    xml—XML (used for SGML-to-XML transformations).

- -o *output_file*—This parameter tells jade to write its output to the named *output_file* instead of the default. The default filename is the name of the last input file with its extension replaced by the name of the type of output (rtf, mif, and so on). If there is no input filename, the extension is added onto the name jade-out.

- -V *variable*—This parameter allows you to set the value of the named variable to true. For example, in the DSSSL style sheet that accompanies Jon Bosak's distribution of Shakespeare's plays in XML form (you can download these for free from http://www.hypermedic.com/style/shakespeare/index.htm) you can specify -V fm to toggle the display of the front matter (the fm element); this content is normally skipped.

- -w—This parameter allows you to specify some XML processing options:

  -wxml switches jade to XML processing mode.

  -wno-valid tells jade that the XML document doesn't have to be valid (the document always has to be well-formed).

jade Error Messages

jade does its best to identify any errors it finds. Listing 19.2 shows an example of a set of output error messages.

OUTPUT   **LISTING 19.2**   JADE ERROR OUTPUT

```
1:  jade:test.xml:7:0:E: DTD did not contain element
➥declaration for document type name
2:  jade:test.xml:9:5:E: element "test" undefined
3:  jade:test.xml:10:10:E: element "a" undefined
4:  jade:test.xml:11:7:E: ID "a1" already defined
5:  jade:test.xml:10:7: ID "a1" first defined here
6:  jade:test.xml:11:10:E: element "b" undefined
7:  jade:test.xml:12:2:E: required attribute "id" not specified
8:  jade:test.xml:12:2:E: element "b" undefined
9:  jade:test.xml:12:28:E: end tag for "b" omitted, but OMITTAG NO
➥was specified
10: jade:test.xml:12:0: start tag was here
11: jade:test.xml:12:28:E: end tag for "b" omitted, but OMITTAG NO
➥was specified
12: jade:test.xml:11:0: start tag was here
13: jade:test.xml:12:28:E: end tag for "a" omitted, but OMITTAG NO
➥was specified
14: jade:test.xml:10:0: start tag was here
15: jade:test.xml:12:28:E: end tag for "test" omitted, but OMITTAG NO
➥was specified
16: jade:test.xml:9:0: start tag was here
```

19

ANALYSIS The error message (see Listing 19.2) gives

- The program (usually jade in this case) that detected the error.
- The name of the file containing the error.
- The number of the line containing the error (this won't always be correct—sometimes it will be impossible for jade to correctly determine where the error *started*—but the description if the error will probably help you to localize it).
- An error code: E for an error (processing will stop), W for a warning (processing will continue, but the output may be useless), I for an information message (you did something wrong, but this is just additional information; an information message often accompanies a warning message), X for an execution error (a serious problem has occurred with jade itself), and nothing (this indicates that something wrong was detected but it is not so serious as to interrupt processing).
- The column (character) number. Again, this won't always be correct. Sometimes it will be impossible for jade to correctly determine where the error *started*, but the description of the error will probably help you to localize it.
- A description of the error.

Viewing jade Output

Obviously, if you are going to convert your XML code into a different format, you must have the matching software on your computer: rtf (Microsoft Word or the free Word Viewer), mif (Adobe FrameMaker or Frame+SGML), html (any Web browser) or tex (a suitable TeX package). This could prove expensive and does force you to keep loading the output file each time (Microsoft Word won't even let you create a new RTF file if the old one is still open).

Fujitsu Labs have released a wonderful package called HyBrick that solves all of these problems. Using this package, you can view the output on your screen (see Figure 19.2). Of course, you still need a development environment. HyBrick can be downloaded from `http://collie.fujitsu.com/hybrick/`. This is a beta test version but is extremely stable. I'm told that they are working on a new version and have plans to support XSL soon.

First Steps in Using jade

Before we get involved in the theory of DSSSL styles, and to convince you that this isn't as difficult as it first seems, let's try a few simple examples.

FIGURE 19.2

*Fujistsu's HyBrick
DSSSL rendering
package.*

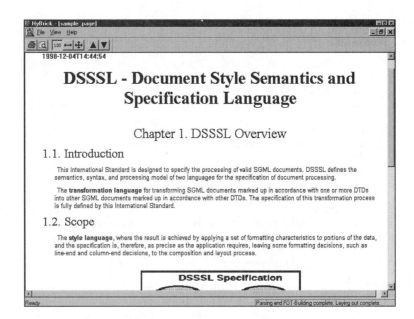

XML to RTF and MIF Conversion

As a first exercise, lets convert a simple XML file into RTF. The XML input file is shown in Listing 19.3.

INPUT **LISTING 19.3** A SIMPLE XML FILE FOR JADE

```
 1: <?xml version="1.0"?>
 2: <!DOCTYPE test [
 3: <!ELEMENT test  (a ¦ b)*>
 4: <!ELEMENT a     (#PCDATA)>
 5: <!ELEMENT b     (#PCDATA)>
 6: ]>
 7: <test>
 8: <a>This is a test</a>
 9: <b>This is also a test</b>
10: <b>And this is another test</b>
11: </test>
```

ANALYSIS As you can see, it's a very simple XML file indeed, using an internal DTD subset to avoid any difficulty with filenames and paths. Now let's try a simple DSSSL style sheet. Have a look at Listing 19.4.

19

INPUT **LISTING 19.4**   A BASIC DSSSL STYLE SHEET FOR XML-RTF CONVERSION

```
1:  <!DOCTYPE style-sheet PUBLIC
2:     "-//James Clark//DTD DSSSL Style Sheet//EN">
3:  (define *rgb-color-space*
4:     (color-space "ISO/IEC 10179:1996//Color-Space Family::Device RGB"))
5:
6:  (define *blue*
7:     (color *rgb-color-space* 0 0 1))
8:
9:  (define *red*
10:    (color *rgb-color-space* 1 0 0))
11:
12: (root                          ;set up the page geometry
13:     (make simple-page-sequence  ;as a simple page
14:     page-width:      8.5in   ;with characteristics
15:         page-height:    11in
16:         top-margin:     1in
17:         bottom-margin:  1in
18:         left-margin:    1in
19:         right-margin:   1in
20:         (process-children))) ;process the content of document
21:
22: (element test
23:     (process-children))
24:
25: (element a
26:     (make paragraph      ; make a paragraph
27:             font-size:      24pt
28:             color:          *blue*
29:             quadding:       'center
30:             space-before:   10pt
31:             line-spacing:   20pt))
32:
33: (element b
34:     (make paragraph    ; make another paragraph
35:             font-size:      18pt
36:             color:          *red*
37:             line-spacing:   30pt))
```

ANALYSIS   It isn't a particularly simple style sheet because it uses colors and the color definitions are something unique to jade. Fortunately, you don't even really have to
understand how the mechanism works.

Note

If you want to color a particular element, all you have to do is declare the color space and then declare the colors that you want to use using the R (red), G (green), and B (blue) values. I use *red* and *blue* for the names of the colors because the asterisks make it easier to find the values when you're changing the style sheet.

Figure 19.3 shows the output RTF file loaded in Microsoft Word.

OUTPUT

FIGURE 19.3

The converted XML file loaded in Microsoft Word.

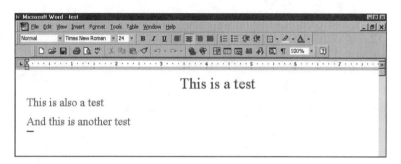

Converting this into MIF format is as simple as changing the `-t rtf` parameter into `-t mif` and then loading the output file into FrameMaker, as demonstrated in Figure 19.4.

OUTPUT

FIGURE 19.4

The converted XML file loaded in Adobe FrameMaker+SGML.

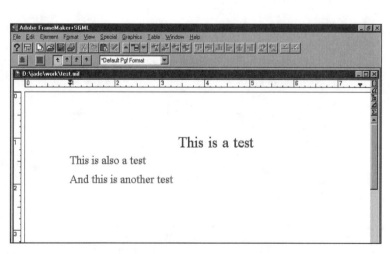

19

XML to HTML Conversion

Converting XML code to HTML code looks pretty scary at first. Fortunately, you don't need to understand a lot of the more complicated code—all you really need to do is copy it as it stands and paste it into your own style sheet. Listing 19.5 shows the XML file we're going to convert.

INPUT   **LISTING 19.5**   XML FILE FOR CONVERSION TO HTML

```
1:  <?xml version="1.0">
2:  <!DOCTYPE DOC [
3:  <!ELEMENT DOC   (TITLE | NOTE | PARA)*>
4:  <!ELEMENT TITLE (#PCDATA)>
5:  <!ELEMENT NOTE (#PCDATA)>
6:  <!ELEMENT PARA (#PCDATA)>
7:  ]>
8:  <DOC>
9:  <TITLE>Simple XML to HTML Conversion</TITLE>
10: <PARA>This sample documents demonstrates not only
11: how you can map XML elements onto HTML elements, but
12: also how you can set attributes as well.</PARA>
13: <NOTE>Note that this paragraph will be set in a
14: different color.</NOTE>
15: <PARA>This second paragraph proves that we have restricted
16: the color change to just the one note paragraph.</PARA>
17: </DOC>
```

ANALYSIS   Basically, what we have to do is map each of the XML elements onto an appropriate HTML element. Some of the mappings are pretty obvious; TITLE to H1 and PARA to P, but the NOTE element gives us a chance to do something more adventurous. Take a look at the DSSSL style sheet shown in Listing 19.6.

INPUT   **LISTING 19.6**   A DSSSL STYLE SHEET FOR XML TO HTML CONVERSION

```
1:  <!DOCTYPE style-sheet PUBLIC
2:     "-//James Clark//DTD DSSSL Style Sheet//EN"[
3:  <!ENTITY lt "&#38;#60;">
4:  <!ENTITY gt "&#62;">
5:  ]>
6:
7:  (declare-flow-object-class element
8:    "UNREGISTERED::James Clark//Flow Object Class::element")
9:  (declare-flow-object-class document-type
10:    "UNREGISTERED::James Clark//Flow Object Class::document-type")
11: (declare-flow-object-class empty-element
12:    "UNREGISTERED::James Clark//Flow Object Class::empty-element")
```

```
13: (declare-flow-object-class formatting-instruction
14: "UNREGISTERED::James Clark//Flow Object
15:             Class::formatting-instruction")
16:
17: (element DOC
18:   (sosofo-append
19:    (make document-type
20:      name:  "HTML"
21:      public-id: "-//W3C//DTD HTML 3.2//EN")
22:        (make element
23:          gi:  "HTML"
24:            (sosofo-append
25:              (make element
26:                gi:  "HEAD"
27:                  (make element
28:                    gi:  "TITLE"
29:                      (sosofo-append
30:                        (literal "Simple XML-to-HTML Conversion")
31:                       )))
32:              (make element
33:                gi:  "BODY"
34:                (process-children))))))
35:
36: (element TITLE
37:   (make element gi: "H1"))
38:
39: (element NOTE (make element gi: "P"
40:     (sosofo-append (literal "Note: "))
41:     (make element
42:       gi: "font"
43:       attributes: '(("COLOR" "RED")))))
44:
45: (element PARA  (make element gi: "P" ))
```

19

ANALYSIS You can ignore the four flow object declarations; these are non-standard DSSSL extensions incorporated into jade to allow us to do things like SGML-SGML and XML-HTML conversions. You also can more or less ignore the specification for the DOC element—this part simply writes out the DTD declaration, the HEAD and TITLE elements, and wraps the rest of the document inside an HTML and a BODY element. The most important declaration you need to remember is this one (Web browsers are so tolerant of bad HTML you could probably get acceptable results by adding one of the statements for each of the XML elements and ignoring the rest of the style sheet):

```
(element xml.element (make element gi: "html.element"))
```

where *xml.element* is the XML element you want to convert and *html.element* is the HTML element you want it to become. Conversion from XML to HTML really can be as easy as that! Listing 19.7 shows the HTML code resulting from the conversion.

OUTPUT **LISTING 19.7** THE CONVERTED XML FILE

```
 1: <!DOCTYPE HTML PUBLIC "-//W3C//DTD HTML 3.2//EN">
 2: <HTML
 3: ><HEAD
 4: ><TITLE
 5: >Simple XML-to-HTML Conversion</TITLE
 6: ></HEAD
 7: ><BODY
 8: ><H1
 9: >Simple XML to HTML Conversion</H1
10: ><P
11: >This sample documents demonstrates not only
12: how you can map XML elements onto HTML elements, but
13: also how you can set attributes as well.</P
14: ><P
15: >Note: <font
16: COLOR="RED"
17: >Note that this paragraph will be set in a different color.</font
18: ></P
19: ><P
20: >This second paragraph proves that we have restricted
21: the color change to just the one note paragraph.</P
22: ></BODY
23: ></HTML
24: >
```

The Web browser's display is shown in Figure 19.5.

OUTPUT

FIGURE 19.5

The converted XML file loaded in Netscape Communicator.

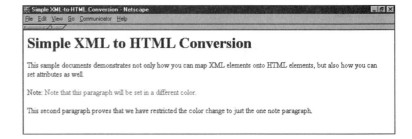

ANALYSIS It's an odd quirk of jade's to break the HTML tags over separate lines, but this has absolutely no effect on the way a Web browser treats the file. Note how the NOTE element from the XML file has been converted into an HTML P element, complete with a prefix text and a color change.

Basic DSSSL

You have already seen some of DSSSL in practice. Now it's time to cover some of the theory. Bear with me; once you get into the theory DSSSL can be very hard to explain and even harder to understand. Don't worry, though; even if you only partially understand what follows you should still grasp enough to build some extremely powerful style sheets. If it all seems too abstract, don't worry either—I'll conclude this chapter with several more practical examples that you can mimic or just copy.

Flow Objects

The basic building block of DSSSL style sheets are called flow objects. Flow objects are presentational objects that end up in the output document. These flow objects can be things like paragraphs, pages, sequences of characters, or elements and attributes.

Each flow object has a display characteristic that determines whether it is displayed (starts on a new line) or is inlined (runs into the container of previous element). In addition, depending on what they are, flow objects have other characteristics such as page margins, font sizes, heights, and widths.

Flow objects are international in nature so that a single style sheet can be used to format documents in natural languages with different writing directions. It is because of this that things like indentations are always given as start and end values rather than as left or right values to reflect the fact that not everyone writes from left to right.

Not all the DSSSL flow object classes are supported by jade. The following ones are:

19

- scroll—A scroll flow object class is used as the top-level flow object for an online display that doesn't divide the output into pages (such as an HTML document). It accepts displayed flow objects. The viewing environment determines the size of the flow object in the direction perpendicular (sideways) to the filling direction (downwards).

- paragraph—A paragraph flow object class represents a paragraph. Its contents may be either inlined or displayed. Inline flow objects are formatted to produce line areas. Displayed flow objects implicitly specify a line break, and their areas are added to the resulting sequence of areas. The paragraph flow object class is the basic flow object for formatting blocks of text.

- paragraph-break—Used with the paragraph-break flow object class, a paragraph flow object class can represent a sequence of paragraphs. The paragraphs are separated by paragraph-break flow objects, which are atomic. Paragraph-break flow objects are allowed only in paragraph flow objects. All the characteristics that apply to a paragraph flow object are also applicable to a paragraph-break flow object. The characteristics of a paragraph-break flow object determine the formatting for the portion of the content of the paragraph flow object following that paragraph-break flow object up to the next paragraph-break flow object, if any.

- character—A character flow object class is formatted to produce a single inline area (character flow objects may only be inlined). The area can be merged with adjacent inline areas. You'd use a character flow object to give a string of characters a different layout or different characteristics from the paragraph in which it is located.

- line-field—The line-field flow object class is inlined and has inline content. It produces a single inline area. The width of this area is equal to the value of the field-width characteristic. If the content of the line-field area can't fit in this width, the area grows to accommodate the content. If the line-field occurs in the paragraph, there's a break after the line-field. You can use these objects to create fixed-width prefixes for items in a list, so that the start of the first character after the prefix doesn't depend on the size of the prefix. This flow object class is useful for things like prefix text in front of indented paragraphs.

- external-graphic—The external-graphic flow object class is used for graphics in an external entity (graphics imported by reference). Flow objects of this class may be inlined or displayed.

- horizontal-rule and vertical-rule—These rule flow object classes specify horizontal rules and vertical rules; they may be inlined or displayed.

- score—The score flow object class is used for underlining and ruling through (scoring) characters.

- embedded-text—The embedded-text flow object class is used for embedding right-to-left text within left-to-right text, or vice-versa. This flow object can only be inlined.

- box—The box flow object class is used to put a box around a sequence of flow objects; this flow object can be either displayed or inlined. If the box is displayed, it accepts any displayed flow objects. If it's inlined, it accepts any inline flow objects.

A `box` flow object may result in more than one area, in which case the border of the box adjacent to the break may be omitted. If the box is inlined, this border is perpendicular to the writing-mode, but if it's displayed, this border is parallel to the writing-mode.

When the box is displayed, the size of the box (the distance between the positions of the borders) in the direction determined by the writing-mode is equal to the box's display size, less the start and end indents. The display size for the box's content is equal to the size of the box.

- `table`—A `table` flow object class contains either all of `table-part` or all of `table-column`, `table-row`, or `table-cell` flow objects. If it contains `table-column` flow objects, they must appear before all the other flow objects. A `table` flow object can only be displayed. A table has two directions associated with it: a row-progression direction and a column-progression direction.

- `table-part`—A `table-part` flow object class is allowed only within a `table` flow object. A `table-part` flow object consists of a table body, a table header, and a table footer. Only `table-column` flow objects are allowed in a table body. A `table-row` and a `table-cell` may be used anywhere in a `table-part`.

  The result of formatting a `table-part` flow object is a sequence of areas. Each area consists of the header's content (unless explicitly omitted), followed by some portion of the table body's content, followed by the table footer's content (unless explicitly omitted). Each row in the table body occurs exactly once, and the order of the rows is kept. The rows in the table header and footer are replicated for each result area (this allows the header to be repeated when a table is divided over more than one page).

- `table-column`—A `table-column` flow object class is an atomic flow object that specifies characteristics applicable to table cells that have the same column and span.

- `table-row`—A `table-row` flow object class groups table cells into rows; all table cells in a `table-row` start in the same geometric row. A `table-row` accepts `table-cell` flow objects. A `table-row` flow object can occur only as the child of a `table-part` or `table` flow object.

- `table-cell`—A `table-cell` flow object class accepts any flow object that can be displayed. A `table-cell` flow object may occur only as the child of a `table-row`, `table-part`, or `table` flow object. The table's width is equal to the sum of the cells' widths.

19

- table-border—A table-border flow object class is used to specify the border of a table cell or an entire table. However, a table-border flow object is not allowed in the content of any flow object. The width of borders doesn't affect the width of the cells, the positioning of the contents of the cells, the table's width, or the size of the area produced by the table.

- sequence—A sequence flow object class is formatted to concatenate the areas produced by each of its children, which can be either inlined or displayed. A sequence flow object is useful for specifying inherited characteristics. Another flow object accepts a sequence flow object only if it would accept each of the flow objects inside that sequence.

- display-group—A display-group flow object class concatenates other flow objects in the same way as sequence flow objects, but it also creates a new display area by starting on a new line and is followed by a new line (even if it has no content). These flow groups are used for controlling the positioning of groups of displayed flow objects.

- simple-page-sequence—A simple-page-sequence flow object class is formatted to produce a sequence of page areas. This flow object accepts any displayed flow object, but it isn't allowed within the content of any other flow object. You'd use this flow object for the root element of a document, or for any element that you want to start at the top of a new page.

  A simple-page-sequence flow object may have a single line header and footer containing text that's constant, except for a page number. A document can contain multiple simple-page-sequences. For example, each chapter of a document could be a separate simple-page-sequence, which would allow the chapter title to be used in a header or footer line.

  The page is filled from top to bottom. The display size for the contents of the simple-page-sequence is the page width, less the left and right margins.

- link—A link flow object class represents a hypertext link that can be interactively traversed, typically by clicking on the areas representing the flow object and its content. However, as you have seen, in XML you don't necessarily have to click on a link to traverse it. A link can contain both inlined and displayed flow objects. Link flow objects can be nested. If they are nested, the innermost link is effective.

DSSSL is easy enough that it's possible to make basic style sheets for simple XML DTDs just by learning the names of a few of these flow objects. All you have to do then is list their mappings in the style sheet to print through construction rules.

Flow Object Characteristics

A flow object is really just a formatting object—a typographic component like a paragraph, a table, an area, a mathematical equation, and so on. Flow objects have specific characteristics according to their nature (there's not much point in specifying a page size for a table!); for details of the characteristics, you should refer to the DSSSL-o specification or the DSSSL specification itself (both are freely available on the Web). However, most of the characteristics are pretty obvious (with the exception of *quadding*, which means the alignment). A summary of the most important flow object classes and their characteristics follows:

- `display`—space-before, space-after, keep-with-previous?, keep-with-next?
- `simple-page-sequence`—page-width, page-height, left-margin, right-margin, top-margin, bottom-margin, header-margin, footer-margin, left-header, center-header, right-header, left-footer, center-footer, right-footer
- `paragraph`—min-leading, line-spacing, first-line-start-indent, last-line-end-indent, font-family-name, font-name, font-size, font-weight, start-indent, end-indent, space-before, space-after, quadding
- `line-field`—field-width, field-align
- `sideline`—sideline-side, sideline-sep, color, line-cap, line-thickness
- `character`—font-family-name, font-name, font-weight, font-size
- `leader`—length
- `rule`—orientation, length, color, line-thickness, start-indent, end-indent, space-before, space-after
- `external-graphic`—scale, max-width, max-height, entity-system-id, notation-system-id, color, start-indent, end-indent, space-before, space-after, position-point-x, position-point-y
- `score`—type, color, line-thickness
- `box`—box-type, background-color, box-size-before, box-size-after, color, length, line-thickness, start-indent, end-indent, space-before, space-after
- `table`—table-width, table-border, before-row-border, after-row-border, before-column-border, after-column-border, start-indent, end-indent, space-before, space-after
- `table-part`—start-indent, end-indent, space-before, space-after
- `table-column`—column-number, *n*-columns-spanned, width, start-indent, end-indent

19

- `table-cell`—column-number, n-columns-spanned, n-rows-spanned, cell-before-row-margin, cell-after-row-margin, cell-before-column-margin, cell-after-column-margin, cell-row-alignment, cell-background?, background-color, cell-before-row-border, cell-after-row-border, cell-before-column-border, cell-after-column-border, starts-row?, ends-row?, line-thickness
- `table-border`—border-present?, color, line-thickness
- `scroll`—background-color, background-tile, start-margin, end-margin
- `link`—destination

In addition to the "official" flow object classes, jade adds a few of its own. While these flow object classes are non-standard, they are extremely useful:

- `heading-level`—A value between 1 and 9 that outputs the paragraph as a header of the specified level. This characteristic allows Microsoft Word to provide useful outline views and a document map.
- `page-number-format`—Controls the format of the number used by page-number-sosofo and current-page-number-sosofo for references to pages in the simple-page-sequence. The initial value is 1. It applies to simple-page-sequence flow objects.
- `page-number-restart?`—If true, then for the purposes of page-number-sosofo and current-page-number-sosofo, the page numbers for this simple-page-sequence restart from 1. The initial value is #f. It applies to simple-page-sequence flow objects.
- `page-`*n*`-columns`—A strictly positive integer giving the number of columns. The initial value is 1. It applies to simple-page-sequence flow objects.
- `page-column-sep`—The separation between columns. The initial value is .5in. It applies to simple-page-sequence flow objects.
- `page-balance-columns?`—If true, the columns on the final page of the page-sequence should be balanced. The initial value is #f. It applies to simple-page-sequence flow objects.
- `superscript-height`—The height of the baseline of a superscript above its parent's baseline. It applies to superscript and script flow objects.
- `subscript-depth`—The depth of the baseline of a subscript below its parent's baseline. It applies to subscript and script flow objects.
- `over-mark-height`—The height of the baseline of the contents of the over-mark area of a mark flow object above the baseline of the contents of the main area. It also controls the height of the contents of the mid-sup area of the script flow object. It applies to mark and script flow objects.

- under-mark-depth—The depth of the baseline of the contents of the under-mark area of a mark flow object below the baseline of the contents of the main area. It also controls the depth of the contents of the mid-sub area of the script flow object. It applies to mark and script flow objects.
- grid-row-sep—The separation between rows of a grid flow object.
- grid-column-sep—The separation between columns of a grid flow object.

If you want to use one of these characteristics, you must add a declaration like this to your DSSSL style sheet for the particular characteristic:

```
(declare-characteristic page-n-columns
"UNREGISTERED::James Clark//Procedure::page-n-columns")
```

Flow Object Tree

The DSSSL style sheet consists of a series of so-called flow object specifications. Each of these specifications (technically one of these specifications is called a *sosofo—a specification of a sequence of flow objects*). The following rule doesn't actually create a flow object; it just specifies how one is to be made using a make statement:

```
(make paragraph font-size: 12pt )
```

Put very simply, jade takes the sosofos and uses them to create flow objects. You can think of the sosofo as being the template and the flow objects as being the result of applying the template to the source document.

Taking all the sosofos together, jade creates what is called a *flow object tree* (fot).

NEW TERM   When jade (or any other DSSSL engine) processes a document, it creates an abstract representation of the result of merging the formatting specification and the source document. This representation is called the *flow object tree* and the nodes of this tree are the *flow objects*.

Figure 19.6 illustrates a typical flow tree that might be produced by jade.

The formatted output, the results that will be printed or displayed, are created by formatting this tree of flow objects.

If you understand the concept of the flow object tree, you understand enough to grasp the essentials of how DSSSL works. If you think of the root of the document tree starting at the root element, you can select an element in that tree and process it in one way to apply one particular formatting specification. Later in the style sheet you can select that element again and apply a different formatting specification. These trees are then merged into the flow output tree, which can include both variations.

19

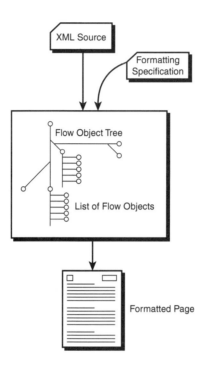

FIGURE 19.6

Processing a document.

Is this explanation too abstract? Let me offer a practical example.

What is a table of contents? You process the document starting at the root element and pick out the headings. You output a paragraph that says something like "Table of Contents" and then you output each heading formatted in a particular way, probably with the page number appended (you could even make this page number an active link). If all you want to do is extract the table of contents, you have already finished. This isn't much use if you want to format the real contents of the document, though. Having processed the whole of the document to create the table of contents, you now have to go back to the root element (or maybe you'd go to the first second level heading and skip what might be the title) and process the whole document to create the actual output.

The merging process that creates the flow output tree allows you to process the source document as many times as you like, in as many ways as you like, so that, from a raw XML document, you can add tables of contents, tables of figures, indexes, glossaries, lists of references, and so on. This is what makes the power and the potential of DSSSL so much more exciting than a simple style language. DSSSL is a processing language; a transformation language and a style language combined. In fact, DSSSL remains a full programming language; you can include procedures, functions, macros, conditional processing, process flow control, expressions—everything that you might expect from a proper programming language. This, however, goes far beyond the scope of this chapter—even beyond the scope of this book, and so we'll come back down to practicalities and return to the mechanics of style sheets.

Element Selection

Each formatting specification consists of a selection rule followed by a construction rule.

A selection rule consists of the keyword `element` and either the name of the element to which the construction rule is to be applied or a clause to select the correct element. The selection syntax is quite simple:

- Element `PARA` simply selects every `PARA` element
- `element (SECTION TITLE)` only selects `TITLE` elements that are inside `SECTION` elements

Construction Rules

A construction rule consists of a `make` expression, followed by the name of a flow object class, a list of any of the characteristics and their values that you want to set for the flow object instance, and then some (optional) processing instructions that select particular child elements for processing.

For example,

```
(root
  (make simple-page-sequence
      (process-children)))
```

This dumps the whole of the document without any particular formatting, whereas the following is quite a different story:

```
(make paragraph
        space-before:          (if (or (equal? (gi (parent)) "A")
                                       (equal? (gi (parent)) "B"))
                              0pt
                              10pt)
        (process-children-trim))
```

DSSSL's syntax takes some getting used to, so let's dissect this expression bit by bit:

- We have an `if` keyword followed by a test expression:

  ```
  (or (equal? (gi (parent)) "A")(equal? (gi (parent)) "B"))
  ```

  If this test expression evaluates to `true` the value of space-before will be 0pt. If it evaluates to `false` the value of space-before will be 10pt.

19

- The test expression is an or expression consisting of two test expressions:

  ```
  (equal? (gi (parent)) "A")
  ```

  and

  ```
  (equal? (gi (parent)) "B")
  ```

- The first test expression is

  ```
  equal? (gi (parent)) "A"
  ```

  or in plain English, "is the parent element of this element an A element?"

- The second test expression is

  ```
  equal? (gi (parent)) "B"
  ```

  or in plain English, "is the parent element of this element a B element?"

So, if the parent of this element is either an A element or a B element, the value of space-before will be 0pt. If it isn't, the space-before value will be 10pt.

As well as using numerical expressions, you can use characters, strings, logical expressions, and even procedures. Expressions in DSSSL can be powerful tools for selecting elements, and you can supplement them by selecting the first element, the last element, and any particular element according to its position in the tree or any of its attributes and attribute values. I won't go into any more detail here, but there are some excellent explanatory documents available on the Web at `http://www.mulberrytech.com/dsssl/dsssldoc`. In the meantime, I suggest you look at other people's examples and try to learn from them.

Cookbook Examples

I'm inclined to believe that the best way to learn is by doing. So, to conclude this chapter I'm simply going to give you a few very basic examples of some common things that you might like to do with DSSSL style sheets.

Prefixing an Element

In Listing 19.5, you already saw how you can use `"(sosofo-append (literal ""))"` to put a text string in front of an element's content. Wouldn't it be nice if you could let the name of the element determine the prefix that gets put in front of the element? Warnings could then be prefixed with the text `"Warning"` and so on. Have a look at the XML code in Listing 19.8.

INPUT   **LISTING 19.8**   XML COOKBOOK FILE 1, PREFIXING AN ELEMENT WITH ITS NAME

```
 1: <?xml version="1.0">
 2: <!DOCTYPE DOC [
 3: <!ELEMENT DOC     (TITLE ¦ CAUTION ¦ NOTE ¦ PARA)*>
 4: <!ELEMENT TITLE   (#PCDATA)>
 5: <!ELEMENT NOTE    (#PCDATA)>
 6: <!ELEMENT PARA    (#PCDATA)>
 7: <!ELEMENT CAUTION (#PCDATA)>
 8: ]>
 9: <DOC>
10: <TITLE>Simple XML to HTML Conversion</TITLE>
11: <PARA>This sample document demonstrates how you can
12: convert the tag name into a piece of text inside an
13: element.</PARA>
14: <NOTE>This is a note.</NOTE>
15: <PARA>This second paragraph proves that normal text is still
16: untouched.</PARA>
17: <CAUTION>This is a caution.</CAUTION>
18: </DOC>
```

Listing 19.9 is the DSSSL style sheet that goes with Listing 19.7:

INPUT   **LISTING 19.9**   DSSSL COOKBOOK FILE 1, PREFIXING AN ELEMENT WITH TEXT

```
 1: <!DOCTYPE style-sheet PUBLIC
 2:     "-//James Clark//DTD DSSSL Style Sheet//EN"[
 3: <!ENTITY lt "&#38;#60;">
 4: <!ENTITY gt "&#62;">
 5: ]>
 6: (declare-flow-object-class element
 7:   "UNREGISTERED::James Clark//Flow Object Class::element")
 8: (declare-flow-object-class document-type
 9:   "UNREGISTERED::James Clark//Flow Object Class::document-type")
10:  (declare-flow-object-class empty-element
11:   "UNREGISTERED::James Clark//Flow Object Class::empty-element")
12: (declare-flow-object-class formatting-instruction
13:   "UNREGISTERED::James Clark//Flow Object
14:     Class::formatting-instruction")
15:
16: (define debug
17: (external-procedure "UNREGISTERED::James Clark//Procedure::debug"))
18:
19: (define (make-special-para)
20:   (make sequence
21:     (make element
22:       gi: "P"
```

continues

19

LISTING 19.9   CONTINUED

```
23:      (make element
24:        gi: "B"
25:        (literal (string-append (gi) ":"))))
26:      (make element
27:        gi: "BLOCKQUOTE"
28:        (process-children))))
29:
30: (element DOC
31:   (sosofo-append
32:     (make document-type
33:       name:  "HTML"
34:       public-id: "-//W3C//DTD HTML 3.2//EN")
35:        (make element
36:          gi:  "HTML"
37:            (sosofo-append
38:              (make element
39:                gi:  "HEAD"
40:                  (make element
41:                    gi:  "TITLE"
42:                      (sosofo-append
43:                        (literal "Simple XML-to-HTML Conversion"))))
44:              (make element gi:  "BODY"
45:                (process-children))))))
46:
47: (element TITLE (make element gi: "H1" ))
48:
49: (element NOTE (make-special-para))
50: (element CAUTION (make-special-para))
51:
52: (element PARA (make element gi: "P" ))
```

ANALYSIS   Ignore the DOC, TITLE, and P elements. The DOC element is messy, but fairly straightforward if you follow the logic step by step; all it does is output the correct HTML code when it sees the DOC element. The TITLE and P elements are just straight mappings.

It is the NOTE and CAUTION elements that are interesting. Because I want them both to be treated as special, I've defined a procedure make-special-para. Taking away the indentation (this helps me to keep track of all the opening and closing brackets), this procedure looks like this:

```
(define (make-special-para)
  (make sequence (make element gi: "P" (make element gi: "B"
    (literal (string-append (gi) ":"))))
    (make element gi: "BLOCKQUOTE" (process-children))))
```

What I do is create a sequence (make sequence). This sequence consists of an element (P), so it's going to wrap what follows in a P element. What follows is a literal composed of the name of the element (gi) with a colon (:) appended to it (hence, string-append). This is also followed by a make element instruction, this time to make a BLOCKQUOTE element and then, finally, the contents of the element (process-children).

Let's have a look at the HTML code this produces—Listing 19.9.

OUTPUT **LISTING 19.10** HTML COOKBOOK FILE 1, PREFIXED ELEMENT OUTPUT

```
 1: <!DOCTYPE HTML PUBLIC "-//W3C//DTD HTML 3.2//EN">
 2: <HTML>
 3: <HEAD>
 4: <TITLE>Simple XML-to-HTML Conversion</TITLE>
 5: </HEAD>
 6: <BODY>
 7: <H1>Simple XML to HTML Conversion</H1>
 8: <P>This sample document demonstrates how you can
 9: convert the tag name into a piece of text inside an
10: element.</P>
11: <P><B>NOTE:</B></P>
12: <BLOCKQUOTE>This is a note.</BLOCKQUOTE>
13: <P>This second paragraph proves that normal text is still
14: untouched.</P>
15: <P><B>CAUTION:</B></P>
16: <BLOCKQUOTE>This is a caution.</BLOCKQUOTE>
17: </BODY>
18: </HTML>
```

And Figure 19.7 shows what the HTML file looks like in a Web browser.

19

OUTPUT

FIGURE 19.7

The prefixed element in the displayed HTML.

Fancy Prefixing

In the previous example we used the name of the element to add a prefix to the element text. Let's take this a step further and do something fancy with these special elements. We'll use the same XML file (Listing 19.5) but a different style sheet, Listing 19.11. To shorten the listing (you will soon get tired of seeing the same old DOC element specification), I'll only include the part of the file that's really relevant (all the code demonstrated in this chapter can be downloaded from the Web site that accompanies this book).

INPUT   **LISTING 19.11**   DSSSL COOKBOOK FILE 2, ADVANCED PREFIXING

```
 1:  <!DOCTYPE style-sheet PUBLIC
 2:           "-//James Clark//DTD DSSSL Style Sheet//EN"[
 3:  <!ENTITY lt "&#38;#60;">
 4:  <!ENTITY gt "&#62;">
 5:  ]>
 6:
 7:  <![CDATA[
 8:  (define RED-ON (make formatting-instruction
 9:           data: "<FONT COLOR='RED'>"))
10:  (define RED-OFF (make formatting-instruction data: "</FONT>"))
11:  (define RULE  (make formatting-instruction
12:           data: "<HR SIZE=5 NOSHADE WIDTH=300>"))
13:  ]]>
14:
15:  (define (make-special-para)
16:    (make sequence
17:      RULE
18:      (make element
19:        gi: "P"
20:        attributes: '(("ALIGN" "center"))
21:      (make element
22:        gi: "B"
23:        (literal (string-append (gi) ":"))))
24:      (make element
25:        gi: "BLOCKQUOTE"
26:        attributes: '(("ALIGN" "center"))
27:        (process-children)
28:        ) RULE ))
29:
30:  (element NOTE (make-special-para))
31:
32:  (element CAUTION (make sequence RED-ON (make-special-para)
33:      RED-OFF))
34:
35:
36:    (element PARA (make element gi: "P" ))
```

ANALYSIS This time I'm using the same `make-special-para` procedure, but I've added to it. First, I've defined a formatting instruction:

```
(define RULE  (make formatting-instruction
        data: "<HR SIZE=5 NOSHADE WIDTH=300>"))
```

This means that I can use `RULE` as shorthand for all that HTML code.

Note

> Note that I use the keyword `data` to prevent the markup from being interpreted. (Remember I said that the style sheet was an SGML document. This means that you have to `hide` any markup that you don't want jade to see.)
>
> I've done the same with the `RED-ON` and `RED-OFF` instructions, but this time I've hidden the markup by putting them both inside a `CDATA` section.

A `NOTE` element now has a rule placed above and below it, and it's centered with the text "NOTE:" above it. A `CAUTION` element is now expanded so that I make a sequence of "`RED-ON make-special-para RED-OFF`" so that cautions are nicely displayed in red, as shown in Figure 19.8.

OUTPUT

FIGURE 19.8

More advanced properties displayed in the HTML code.

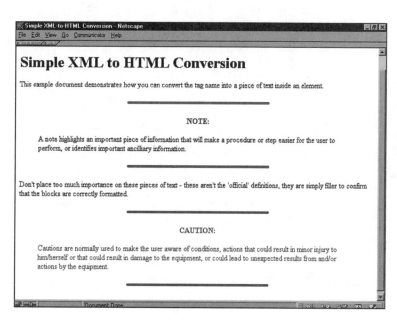

19

Tables

The two earlier examples were both for the conversion of XML into HTML. Now it's time to convert an XML file into RTF. For this example, I thought I'd choose something that is often irritatingly difficult: a table. The XML input document is shown in Listing 19.12 and the DSSSL style sheet is shown in Listing 19.13.

INPUT   **LISTING 19.12**   XML COOKBOOK FILE 3 (TABLES)

```
1:  <?xml version="1.0">
2:  <!DOCTYPE DOC [
3:  <!ELEMENT DOC   (TITLE ¦ TABLE ¦ PARA)*>
4:  <!ELEMENT TITLE (#PCDATA)>
5:  <!ELEMENT TABLE (ROW)* >
6:  <!ELEMENT ROW    (CELL)*>
7:  <!ELEMENT CELL (#PCDATA)>
8:  <!ELEMENT PARA (#PCDATA ¦ TITLE)*>
9:  <!ELEMENT CAUTION (#PCDATA)>
10: ]>
11: <DOC>
12: <TITLE>Simple XML to RTF Conversion</TITLE>
13: <PARA>This sample document demonstrates how you can
14: create tables.</PARA>
15:
16: <TABLE>
17: <ROW><CELL>Cell 1.1</CELL><CELL>Cell 1.2</CELL>
18:     <CELL>Cell 1.3</CELL></ROW>
19: <ROW><CELL>Cell 2.1</CELL><CELL>Cell 2.2</CELL>
20:     <CELL>Cell 2.3</CELL></ROW>
21: <ROW><CELL>Cell 3.1</CELL><CELL>Cell 3.2</CELL>
22:     <CELL>Cell 3.3</CELL></ROW>
23: <ROW><CELL>Cell 4.1</CELL><CELL>Cell 4.2</CELL>
24:     <CELL>Cell 4.3</CELL></ROW>
25: <ROW><CELL>Cell 5.1</CELL><CELL>Cell 5.2</CELL>
26:     <CELL>Cell 5.3</CELL></ROW>
27: <ROW><CELL>Cell 6.1</CELL><CELL>Cell 6.2</CELL>
28:     <CELL>Cell 6.3</CELL></ROW>
29: <ROW><CELL>Cell 7.1</CELL><CELL>Cell 7.2</CELL>
30:     <CELL>Cell 7.3</CELL></ROW>
31: </TABLE>
32:
33: <PARA>Now we're back to normal text again.</PARA>
34: </DOC>
```

```
1:   <!DOCTYPE style-sheet
2:      PUBLIC "-//James Clark//DTD DSSSL Style Sheet//EN">
3:   (define debug
4:  (external-procedure "UNREGISTERED::James Clark//Procedure::debug"))
5:
6:   (root
7:      (make simple-page-sequence
8:      left-margin:              2cm
9:      font-size:               12pt
10:     line-spacing:            14pt
11:      right-margin:            2cm
12:       top-margin:            2cm
13:       bottom-margin:         2cm
14:      (process-children)))
15:
16:  (element (DOC TITLE)
17:       (make paragraph
18:          quadding:             'center
19:          font-size:            24pt
20:          line-spacing:         36pt
21:          space-after:          12pt
22:          font-weight:          'bold
23:          keep-with-next?:      #t
24:          (process-children)))
25:
26:  (element PARA
27:       (make paragraph
28:          font-size:             12pt
29:          line-spacing:          16pt
30:          (process-children)))
31:
32:  (element TABLE                       ;the processing of the table element
33:      (make table                      ;a data-driven table
34:          space-before: .25in
35:          space-after: .5in
36:          table-border:  (make table-border line-thickness: 3pt)
37:          (make table-column width: 1.5in)   ;all columns before any rows
38:          (make table-column width: 1.5in)
39:          (make table-column width: 1.5in)
40:          (process-children)))  ;child elements make row flow objects
41:
42:  (element ROW                          ;a row in the table
43:       (make table-row
44:            (process-children)))  ;child elements make cell flow objects
45:
46:  (element CELL                          ;a column in the row
```

continues

LISTING 19.13 CONTINUED

```
47:      (make table-cell
48:          cell-before-row-border:    #t
49:          cell-before-column-border: #t
50:      (make paragraph
51:          quadding:          'center
52:          (process-children)))) ;content of the table cell
```

ANALYSIS   As you can see from Listing 19.12, I haven't needed to perform any special tricks to format the XML table. There's no point in looking at the RTF code, so Figure 19.9 simply shows the converted XML file loaded into Microsoft Word.

OUTPUT

FIGURE 19.9

The tables displayed in RTF.

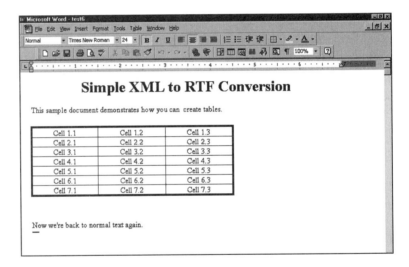

Table of Contents

Earlier, I mentioned the possibility of processing a document more than once to format the contents in different ways. That's what I'm going to do this time. I kept this example intentionally ultra-simple because I want to concentrate on the mechanics of modes rather than confuse the issue by making hyperlinks from the table of contents to the entries. I've also chosen to add information in the table of contents that isn't explicitly present in the XML document itself. The XML input document is shown in Listing 19.14 and the DSSSL style sheet is shown in Listing 19.15.

INPUT   **LISTING 19.14**   XML COOKBOOK FILE 4 (TABLE OF CONTENTS)

```
 1: <?xml version="1.0">
 2: <!DOCTYPE DOC [
 3: <!ELEMENT DOC   (TITLE | SECTION)*>
 4: <!ELEMENT SECTION (TITLE | CAUTION | NOTE | PARA)*>
 5: <!ELEMENT TITLE (#PCDATA)>
 6: <!ELEMENT NOTE (#PCDATA)>
 7: <!ELEMENT PARA (#PCDATA | TITLE)*>
 8: <!ELEMENT CAUTION (#PCDATA)>
 9: ]>
10: <DOC>
11: <TITLE>Simple XML to HTML Conversion</TITLE>
12: <SECTION>
13: <TITLE>Introduction</TITLE>
14: <PARA>This sample document demonstrates how you can
15: create a table of contents. This code uses two DSSSL modes. The
16: most important (toc) model allows us to process the document twice,
17: once to extract the text we need for the TOC and once for
18: the normal document formatting.
19: element.</PARA>
20: <NOTE>This is an extremely powerful feature of DSSSL that is well
21: worth learning.</NOTE>
22: <PARA>This second paragraph proves that normal text is still
23: untouched.</PARA>
24: </SECTION>
25: <SECTION><TITLE>Going Further</TITLE>
26: <CAUTION>Don't forget to use the debug features when developing
27: DSSSL style sheets with jade.</CAUTION>
28: <PARA>If you look at the code, you'll see I used two modes, not one,
29: I use a toc mode on the document to extract the TITLE elements to
30: include them in the TOC, and another mode to extract the text
31: contained within the TITLE element since I don't want
32: them to be formatted.</PARA>
33: </SECTION>
34: <SECTION><TITLE>And then?</TITLE>
35: <PARA>Even when XSL takes off, DSSSL is going to
36: be around for a long time yet (if for no other reason than
37: that it is an ISO standard). DSSSL (with jade) is still worth
38: learning.</PARA>
39: </SECTION>
40: </DOC>
```

19

```
 1: <!DOCTYPE style-sheet
 2:     PUBLIC "-//James Clark//DTD DSSSL Style Sheet//EN">
 3: <!DOCTYPE style-sheet
 4:     PUBLIC "-//James Clark//DTD DSSSL Style Sheet//EN">
 5: (declare-flow-object-class element
 6:   "UNREGISTERED::James Clark//Flow Object Class::element")
 7: (declare-flow-object-class document-type
 8:   "UNREGISTERED::James Clark//Flow Object Class::document-type")
 9: (declare-flow-object-class empty-element
10:   "UNREGISTERED::James Clark//Flow Object Class::empty-element")
11: (declare-flow-object-class formatting-instruction
12:   "UNREGISTERED::James Clark//Flow Object
13:            Class::formatting-instruction")
14: (define debug
15:   (external-procedure "UNREGISTERED::James Clark//Procedure::debug"))
16:
17: <![CDATA[
18: (define RED-ON (make formatting-instruction
19:     data: "<FONT COLOR='RED'>"))
20: (define RED-OFF (make formatting-instruction data: "</FONT>"))
21: (define RULE  (make formatting-instruction data: "<HR>"))
22: (define START (make formatting-instruction data: "<P>"))
23: (define STOP (make formatting-instruction data: "</P>"))
24: ]]>
25:
26: (define (make-special-para)
27:   (make sequence
28:     (make element
29:      gi: "P"
30:     (make element
31:      gi: "B"
32:     (literal (string-append (gi) ":"))))
33:     (make element
34:      gi: "BLOCKQUOTE"
35:     (process-children))))
36:
37: (element DOC
38:   (sosofo-append
39:     (make document-type name: "HTML"
40:           public-id: "-//W3C//DTD HTML 3.2//EN")
41:     (make element gi:  "HTML"
42:       (sosofo-append
43:         (make element gi:  "HEAD"
44:           (make element gi: "TITLE" (sosofo-append
45:                   (literal "Simple XML-to-HTML Conversion")))
46:         ))
47:       (make element gi:  "BODY"
48:         (make sequence
```

```
49:                    (make element gi:  "H2"  (sosofo-append
50:                        (literal "Table of Contents")))
51:                    (with-mode toc (process-matching-children 'section))
52:                    (process-children))))))
53:
54: (mode extract-title-text (element (TITLE) (process-children)))
55:
56: (mode toc
57:    (element section
58:      (make sequence
59:        START
60:        (literal "Section ")
61:        (literal (format-number (child-number) "1"))
62:        (literal " ... ... ... ... ... ")
63:        (with-mode extract-title-text
64:      (process-first-descendant "TITLE"))
65:        STOP)))
66:
67: (element (DOC TITLE)
68:    (make sequence RULE (make element gi: "H2" )))
69:
70: (element (SECTION TITLE) (make element gi: "H3" ))
71:
72: (element NOTE   (make-special-para))
73:
74: (element CAUTION
75:    (make sequence
76:      RED-ON (make-special-para) RED-OFF))
77:
78: (element PARA (make element  gi: "P"))
```

19

ANALYSIS The secret to making all this work is to use a thing called a *mode*. A mode is basically a different way of processing the document. To make the table of contents I need two modes.

NEW TERM A *mode* is a named set of processing instructions. By setting conditions for when a mode is triggered, you can implement conditional processing. By including several modes you can process a document several times, but in different ways. For example, you would use one mode to process the complete contents of a document to format it, but another mode to extract and format only selected elements to generate a table of contents or an index.

The sole purpose of the first mode is to extract the children of the title elements. Because these elements don't have any child elements, the process-children instruction simply processes the text that they contain:

```
(mode extract-title-text
    (element (TITLE)
        (process-children)))
```

Now I need a second mode that specifies how to handle this extracted text. This is the mode that actually creates the table of contents:

```
(mode toc
  (element section
    (make sequence
      START
      (literal "Section ")
      (literal (format-number (child-number) "1"))
      (literal " ... ... ... ... ... ")
      (with-mode extract-title-text
        (process-first-descendant "TITLE"))
      STOP)))
```

The formatting specification is triggered by a SECTION element. I then create a sequence consisting of an opening P tag, using the START procedure, some literal text, the section number, the text from the title, and a closing P tag using the STOP procedure. There are two special things about the contents of this specification:

- The number—Even though I haven't numbered the sections (I could use the style sheet to do this too), each element still has its place in the tree: the child-number. I wrap the child-number in a format-number that specifies how I want the number displayed. This could be 1 (decimal numbers: 1, 2, 3), "A" (uppercase alphabet: A, B, C), "a" (lowercase alphabet: a, b, c), "I" (uppercase roman: I, II, III, IV), or "i" (lowercase roman: i, ii, iii, iv).

- Using the mode—I tell the DSSSL engine to use the mode with the with-mode keyword and then I tell it to only process the first child TITLE element. There won't actually be any other child TITLE elements, but I don't want to include all the paragraph text (which is what I'd get if I said process-children).

This is an XML-to-HTML conversion so we can look at the output code again, shown in Listing 19.14. The Web browser display is shown in Figure 19.10.

Cross References

For the last of these examples I'd like to return to an XML-to-RTF conversion.

So far I've only been using elements, although in the last example I did use the position of the element in the document tree to extract extra information. This extra information comes close to being attribute information.

In this example I'd like to go one step further and really use information contained in attributes. Let's look at the XML document first, Listing 19.16.

FIGURE 19.10

The generated table of contents.

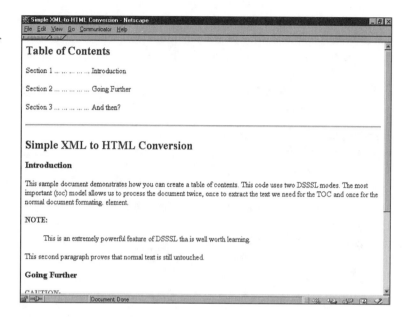

LISTING 19.16 XML COOKBOOK FILE 5 (CROSS REFERENCES)

```
1:  <?xml version="1.0">
2:  <!ELEMENT doc (TITLE | SECTION)*>
3:  <!ELEMENT SECTION (TITLE | PARA)*>
4:  <!ELEMENT TITLE (#PCDATA)>
5:  <!ELEMENT PARA (#PCDATA | NOTE | XREF)*>
6:  <!ELEMENT NOTE (#PCDATA)>
7:  <!ATTLIST NOTE ID ID #IMPLIED>
8:
9:  <!ELEMENT XREF EMPTY>
10: <!ATTLIST XREF REF CDATA #IMPLIED>
11: ]>
12: <doc>
13: <TITLE>Test Document</TITLE>
14: <SECTION><TITLE>Starting</TITLE>
15: <PARA>This paragraph simply contains some text
16: (<NOTE ID="N1">Note 1 </NOTE>
17: this is an embedded note) that we will use to wrap the
18: note we're going to cross-reference.</PARA></SECTION>
19: <SECTION><TITLE>Going On</TITLE>
20: <PARA>In this second paragraph, we'll include a cross-reference
21: <XREF REF="N1"> to the previous note.</PARA>
22: </SECTION>
23: </DOC>
```

ANALYSIS There aren't any real surprises in the XML code, but note how in the DTD I have added an ID attribute to the NOTE element and created a new XREF element that has a REF attribute. In the document itself, the NOTE element has an ID attribute value of N1 and this is the same value given to the REF attribute of the XREF element. In the DSSSL style sheet I use this to extract the text contained inside the NOTE. The DSSSL style sheet is shown in Listing 19.17.

INPUT   **LISTING 19.17**   DSSSL COOKBOOK FILE 5 (CROSS REFERENCES)

```
 1:  <!DOCTYPE style-sheet
 2       PUBLIC "-//James Clark//DTD DSSSL Style Sheet//EN">
 3:  <!DOCTYPE style-sheet
 4:      PUBLIC "-//James Clark//DTD DSSSL Style Sheet//EN">
 5:
 6:  (define debug
 7:   (external-procedure "UNREGISTERED::James Clark//Procedure::debug"))
 8:
 9:  (element doc
10:     (make simple-page-sequence
11:      page-width: 15cm
12:      page-height: 20cm
13:      left-margin: .5cm
14:      right-margin: .5cm
15:      top-margin: 2cm
16:      bottom-margin: 2cm
17:      header-margin: 1cm
18:      footer-margin: 1cm
19:      center-footer:   (make sequence
20:                          (literal "Page " )
21:                          (page-number-sosofo))
22:     left-header:  (with-mode head (make sequence
23:              font-size: 10pt
24:              line-spacing: 14pt
25:              font-posture: 'italic
26:              (process-first-descendant "TITLE")))))
27:
28:  (element PARA (make paragraph font-size: 14pt space-after: 5pt))
29:
30:  (element (DOC TITLE) (make paragraph font-size: 18pt
31:           space-before: 6pt space-after: 10pt))
32:  (element (SECTION TITLE) (make paragraph font-size: 14pt
33:           space-before: 6pt space-after: 10pt))
34:
35:  (mode head
36:     (element TITLE
37:        (make paragraph font-size: 10pt space-before: 6pt
38:           space-after: 10pt)))
39:
```

```
40: (element NOTE
41:    (make sequence
42:      font-posture: 'italic
43:      font-size: 12pt
44:      (process-children)))
45:
46: (element XREF
47:    (make sequence
48:      (literal "(see ")
49:      (with-mode #f (process-children-trim)))
50:      (process-element-with-id
51:       (attribute-string "REF"))
52:      (literal ")")))
```

ANALYSIS To get the XREF element to show the string 'Note 1', which it extracts from the NOTE element with the matching ID attribute value, I use the following specification:

```
(element XREF
  (make sequence
    (literal "(see ")
    (with-mode #f (process-children-trim)))
    (process-element-with-id
     (attribute-string "REF"))
    (literal ")")))
```

I'm using a mode, or rather explicitly not using a mode, so I set with-mode to false (#f). I then process the element with the id (process-element-id) that matches the value in the string in the REF attribute (attribute-string "REF"). Notice that I use process-children-trim instead of just process-children; this trims off any extra spaces, tabs, or carriage returns around the string I'm extracting.

There are two more things I snuck in at the last moment, a page header and a footer.

The footer is extremely easy because a simple-page-sequence already has three footer characteristics. All I have to do is choose the one I want and attach another ready-made flow object, a page-number-sosofo:

```
center-footer:  (make sequence
                  (literal "Page " )
                  (page-number-sosofo))
```

I thought I'd be a little more adventurous with the page header, so I created a mode to format the document's title element:

```
(mode head
  (element TITLE
    (make paragraph font-size: 10pt space-before: 6pt
space-after: 10pt)))
```

19

The mode itself is nothing special—it's just enough to give some basic formatting to the text. The real work is done in specifying the appropriate header characteristic, which is where I call the mode:

```
left-header:  (with-mode head (make sequence
                    font-size: 10pt
                    line-spacing: 14pt
                    font-posture: 'italic
                    (process-first-descendant "TITLE")))
```

We're done. This is an XML-to-RTF conversion, so we can skip looking at the RTF code and just look at the layout when it's loaded into Microsoft Word (believe me, the header and footer are there even if you can't see them), shown in Figure 19.11.

FIGURE 19.11

RTF cookbook file 5 displayed (Cross References).

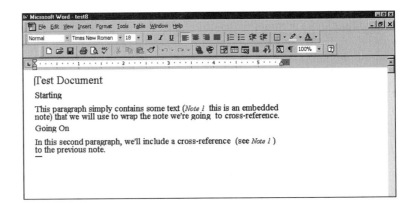

Summary

This chapter looked at XML and DSSSL and demonstrated how you can use jade to convert XML code into RTF (for display in Microsoft Word), into MIF (for display in Adobe FrameMaker), or even into HTML. I haven't covered all the conversions that jade can handle (there is also, for example, a very good TeX backend). I haven't even taught you very much about DSSSL itself, and I have intentionally kept the technical details to a bare minimum. However, with the help of a few cookbook examples (there are quite a few more available on the Web, as well as a DSSSL mailing list that is a ready source of help and advice from some of the best experts out there), I hope I have demonstrated that whatever happens with XSL, DSSSL is here and you can easily do some exciting things with it.

Q&A

Q **Why and when should you use the `-wxml` and `-wno-valid` parameters when running jade?**

A jade is really an SGML tool and it expects you to use the tag minimization symbols in your DTD. To stop jade complaining, use the `-wxml` parameter.

Jade also normally validates documents before it processes them. Unlike SGML, XML documents do not have to be valid, although they must be well-formed. To suppress jade's validation, use the `-wno-valid` parameter.

Q **Why do you have to hide markup characters (like <) in a DSSSL style sheet?**

A The DSSSL style sheet used by jade is a perfectly standard SGML document. That's why you have to edit or specify the catalog file when you run jade to make sure it can find the DTD for style sheets. Because it is a standard SGML document, the normal rules apply for escaping markup characters that you don't want jade to interpret, but because you cannot escape them using the normal approaches (character entities, for example) you have to hide the markup inside a data keyword or CDATA section.

Q **Why does a DSSSL style sheet use `start` and `end` instead of `left` and `right`?**

A DSSSL is completely international. A style sheet can be used to format text from left to right, from right to left, or even vertically. The notions of left and right would be very confusing in this context and so the style sheets use direction-neutral terms such as `start`, `end`, `before` and `after`.

Exercises

1. Download jade and run the test sample that's included in the distribution.

2. To give yourself an idea of just how powerful a DSSSL style sheet can be, pick any HTML document you like. Download jade and look for the html32hc.dsl style sheet. Use this style sheet to convert the HTML into either RTF or MIF and view the result in the appropriate software package.

3. Take the cookbook example style sheet for the table of contents (number 3) and see if you can improve the style sheet so that there's an active link between the table of contents entry and the section title itself. You need a `link` flow object and a `current-node-page-number-sosofo`; the html32hc style sheet may give you some clues.

19

4. Take the cross references cookbook example (number 5) and see if you can add the HTML markup to turn the cross reference into a hyperlink. Use an "A HREF=" element around the source an "A NAME=" element around the target, where the value HREF attribute matches the value of the NAME attribute.

DAY **20**

Rendering XML with XSL

On Day 18, "Styling XML with CSS," you learned about cascading style sheets (CSS) and how CSS code can be used for formatting XML documents, despite the fact that it is really intended for use with HTML documents. Then, in yesterday's chapter, you learned about DSSSL and how jade can be used to produce far more sophisticated layouts of XML documents. Today we will complete the tour of XML related style languages by looking at the extensible style language, XSL, itself.

In this chapter you will:

- Learn briefly about the first version of XSL
- Learn how to do simple rendering with XSL2 using formatting objects
- Learn about element and attribute selection
- Be introduced to XSL's powerful conditional processing capabilities.

XSL1

The first version of XSL (released as an unofficial committee draft in October 1997) was a strange mixture of the conceptual models and flow objects from DSSSL-o and a new set of flow objects that mapped the suite of HTML elements, all formulated in XML syntax.

NEW TERM In earlier chapters, I have used the terms displaying and formatting fairly indiscriminately. Throughout this chapter, when discussing *rendering* text for display on a screen and formatting text for printing, I will keep to the more neutral term of *rendering*.

Once you got used to the power of DSSSL (and fought your way around learning its strange syntax), the trade-down to this first version of XSL felt like an acceptable compromise. Compare Listing 20.1, which shows a fragment of XSL1 code, with Listing 20.2, which shows the equivalent code in DSSSL-o.

LISTING 20.1 A FRAGMENT OF XSL1 CODE

```
1: <rule>
2:   <target-element type="DOC"/>
3:   <scroll>
4:     <children/>
5:   </scroll>
6: </rule>
```

LISTING 20.2 THE EQUIVALENT OF LISTING 20.1 IN DSSSL-o CODE

```
1: (element DOC
2:   (make scroll
3:     (process-children)
4:   )
5: )
```

ANALYSIS The code fragments shown in Listing 20.1 and 20.2 do exactly the same thing; they simply select the DOC element, create a scroll flow object, and then process the elements that are children of the DOC element. As far as features are concerned, XSL1 was a small step in the right direction. It managed to combine a lot of the DSSSL-o flow objects (though a few useful ones were omitted) with HTML flow objects, which gave it a certain degree of backward compatibility with CSS. The important advance was that instead of forcing you to learn a completely separate syntax, XSL1 was formulated in standard XML syntax. This opened up all sorts of possibilities in that it now became feasible to consider creating not just XML code automatically but also its style code as well.

I'm not going to go into any further detail about XML1 because it no longer really exists. With the appearance of XSL2, the older version of XSL is completely obsolete.

XSL2

XSL2 was first released in draft form in July 1998. The latest and current version was released as a working draft on December 16, 1998 (from now on I shall simply refer to it as XSL because it makes all earlier versions obsolete).

There are quite a few sections of the draft still unfinished and several questions that still need to be answered before the proposal can be properly adopted as a standard. As was also true of the previous release, publication was already a month late by the time the draft came out and I suppose the authors felt that it was better to let everyone see at least a partial version. Fortunately, this hasn't stopped software developers. Within a month of the last release there was an XSL processor available for free download (imaginatively called XSLProcessor, available from `http://www.inria.fr/koala/XML/xslProcessor`). This tool is a Java XSL processor that takes an XSL file and an XML file and creates one or more HTML files.

> **Note**
> In between this release and the last, Microsoft released a second beta preview of Internet Explorer 5. Microsoft incorporated some changes that were not made public until the latest release of the XSL draft and so for a short time it appeared as if they had implemented a private version of XSL.

More interestingly, Indelv (`http://www.indelv.com`) released a so-called Technology Introduction Preview Release package that processes and displays XML code using XSL code. The current release of this software is extremely limited (some of the editing functions have been disabled, although it does have limited VML support, which is quite exciting to see), but with a little hacking it's possible to get the software to process your own code.

20

Tip

The key to *hacking* (I use the word in its original sense of experimenting with software) is to edit the file `navigation.xml`. If you add the following lines to the end of this file:

```
<branch collapsed="no">
  <branch-title
     href="simon.xml">Simon's Files
  </branch-title>
  <branch>
    <branch-title
       href="simon1.xml">File 1
    </branch-title>
  </branch>
  <branch>
    <branch-title
       href="simon2.xml">File 2
    </branch-title>
  </branch>
</branch>
```

Where you replace the filenames `simon1.xml` and `simon2.xml` with the name of your files, you can get Indelv to read any XML file you want.

Before we get too involved in the theory, let's look at a short example of an XML file and its associated XSL file. Listing 20.3 shows an XML example, Listing 20.4 shows the XSL code, and Figure 20.1 shows what the result looks like in Indelv.

INPUT   **LISTING 20.3**   A SAMPLE XML FILE

```
 1: <?xml version="1.0"?>
 2: <?xml:stylesheet type="text/xsl" href="simon1.xsl"?>
 3: <content>
 4:
 5: <hr/>
 6:
 7: <title>THE MORON</title>
 8: <poem>
 9: <line>See the happy moron</line>
10: <line>He doesn't give a damn.</line>
11: <line>I wish I were a moron,</line>
12: <line><stress>My God! perhaps I am.</stress></line>
13: </poem>
14:
15: </content>
```

Note how the XSL style sheet is linked to the XML document by means of an XML processing instruction (this is the approved manner of linking the two together). You can also link a CSS style sheet to an XML file using the same mechanism (the file would then be a CSS file and the type would be text/css).

Caution

The latest release of the XSL working draft is so new that few tools have had a chance to implement the changes in the syntax of XSL. Generally, to make the code examples shown in this chapter comply with the new syntax, you should replace all occurrences of xsl:process-childen with xsl:apply-templates.

Note, though, that IE5 doesn't support flow objects and so you won't be able to display much of this code anyway.

INPUT **LISTING 20.4** THE ASSOCIATED XSL FILE

```
1:  <xsl:stylesheet
2:    xmlns:xsl="http://www.w3.org/TR/WD-xsl"
3:    xmlns:fo="http://www.w3.org/TR/WD-xsl/FO"
4:    result-ns="fo">
5:
6:  <xsl:template match="/">
7:    <fo:sequence
8:        font-size="12pt"
9:        indent-end=8pt
10:       indent-start=8pt>
11:    <xsl:process-children/>
12:    </fo:sequence>
13:  </xsl:template>
14:
15:  <xsl:template match="hr">
16:    <fo:rule-graphic
17:        space-before-optimum="12pt"
18:        space-after-optimum="12pt"
19:        graphic-line-thickness='2pt'>
20:      <xsl:process-children/>
21:    </fo:rule-graphic>
22:  </xsl:template>
23:
24:  <xsl:template match="poem">
25:    <fo:block-level-box
26:        indent-start="1in"
27:        indent-end="1in"
28:        background-color='blue'
```

20

continues

LISTING **20.4**   CONTINUED

```
29:              graphic-line-thickness='3pt'>
30:        <xsl:process-children/>
31:        </fo:block-level-box>
32:   </xsl:template>
33:
34:   <xsl:template match="line">
35:      <fo:block
36:         font-style="italic"
37:         space-before-optimum="2pt"
38:         space-after-optimum="2pt">
39:        <xsl:process-children/>
40:      </fo:block>
41:    </xsl:template>
42:
43:   <xsl:template match="title">
44:      <fo:block
45:         font-size="14pt"
46:         font-weight="bold"
47:         space-before-optimum="12pt"
48:         space-after-optimum="8pt">This poem is called '
49:        <xsl:process-children/>
50:        <xsl:text> '</xsl:text>
51:      </fo:block>
52:   </xsl:template>
53:
54:   <xsl:template match="stress">
55:      <fo:sequence
56:         font-size="14pt"
57:         font-weight="bold"
58:         font-style="normal"
59:         color='white'>
60:        <xsl:process-children/>
61:      </fo:sequence>
62:   </xsl:template>
63:
64: </xsl:stylesheet>
```

ANALYSIS   Note how the XSL style sheet is a well-formed XML document. In fact, the style
sheet can also be validated because there's a style sheet DTD included as an
appendix to the working draft. (This alone is a major step forward because you can now
check that the syntax of your style sheets is correct by using the same tools that you use
for your XML files—an option that was sadly missing from CSS.)

Tip

The great thing about this new style sheet syntax is that it is not only well-formed, it should also be valid. If you point your Web browser to the XSL proposal (http://wwww.w3c.org/TR/WD-xsl) and save the file to your hard disk, you can extract the DTD contained in Appendix A and use it to debug your style sheets. This will save you a lot of effort in trying to check for those annoyingly simple syntax errors that seem to be so easy to make, but so hard to find.

The first part of the style sheet is more or less standard. This prologue is the standard XML document prologue plus some namespace declarations. The XSL namespace should always be used as it is shown here, but the result namespace can really be anything you like.

Note

There are still a lot of issues to be solved concerning namespaces, but for the time being we have to go ahead with what we've got. In theory, if you declare your own namespace there should be an accompanying URL that points to an explanation of the semantics of the elements. This, however, is not checked and so any URL is acceptable until a resolution mechanism is found.

OUTPUT

FIGURE 20.1

A rendered XML file showing properties applied by an XSL file.

20

Template Rules

The basic XSL style sheet building block is a template rule. A template rule describes how an XML element node (that element and all the elements it contains) is converted into an XSL element node that can be rendered. Don't forget that you can construct new trees out of parts of the document tree (discussed on Day 19, "Converting XML with DSSSL"). The element node could be a whole branch of the document tree, or it could even be the whole of the XML document processed in a different way (for example, when creating a table of contents).

A template rule consists of two parts:

1. A pattern that identifies the XML node (element) in the XML document.
2. An action (rendering or processing part) that details the transformation and rendering of the resulting node (the element or elements that you have identified).

If all you wanted to do was pass the XML document through untouched, the following would probably be enough, although another instruction (xsl:copy) that you will learn later in this chapter can be used to pass XML code through or even to make a hybrid XML/HTML mix:

```
<xsl:template match="/">
  <fo:page-sequence>
    <xsl:apply-templates/>
  </fo:page-sequence>
</xsl:template>
```

Note

Many of the XSL code fragments shown here rely on flow objects because this is the easiest and preferred way to render XML code. It is, however, not the only way, and flow objects are not currently supported in Internet Explorer 5. (There is some public doubt that they ever will be supported because they aren't relevant to Microsoft's express purpose of converting XML code into HTML code for display in a Web browser). Later in this chapter you will see some examples of XSL style sheets that do not rely on flow objects and that can actually be used in IE5.

Caution

The process-children element is used in some of the examples in this chapter because this is what is currently supported. In the latest XSL working draft this element is changed to xsl:apply-templates, and it is this element that is supported in the beta preview 2 release of Microsoft Internet Explorer 5.

It is often useful to put all the basic style properties on the root of the document so that all the descendant elements inherit the properties. This is done by using a single forward slash to represent the root element:

```
<xsl:template match= "/">
```

There are many ways of matching elements, including:

- Matching by ID
- Matching by element name
- Matching by ancestry
- Matching by children
- Matching by attributes

Matching an Element by its ID

The syntax for matching an element by its ID is the same as the syntax for an Xpointer:

```
<xsl:template match="id([id-value])">
```

where *id-value* is the specific value of the ID attribute that you want to select by. This fragment of XSL code in the style sheet:

```
<xsl:template match= "id(1)">
```

could select this fragment of XML code in the XML document:

```
<line id="1">See the Happy Moron!</line>
```

Matching an Element by its Name

This is the simplest match—the source element is identified by its name using the match attribute.

The following XSL code would select all the line elements in the XML document:

```
<xsl:template match="line">
```

Matching an Element by its Ancestry

In XSL you can match an element according to what its parent element is (a context-sensitive match). For example:

```
<xsl:template match="line/stress">
```

matches any stress element that has a line element as its parent.

Instead of the immediate relationship of parent/child, you can select by the less precise ancestor selector. For example, the following would select a stress element that has a line element somewhere in the tree directly above it (great grandparent, grandparent, and so on). Note that there are two slashes, not one:

```
<xsl:template match="line//stress">
```

20

You can also make nested selections consisting of more than one parent. For example, the following would match a stress element that has a line element as its parent, and that line element has a poem element as its parent (the poem element must be the stress element's grandparent):

```
<xsl:template match="poem/line/stress">
```

Matching Several Element Names

If you want to select more than one element at the same time, simply separate the names of the elements with a vertical line character "¦". For example,

```
<xsl:template match="poem ¦ line ¦ stress">
```

matches all of the poem, line, and stress elements.

Matching an Element by its Attributes

The syntax for matching by an attribute is

```
<xsl:template match="element-name[@attribute-name="attribute-value"]">
```

Consider the XML document shown in Listing 20.5.

LISTING 20.5   A SIMPLE XML FILE WITH ATTRIBUTES

```
 1: <chapter>
 2:   <section number="1">
 3:     <title>first</title>
 4:     <para type="first">Some text</para>
 5:     <para>Some <em>emphasized</em> text</para>
 6:     <para>Another para with no attributes</para>
 7:     <para type="last">Some more text</para>
 8:   </section>
 9:
10:   <section number="2">
11:     <title>two</title>
12:     <para type="first">Some text</para>
13:     <para>Some <em>emphasized</em> text</para>
14:     <para>Another para with no attributes</para>
15:     <para type="last">Some more text</para>
16:   </section>
17: </chapter>
```

The following examples demonstrate how you can use the attributes and their values to select elements from the XML file shown in Listing 20.5:

- `<xsl:template match="para">`—Matches all the para elements (with and without attributes).

- `<xsl:template match="para[@type)]">`—Matches all the para elements that have a type attribute (the value of the attribute doesn't matter).

- `<xsl:template match="para[@type='first']">`—Matches all the para elements that have a type attribute with a value of "first".

- `<xsl:template match="section[@number= '1']/para[@type='first']">`—Matches all the para elements with a type attribute whose value is "first", and that have a parent of section with a number attribute with a value of 1 (the very first para element in Listing 20.5).

Matching an Element by its Children

Elements can also be matched according to their child elements (the elements they contain).

The syntax for this is

```
<xsl:template match="element-name[child-name]">
```

For example, the following matches all the line elements that have a stress element child.:

```
<xsl:template match="line[stress]">
```

Matching an Element by its Position

You can also match elements based on a pattern using position qualifiers.

The syntax for matching an element by its position is

```
<xsl:template match="element[position-description]"
```

You can use the following position descriptions:

- `first-of-any()`—The element must be the first sibling element.
- `first-of-type()`—The element must be the first sibling of its type.
- `last-of-any()`—The element must be the last sibling element.
- `last-of-type()`—The element must be the last sibling of its type.

20

- `only-of-any()`—The element must not have any sibling elements.
- `only-of-type()`—The element must not have any sibling elements of the same type.
- `not-first-of-any()`—The element must not be the first sibling element.
- `not-first-of-type()`—The element must not be the first sibling of its type.
- `not-last-of-any()`—The element must not be the last sibling element.
- `not-last-of-type()`—The element must not be the last sibling of its type.
- `not-only-of-any()`—The element must have one or more sibling elements.
- `not-only-of-type()`—The element must have one or more element siblings of the same type.

For example, the XML template matches the last `line` element:

```
<xsl:template match= "line[last-of-type()]"
```

You can qualify these selectors by using the `not` keyword, so that the previous example could be rewritten so that it matches everything but the last `line` element:

```
<xsl:template match= "line[not last-of-type()]"
```

Wildcard Matches

A wildcard match will select any element. A wildcard match rule is useful for designating a rule to apply if no other rule applies. (The XSL processor is actually required to assume a default rule when there is no specific rule, as you will learn later in this chapter.)

The syntax for a wildcard selection is

```
<xsl:template match="*">
```

You can also specify the following rule to match the whole of a document if you want to make absolutely sure you capture everything:

```
<xsl:template match="/ ¦ *">
```

Resolving Selection Conflicts

It's possible for more than one template rule to apply to the same source element. When this occurs, the more specific rule applies. For example, the following rules that select the same element are given in decreasing order of specificity.

1. `id(line1)`—The ID attribute value is the most specific (remember that ID values have to be unique).

2. `line[attribute(type)='line-no',attribute(line-no)='1']`—Selects any element with a specific attribute and attribute value pair (because it isn't an ID attribute the attribute value doesn't have to be unique).

3. `line[attribute(type)='line-no']`—Selects any element with a specific attribute name.

4. `line`—Selects all the elements with that element name.

5. `*`—Selects any element (a wildcard is the least specific).

If you want more control over the applicability of a template, you can specify a template priority attribute and assign it a positive integer value:

```
<xsl:template match="section/title" priority="1">
  <fo:block>
    <xsl:apply-templates/>
  </fo:block>
</xsl:template>
```

The higher the priority value, the higher the priority of the template rule. The default value (used if you do not specify a priority value) is 0.

The Default Template Rule

The XML processor recursively processes the XML document tree to produce an output tree. To prevent this recursive process from stalling when there isn't a suitable selection rule, the XSL procesor assumes a default template rule if it cannot find a suitable rule. The syntax of this rule is

```
<xsl:template match="/¦*">
        <xsl:apply-templates/>
</xsl:template>
```

Tip

You can write your own rule to override the default template rule. For example:

```
<xsl:template match= "/¦*">
        [missing rule]
</xsl:template>
```

would stop the processing of all the elements for which a style rule had not been provided and would substitute the string [missing rule] in the output tree. This can be extremely useful for highlighting elements that you have missed.

20

Formatting Objects

You will remember from Day 19 that DSSSL-o uses flow objects and that XLS1 used a group of DSSSL and HTML flow objects. The latest version of XSL also provides its own list of flow objects, but they are now called *formatting objects*. Formatting objects are referred to by the fo namespace.

The formatting object is applied to the result tree node by being contained in the pattern part of the element:

```
<xsl:template match="[pattern]">
    <fo:[formatting-object] ([style-property]="[value]")*>
        [processing-instructions]*
    </fo:[formatting-object]>
</xsl:template>
```

Layout Formatting Objects

The current XSL working draft describes only the page-sequence object and the simple-page-master object. More formatting objects will be added as the draft gains more form. These are the formatting objects that have been specified so far:

- page-sequence—A page-sequence object acts as an ancestor to a series of pages, either printed pages or screen display pages.

  A page-sequence object contains one or more formatting objects or page-sequences. It can hold one or more single-page-master children, or up to six child queues.

  In practice a page-sequence acts as a container for style rules that can be inherited by the rest of the document. For example, the template rule

  ```
  <xsl:template match="/">
      <fo:page-sequence
          font-family="times new roman,serif"
          font-size="12pt"
          background-color= "white'
          color= "black">
          <xsl:apply-templates/>
      </fo:page-sequence>
  </xsl:template>
  ```

  sets the font and color for the other formatting objects in the result tree, unless alternates are specified.

- simple-page-master—A simple-page-master formatting object describes a simple page that can be divided into six areas. This model can be used for either print or screen rendering.

The element must have a master-name attribute, which can have one of the following values:

first—Formatting for the first page of a series of pages.

odd—The equivalent of the left-hand page in print (verso).

even—The equivalent of right-hand page in print (recto).

scrolling—The type of page used for screen display.

Content Formatting Objects

The following are some of the more common content formatting objects:

- queue—A queue flow object isn't really a formatting object at all, but a container for other formatting so that they can be assigned to a specific area on the page (or screen).

  A queue can only be a child of a page-sequence. It has a queue-name attribute with a value that is title, header, body, footer, start-side, or end-side. The body is where the main content of the XML document goes. Figure 20.2 shows the arrangement of the six queue areas on a page. Note that the title queue area only applies to scrollable (screen display) media.

FIGURE 20.2

The six queue areas used for constructing a page with XSL.

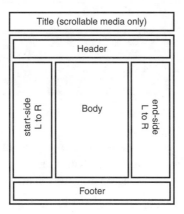

- sequence—A sequence formatting object is used to group formatting objects that share an inherited set of properties. The following code fragment renders all the elements enclosed in an em element in italic:

```
<xsl:template match="em">
  <fo:sequence font-style="italic">
    <xsl:apply-templates/>
  </fo:sequence>
</xsl:template>
```

20

- `block`—A block formatting object simply puts a line break both before and after the block (like a paragraph). The opposite of a block formatting object is an inline formatting object. For example, Listing 20.6 shows the template for a block formatting object and Figure 20.3 shows the result when applied to two p elements.

Note that in Listings 20.6 through 20.9, when describing the XSL code I use `xsl:apply-templates`, but in the practical examples I use `xsl:process-children` because the newer `xsl:apply-templates` element is not yet supported by many packages.

INPUT   **LISTING 20.6**   A BLOCK FORMATTING OBJECT TEMPLATE

```
1:  <xsl:template match="p">
2:    <fo:block
3:       indent-start="1.5in"
4:       indent-end="1.5in"
5:       space-before-optimum="6pt"
6:       space-after-optimum="6pt">
7:       <xsl:process-children/>
8:    </fo:block>
9:  </xsl:template>
```

OUTPUT

FIGURE 20.3

A rendered block formatting object.

- `inline-box`—Acts as an inline container so that you can highlight text or graphics, produce borders and backgrounds, or just control the spacing surrounding an element or piece of text. For example, Listing 20.7 shows the template for an inline-box formatting object and Figure 20.4 shows the result when applied to a p element.

INPUT   **LISTING 20.7**   AN INLINE-BOX FORMATTING OBJECT TEMPLATE

```
1:  <xsl:template match="em">
2:    <fo:inline-box
3:      background-color='yellow'
4:      graphic-line-thickness='0pt'>
5:      <xsl:process-children/>
6:    </fo:inline-box>
7:  </xsl:template>
```

OUTPUT

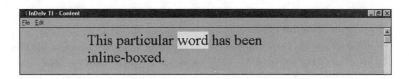

FIGURE 20.4

The rendered inline-box formatting object.

- list—A list formatting object acts as a container for the list-item, list-item-label, and list-item-body formatting objects. If you want to nest lists, the second list must be a child of the list-item-body formatting object.

- rule-graphic—A rule-graphic formatting object corresponds to the HR (horizontal rule) element in HTML, but it can either be an inline or a block formatting object. For example, Listing 20.8 shows the template for a block formatting object and Figure 20.5 shows how the horizontal line is rendered.

INPUT   **LISTING 20.8**   A RULE-GRAPHIC FORMATTING OBJECT TEMPLATE

```
1:  <xsl:template match="hr">
2:    <fo:rule-graphic
3:      space-before-optimum="12pt"
4:      space-after-optimum="12pt"
5:      graphic-line-thickness='3pt'>
6:      <xsl:process-children/>
7:    </fo:rule-graphic>
8:  </xsl:template>
```

20

- graphic—A graphic formatting object corresponds to the IMG element in HTML but it can be either an inline or a block formatting object. For example:

```
<xsl:template match="display-graphic">
  <fo:graphic
      graphic-max-width="2in"
      graphic-max-height="2in"/>
</xsl:template>
```

FIGURE 20.5

The rendered rule-graphic formatting object.

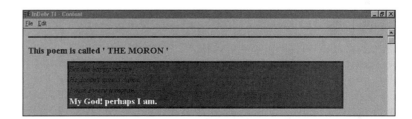

- score—A score flow object is a formatting object that can take text decoration, such as underlines, strikethroughs, overbars, and so on. A score is an inline formatting object.

- block-level-box—A box provides borders, margins, and backgrounds and provides spacing between the border of a box and its content. A box can be an inline or block formatting object. For example, Listing 20.9 shows the template for a block formatting object and Figure 20.6 shows the result when applied to two p elements.

INPUT   **LISTING 20.9**   A BLOCK-LEVEL-BOX FORMATTING OBJECT TEMPLATE

```
1:   <xsl:template match="p">
2:     <fo:block-level-box
3:        indent-start="1in"
4:        indent-end="1in"
5:        background-color='blue'
6:        graphic-line-thickness='3pt'>
7:        <xsl:process-children/>
8:     </fo:block-level-box>
9:   </xsl:template>
```

OUTPUT

FIGURE 20.6

The rendered block-level-box formatting object.

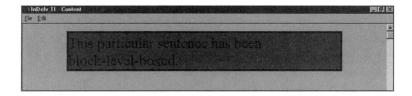

- page-number—A page-number formatting object is used to instruct the rendering engine to construct and display a page-number.

- link—A link creates an area in which you can put link-end-locator flow objects.

- link-end-locator—Link-end-locator flow objects provide information about the destination of a link (this is equivalent to HREF= "[URI]" in HTML).

- character—Allows you to treat a single character as a flow object. Each formatting object may take certain style properties.

Processing

As you have just seen, the first part of the action involves describing the resulting rendering actions. The second part of the action involves processing or building a result tree formatting object from the source tree.

The standard instruction to the XSL processor follows:

```
<xsl:apply-templates/>
```

The XML processor processes all the children of the source element that is matched.

Direct Processing

If your source XML document has a known, regular structure (such as you usually see in tables and catalogs), you can use the for-each statement to recursively process down the tree. Listing 20.10 shows a sample XML file taken from a database containing listings of the names of tracks in a CD collection.

LISTING 20.10 A REGULARLY STRUCTURED XML FILE

```
 1:  <?xml version="1.0"?>
 2:  <?xml:stylesheet type="text/xsl" href="cd1.xsl"?>
 3:  <CDs>
 4:    <CD>
 5:      <title>Boys for Pele</title>
 6:      <artist>Tori Amos</artist>
 7:      <tracks>
 8:        <track>Horses</track>
 9:        <track>Blood Roses</track>
10:        <track>Father Lucifer</track>
11:        <track>Professional Widow</track>
12:        <track>Mr. Zebra</track>
13:        <track>Marianne</track>
14:        <track>Caught a Lite Sneeze</track>
15:        <track>Muhammad My Friend</track>
16:        <track>Hey Jupiter</track>
17:        <track>Way Down</track>
18:        <track>Little Amsterdam</track>
```

20

continues

LISTING 20.10 CONTINUED

```
19:        <track>Talula</track>
20:        <track>Not the Red Baron</track>
21:        <track>Agent Orange</track>
22:        <track>Doughnut Song</track>
23:        <track>In the Springtime of his Voodoo</track>
24:        <track>Putting the Damage on</track>
25:        <track>Twinkle</track>
26:      </tracks>
27:    </CD>
28:    <CD>
29:      <title>The Ghosts that Haunt Me</title>
30:      <artist>Crash Test Dummies</artist>
31:      <tracks>
32:        <track>Winter Song</track>
33:        <track>Comin' Back Soon (The Bereft Man's Song)</track>
34:        <track>Superman's Song</track>
35:        <track>The Country Life</track>
36:        <track>Here on Earth (I'll have my Cake)</track>
37:        <track>The Ghosts that Haunt Me</track>
38:        <track>Thick-Necked Man</track>
39:        <track>Androgynous</track>
40:        <track>The Voyage</track>
41:        <track>At My Funeral</track>
42:      </tracks>
43:    </CD>
44: </CDs>
```

The XSL style sheet shown in Listing 20.11 creates an HTML document containing a table with a row for each track element.

LISTING 20.11 USING for-each TO RECURSIVELY PROCESS THE XML FILE

```
 1:  <?xml version="1.0"?>
 2:  <xsl:stylesheet xmlns:xsl="http://www.w3.org/TR/WD-xsl">
 3:
 4:  <xsl:template match="/">
 5:    <xsl:apply-templates/>
 6:  </xsl:template>
 7:
 8:  <xsl:template match="track">
 9:      <xsl:apply-templates/>, </xsl:template>
10:
11:  <xsl:template match="track[end()]">
12:    <xsl:apply-templates/>. </xsl:template>
13:
14:  <xsl:template match="textnode()">
```

```
15:    <xsl:get-value/></xsl:template>
16:
17: <xsl:template match="/">
18:    <HTML>
19:      <HEAD>
20:        <TITLE>My CD Collection</TITLE>
21:      </HEAD>
22:      <BODY>
23:        <H1>My CD Collection</H1>
24:        <TABLE BORDER="3" CELLSPACING="2" CELLPADDING="6">
25:          <col bgcolor="yellow"/>
26:          <THEAD align="left" bgcolor="silver">
27:            <TH>Artist</TH><TH>Album Title</TH><TH>Tracks</TH>
28:          </THEAD>
29:          <TBODY>
30:            <xsl:for-each select="CDs/CD">
31:            <TR>
32:              <TD><font color="red" size="5">
33:                <B><xsl:value-of select="artist"/></B></font></TD>
34:              <TD><B><I><xsl:value-of select="title"/></I></B></TD>
35:              <TD><xsl:apply-templates select="tracks/track"/></TD>
36:            </TR>
37:            </xsl:for-each>
38:          </TBODY>
39:        </TABLE>
40:      </BODY>
41:    </HTML>
42: </xsl:template>
43:
44: </xsl:stylesheet>
```

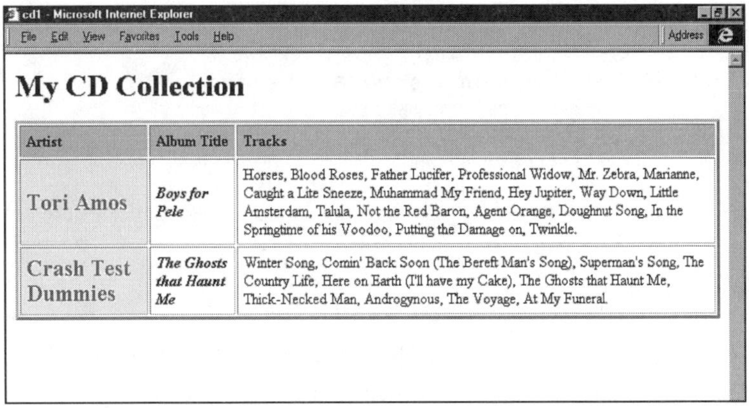

FIGURE 20.7

The XML code rendered as HTML in IE5.

Artist	Album Title	Tracks
Tori Amos	*Boys for Pele*	Horses, Blood Roses, Father Lucifer, Professional Widow, Mr. Zebra, Marianne, Caught a Lite Sneeze, Muhammad My Friend, Hey Jupiter, Way Down, Little Amsterdam, Talula, Not the Red Baron, Agent Orange, Doughnut Song, In the Springtime of his Voodoo, Putting the Damage on, Twinkle.
Crash Test Dummies	*The Ghosts that Haunt Me*	Winter Song, Comin' Back Soon (The Bereft Man's Song), Superman's Song, The Country Life, Here on Earth (I'll have my Cake), The Ghosts that Haunt Me, Thick-Necked Man, Androgynous, The Voyage, At My Funeral.

My CD Collection

20

Note Listing 20.11 uses end() in line 11. This is unfortunately one of the incorrect changes that Microsoft implemented in IE5 before the latest version of the XSL syntax proposal was released. According to the formal proposal this should be last-of-type() but IE5 does not recognize this selector.

ANALYSIS Note how surprisingly easy it is to convert XML code into HTML using XSL style sheets! All you have to do is select the element or elements that you are interested in, insert the HTML starting tag, process the element content, then insert the HTML closing tag. This is probably the simplest method that you will see in this whole book and an excellent reason for learning XSL.

Note Matching XML elements to HTML elements using XSL is a simple way of rendering XML, but there is an easier way using xsl:copy that will be explained later in this chapter. The xsl:copy instruction enables you to use HTML markup in an XML file and simply pass it through verbatim to the Web browser.

Restricted Processing

If you only want to process certain children of an element, use the xsl:apply-templates element and then select the elements to be processed by their names. The following example could be used to process all the title elements to make a table of contents:

```
<xsl:template match="section">
  <fo:block font-size="12pt">
    <xsl:apply-templates select="title"/>
  </fo:block>
</xsl:template>
```

Selection patterns can also be used in the same manner as the select value to be even more selective.

Conditional Processing

There are two instructions in XSL that allow you to conditionally process an element according to certain test conditions: xsl:if and xsl:choose.

The xsl:if instruction provides simple if (a), then (b) conditionality. The xsl:choose instruction enables you to select one choice when there are several possibilities.

The xsl:if element has a single test attribute, which specifies a test pattern. The content is a template. If the pattern selects a non-empty list of elements, the content is instantiated; otherwise nothing is created.

In the following example, the names in a group of names are formatted as a comma-separated list:

```
<xsl:template match="namelist/name">
  <xsl:apply-templates/>
  <xsl:if test=".[not(last-of-type())]">, </xsl:if>
</xsl:template>
```

The xsl:choose element selects one from among a number of possible alternatives. It consists of a series of xsl:when elements followed by an optional xsl:otherwise element.

Each xsl:when element has a single test attribute, which specifies a test pattern. The result of the test is true if the pattern selects a non-empty list of elements.

The content of the xsl:when and xsl:otherwise elements is a template. When an xsl:choose element is processed, each of the xsl:when elements is tested in turn. The content of the first, and only the first xsl:when element whose test is true is used. If no xsl:when element is true, the content of the xsl:otherwise element is used. If no xsl:when element is true, and no xsl:otherwise element is present, nothing is created. You should therefore make a habit of always specifying an xsl:otherwise element.

The example XSL style sheet shown in Listing 20.12 enumerates items in an ordered list using Arabic numerals, letters, or roman numerals depending on the depth to which the ordered lists are nested.

LISTING 20.12 CONDITIONAL PROCESSING IN AN XSL FILE

```
 1: <xsl:template match="list/item">
 2:   <fo:list-item indent-start='12pt'>
 3:     <fo:list-item-label>
 4:       <xsl:choose>
 5:
 6:         <xsl:when test='ancestor(list/list)'>
 7:           <xsl:number format="i"/>
 8:         </xsl:when>
 9:
10:         <xsl:when test='ancestor(list)'>
11:           <xsl:number format="a"/>
12:         </xsl:when>
13:
14:         <xsl:otherwise>
```

20

continues

```
15:                 <xsl:number format="1"/>
16:             </xsl:otherwise>
17:
18:         </xsl:choose>
19:
20:         <xsl:text>. </xsl:text>
21:     </fo:list-item-label>
22:
23:     <fo:list-item-body>
24:         <xsl:apply-templates/>
25:     </fo:list-item-body>
26:
27:   </fo:list-item>
28:
29: </xsl:template>
```

Computing Generated Text

Within a template, the xsl:value-of element can be used to compute generated text, for example, by extracting text from the source tree or by inserting the value of a string constant.

The xsl:value-of element computes the text by using a string expression that is specified as the value of the select attribute. String expressions can also be used inside attribute values of literal result elements by enclosing the string expression in curly braces ({}).

Let's suppose that you have a fragment of XML code that says this:

```
<link target="http://my.home.com/~simon">My Diary</link>
```

You want to convert the attribute into an element:

```
My Diary <address>http://my.home.com/~simon</address>
```

Listing 20.13 shows the XSL code to achieve this.

LISTING 20.13   USING xsl:value-of

```
1:     <xsl:template match="link">
2:       <xsl:apply-templates/>
3:         <address>
4:           <xsl:value-of select="attribute(link)"/>
5:         </address>
6:     </xsl:template>
```

You can just as easily go the other way and convert an element into an attribute. Imagine that you have the following XML code:

```
<image>
  <file>my-smiling-face.gif</file>
  <size width="100"/>
</image>
```

and you want to convert it into this:

```
<graphic src="my-smiling-face.gif" width="100"/>
```

Listing 20.14 shows how you could achieve this.

LISTING 20.14 USING AN ATTRIBUTE VALUE TEMPLATE

```
1:    <xsl:template match="image">
2:        <graphic src="{file}" width="{size/@width}"/>
3:    </xsl:template>
```

Adding a Text Formatting Object

You can add a text formatting object by including it in the processing model, as shown in Listing 20.15.

LISTING 20.15 USING xsl-text TO INSERT TEXT INTO THE OUTPUT XML FILE

```
1:    <xsl:template match="title">
2:        <fo:block
3:            font-size="14pt"
4:            font-weight="bold"
5:            space-before-optimum="12pt"
6:            space-after-optimum="8pt">This poem is called '
7:            <xsl:process-children/>
8:            <xsl:text> '</xsl:text>
9:        </fo:block>
10:   </xsl:template>
```

20

Numbering

You can automatically number elements in the XML input file by using the xsl:number element.

You can control the numbering using the level, count, and from attributes:

- When level="single" is used, the count starts at the nearest ancestor (including the current node as its own ancestor) that matches the count pattern. It constructs a list of length one containing one plus the number of preceding siblings of that ancestor that match the count pattern. If there is no such ancestor, the list is empty. If the from attribute is specified, the only ancestors that are searched are those that are descendants of the nearest ancestor that matches the from pattern.

- When level="multi" is used, all the ancestors of the current node in document order followed by the element itself are counted first. The elements that match the count pattern are selected and mapped to one plus the number of preceding siblings of that element that match the count pattern. If the from attribute is specified, then the only ancestors that are searched are those that are descendants of the nearest ancestor that matches the from pattern.

- When level="any" is used, the count contains one plus the number of elements at any level of the document that start before this node and that match the count pattern. If the from attribute is specified, then only the elements after the first element that come before this element and match the from pattern are counted.

As an example, the following XSL template numbers the item elements in a list:

```
<xsl:template match="list/item">
        <fo:block>
            <xsl:number/>
            <xsl:text>. </xsl:text>
            <xsl:process-children/>
        </fo:block>
    <xsl:template>
```

To illustrate a more practical use of numbering, Listing 20.16 shows two rules for numbering title elements. This is intended for a document that contains a sequence of chapters followed by a sequence of appendices, where both chapters and appendices contain sections with subsections. Chapters are numbered 1, 2, 3. Appendices are numbered A, B, C. Sections in chapters are numbered 1.1, 1.2, 1.3 and sections in appendices are numbered A.1, A.2, A.3.

LISTING 20.16   USING xsl:number TO CREATE MULTI-LEVEL NUMBERING

```
1:  <xsl:template match="title">
2:    <fo:block>
3:      <xsl:number level="multi"
4:            count="chapter ¦ section ¦ subsection"
5:            format="1.1. "/>
6:      <xsl:apply-templates/>
```

```
7:    </fo:block>
8:  </xsl:template>
9:
10: <xsl:template match="appendix//title">
11:   <fo:block>
12:     <xsl:number level="multi"
13:       count="appendix ¦ section ¦ subsection"
14:       format="A.1. "/>
15:     <xsl:apply-templates/>
16:   </fo:block>
17: </xsl:template>
```

Sorting

Sorting is specified by adding xsl:sort elements as children of xsl:apply-templates or xsl:for-each elements. The first xsl:sort child specifies the primary sort key, the second xsl:sort child specifies the secondary sort key and so on.

When an xsl:apply-templates or xsl:for-each element has one or more xsl:sort children, then instead of processing the selected elements in the order they appear in the XML document order, the XML processor sorts the elements according to the specified sort keys and processes them in the sorted order.

When used in an xsl:for-each element, xsl:sort elements must occur first.

An xsl:sort element has a select attribute with a value that is a select pattern. For each element to be processed, the select pattern is evaluated with that element as the current element. The value of the first selected element is used as the sort key for that element. The default value of the select attribute is '.' (the current element).

The select string serves as the sort key. The following optional attributes on the xsl:sort element control how the list of sort keys is sorted:

- order—Specifies whether the strings should be sorted in ascending or descending order; ascending specifies ascending order; descending specifies descending order; the default is ascending.
- lang—Specifies the language of the sort keys; it has the same range of values as the xml:lang attribute; if no lang value is specified, the language is determined from the system environment.
- data-type—Specifies the data type of the sort strings; the following values are allowed:

> text—Specifies that the sort keys should be sorted alphabetically in the correct manner for the language specified by lang

20

number—Specifies that the sort keys are to be converted into numbers and then sorted according to their numeric values; the value specified by lang can be used to help convert the values into numbers. The default value is text.

• case-order—This can have the value upper-first or lower-first. This value applies when data-type="text", and specifies that the uppercase characters should be sorted before the lowercase letters, or vice versa respectively. For example, if lang="en" then A B a A becomes A a B b when sorted with case-order="upper-first". It becomes a A b B when sorted with case-order="lower-first". The default value depends on the language specified.

For example, suppose you have a CD database marked up in XML:

```
<CDs>
        <CD>
          <artist>Tori Amos</artist>
          <title>Boys for Pele</title>
        </CD>
</CDs>
```

You can then generate a list of the CDs sorted by artist using the XSL code shown in Listing 20.17.

LISTING 20.17 USING XSL TO SORT ELEMENTS

```
1:  <xsl:template match="CDs">
2:    <ul>
3:      <xsl:apply-templates select="CD">
4:        <xsl:sort select="artist"/>
5:        <xsl:sort select="title"/>
6:      </xsl:apply-templates>
7:    </ul>
8:  </xsl:template>
9:
10: <xsl:template match="CD">
11:   <li>
12:     <xsl:value-of select="artist"/>
13:       <xsl:text> </xsl:text>
14:     <xsl:value-of select="title"/>
15:   </li>
16: </xsl:template>
```

Whitespace

If it is important to you to keep the whitespace inside an xsl:text element, set the xml:space attribute value to preserve:

```
<xsl:text xml:space="preserve">
   The spaces       in     this   t e x t
   will n o  t be         removed.
</xsl:text>
```

If, on the other hand, you know there is whitespace inside an element that is simply "noise" you can remove it automatically by declaring xml:space="strip".

At a higher level, to affect all the elements of a particular type, you can also include separate instructions in the XSL style sheet:

```
<xsl:strip-space element="para">
<xsl:preserve-space element="code">
```

Macros

Macros allow you to reuse parts of your style sheet by breaking it up in named parts. Listing 20.18 shows a simple macro that sets the content inside a box.

LISTING 20.18   A SIMPLE XSL MACRO

```
1: <xsl:define-macro name="special-para">
2:   <fo:block-level-box
3:     space-before-optimum="8pt"
4:     space-after-optimum="8pt"
5:     graphic-line-thickness='1.5pt'>
6:       <xsl:contents/>
7:   </fo:block-level-box>
8: </xsl:define-macro>
```

You can then call this macro whenever you need it, as shown in Listing 20.19.

20

LISTING 20.19   CALLING AN XSL MACRO

```
1: <xsl:template match="para">
2:   <xsl:invoke macro="special-para">
3:     <xsl:apply-templates/>
4:   </xsl:invoke>
5: </xsl:template>
```

Formatting Object Properties

Each formatting object has its own set of properties. There isn't room here to list them all in detail, much less describe them. The following lists are therefore very brief summaries of some of the formatting objects and some of their properties and values. If only one value is shown (such as a measurement), this is the default value, otherwise the default values are shown in bold text. You have seen some of them used in the examples in this chapter.

> **Caution**
>
> Formatting objects are currently the least supported feature of XSL, and are the most prone to change (which is probably why they are so poorly supported). The following list is not meant to be complete or definitive; it is meant to give you an impression of the richness that XSL has to offer. To check the latest status of the formatting objects and their properties you should download the latest XSL working draft (at http://www.w3.org/WD/WD-xsl).

- Simple-page-master:

  A simple-page-master defines the layout of a page area. You can repeat simple-page-masters by using a page-sequence specification.

  ```
  master-name = name-specifier
  background-attachment = ( scroll ¦ fixed )
  background-color = a color-specifier or transparent
  background-image = a URI or none
  background-position-x = ( a length-specifier ¦ left ¦ center ¦
  ➡right )
  background-position-y = ( a length-specifier ¦ top ¦ middle ¦
  ➡bottom )
  background-repeat = ( no-repeat ¦ repeat ¦ repeat-x ¦ repeat-y )
  page-height = length-specifier ¦ auto
  page-width = length-specifier ¦ auto
  page-writing-mode = writing-mode-specifier  lr-tb
  margin-bottom  =  36.0pt
  margin-left =  36.0pt
  margin-right  = 36.0pt
  margin-top = 36.0pt
  body-overflow  = ( visible ¦ hidden ¦ scroll ¦ auto )
  body-writing-mode = a writing-mode-specifier ¦ use-page-writing-mode
  end-side-overflow = ( visible ¦ hidden ¦ scroll ¦ auto )
  end-side-separation (0.0pt
  end-side-size 0.0pt
  end-side-writing-mode = a writing-mode-specifier ¦ use-page-writing-
  ➡mode
  ```

```
footer-overflow = ( visible ¦ hidden ¦ scroll ¦ auto )
footer-precedence = ( true ¦ false )
footer-separation 18.0pt
footer-size 36.0pt
footer-writing-mode = a writing-mode-specifier ¦ use-page-writing-
➡mode
header-overflow = ( visible ¦ hidden ¦ scroll ¦ auto )
header-precedence = ( true ¦ false )
header-separation 18.0pt
header-size  36.0pt
header-writing-mode = a writing-mode-specifier ¦ use-page-writing-
➡mode
start-side-separation 0.0pt
start-side-size 0.0pt
start-side-overflow = ( visible ¦ hidden ¦ scroll ¦ auto )
start-side-writing-mode = a writing-mode-specifier
       ¦ use-page-writing-mode
```

- Block:

  A block formatting object is used to create a block-level area that contains text lines. Blocks are commonly used for formatting paragraphs, titles, headlines, figure and table captions, and so on. It normally specifies a rectangular area that occupies the width of the containing area and a height that is determined by the amount of text that the block contains.

```
language = ( none ¦ use-document ¦ an xml:lang specifier )
background-attachment = ( scroll ¦ fixed )
background-color = a color-specifier or transparent
background-image = a URI or none
background-position-x = ( a length-specifier ¦ left ¦ center ¦
➡right )
background-position-y = ( a length-specifier ¦ top ¦ middle ¦
➡bottom )
background-repeat = ( no-repeat ¦ repeat ¦ repeat-x ¦ repeat-y )
font-family = font-name or font-name-list any
font-style = ( normal ¦ italic ¦ oblique )
font-stretch = ( ultra-condensed ¦ extra-condensed ¦ condensed ¦
            semi-condensed ¦ normal ¦ semi-expanded ¦ expanded ¦
            extra-expanded ¦ ultra-expanded)
font-size 10.0pt
font-variant = ( normal ¦ small-caps )
font-weight = ( any ¦ not-applicable ¦ ultra-light ¦ extra-light ¦
            light ¦ semi-light ¦ book ¦ normal ¦ medium ¦
➡semi-bold ¦
            bold ¦ extra-bold ¦ ultra-bold  )
glyph-alignment-mode  = ( base ¦ center ¦ top ¦ bottom ¦ font )
indent-end 0.0pt
indent-start 0.0pt
indent-first-line-start 0.0pt
break-after = ( none ¦ page ¦ page-odd ¦ page-even )
```

20

```
break-before = ( none ¦ page ¦ page-odd ¦ page-even )
keep = ( auto ¦ no-break ¦ page )
orphans = 2
widows = 2
keep-with-next = ( true ¦ false )
keep-with-previous = ( true ¦ false )
block-line-breaking = ( wrap ¦ asis ¦ as-is-wrap ¦ asis-truncate ¦
➥none )
block-asis-truncate-indicator = ( none ¦ a character )
block-asis-wrap-indicator = ( none ¦ a character )
block-asis-wrap-indent 0.0pt
hyphenation-keep = ( none ¦ spread ¦ page ¦ column )
hyphenation-ladder-count  2
text-align = ( start ¦ end ¦ left ¦ right ¦ spread-inside ¦
               spread-outside ¦ page-inside ¦ page-outside ¦
               center ¦ justify ¦ justify-force )
text-align-last = ( auto ¦ start ¦ end ¦ left ¦ right ¦
                    spread-inside ¦ spread-outside ¦
                    page-inside ¦ page-outside ¦ center ¦ justify )
linespacing-strategy = ( fixed ¦ auto )
linespacing 12.0pt
space-after-maximum  0.0pt
space-after-minimum 0.0pt
space-after-optimum 0.0pt
space-before-maximum 0.0pt
space-before-minimum 0.0pt
space-before-optimum 0.0pt
writing-mode = writing-mode-specifier  lr-tb
```

- Character:

  Use a character formatting object when you need to explicitly override a specific character or array of characters with a specific glyph.

```
background-attachment = ( scroll ¦ fixed )
background-color = a color-specifier or transparent
background-image = a URI or none
background-position-x = ( a length-specifier ¦ left ¦ center ¦
➥right )
background-position-y = ( a length-specifier ¦ top ¦ middle ¦
➥bottom )
background-repeat = ( no-repeat ¦ repeat ¦ repeat-x ¦ repeat-y )
text-shadow = see the CSS proposal
text-transform = ( as-entered ¦ lower ¦ upper ¦ title ¦ (see CSS) )
char
char-kern
char-kern-mode
char-ligature
color
font-specification
glyph-alignment-mode
```

```
hyphenate
hyphenation-char
inhibit-wrap
language
position-point-shift
letterspace-after-maximum
letterspace-after-minimum
letterspace-after-optimum
wordspacing-maximum
wordspacing-minimum
wordspacing-optimum
text-shadow
text-transform: capitalize ¦ uppercase ¦ lowercase ¦ none
writing-mode
```

- List:

  Creates a block-level area containing a list. Its allowed children are either only list-item-label, list-item pairs, or only list-item-body objects.

  ```
  background-attachment = ( scroll ¦ fixed )
  background-color = a color-specifier or transparent
  background-image = a URI or none
  background-position-x = ( a length-specifier ¦ left ¦ center ¦
  ➥right )
  background-position-y = ( a length-specifier ¦ top ¦ middle ¦
  ➥bottom )
  background-repeat = ( no-repeat ¦ repeat ¦ repeat-x ¦ repeat-y )
  break-before = ( none ¦ page ¦ page-odd ¦ page-even )
  break-after = ( none ¦ page ¦ page-odd ¦ page-even ¦),
  indent-start 0.0pt
  indent-end 0.0pt
  space-before-maximum  0.0pt
  space-before-minimum 0.0pt
  space-before-optimum 0.0pt
  space-after-maximum  0.0pt
  space-after-minimum 0.0pt
  space-after-optimum  0.0pt
  ```

- List-item:

  A list-item flow object contains the label and the body of each item. Use a list-item to override and modify some of the list's properties on a case-by-case basis. A list-item flow object can only be contained by a list. It is a wrapper for a list-item-label and a list-item-body.

  ```
  background-attachment = ( scroll ¦ fixed )
  background-color = a color-specifier or transparent
  background-image = a URI or none
  background-position-x = ( a length-specifier ¦ left ¦ center ¦
  ➥right )
  ```

20

```
background-position-y = ( a length-specifier ¦ top ¦ middle ¦
➥bottom )
background-repeat = ( no-repeat ¦ repeat ¦ repeat-x ¦ repeat-y )
indent-start 0.0pt
indent-end 0.0pt
item-space-before-maximum 0.0pt
item-space-before-minimum 0.0pt
item-space-before-optimum  0.0pt
item-space-after-maximum  0.0pt
item-space-after-minimum  0.0pt
item-space-after-optimum 0.0pt
```

- List-item-label:

  Use a list-item-label to either enumerate, identify, or adorn the list-item's body. A list-item-label can be contained only in a list-item. The label has content, and is formatted to become the adornment or enumeration of the list-item.

```
background-attachment = ( scroll ¦ fixed )
background-color = a color-specifier or transparent
background-image = a URI or none
background-position-x = ( a length-specifier ¦ left ¦ center ¦
➥right )
background-position-y = ( a length-specifier ¦ top ¦ middle ¦
➥bottom )
background-repeat = ( no-repeat ¦ repeat ¦ repeat-x ¦ repeat-y )
label-width 0.0pt
space-end 0.0pt
label-separator 12.0pt
```

- List-item-body:

  The list-item-body flow object holds the components (usually blocks) for a list item. It controls styling defaults for the body, the spacing between lines and between paragraphs within the list item, and the break precedence for line and paragraphs within the list item.

```
background-attachment = ( scroll ¦ fixed )
background-color = a color-specifier or transparent
background-image = a URI or none
background-position-x = ( a length-specifier ¦ left ¦ center ¦
➥right )
background-position-y = ( a length-specifier ¦ top ¦ middle ¦
➥bottom )
background-repeat = ( no-repeat ¦ repeat ¦ repeat-x ¦ repeat-y )
```

- Rule-graphic:

  A graphic representation of a line-segment used for rules and scores.

```
background-attachment = ( scroll ¦ fixed )
background-color = a color-specifier or transparent
background-image = a URI or none
```

```
background-position-x = ( a length-specifier ¦ left ¦ center ¦
➥right )
background-position-y = ( a length-specifier ¦ top ¦ middle ¦
➥bottom )
background-repeat = ( no-repeat ¦ repeat ¦ repeat-x ¦ repeat-y )
color
block-level-alignment
break-after
break-before
graphic-line-thickness
indent-end
indent-start
inhibit-wrap
keep
keep-with-previous
keep-with-next
rule-graphic-length
rule-graphic-orientation
position-point-shift
space-after-maximum
space-after-minimum
space-after-optimum
space-before-maximum
space-before-minimum
space-before-optimum
writing-mode
```

- Display-graphic:

   Use this object to create a block-level area that contains a graphic.

```
background-attachment = ( scroll ¦ fixed )
background-color = a color-specifier or transparent
background-image = a URI or none
background-position-x = ( a length-specifier ¦ left ¦ center ¦
➥right )
background-position-y = ( a length-specifier ¦ top ¦ middle ¦
➥bottom )
background-repeat = ( no-repeat ¦ repeat ¦ repeat-x ¦ repeat-y )
inline
block-level-alignment
break-after
break-before
color
external-graphic-id
graphic-max-height
graphic-max-width
graphic-scale
indent-end
indent-start
inhibit-wrap
keep
```

20

```
keep-with-previous
keep-with-next
position-point-x
position-point-y
position-preference
space-after-maximum
space-after-minimum
space-after-optimum
space-before-maximum
space-before-minimum
space-before-optimum
writing-mode
```

- Inline-box:

```
background-attachment = ( scroll ¦ fixed )
background-color = a color-specifier or transparent
background-image = a URI or none
background-position-x = ( a length-specifier ¦ left ¦ center ¦
➥right )
background-position-y = ( a length-specifier ¦ top ¦ middle ¦
➥bottom )
background-repeat = ( no-repeat ¦ repeat ¦ repeat-x ¦ repeat-y )
box-reserve-space
box-open-end
box-size-after
box-size-before
box-type
break-after
break-before
color
graphic-line-thickness
indent-end
indent-start
inhibit-textline-breaks?
keep
keep-with-previous?
keep-with-next?
space-after-maximum
space-after-minimum
space-after-optimum
space-before-maximum
space-before-minimum
space-before-optimum
writing-mode
```

- Block-level-box:

```
background-attachment = ( scroll ¦ fixed )
background-color = a color-specifier or transparent
background-image = a URI or none
background-position-x = ( a length-specifier ¦ left ¦ center ¦
➥right )
```

```
background-position-y = ( a length-specifier | top | middle |
➥bottom )
background-repeat = ( no-repeat | repeat | repeat-x | repeat-y )
box-reserve-space
box-size-after
box-size-before
box-type
break-after
break-before
color
graphic-line-thickness
indent-end
indent-start
inhibit-textline-breaks?
keep
keep-with-previous?
keep-with-next?
space-after-maximum
space-after-minimum
space-after-optimum
space-before-maximum
space-before-minimum
space-before-optimum
writing-mode
```

- Link:

  A link can be either a display-link (block-level) or an inline-link.

```
background-attachment = ( scroll | fixed )
background-color = a color-specifier or transparent
background-image = a URI or none
background-position-x = ( a length-specifier | left | center |
➥right )
background-position-y = ( a length-specifier | top | middle |
➥bottom )
background-repeat = ( no-repeat | repeat | repeat-x | repeat-y )
merge-link-end-locators = ( true | false )
```

- Link-end-locator:

  Represents a target for link.

```
background-attachment = ( scroll | fixed )
background-color = a color-specifier or transparent
background-image = a URI or none
background-position-x = ( a length-specifier | left | center |
➥right )
background-position-y = ( a length-specifier | top | middle |
➥bottom )
background-repeat = ( no-repeat | repeat | repeat-x | repeat-y )
href = ( XPointer )
show-content = ( true | false )
```

20

Avoiding Flow Objects

In an earlier example, you saw how you to use an XSL style sheet to convert XML code into HTML code. A possibly improper logical extension of this feature (improper because it runs rather counter to the spirit of XSL) is the use of XSL style sheets to allow HTML markup to be mixed with "true" XML markup. This mix creates a kind of hybrid XML/HTML similar to that described in earlier chapters.

Listing 20.20 shows a simple XML document that uses known HTML tags to mark up a table. After all, tables are handled quite well in HTML and offer an easy way to apply table formatting in XSL.

LISTING 20.20   EMBEDDING HTML MARKUP IN AN XML FILE

```
 1:  <?xml version="1.0"?>
 2:  <?xml:stylesheet type="text/xsl" href="page.xsl"?>
 3:  <PAGE>
 4:    <PARA>
 5:      These are the "new" CDs I found in CD-Warehouse.
 6:    </PARA>
 7:    <PARA>
 8:      <TABLE>
 9:        <TITLE>List of New CDs</TITLE>
10:        <TR valign="top">
11:          <TH>Artist</TH><TH>Album Title</TH>
12:        </TR>
13:        <TR valign="top">
14:          <TD>Anouk</TD>
15:          <TD>Together Alone</TD>
16:        </TR>
17:        <TR valign="top">
18:          <TD>Tori Amos</TD>
19:          <TD>Boys for Pele</TD>
20:        </TR>
21:        <TR valign="top">
22:          <TD>Crash Test Dummies</TD>
23:          <TD>The Ghosts that Haunt Me</TD>
24:        </TR>
25:        <TR valign="top">
26:          <TD>Crash Test Dummies</TD>
27:          <TD>A Worm's Life</TD>
28:        </TR>
29:      </TABLE>
30:    </PARA>
31:  </PAGE>
```

If I now develop an XSL style sheet to render this XML inside Internet Explorer 5 (beta preview 2), I can use xsl:copy to pass this XML table code through to the browser and let it apply its default HTML rendering, saving me a lot of effort. Listing 20.21 shows the XSL style sheet and Figure 20.8 shows the resulting display in Internet Explorer 5.

LISTING 20.21   USING AN XSL STYLE SHEET TO PASS HTML THROUGH UNTOUCHED

```
 1:  <?xml version="1.0"?>
 2:  <xsl:stylesheet xmlns:xsl="http://www.w3.org/TR/WD-xsl">
 3:
 4:  <xsl:template><xsl:value-of/></xsl:template>
 5:
 6:  <xsl:template match="/">
 7:    <HTML>
 8:      <BODY BGCOLOR="#FFFFFF" LINK="#000066"
 9:            VLINK="#666666" TEXT="#000000">
10:        <xsl:for-each select="PAGE">
11:          <xsl:apply-templates/>
12:        </xsl:for-each>
13:      </BODY>
14:    </HTML>
15:  </xsl:template>
16:
17:  <xsl:template match="PAGE/PARA">
18:    <P><xsl:apply-templates/></P>
19:  </xsl:template>
20:
21:  <xsl:template match="TABLE">
22:    <TABLE border="1">
23:      <xsl:apply-templates>
24:        <xsl:template>
25:          <xsl:copy>
26:            <xsl:for-each select="@*">
27:              <xsl:attribute>
28:                <xsl:value-of/>
29:              </xsl:attribute>
30:            </xsl:for-each>
31:            <xsl:apply-templates/>
32:          </xsl:copy>
33:        </xsl:template>
34:      </xsl:apply-templates>
35:    </TABLE>
36:  </xsl:template>
37:
38:  </xsl:stylesheet>
```

20

FIGURE 20.8

*The XML/HTML table
code rendered as
HTML in IE5*

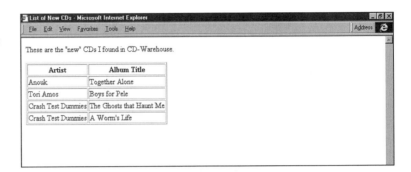

ANALYSIS There are a couple of features in Listing 20.22 that deserve a special mention. The major part of the work is done by the xsl:copy element (lines 24 to 31). Note, though, that I use an xsl:for-each element (lines 26 to 30) to step through the attributes of each element inside the TABLE element. Using select="@*", I select each of the attributes (of any type) and use the xsl:attribute element (lines 27 to 29) to copy each attribute and its value from the XML element in the input document across to the rendered display in Internet Explorer.

Summary

In this chapter you were very briefly introduced to XSL1 before we moved on to the version of XSL that superceded it. You were shown the structure of an XSL style sheet and its templates and you saw how you can not only select elements, but apply sophisticated rules for conditional selection. Many additional complex examples given in the XSL working draft are well worth experimenting with. Finally, you were introduced to XSL's formatting objects and saw practical examples of how you can use them to render your XML code.

The beta preview 2 release of Microsoft Internet Explorer 5 already supports much of the transformation part of XSL, although it doesn't support flow objects. However, with a little care in taking note of Internet Explorer's deviations from the standard, and armed with this chapter, you should know enough to start polishing your skills.

Q&A

Q What happens when there is more than one style sheet rule that matches an element?

A All of the rules are checked and only the most specific rule is applied. So, for example, select="a/b" would take precedence over select="a". You can control this by explicitly declaring a priority attribute for a rule.

Q What happens if you do not supply any rule at all for an element?

A The default processing action is applied according to the (implied) default rule. This action simply looks for any elements inside the element:

```
<xsl:apply-templates>
```

Q How can you skip elements in the source XML file?

A There are two main ways: You can either not specify a rule for the element, or you can select the element and explicitly output an empty string (the latter is preferable because the element markup would be retained so that you can check that you have actually processed the element).

Exercises

1. You have seen how you can use select to capture a specific element. Given the following fragment of XML code, write the XSL template to reverse the order and output the string (use a sequence formatting object) "cccbbbaaa":

```
<list>
  <itema>aaa</itema>
  <itemb>bbb</itemb>
  <itemc>ccc</itemc>
</list>
```

2. Using the same XML fragment used for the previous exercise, write the XSL template to skip the itemb element and output the string "aaaccc".

3. Given the following XML file, write an XSL style sheet to convert it into an HTML document:

```
<?xml version="1.0"?>
<!DOCTYPE page [
    <!ELEMENT page (#PCDATA, page)*>
    <!ELEMENT para (#PCDATA, image)*>
    <!ELEMENT image (#PCDATA)>
]>
<page>
  <title>My Home Page</title>
  <para>This is my first basic home page
            created in XML.</para>
  <para>It even includes an image:
      <image>logo.gif</image>.</para>
</page>
```

20

DAY 21

Real World XML Applications

Although I have tried to relate everything you have learned about XML in this book to something practical, and preferably something visible, that hasn't always been easy. In today's lesson I'm going to stick to that policy and, although I will review some of the more esoteric applications, I will try to concentrate on XML applications that already work. In some cases the actual implementation of these applications may be a little less than perfect.

In this chapter you will:

- Learn what the major XML applications are
- Learn some of the basics of the Mathematics Markup Language (MathML) and see how you can view your code
- Learn about structured graphics and review some of the pending developments
- Be introduced to behaviors and Microsoft's planned CSS extension
- Be introduced to Chrome and learn of Microsoft's impressive 2D and 3D interactive XML browsing environment

The State of the Game

The list of possible uses for XML is almost endless, and new applications are being added all the time. The current roll call of XML applications includes, in no particular order of importance, the following items. This list is by no means complete, but it does include the most important or the most promising applications:

- The Open Software Description (OSD) format software distribution and update—Microsoft has a vision of zero install software; software that can be downloaded from the Internet, used, and then discarded.

  Have you ever thought about the fact that when your Web browser downloads a Java applet or executes a piece of JavaScript code, you have in essence downloaded a piece of software, used it and, when you close the browser, thrown it away? By extending CSS (and you will see an example of this later in this chapter), Microsoft and Marimba would like to distribute software, even binary code, via the Internet.

- The Internet Open Trading Protocol (OTP)—An XML protocol for the exchange of financial transaction information, electronic payment, credit card information, and bank account details.

- The Java Speech Markup Language (JSML)—Adds structural information to synthesized speech so that it can sound more natural.

- The Health Level 7 (HL7) initiative for formatting electronic patient records—This doesn't just mean medical records, it means insurance information and treatment and billing details. This is probably one of the least publicized applications, but it is probably the one with the most far-reaching consequences. It comes at a time when most of the Western countries are struggling to gain control of their medical care costs: an area where administration costs seem to threaten dominance over actual medical costs.

- The Open Financial Exchange Specification (OFE)—This is another candidate format and protocol for e-commerce.

- The Handheld Device Markup Language (HDML)—This is a sort of mini-HTML that would allow hand-held devices (PDAs like the PalmPilot, mobile telephones, and palm computers) to browse the Web and communicate over the Internet.

- The Channel Definition Format (CDF)—Though once trumpeted as the breakthrough in a new model for Web publishing called *Push Media*, CDF has become a useful way of subscribing through Internet Explorer to Web sites that provided regularly updated information (news, stock price quotations, and so on).

- Visual XML (VXML)—A way of describing Web sites and publishing them in the Virtual Reality Modeling Language (VRML). This gives the browser a virtual 3D navigation experience (similar to what has already been done for some years by the Hyperwave people).

- The Signed Document Markup Language (SDML)—A means to electronically sign and verify electronic documents (a little similar to public key encryption mechanisms like those that form the heart of PGP (Pretty Good Privacy)).

- The Translation Memory Exchange (TMX)—A way to exchange vocabulary databases between (high-end) translation and localization software packages.

- OpenTag—A method for inserting XML tags in text to allow the extraction, translation, and re-insertion of translated material.

- The Platform for Privacy Preferences (P3P)—A method for Web sites to use RDF and XML to identify the nature of their content (such as adults only material).

- WebBroker—A means for distributed software components to communicate over the Internet with each other.

- The Development Markup Language (DML)—A means for development organizations (such as the WHO, UNESCO, the OECD, the Rockefeller Foundation and the World Bank) to exchange information.

- The XML Query Language (XML-QL)—An implementation of SQL in XML.

- The Bioinformatic Sequence Markup Language (BSML)—Represents and displays genetic sequence information.

- The Chemical Markup Language (CML)—Represents and displays chemical molecule information.

- The Synchronized Multimedia Integration Language (SMIL)—Integrates independent multimedia objects (video, graphics, audio, and so on) into a synchronized multimedia presentation.

This is just a small sample of the many applications that people have thought up for XML. Some of them have the backing of the largest companies (Visa, Microsoft, Oracle, to name just a few), others are personal interest involving just a few people.

I don't have the space here to go into the details of all of these applications. I have therefore picked one of the most interesting, the Mathematics Markup Language (MathML). I will also focus on two application areas (graphics and behaviors) where XML will most probably have the greatest impact on non-specialist audiences.

21

Mathematics Markup Language

One of the reasons that the TeX computer-typesetting package continues to be popular, despite being about as user-friendly as a rattlesnake, is that there are very few other affordable ways for typesetting mathematics.

Somehow, mathematics and HTML have never quite managed to live together. The extension of HTML was "on the way" for so long that now that XML has "arrived" HTML will probably never be extended to include mathematics. Even now, if you want to display basic mathematical equations in a Web page, you can choose between making a screen capture and importing it into your document as a graphics file, or wasting hours on the extremely frustrating exercise of trying to find the right symbol in the right font. (You then have to hope that readers will be prepared to go through almost as much pain to find the right fonts at their end.)

MathML attempts to correct this by providing a markup language for mathematics. There is even a Web browser that supports part of MathML; the Amaya browser can be down-loaded from the W3C site (`http://www.w3c.org/`).

MathML represents a very interesting variation on a theme that has pervaded the SGML world since the very beginning: the seemingly conflicting interests of presentation and semantic (information-based) markup. MathML combines these interests, in parallel, in the same document.

 Presentation markup is primarily concerned with the appearance of the final result. The HTML elements <HR> and <BLINK> are presentation elements.

Semantic markup is far more interested in identifying the information content of a document. This makes it possible to do other things with the data, such as render it audibly for the sight-impaired, or even (in the case of MathML) submit it to a computer algebra system so that it can plot or even solve the equation for you.

Perhaps recognizing that a picture really is worth a thousand words, MathML intends to incorporate both presentation-based and content-based markup schemes. Consider the simple equation: $x(x + 4) = 1$. Multiplying out the brackets, this gives $x^2 + 4x -1 =0$, which can be written using only presentation codes, as shown in Listing 21.1.

LISTING 21.1   AN EXAMPLE OF MATHML PRESENTATION MARKUP

```
1:  <MROW>
2:    <MROW>
3:      <MSUP>
4:        <MI>x</MI>
5:        <MN>2</MN>
```

```
 6:      </MSUP>
 7:      <MO>+</MO>
 8:      <MROW>
 9:        <MN>4</MN>
10:        <MO>&InvisibleTimes;</MO>
11:        <MI>x</MI>
12:      </MROW>
13:        <MO>-</MO>
14:        <MN>1</MN>
15:    </MROW>
16:    <MO>=</MO>
17:    <MN>0</MN>
18: </MROW>
```

Here the codes merely describe the appearance of the symbols on the page. Now compare this with Listing 21.2, where the same equation is marked up using semantic markup elements.

LISTING 21.2   AN EXAMPLE OF MATHML SEMANTIC MARKUP

```
 1:  <EXPR>
 2:    <EXPR>
 3:      <EXPR>
 4:        <MI>x</MI>
 5:        <POWER>
 6:        <MN>2</MN>
 7:      </EXPR>
 8:      <PLUS/>
 9:      <EXPR>
10:        <MN>4</MN>
11:        <TIMES>
12:        <MI>x</MI>
13:      </EXPR>
14:      <MINUS/>
15:      <MN>1</MN>
16:    </EXPR>
17:    <E/>
18:    <MN>0</MN>
19: </EXPR>
```

ANALYSIS   Listings 21.1 and 21.2 show two sets of markup that give completely different views of the same objects. One is a set of pretty meaningless symbols that are positioned in relation to each other, where terms such as superscript (element <MSUP>) and subscript (element <MSUB>) have predominated. The other displays markup that makes a semantically meaningful statement consisting of expressions (element <EXPR>).

21

These two views of markup are, however, not irreconcilable and both have their place. Presentation markup is ideally suited for display and even provides a means for an expression to make sense when it is read out loud. In contrast, content markup represents the mathematical meaning of an expression so that the statements can be understood.

Recognizing the need for both types of markup, MathML uses a sort of super element—the <SEMANTIC> element. This element has two children. The first child is the presentation markup, and the second child is the semantic markup. Within MathML, the semantic markup would be a set of MathML content tags, but it doesn't have to be (it could be code that makes sense to some other program). The content of the semantic markup could be a computer algebra expression, or it could even be computer program source code (in C or even Java).

At the moment there is no support for the semantic part of XML, although there are a few individuals who are experimenting with it. The Amaya browser, however, does support the presentation part of XML. Listing 21.3 shows some simple examples of one of the most basic features of all mathematics (and a lot of other text), superscripts, and subscripts, and Figure 21.1 shows what it looks like in Amaya.

INPUT

LISTING 21.3 THE MATHML PRESENTATION MARKUP FOR SUBSCRIPTS AND SUPERSCRIPTS

```
 1: <html>
 2: <head>
 3: <title>MathML Examples 1</title>
 4: </head>
 5: <body>
 6: <h1>Subscripts and Superscripts</h1>
 7: <hr>
 8: <h4>A Simple Subscript</h4>
 9:
10: <math>
11:   <msub>
12:     <mi>x</mi>
13:     <mn>y</mn>
14:   </msub>
15: </math>
16:
17: <hr>
18: <h4>A Simple Superscript</h4>
19: <math>
20:   <msup>
21:     <mi>x</mi>
22:     <mn>a</mn>
23:   </msup>
24: </math>
```

```
25:
26: <hr>
27: <h4>A Subscript Squared</h4>
28: <math>
29:   <msup>
30:     <msub>
31:       <mi>x</mi>
32:       <mn>n</mn>
33:     </msub>
34:     <mn>2</mn>
35:   </msup>
36: </math>
37: <p></p>
38: <hr>
39: <h4>A Subscript and a Superscript Combined</h4>
40:
41: <math>
42:   <msubsup>
43:     <mi>x</mi>
44:     <mn>a</mn>
45:     <mn>b</mn>
46:   </msubsup>
47: </math>
48: <p></p>
49: <hr>
50: </body>
51: </html>
```

OUTPUT

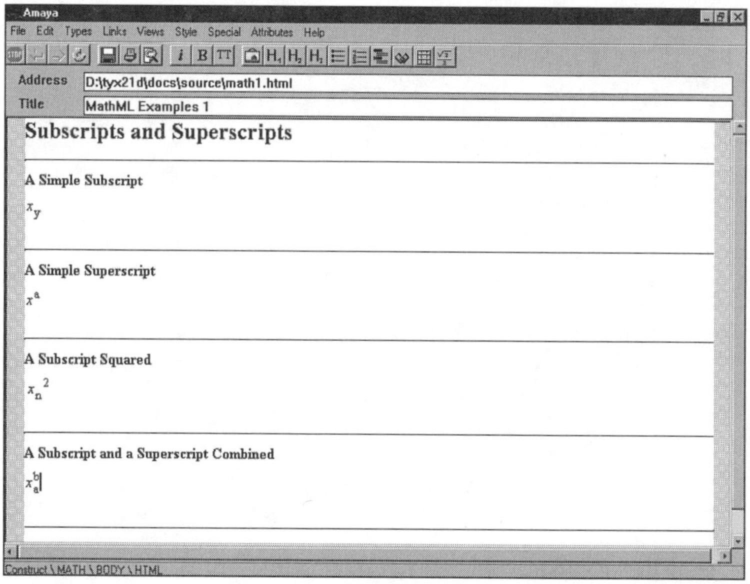

FIGURE 21.1

This is how Amaya displays the MathML code from Listing 21.3.

21

ANALYSIS Superscripts and subscripts aren't really that demanding. There are even HTML character codes that allow you to insert the small numbers. Listing 21.4 shows something a little more demanding—an example of the MathML code for some simple matrices. Figure 21.2 shows what the code looks like in Amaya.

INPUT   **LISTING 21.4**   THE MathML PRESENTATION MARKUP FOR MATRICES

```
 1: <!DOCTYPE HTML PUBLIC "-//W3C//DTD HTML 4.0 Transitional//EN">
 2: <html>
 3: <head>
 4: <title>
 5: MathML Examples 2</title>
 6: </head>
 7: <body>
 8: <h1>Matrices</h1>
 9: <hr>
10:
11: <h4>A Simple Matrix</h4>
12: <math>
13:   <mfenced open="[" close="]">
14:     <mfrac>
15:       <mi>a</mi>
16:       <mi>b</mi>
17:     </mfrac>
18:   </mfenced>
19: </math>
20: <hr>
21:
22: <h4>Complex Braces (fences)</h4>
23: <math>
24:   <mfenced open="(" close="]">
25:     <mfrac>
26:       <mi>a</mi>
27:       <mi>b</mi>
28:     </mfrac>
29:   </mfenced>
30: </math>
31: <hr>
32:
33: <h4>A More Complex Matrix (math table)</h4>
34: <math>
35:   <mfenced open="(" close=")">
36:     <mtable>
37:       <mtr>
38:         <mtd>
39:           <mn>1</mn>
```

```
40:           </mtd>
41:           <mtd>
42:             <mn>0</mn>
43:           </mtd>
44:           <mtd>
45:             <mn>0</mn>
46:           </mtd>
47:         </mtr>
48:         <mtr>
49:           <mtd>
50:             <mn>0</mn>
51:           </mtd>
52:           <mtd>
53:             <mn>1</mn>
54:           </mtd>
55:           <mtd>
56:             <mn>0</mn>
57:           </mtd>
58:         </mtr>
59:         <mtr>
60:           <mtd>
61:             <mn>0</mn>
62:           </mtd>
63:           <mtd>
64:             <mn>0</mn>
65:           </mtd>
66:           <mtd>
67:             <mn>1</mn>
68:           </mtd>
69:         </mtr>
70:       </mtable>
71:     </mfenced>
72: </math>
73: <hr>
74: </body>
75: </html>
```

21

OUTPUT

FIGURE 21.2

This is how Amaya displays the MathML code from Listing 21.4.

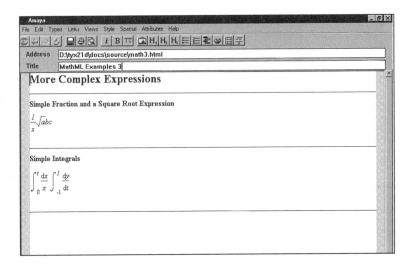

ANALYSIS Matrices, arrangements of characters or digits that are enclosed by brackets and braces, are notoriously difficult to get right. The brackets and braces have to be scaled to fit the contents, and normally this means trying to build up composites using separate characters for the ends and vertical lines for the center pieces. Listing 21.4 shows how easy it can be to specify any kind of bracket or brace you want. They can even be scaled automatically, as shown in Figure 21.2.

Matrices alone are quite an achievement, but what would mathematics be without integrals and all those other awkward symbols? Listing 21.5 shows a couple of more complex equations. Figure 21.3 shows what they look like in Amaya.

INPUT   **LISTING 21.5**   THE MATHML PRESENTATION MARKUP FOR MORE COMPLEX MATH

```
1:  <!DOCTYPE HTML PUBLIC "-//W3C//DTD HTML 4.0 Transitional//EN">
2:  <html>
3:  <head>
4:  <title>MathML Examples 3</title>
5:  <body>
6:  <h1>More Complex Expressions</h1>
7:  <hr>
8:  <h4>Simple Fraction and a Square Root Expression</h4>
9:  <math>
10:   <mfrac>
11:     <mi>1</mi>
12:     <mi>x</mi>
13:   </mfrac>
```

```
14:    <msqrt>
15:      <mi>a</mi>
16:      <mi>b</mi>
17:      <mi>c</mi>
18:    </msqrt>
19: </math>
20: <p></p>
21: <hr>
22: <h4>Simple Integrals</h4>
23: <math>
24:    <mrow>
25:      <msubsup>
26:        <mo>&int;</mo>
27:        <mn>0</mn>
28:        <mi>t</mi>
29:      </msubsup>
30:      <mfrac>
31:        <mrow>
32:          <mo>&dd;</mo>
33:          <mi>x</mi>
34:        </mrow>
35:        <mi>x</mi>
36:      </mfrac>
37:    </mrow>
38:    <mrow>
39:      <msubsup>
40:        <mo>&int;</mo>
41:        <mn>-1</mn>
42:        <mi>1</mi>
43:      </msubsup>
44:      <mfrac>
45:        <mrow>
46:          <mo>&dd;</mo>
47:          <mi>y</mi>
48:        </mrow>
49:        <mi>dt</mi>
50:      </mfrac>
51:    </mrow>
52: </math>
53: <p></p>
54: <hr>
55: </body>
56: </html>
```

21

FIGURE 21.3

This is how Amaya displays the MathML code from Listing 21.5.

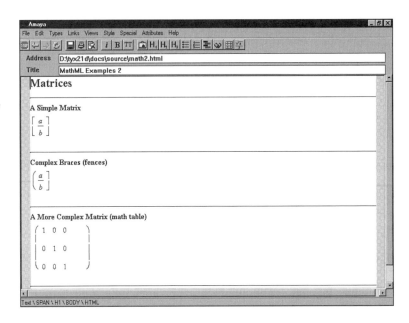

As you can see, Amaya makes pretty light work of displaying additional mathematical symbols.

MathML is not yet finished—it still has a number of features that need to be worked out. It is also a long way from being supported in the major Web browsers. However, there is a browser plug-in called EzMath that uses a proprietary math code, but the editor can create MathML code too (you can download this free software from `http://www.w3.org/People/Raggett/EzMath.zip`).

Structured Graphics

As soon as Web browsers started to be able to display graphics, people wanted it to be possible for something to happen if you clicked on them. Linked images followed, then buttons, and then HTML image maps—first those interpreted by the server (server-side) and then those interpreted by the browser itself (client-side).

Image maps allow the link to depend on where you click in the image. Unfortunately, these image maps are simple lists of very simple objects (circles, squares, and regular polygons) with fixed coordinates. Listing 21.6 shows an example of an HTML client-side image map.

LISTING 21.6   A TYPICAL HTML CLIENT-SIDE IMAGE MAP

```
1: <map name="map">
2: <area shape="rect" coords="33,78,58,88" href="1.html">
3: <area shape="circle" coords="164,207,57" href="2.html">
4: <area shape="poly" coords="146,35,165,69,134,127,123,96,
5:    105,77,69,82,39,81,20,66,19,55,51,54,118,31,0,19474"
6:    href="3.html">
```

As anyone who's tried can tell you, maintaining these kinds of coordinate graphics is a nightmare. Each time the graphics change, you basically have to re-create the image map from scratch (there are a few tools that can read in and modify an image map, but you still have to replace the map in the HTML file).

Now, add to the problem the fact that most graphics are bitmaps. Bitmaps are essentially binary data that represents the color of the dots (pixels) on the computer screen. Because they address specific dots of light, bitmaps are very sensitive to what resolution of screen you are using. For example, I currently have a screen resolution of 1152×864 pixels with 65,536 colors. When I want to capture a screen to show it in this book, for technical reasons I have to drop down to 800×600 pixels and 256 colors. What looks great at the higher resolution can look absolutely terrible at low resolution, and vice versa. The situation is almost exactly the same if I want to zoom in on a graphic, no matter what the resolution. Sooner or later, using a bitmap graphic will just become a blur of colored blocks as you start to be able to pick out the individual pixels of color. This problem is demonstrated in the grossly magnified digital photograph shown in Figure 21.4.

FIGURE 21.4

A Photograph magnified so that the individual pixels are visible.

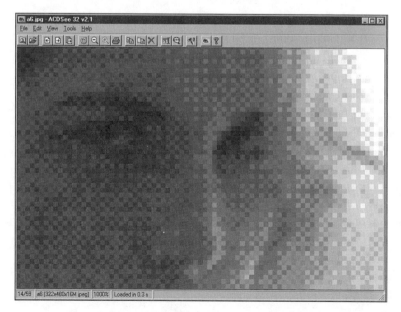

21

There are many alternative formats for bitmaps (such as TIFF, GIF, JPEG, and BMP, to name just a few). Each of these formats has its own strengths and weaknesses and therefore each has its own special area for which it is most suitable. For vector graphics, there are two competing formats: Windows Metafile (WMF) and Computer Graphics Metafile (CGM).

NEW TERM Instead of describing individual pixels, *vector graphics* use primitive objects such as lines and arcs. These objects are described by means of starting points, directions, and lengths (vectors). The display software has to translate this data into something you can see (on a screen or on a piece of paper, for example) which makes vector graphics completely independent of the output device resolution. Vector graphics can be scaled almost endlessly (certainly to the point where what you see no longer makes any sense at all).

Bitmaps are *raster formats* that break an image into a grid of equally sized pieces, called pixels, and record color information for each pixel.

There is a third sort of format. Meta formats can contain vector data and a raster image. A Windows metafile (WMF) format file, for example, can contain a bitmap, vector information, and text, with the bitmap forming the major part of the image and the vector and text data being used for annotations.

Vector graphics can easily be expressed in a plain text (ASCII) format. This immediately begs the question of whether they can then be expressed in XML. The answer to that question is a resounding yes and there are several initiatives that are addressing that very idea.

WebCGM

WebCGM is not an XML application and so I won't go into much detail about it here, but it does at least deserve a mention.

CGM (Computer Graphics Metafile) has been an ISO standard since 1987, and it's been a recognized Internet format (MIME type) since 1995. However, although it is the preferred format for technical documentation it hasn't made much of an impact on the Web (there is a browser plug-in that allows you to view CGM data). There isn't that much mass-market software that fully supports it either. Most graphics packages allow you to view, and possibly write, CGM raster data, but there are very few packages that can deal with CGM vector data. Nevertheless, Boeing (one of the major users) and some of the leading software companies in this area (including Intercap, Inso, and ITEDO) have proposed a profile of CGM called WebCGM that introduces metadata that can be used for hyperlinking, document navigation, and searching based on picture content.

Precision Graphics Markup Language

PGML is Adobe's expansion of the PostScript/PDF format. Put very simply, PGML translates PostScript commands into XML elements and attributes.

NEW TERM Many people are aware that *PostScript* is a page description language—a formal description of the layout of ink on a page. When you print a PostScript document, you send a series of PostScript commands in which your data is embedded to a dedicated processor in the printer. The processor then interprets and executes the commands.

To demonstrate, Listing 21.7 shows the PostScript code taken from a small test file that prints out the characters in a font in various sizes. The resulting display is shown in Figure 21.5.

INPUT   **LISTING 21.7**   A TYPICAL POSTSCRIPT FILE

```
 1:  % Check for command line parameters:
 2:  %        Name, FirstSize, Ratio, NumSizes, UseOutline.
 3:
 4:  /FontName where { pop } { /FontName (Palatino-Italic) def } ifelse
 5:  /FirstSize where { pop } { /FirstSize 15 def } ifelse
 6:  /Ratio where { pop } { /Ratio 1.6 def } ifelse
 7:  /NumSizes where { pop } { /NumSizes 3 def } ifelse
 8:  /UseOutline where { pop } { /UseOutline false def } ifelse
 9:
10:  /Strings FirstSize 20 gt
11:  { [
12:          (ABCDEFGHIJ) (KLMNOPQR) (STUVWXYZ)
13:          (abcdefghijklm) (nopqrstuvwxyz)
14:          (0123456789<=>) (:;?@  !"#$%&')
15:          (\(\)*+,-./[\\]^_) (`{|}~)
16:  ] }
17:  { [
18:          (ABCDEFGHIJKLMNOPQRSTUVWXYZ)
19:          (abcdefghijklmnopqrstuvwxyz)
20:          (0123456789<=>:;?@  !"#$%&')
21:          (\(\)*+,-./  [\\]^_  `{|}~)
22:  ] }
23:  ifelse def
24:
25:  /sshow
26:  { gsave UseOutline
27:      { { gsave ( ) dup 0 4 -1 roll put
28:          false charpath pathbbox 0 setlinewidth stroke grestore
29:          pop 8 add currentpoint exch pop moveto pop
30:        } forall
31:      }
```

21

LISTING 21.7 CONTINUED

```
32:    { 2 0 3 -1 roll ashow }
33:    ifelse grestore
34: } def
35:
36: FontName findfont FirstSize scalefont setfont
37:
38: clippath pathbbox /top exch def pop pop pop newpath
39: 10 10 moveto
40: NumSizes
41: { gsave nulldevice (Q) false charpath pathbbox grestore
42:    exch pop exch sub exch pop 1.25 mul /height exch def
43:    Strings
44:    { currentpoint exch pop top height 3 mul sub gt
45:       { showpage 10 10 height sub moveto
46:       }
47:    if
48:    dup sshow
49:    UseOutline not
50:       { 0 height rmoveto gsave 0.01 rotate sshow grestore }
51:    if
52:    0 height rmoveto
53:    } forall
54:    Ratio dup scale
55: } repeat
56: showpage
```

OUTPUT

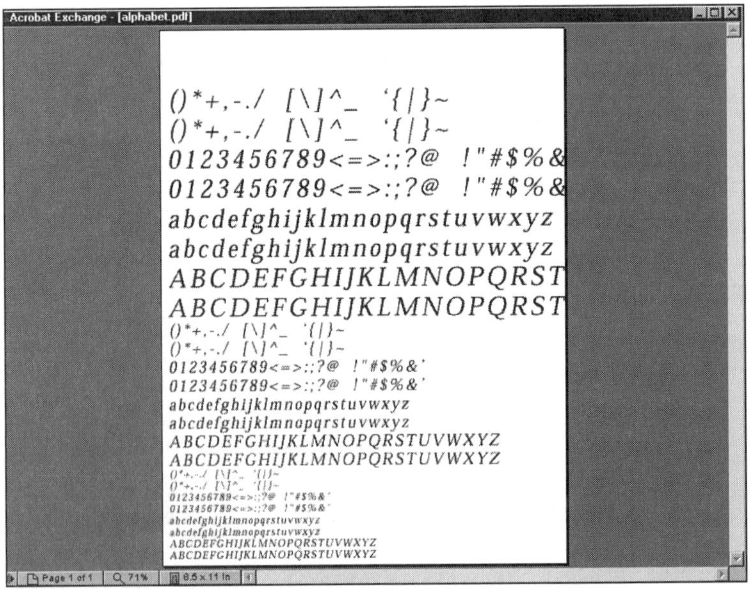

FIGURE 21.5

The PostScript code from Listing 21.7 looks like this when displayed as an Adobe Acrobat (PDF) File.

ANALYSIS As you can see from Listing 21.7, there are quite clearly commands being sent. Indeed, although Adobe's PDF format is a binary format, if you filter out the binary codes you can still detect some of the remnants of the original PostScript commands, as shown in Listing 21.8.

OUTPUT **LISTING 21.8** A FRAGMENT OF POSTSCRIPT FILE OF LISTING 21.7 AFTER CONVERSION INTO ADOBE ACROBAT (PDF) FORMAT

```
 1: <<
 2: /ProcSet [/PDF /Text ]
 3: /Font <<
 4: /F2 4 0 R
 5: >>
 6: /ExtGState <<
 7: /GS1 5 0 R
 8: >>
 9: >>
10: endobj
11: 7 0 obj
12: <<
13: /Type /Halftone
14: /HalftoneType 1
15: /HalftoneName (Default)
16: /Frequency 60
17: /Angle 45
18: /SpotFunction /Round
19: >>
20: endobj
21: 5 0 obj
22: <<
23: /Type /ExtGState
24: /SA false
25: /OP false
26: /HT /Default
27: >>
28: endobj
29: 8 0 obj
30: <<
31: /Type /FontDescriptor
32: /Ascent 733
33: /CapHeight 692
34: /Descent -276
35: /Flags 98
36: /FontBBox [-170 -276 1010 918]
37: /FontName /Palatino-Italic
38: /ItalicAngle -10
39: /StemV 84
40: /XHeight 482
41: >>
42: endobj
```

21

I won't go into the technical details of PostScript here, but it's enough to say that it uses a very few basic commands consisting of path instructions (such as moveto, lineto, and curveto) and attributes (such as height, linewidth, and rgbcolor). These instructions are actually quite simple to translate into XML elements and attributes. Listing 21.9 shows a very simple PGML file.

INPUT   **LISTING 21.9**   A SAMPLE PGML FILE

```
1:   <?XML version="1.0"?>
2:   <!DOCTYPE PGML SYSTEM "pgml1.0.dtd">
3:   <pgml boundingbox="0 0 300 300">
4:     <path fill="1" fillcolor="100 0 0">
5:       <moveto x="100" y="100"/>
6:       <lineto x="150"/>
7:       <lineto y="150"/>
8:       <lineto x="100"/>
9:       <lineto y="100"/>
10:    </path>
11: </pgml>
```

ANALYSIS   The PGML code shown in Listing 21.9 produces a small, solid red box: bound-ingbox declares the x and y coordinates of the area in which the drawing will be done (0,0—the bottom left-hand corner, to 300,300). The fillcolor instructions sets the Red, Green, and Blue color values (100,0,0) of the color that will be used to fill the object, and moveto sets the starting point to (100,100). Finally, the four lineto instructions draw the sides; the corners are at (100,100), (150,100), (150,150), and (100,150).

Adobe has been extremely adventurous and, as an outsider, I'd say that they'd decided that if they were going to do it all then they decided they were going to do it right. PSGML doesn't stop with just converting PostScript into XML; it takes the development several exciting steps further. It allows you to:

- Name objects and groups of objects so that they can easily be found by software for applying links or searching

- Embed XML links inside objects

- Embed scripting into the PSGML file so a browser will behave just as if the script-ing commands had been placed in the enveloping HTML file

- Embed event handling (based on the Document Object Model that you learned about on Day 16, "Programming with the Document Object Model") to enable interaction and animation

There are as yet no software packages that support the creation of PGML code, and there is no way to display or use the code once it has been written. Indeed, less than half of the PGML specification has been written. However, every indication is that Adobe takes it very seriously and it cannot be too long before the first packages appear.

Vector Markup Language

When Microsoft brought out Internet Explorer version 4, it also brought out a development called structured graphics. Structured graphics are an ASCII vector format for describing drawings. This format is really of historical interest only, but it is supported by Internet Explorer version 4 and will still be supported in Internet Explorer version 5. There is a tool available from Microsoft, called wmfcnv.exe, that can convert vector Windows Metafile format (WMF) files into structured graphics format.

Note

Note that you must use vector format metafiles. A lot of common graphics packages (such as PaintShop Pro) can only write the raster version of these files. You will not be able to convert these files (wmfcnv is a very small and simple utility—it will not tell you anything but the output file will be empty).

There aren't many packages that can create these vector format files; one that can is CorelDraw.

If you want a ready source of true vector format metafiles, check the clip art library supplied with Microsoft Word or Microsoft Office, or check the live clip art Web pages on Microsoft's Web site (www.microsoft.com).

Listing 21.10 is a very simple structured graphics file for the creation of a yin-yang symbol embedded in an HTML file.

INPUT   **LISTING 21.10**   A YIN-YANG SYMBOL IN STRUCTURED GRAPHICS FORMAT

```
1:  <html>
2:  <head>
3:  <title>Structured Graphic</title>
4:  </head>
5:  <body>
6:  <H1>Animated Yin-Yang</H1>
7:  <p>
8:  <object ID="yin-yang"
9:  CLASSID="CLSID:369303C2-D7AC-11D0-89D5-00A0C90833E6"
10: STYLE="height: 200; width:200; zindex:10">
```

21

continues

LISTING **21.10**   CONTINUED

```
11: <PARAM NAME="Line0001" VALUE="SetLineColor(0,0,0)">
12: <PARAM NAME="Line0002" VALUE="SetFillColor(255,0,0)">
13: <PARAM NAME="Line0003" VALUE="SetLineStyle(6)">
14: <PARAM NAME="Line0004" VALUE="Polygon(102,2,5,-1,3,-3,1,-8,-3,-11,
15: -5,-12,-8,-14,-11,-15,-14,-17,-18,-17,-20,-17,-23,-17,-26,-16,-29,
16: -15,-32,-14,-35,-12,-38,-9,-41,-7,-43,-5,-44,-3,-46,-1,-47,2,-47,4,
17: -48,6,-48,8,-48,13,-48,9,-49,7,-49,4,-49,1,-49,-2,-49,-5,-49,-7,-49,
18: -10,-49,-13,-48,-17,-47,-20,-46,-23,-44,-26,-43,-29,-41,-31,-39,-33,
19: -37,-35,-35,-37,-33,-39,-31,-41,-29,-42,-27,-44,-24,-45,-22,-46,-19,
20: -47,-17,-48,-14,-49,-11,-50,-8,-50,-5,-50,-2,-50,1,-50,4,-50,7,-49,11
21: ,-49,14,-48,17,-47,19,-46,22,-45,24,-43,27,-41,29,-39,32,-38,34,-36,
22: 36,-34,38,-32,39,-30,41,-27,43,-26,44,-24,45,-22,46,-20,46,-17,47,
23: -15,47,-13,47,-11,47,-8,47,-6,46,-3,45,1,44,1,43,3,41,4,40,6,
24: 38,7,35,8,33,9,31,10,28,10,25,10,23,10,20,9,17,8,14,7,12
25: ,6,10,4,7)">
26: <PARAM NAME="Line0005" VALUE="SetFillColor(255,255,0)">
27: <PARAM NAME="Line0006" VALUE="Polygon(102,-3,-4,0,-2,
28: 2,0,7,4,10,6,11,9,13,12,14,15,16,18,16,21,16,24,16,27,
29: 15,30,14,33,13,36,11,39,8,42,6,44,4,45,2,47,0,48,-3,48,
30: -5,49,-7,49,-9,49,-14,49,-10,49,-8,50,-5,50,-2,50,1,50,4,
31: 50,6,50,9,50,12,49,16,48,19,47,22,45,25,44,28,42,30,40,32,
32: 38,34,36,36,34,38,32,40,30,41,28,43,25,44,23,45,20,46,18,
33: 47,15,48,12,49,9,49,6,49,3,50,0,49,-3,49,-6,48,-10,48,-13,
34: 47,-16,46,-18,45,-21,44,-23,42,-26,40,-28,38,-31,37,-33,35,
35: -35,33,-37,31,-38,29,-40,26,-42,25,-43,23,-44,21,-45,19,-45,
36: 16,-46,14,-46,12,-46,10,-46,7,-46,5,-45,2,-44,0,-43,-2,-42,-4,
37: -40,-5,-39,-7,-37,-8,-35,-9,-32,-10,-30,-11,-27,-11,-24,-11,
38: -22,-11,-19,-10,-16,-9,-13,-8,-11,-7,-9,-5,-6)">
39: </object>
40: </body>
41: </html>
```

This file, displayed in Internet Explorer 5, is shown in Figure 21.6.

OUTPUT

FIGURE 21.6

This is what Listing 21.10 looks likes like in Internet Explorer 5.

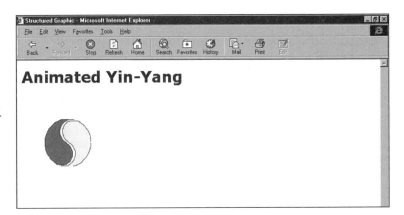

ANALYSIS The structured graphics format shown in Listing 21.10 obviously doesn't have the high information content of PGML, but it does work. Generally, this structured graphics file format is about 20% smaller than the equivalent Windows Metafile format file, which, if it only contains a vector image, is already very compact. The bigger the file, the larger the space saving.

One of the interesting features of this format is that it is very easy to animate. By adding just nine lines, I can animate this drawing so that it will rotate when you click the button, as shown in Listing 21.11.

INPUT **LISTING 21.11** ANIMATING THE YIN-YANG SYMBOL

```
 1:  <html>
 2:  <head>
 3:  <title>Structured Graphic</title>
 4:  <SCRIPT LANGUAGE="JavaScript">
 5:  <!--
 6:  function Rotate(degVar){
 7:    widget.rotate(0,degVar,0);
 8:    window.setTimeout("Rotate(5)",040,"JavaScript");
 9:  }
10:  -->
11:  </script>
12:  </head>
13:  <body>
14:  <H1>Animated Yin-Yang</H1>
15:  <p>
16:  <object
17:  ID="widget"
18:
19:  .
20:  . put object code here
21:  .
22:
23:  </object>
24:  <p>
25:  <INPUT TYPE=button ID=rotate VALUE="ROTATE" onclick="Rotate(0)">
26:  </body>
27:  </html>
```

Three illustrations of the rotating image are shown in Figures 21.7, 21.8, and 21.9.

21

OUTPUT

FIGURE 21.7

*This is a view of the
rotating Yin-Yang
symbol in Internet
Explorer 5.*

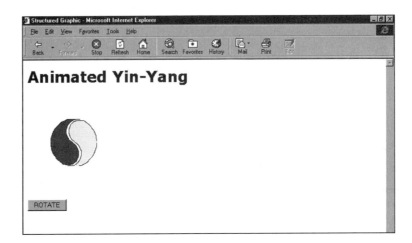

FIGURE 21.8

*This is another view
of the rotating Yin-
Yang Symbol in
Internet Explorer 5.*

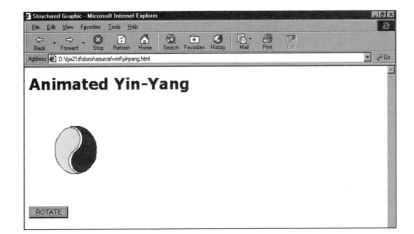

FIGURE 21.9

*A third view of the
rotating Yin-Yang
Symbol in Internet
Explorer 5.*

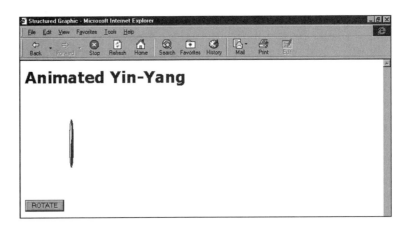

Curiously, the more times you click the button, the faster the image appears to rotate but, because there is internal processing rather than file loading to be done, the speed at which the image is redrawn is quite fast. Structured graphics were a forerunner of Microsoft's Vector Markup Language (VML). VML takes the basics of structured graphics but puts them inside XML elements (taken from the VML namespace). If I were to take my yin-yang symbol from Listing 21.10 (I won't since I'd have to do it by hand and there are no tools to check the results afterwards), part of it might look something like this:

```
<v:line id="Line0002" from="0 0 " to="100 100"
   style="visibility: visible"
   stroke="true" strokecolor="black">
<v:curve from="0 0" to="0 0" style="visibility: visible">
```

I won't go into any more detail about VML here because there's no way to guarantee that any code I produce is correct. Furthermore, the submission to the W3C is (October 1998) still only a note, which has precious little official standing. However, informed sources say that Microsoft intends to go ahead and implement VML, regardless of what the W3C does. I gather from a visit to the Microsoft campus in Redmond that we may even hope to see it in Microsoft Office 2000 and that conversion tools from existing graphics formats are on their way.

Behaviors

One of the major practical breakthroughs that resulted from the introduction of SGML was that it was possible to separate the appearance of text information from the information itself. For many professional technical writers (myself included), it meant that they no longer had to care whether they'd used the right font or not, or whether a product name should be in italic or bold. All the writer had to do was select the right element in which to wrap a certain piece of text and the authoring software would automatically choose the right appearance. Better still, it meant that the graphic designers responsible for the layout of documents could work independently, in parallel with the writers, without either party having to wait for the other.

Web pages have evolved in a similar fashion. Graphics and content came under the same roof until style sheets were developed, although many HTML pages still do not use style sheets. The appearance of style sheets meant that graphic designers and the content writers were able to divide the work between them. However, then people discovered interaction and animation; they wanted text that moved, and zoomed. Almost overnight a new bottleneck was created as everyone had to wait for the programmer to add the script, tweak the code, test the page, then hand it over for uploading to the server. Then there came the chaos associated with what script was best to use (Jscript, JavaScript, ActiveX,

21

Java?) and where one found these script writers. Furthermore, you had to consider code re-use (the heart and soul of modern software development). Forget it—the closest you can get to that is good-old cut and paste!

It was only a matter of time before someone proposed a method of externalizing the behavior of HTML code—and both Netscape and Microsoft have tables their own solutions.

Action Sheets

Action sheets, or more properly, *Cascading Action System* (CAS), are Netscape's proposal for attaching behaviors to XML elements.

CAS works in two ways; for HTML an action sheet is attached to an element by using a minor extension of the Cascading Stylesheet (CSS) syntax. In the HTML code, you'd simply add another LINK element to point to the style sheet, like this:

```
<LINK REL="ActionSheet" TYPE="text/act" HREF="flip.act">
```

The behavior that you want to add to the page (or part of it) is encapsulated in the external script file `flip.act`, which can be in any language the browser can handle.

The elements that you want to have this behavior can simply be given the right class attribute, like this:

```
<P CLASS="flip">This paragraph will flip when you click on it<P>
```

For XML, Netscape proposes creating an action sheet as an XML document and then associating it with the target XML document in the same way as is currently done for CSS style sheets (using processing instructions as you saw on Days 13, "Viewing XML in Other Browsers" and 18, "Styling XML with CSS"). A typical action sheet could then look a little like the sketch shown in Listing 21.12.

INPUT   **LISTING 21.12**   A TEMPLATE ACTION SHEET DOCUMENT

```
1:  <!DOCTYPE actionsheet SYSTEM "asheet.dtd">
2:  <actionsheet>
3:
4:  <action type="text/cas" codetype="text/javascript">
5:  @import url(http://purl.org/simonscripts/flip.cas")
6:  .flip ( onMouseover: "flip(event)"; onMouseOut: "flop(event)")
7:  </action>
8:
9:  <script type="text/javascript" src="flip.js">
10: </script>
11:
```

```
12: <script type="text/javascript">
13: function flip(e) { … }
14: function flop(e) { … }
15: </script>
16: </actionsheet>
```

There are no implementations of action sheets yet.

CSS Behavior

Microsoft calls this method for adding behavior *DHTML Behaviors*. As far as I know it has not (yet) been submitted to the W3C for consideration, and I'm not sure if it ever will.

The principle of this mechanism is very simple. All you have to do is add the script to the XML element, as shown in Listing 21.13.

LISTING 21.13   AN HTML FILE WITH DYNAMIC BEHAVIOR

```
 1:  <html>
 2:  <head>
 3:  <title>Jumping XML</title>
 4:  <XML:namespace prefix="IE5"/>
 5:  <style>
 6:  @namespace IE5 {
 7:    getsclass {
 8:      font-family: courier; color: red; font-weight: bold;
 9:      border-style: solid;  background-color: yellow;
10:      border-color: black; border-width: 3; width: 240;
11:      height: 140; padding: 10
12:      }
13:    }
14:  </style>
15:  </head>
16:  <body>
17:  <h1>Application of CSS Behavior to XML</h1>
18:  <P>This paragraph is standard HTML code.</p>
19:  <IE5:getsclass onclick="this.style.position = 'static';"
20:    style="position: absolute;
21:    top: 200; left: 200">This paragraph is XML code, with behavior
22:    attached to it by a style.
23:  Click on it, and it will jump
24:    to a new position.</IE5:getsclass>
25:  <P>This paragraph is also standard HTML code,
26:    it will make room for the XML
27:  paragraph when it moves.</p></body>
28:  </html>
```

21

Figures 21.10 and 21.11 illustrate what the browser displays before and after the addition of the script to the XML element.

The dynamic XML paragraph in Internet Explorer 5 before it's clicked.

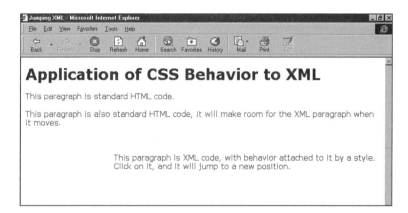

The dynamic XML paragraph in Internet Explorer 5 after it's been clicked.

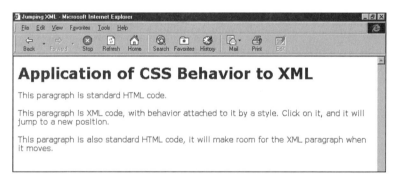

ANALYSIS Embedding the behavior works, as you can see from the before and after illustrations (Figures 21.10 and 21.11). However, it only gets us part of the way there because the code is still inside the HTML/XML document.

Microsoft's solution for importing externally defined behavior, like Netscape's solution, is to use the existing CSS style sheet mechanism. Microsoft, though, has also slightly extended the CSS syntax to add a new behavior property. I have rewritten Listing 21.13 to externalize this behavior and titled it Listing 21.14.

INPUT **LISTING 21.14** AN HTML FILE WITH DYNAMIC BEHAVIOR

```
1:  <html>
2:  <head>
3:  <title>Jumping XML</title>
4:  <XML:namespace prefix="IE5"/>
5:  <style>
```

```
6:   IE5\:jump {style="font-color: red"; behavior: url(jump.sct);}
7:   </style>
8:   </head>
9:   <body>
10:  <h1>Application of CSS Behavior to XML</h1>
11:  <P>This paragraph is standard HTML code.</p>
12:  <IE5:jump>This paragraph is XML code, with behavior
13:  attached to it by a style.
14:  style. Click on it, and it will jump
15:   to a new position.</IE5:getsclass>
16:  <P>This paragraph is also standard HTML code,
17:   it will make room for the XML
18:  paragraph when it moves.</p></body>
19:  </html>
```

ANALYSIS Listing 21.14 behaves exactly the same way as Listing 21.13 (I do, of course have to shift the behavior code into the file pointed to by the URL in the behavior property). Note that in Listing 21.14, I have used an embedded style sheet (using the STYLE tag), but I could just as easily have moved this to an external style sheet.

Microsoft seems to have great plans for behaviors. One of the many things rumored to be on the way is the ability to not just use scripts to attach behavior to elements, but also ActiveX controls. In practice, this could have much the same effect as allowing a Web page to run a normal program on your computer. While it opens up exciting possibilities for extending the capabilities of Web pages (imagine logging into a help desk for a software package and having an interactive demonstration of how to use a feature on your own screen), the thought of allowing this kind of access does raise the usual questions concerning security. Whatever happens, it will most certainly be interesting.

Microsoft's Chrome

For a company that discovered the Internet so late, Microsoft has caught up quickly. Indeed, in some areas they are now so far ahead of the rest of the pack that it's almost breathtaking to watch. Chrome is one of these areas. Unfortunately, Chrome is not for the less dedicated—it requires a 350 MHz Pentium computer with at least 64 MB of RAM, a minimum of a 100 MHz bus speed, an AGP graphics card, and Windows 98.

Chrome is an XML application that allows you to make 2D and 3D interactive animations. Yes, I know VRML can do this already, and I already mentioned another attempt to achieve something similar earlier in this chapter (VXML). Picture a three-dimensional cube floating in the center of your Web browser's window. You can rotate the cube as you want by moving your mouse to the left and right, or up and down. You can zoom in on one of the faces by using the scroll dial on the mouse. Each of the faces of the cube

21

has a Web page on it, in perfect miniature: text, graphics, the works. (Chrome allows you to add any texture to any surface and that texture can also be an HTML Web page.) Rotate an interesting face to the front and click on it; the cube explodes outward to show six more pages textured onto the inside surfaces.

There are two major challenges to face in Chrome; the technical one (getting it to work), and the practical one of how on earth do we use this—how are we going to create applications that use it? There are a million questions to ask and it's going to be some time before we learn to master this new kind of user interaction.

Summary

In today's chapter I have taken you from the down-to-earth problems of displaying mathematical equations to the almost science fiction vision of interactive 3D XML experiences. Along the way you learned about graphics applications and how XML is going to provide solutions to some very old problems, as well as how XML and behaviors may solve some of the more recent problems of code re-use and distribution.

Q&A

Q Why is MathML so different from the other markup languages?

A Markup languages often have to make a choice between being purely presentational or being semantic (information oriented). Many find an uneasy compromise by mixing the two. MathML is unique in that it still mixes presentational and semantic markup, but it does it with two parallel markup sets.

Q Why are graphics such an important area for XML?

A Graphics are a sort of black hole on the Web. You can't link into them and you can't link out of them (although you can link to them and you can link from them). Worse, it's almost impossible to include them in searches unless, for example, someone happened to name the graphic file something useful. XML has the potential to make graphics as accessible as XML markup.

Q Why are behaviors such a profitable application area for XML?

A Adding code (scripts and so on) to HTML pages is becoming a bottleneck in the Web page production line. The current method of simply putting code in pages also makes re-use almost impossible. XML and CSS make it possible to externalize the behavior of elements, allowing the development effort to be shared and code to be re-used.

Exercises

1. Download Amaya from the W3C site and experiment with MathML code (the browser includes a math editor).

2. Visit Microsoft's Internet Explorer pages and hunt out the material on structured graphics (it's located with the Internet Explorer 4 material). You will also find a few example graphics.

3. Visit Microsoft's Chrome pages (`http://www.microsoft.com/sitebuilder/`) and read more about Chrome. If you have the necessary hardware, try it.

21

APPENDIXES

A   Glossary   527

B   XML Resources   533

APPENDIX **A**

Glossary

application   A piece of software on behalf of which an XML processor processes XML documents. More generally, a usage of the generic XML framework for a particular purpose, with its own DTD, linking conventions, and style sheets.

attribute   A name-value pair that is associated with an element and provides more information about the content of that element. Attribute values can be specified in the element's start tag, or default values can be inherited from the DTD.

attribute declaration   A declaration in a DTD specifying an attribute's name, type, and default value, if any.

attribute-list declaration   In a DTD, a list of attribute declarations for a particular element type.

cascading style sheets (CSS)   A style sheet language for rendering HTML documents.

CDATA section   A part of an XML document in which markup (apart from that indicating the end of the CDATA section) is not interpreted as markup, but is passed to the application as-is.

character   An atomic unit of text represented by a bit string.

character data   The actual text of an XML document, as opposed to the markup of the document.

character reference   An escape code for a single Unicode character that quotes the numerical value of its bit string.

comment   A piece of markup within an XML document containing text that is not to be treated as part of the document.

conditional section   In the DTD, a piece of markup that can be included in, or excluded from, the logical structure of the DTD, depending on the keyword at its start.

content model   In the DTD, a description of what might occur within instances of a given element type.

document   See *XML document*.

document element   The single element that contains all the other elements and character data that make up an XML document, also known as the root element.

document type declaration   A declaration at the start of an XML document that specifies where the external DTD subset can be found and includes the internal DTD subset.

document type definition   See *DTD*.

DSSSL   Document Style Semantics and Specification Language. An International Standard (ISO/IEC 10179:1996) that defines a transformation language and a style language for the processing of valid SGML documents.

DSSSL-o   A subset of DSSSL, called the online profile, proposed as a cut-down version of DSSSL suitable for rendering XML documents.

DTD   A set of rules governing the element types that are allowed within an XML document and specifying the allowed content and attributes of each element type. The DTD also declares all the external entities referenced within the document and the notations that can be used. See also *external DTD subset*.

element   A logical unit of information within an XML document.

element construction rule   An instruction in an XSL stylesheet that specifies which flow objects are to be constructed when a particular element type is encountered.

A

element content   In a DTD, a content model that allows other elements only inside instances of a given element type. (Compare with *mixed content*.)

element type   A particular type of element, such as *paragraph*. An element's type is indicated by the name that occurs in its start tag and end tag.

empty element   An element containing no sub-elements or character data.

encoding declaration   A declaration of the character encoding scheme used for a particular text entity.

end tag   A tag that marks the end of an element, such as `</section>`.

entity   Any data that can be treated as an object, such as an external file containing an image.

entity declaration   Part of the DTD. An entity declaration declares a name for an entity and associates it with a replacement string or externally stored data identified by a URL.

entity reference   A reference within the text of an XML document to a previously declared entity, signifying that the contents of the entity are to be processed at this point (processing can also mean simple inclusion).

extended link   A link that can involve any number of resources. An extended link doesn't need to be co-located with any of the resources involved in the link.

external DTD subset   The part of the DTD that is held in a separate resource addressed by a URL. The external DTD subset is often referred to as the DTD of a class of documents. See also *DTD*.

external entity   An entity whose contents are contained in an external XML resource, such as an image file, referred to from within an XML document.

flow object   A formatting feature, such as a paragraph or a table cell, into which the content of an XML document is flowed under the control of an XSL style sheet.

flow object tree   The complete set of flow objects into which an XML document is converted by an XSL stylesheet.

generic identifier   The name assigned to an element type.

grove   A representation of an XML document in which each node represents a property of the document.

HTML   Hypertext Markup Language. An encoding scheme for displaying and hyperlinking pages of information on the World Wide Web. Some versions of HTML are applications of SGML.

HyTime   ISO/IEC 10744 Hypermedia/Time-based Structuring Language. An SGML application that extends SGML capabilities to allow such things as multimedia capabilities and advanced addressing mechanisms.

inline link   See *simple link.*

internal DTD subset   The part of the DTD that is declared within the XML document itself, before the first start tag.

internal entity   An entity whose value is given in its entity declaration in the DTD.

locator   A character string that identifies one end of a link.

logical structure   The declarations, elements, character references, processing instructions, and so on that make up an XML document. These are all indicated by explicit markup.

markup   Information that is intermingled with the text of an XML document to indicate its logical and physical structure.

mixed content   In the DTD, a content model that allows character data to be mixed with sub-elements in any order. (Compare with *element content.*)

name   Within an XML DTD, a letter or underscore followed by zero or more name characters.

name character   A letter, digit, hyphen, underscore, full stop, or one of a set of special characters specified in the XML standard.

name token   Any mixture of name characters.

namespace   A method for qualifying the names used in XML documents by associating them with contexts identified by URIs.

non-validating XML processor   An XML processor that checks whether XML documents are well-formed but not whether they are valid.

notation   The format of an external entity, such as a GIF image or an MPEG video.

out-of-line link   A link that does not serve as one of its own resources.

parameter entity   A text entity used within a DTD or used to control processing of conditional sections.

physical structure   The arrangement of physical storage units (entities) in which an XML document is held.

processing instruction (PI)   A piece of markup that gives information or instructions to software that will process an XML document. A PI does not form part of the document's character data.

prolog   The part of an XML document, including the XML declaration and DTD, that precedes the actual document element.

rendering   The act of processing a document so that it can be viewed. Rendering normally implies display on a screen but could also mean other forms of processing, such as text-to-speech conversion for the blind.

resource   Any addressable unit of information that can participate in a link. A resource can include complete XML documents, elements (or spans of elements) within them, and chunks of text.

root element   See *document element*.

SGML   Standard Generalized Markup Language. An International Standard (ISO 8879:1986) that describes a generalized markup scheme for representing the logical structure of documents in a system- and platform-independent manner.

simple link   An inline link, such as the familiar `<A HREF="">` tag in HTML, that links a specific point in an XML document to some target.

start tag   A tag that marks the start of an element, such as `<para>`.

style sheet   A set of instructions specifying how each element within a document is to be formatted.

traversal   Use of a link to access the resource at its other (or another) end. For simple links, traversal can be thought of as the action of following a link.

valid XML document   A well-formed XML document that also conforms to all the rules governing the structure of its content expressed in its DTD.

W3C   World Wide Web Consortium. A group of vendor companies that acts as a sort of standards body for the Web.

Web   A common name for the World Wide Web. An Internet service that uses the HTTP protocol and the HTML format to deliver documents.

well-formed XML document   An XML document that consists of a single (root) element containing correctly nested sub-elements. All entity references within a well-formed XML document refer to entities that have been declared in the DTD or are one of a small set of default entities, and all attribute values are enclosed in quotes. A well-formed XML document also obeys a few other rules.

XML   Extensible Markup Language. A profile, or simplified subset, of SGML.

XML declaration   A processing instruction at the start of an XML document that declares it to be XML code.

XML document   A document consisting of an optional XML declaration, followed by an optional document type declaration, and then followed by a document element.

XML processor   A program that reads XML documents, checks whether they are valid and well-formed, and makes their contents available to XML applications.

XPointer   A syntax for identifying the element, range of elements, or text within an XML document that is the target resource of a link.

XSL   The XML style language.

APPENDIX B

XML Resources

XML is concerned most with the distribution of information over the Internet, so it should hardly come as a surprise that the majority of information about XML is also available on the World Wide Web. I have spent many hours scouring the Web to assemble the listings included here, but it's impossible to avoid missing something. To try to be as thorough as possible, and to avoid directing you to sites that are already out of date by the time you read this, I have tried to include the addresses of Web sites that include pointers to other sites.

Books

Because XML is so new, there aren't very many books about it. I have therefore chosen a few selected SGML books that may also be of assistance to someone who is predominantly interested in XML, and is only interested in SGML as far as it affects XML.

(I have not included any books on HTML. There are simply too many books on the subject and often far better sources of information on the Web.)

- *The SGML Handbook*, Charles F. Goldfarb, 1990, Oxford University Press (ISBN 0-19-853737-1). This is probably the most definitive book on the SGML standard, and is written by someone who really ought to know. Be warned that this is not light reading, but it makes a very good technical reference thanks to its excellent index.

- *Practical SGML*, Eric van Herwijnen, 1994, Kluwer Academic Publishers (ISBN 0-7923-9434-8). This is probably the best and the most accessible introduction to SGML that exists.

- *SGML on the Web Small Steps Beyond HTML*, Murray, Maloney, and Yuri Rubinski, 1997, Prentice Hall PTR (ISBN 0-13-519984-0). Apart from being interesting historically and a tribute to the sad loss of Yuri Rubinski, this book gives some interesting insights into the reasons for using SGML, rather than HTML, on the Web. The book includes a copy of SoftQuad's Panorama SGML Browser/plug-in.

- *Developing SGML DTDs: From Text to Model to Markup*, Jeanne El Andaloussi and Eve Maler, 1996, Prentice Hall PTR (ISBN 0-13-309881-8). Although focused entirely on SGML, this is one of the few books that adequately cover the subject of DTD development. It will also be of interest to anyone interested in developing serious XML DTDs.

- *Structuring XML Documents*, David Megginson, 1998, Prentice Hall PTR (ISBN 0-13-642299-3). David is one of the leading experts on SGML. Aimed more at programmers, this book is the definitive source for information about architectural forms and DTD manipulation.

- *Presenting XML*, Richard Light, 1997, Sams.Net (ISBN 0-7923-9943-9). Although I have to admit to some bias here (I coauthored this book), this was the first book on XML. Although it is somewhat out of date now, it is still one of the best semi-technical introductions to XML.

- *Designing XML Internet Applications*, Michael Leventhal, David Lewis and Matthew Fuchs, 1998, Prentice Hall PTR (ISBN 0-13-616822-1). One of the best books currently available on programming XML using Perl and Java.

Online Resources

If you remember only a few addresses after scanning through this appendix, I hope it will be the following. These are probably the most complete reference sites for absolutely anything connected with XML (sometimes quite remotely connected):

- *The SGML Bibliography*—Robin Cover has been collecting bibliographic data on SGML and related topics since 1986. Robin claims that the searchable online listings are merely a subset of the database, but even so, the online listings appear to cover nearly every kind of print media. This site is a must and can be reached at `http://www.oasis-open.org/sgml/biblio.html`.

- *The XML site*—This is one of the most definitive sites for XML information and includes Tim Bray's excellent annotated version of the XML syntax recommendation. It's at `http://www.xml.com`.

- *The Whirlwind Guide to SGML Tools and Vendors*—Steve Pepper started compiling this guide in 1992, back in the days when it was easy to do so in your spare time. The rapidly expanding market has forced him to become somewhat more selective in his entries, but it is still one of the definitive sources. It can be reached at `http://www.infotek.no/sgmltool/guide.htm`.

Articles

Some of the articles XML can often seem more like advertisements than serious attempts to inform, but there are still quite a few that are worth reading. The following is a selection of some of the best:

- "The Case for XML" and others—Dianne Kennedy is an SGML consultant and writer of some repute. She has written several well-informed and highly informative articles about XML matters that can be accessed online at `http://www.mcs.net/~dken/xml.htm`.

- "Multidimensional Files: There's a Bright Future Beyond HTML"—This is a very good article covering not just XML, but CDF and the Document Object Model as well. You can access it online at `http://webreview.com/97/05/16/feature/xmldim.html`.

- "XML: Adding Intelligence to Your Business-Critical Documents"—This white paper from Grif discusses the place for XML in intranets. It can be reached at `http://www.grif.fr/newsref/xml.htm`.

- "Some Thoughts and Software on XML"—Bert Bos provides this very short article containing some public thoughts about XML and links to some software. You can reach it at `http://www.w3.org/XML/notes.html`.

- "XML: A Professional Alternative to HTML"—Aimed at HTML authors, this technical article by Ingo Macherius gives a fairly thorough picture of XML as an HTML replacement. You can access it online at `http://www.heise.de/ix/artikel/E/1997/06/106/artikel.htm`.

- "Building Blocks, Turning the Web Into a Data Source"—This is a brief description of how XML (and WebMethod's server software) can bridge the gap between HTML and databases. You can access it online at `http://tni.webmethods.com/news/stories/turning.html`.

- "XML, Java, and the Future of the Web"—This is Jon Bosak's milestone article, originally written in October 1996, and has been updated since then. You can access it at `http://sunsite.unc.edu/pub/sun-info/standards/xml/why/xmlapps.htm`.

- "XML White Paper"—This is Microsoft's policy on XML, but still is an excellent description of what XML is and how it works. It can be accessed at `http://www.microsoft.com/standards/xml/xmlwhite.htm`.

- "An Introduction to Structured Documents"—This is Peter Murray-Rust's extremely readable discussion of the reasons for using XML and CML, and can be accessed at `http://www.sil.org/sgml/murrayRustECHET.html`.

- BUILDER.COM, "20 Questions on XML"—Gives a fairly useful overview for developers at `http://www.cnet.com/Content/Builder/Authoring/ Xml20/`.

- Developer Zone, "XML Basics"—Has a fairly good introduction to the basics of XML at `http://www.projectcool.com/developer/xmlpub/xmlbasics/`.

- *Project Cool XML Zone*—Contains a lot of useful XML information, but is also one of the very best sites for developers. Contains a lot of useful XML code examples. It can be found at `http://www.projectcool.com/developer/xmlpub/`.

- "WebDeveloper.com's Guide to XML"—A very professional XML introduction that can be found at `http://www.webdeveloper.com/categories/html/`.

- *What the ?XML! Home Page*—A very accessible introduction to XML that can be found at `http://www.geocities.com/SiliconValley/Peaks/5957/xml.html`.

- "XML Reference Guide"—Close to a definitive description, which can be found at `http://webreview.com/xml/`.

- "XML for Structured Data"—This is a very interesting open discussion about the use of XML for representing structured data. It can be reached at `http://207.201.154.232/murray/specs/xml-sd.html`.

Applications

These are the Web sites containing descriptions of the XML applications as of this writing. New applications are being added all the time, which is hardly surprising when you review this short list and consider the incredibly wide and varied assortment of application fields it represents.

- Bioinformatic Sequence Markup Language (BSML)—This is concerned with the encoding and exchange of genetic information using XML. It can be found at `http://www.topogen.com/sbir/rfc.html`.

- CDIF Home Page—The Computer Aided Software & Systems Engineering (CASE) Data Interchange Format is intended to facilitate the exchange of software development information between CASE software tools. This site can be found at `http://www.cdif.org/`.

- CHIP Info Production's Hypertext Management System (HTM-S)—This is a commercial initiative to use XML to manage Web sites. Details can be found at `http://www.chipinfo.com/products/htms.htm`.

- Chrome—Microsoft's two- and three-dimensional XML modeling technology. Details can be found at `http://www.microsoft.com/workshop/imedia/chromeffects/down_default.asp`.

- Conceptual Knowledge Markup Language DTD—This is concerned with applying XML to artificial intelligence. It can be found at `http://wave.eecs.wsu.edu/WAVE/Ontologies/CKML/CKML-DTD.html`.

- Development Markup Language (DML)—An XML application for the exchange of information between agencies and organizations concerned with providing assistance to developing countries. Information can be found at `http://resources.bellanet.org/xml/index.cfm`.

- Document Interchange Initiative—An XML application for the electronic interchange of documents. Details can be found at `http://interaction.in-progress.com/interchange/index`.

- Extensible Log Format Initiative—The use of XML to encode Web server logs to make them easier to process and interrogate. Details can be found at `http://www.docuverse.com/xlf/`.

- FlixML Home Page—A semi-serious attempt by XML author John E. Simpson to represent his database of B-movie reviews in XML. Details can be found at `http://www.flixml.org/`.

- Genealogical Data in XML (GedML)—An attempt to use XML to make it easier to trace and record your family tree. Details can be found at `http://home.iclweb.com/icl2/mhkay/gedml.html`.

- Handheld Device Markup Language (HDML)—A miniature version of HTML in XML that would allow PDAs and cellular phones to be used for email and Web applications. The home page is at `http://www.uplanet.com/pub/hdml_w3c/`.

- HL7 SGML SIG—A massive initiative to present health information (patient, medical, treatment, insurance, and financing information) in XML. The major starting point can be found at `http://www.mcis.duke.edu/standards/HL7/committees/sgml/`.

- Information & Content Exchange (ICE)—An attempt to provide a more usable description of a Web site's contents. The home page can be found at `http://www.vignette.com/`.

- Internationalization and Localization Tools (ILE)—The use of XML for software and software documentation localization into foreign languages. Details can be found at `http://www.ile.com/tools/`.

- Instructional Management System (IMS) Meta-data—An initiative to use XML to support Internet-based learning. The project home page is at `http://www.imsproject.org/md_overview.html`.

- Java Speech Markup Language—Sun's effort to use XML to encode voice data. Details and software can be found at `http://java.sun.com/products/java-media/speech/forDevelopers/JSML/`.

- MathML—A DTD application to (finally!) allow mathematics to be marked up in XML. Other than the Web site itself (`http://www.w3c.org`), useful extra information can be found at `http://www.nag.co.uk/projects/OpenMath/mml-files`.

- Motorola VoxML—Motorola's application of XML to voice data application development. Details can be found at `http://VoxML.mot.com/`.

- The News Industry Text Format initiative (NITF) —An application for using XML to transmit news reports. Details can be found at `http://www.iptc.org/iptc/orddocs.htm#nitf`.

- NuDoc Technology Brief—Bitstream's application of XML to encode document font information. Discussion papers and press releases can be found at `http://www.bitstream.com/nudoc/nudoctb.html`.

- OpenFilter—A means of exchanging filter information. Details can be found at `http://www.ile.com/tools/openfilter.htm`.

- Open Financial Exchange Specification—Microsoft's application of XML for the exchange of financial transaction information. Details and specifications can be found at `http://www.microsoft.com/finserv/ofxdnld.htm`.

- Open Software Description (OSD)—An application of XML to allow software to be distributed via the Internet. Details can be found at `http://www.microsoft.com/standards/osd/`.

- OpenTag—An application of XML that allows the exchange of translation database information. The home page can be found at `http://www.opentag.org/`.

- Open Trading Protocol—XML applied to the exchange of commercial information. Details can be found at `http://www.otp.org:8080/`.

- OMG TC Work in Progress—The Object Management Group (OMG) is one of the leading bodies in the field of component-based software. This is an initiative to use XML to implement distributed software components. The project home page can be found at `http://www.omg.org/library/schedule/Stream-based_Model_Interchange.htm`.

- Process Interchange Format - XML—An attempt to use XML to encode commercial process information. Details can be found at `http://www.xmls.com/pif/`.

- Python/XML How-to—The application of the Python scripting language to processing XML data. Details can be found at `http://www.python.org/doc/howto/xml/`.

- Q&A Markup Language (QAML)—A semi-serious attempt to use XML to make it easier to author and exchange Internet Frequently Asked Question (FAQ) documents. Details can be found at `http://www.faq.org/qaml/`.

- RDF Made (Fairly) Easy—An excellent attempt to explain the Resource Description Format (RDF) in an accessible manner. The base page can be found at `http://www.ccil.org/~cowan/XML/RDF-made-easy.html`.

- Schema for Object-Oriented XML—One of the many possible XML schemas vying to be the successor to the DTD. The home page can be found at `http://www.w3.org/TR/NOTE-SOX/`.

- Software Component Interface Description in SGML—An academic project to apply XML to the description of software component interfaces. The project home page can be found at `http://www.cgl.uwaterloo.ca/Projects/meta/sgml97/mmccool/index.html`.

- TCIF Information Product Interchange Committee—A commercial initiative to apply XML to product information interchange. Details can be found at `http://www.atis.org/atis/tcif/ipi/5tc60hom.htm`.

B

- VXML (now 3DXML)—An attempt to use XML to publish VRML (virtual reality modeling language) information. The discussion papers can be found at `http://www.ultrablue.com/dan/vxml/printable.html`.

- X-ACT—ActiveX Content Technologies' approach to the use of XML for business activities. Details can be found at `http://www.x-act.org/`.

- XML/EDI Group's Home Page—SGML has long been used for Electronic Data Interchange (EDI), and this is an initiative aimed at doing the same with XML. Details can be found at `http://www.geocities.com/WallStreet/Floor/5815/`.

- XML File System—A proposal to use XML to describe computer file system organization. Details can be found at `http://www.gefen.co.il/xml/whole.html`.

- Extended Forms Description Language (XFDL)—An application of XML to expand on HTML's limited form-handling capabilities. The home page can be found at `http://www.uwi.com/xfdl/`.

- XML-Based Components - Coins—An initiative to apply XML to the management of Java components. The home page can be found at `http://www.jxml.com/coins/presentations/Coins980616/index.htm`.

- XML-QL: A Query Language for XML—An initiative to implement the capabilities of the SQL database query language in XML. The draft proposal can be found at `http://www.w3.org/TR/NOTE-xml-ql/`.

Standards

ISO standards are copyrighted documents and represent a major source of income for ISO, so it is understandable that copies are not too easy to find in the public domain. For paper copies of the definitive versions of these standards, you should contact your local national standards organization (all national bodies are authorized to sell copies of ISO and other international standards documents). Having said that, drafts of some of the ISO and non-ISO standards are readily available on the Internet. The following are some of the most important standards and other semi-official documents available online:

- *Submissions to W3C*—All new proposals to the W3C are listed at `http://www.w3.org/pub/WWW/Submission/`.

- *Extensible Markup Language Proposal, Version 1.0*—The definitive W3C source can be reached at `http://www.w3.org/pub/WWW/TR/PR-xml`.

- *Action Sheets*—`http://www.w3.org/TR/NOTE-AS`.

- *Cascading Style Sheets*, level 1—`http://www.w3.org/pub/WWW/TR/PR-CSS1`.

- *Cascading Style Sheets*, Level 2—`http://www.w3.org/TR/REC-CSS2`.

- *Comparison of SGML and XML*—`http://www.w3.org/TR/NOTE-sgml-xml.html`.

- *Draft specification on channel definition format*—`http://www.microsoft.com/standards/cdf.htm`.

- *Document Content Description for XML*—`http://www.w3.org/TR/NOTE-dcd`.

- *Document Object Model Specification*—`http://www.w3.org/TR/WD-DOM/`.

- *The Annotated XML Specification*—`http://xml.com/axml/axml.html`.

- *HDML Language Specification*—`http://www.uplanet.com/pub/hdml_w3c/hdml20-1.html`.

- *User's Guide to ISO/IEC 15445:1998 HTML* (Work in progress)—`http://www.ornl.gov/sgml/wg8/document/n1966/UG.html`.

- *HTML 3.2 Reference Specification*—`http://www.w3.org/pub/WWW/TR/WD-html`.

- *HTML 4.0 Specification*—`http://www.w3.org/TR/WD-html40/`.

- *Hyper Graphics Markup Language (HGML)*—`http://www.w3.org/TR/NOTE-HGML`.

- *Mathematical Markup Language (MathML)*—`http://www.w3.org/TR/REC-MathML`.

- *Meta Content Framework Using XML*—`http://www.textuality.com/sgml-erb/w3c-mcf.html`.

- *Namespaces in XML*—`http://www.w3.org/TR/WD-xml-names`.

- *Open Software Description Specification*—`http://www.w3.org/TR/NOTE-OSD.html`.

- *Open Financial Exchange Specification*—`http://www.microsoft.com/finserv/ofxdnld.htm`.

- *P3P* (Platform for Privacy Preferences)—`http://www.w3c.org/TR/WD-P3P10-syntax`.

- *PICS-NG Metadata Model and Label Syntax* (Platform for Internet Content Selection)—`http://207.201.154.232/murray/specs/WD-pics-ng-metadata-970514.html`.

- *Precision Graphics Markup Language (PGML)*—`http://www.w3.org/TR/1998/NOTE-PGML`.

- *Resource Description Framework (RDF) Model and Syntax*—`http://www.w3.org/TR/WD-rdf-syntax/`.

- *SDML - Signed Document Markup Language* – Version 2.0—`http://www.w3.org/TR/NOTE-SDML/`.

- *Synchronized Multimedia Integration Language*—`http://www.w3.org/TR/WD-smil`.

B

- *Translation Memory Exchange (TMX) Format Specifications*—`http://www.lisa.org/tmx/tmx.htm`.
- *Unicode Home Page*—`http://www.unicode.org/`.
- *WebBroker* - Distributed Object Communication on the Web—`http://www.w3.org/TR/1998/NOTE-webbroker-19980511/`.
- *Schematic Graphics*—`http://www.w3.org/TR/1998/NOTE-WebSchematics/`.
- *WebCGM Profile*—`http://www.w3.org/TR/NOTE-WebCGM/`.
- *Web Interface Definition Language (WIDL)*—`http://www.oasis-open.org/sgml/xml.html#widl`.
- *Web Collections using XML Submission*—`http://www.w3.org/pub/WWW/TR/NOTE-XMLsubmit.html`.
- *XAPI-J* - Standardized XML API in Java—`http://www.datachannel.com/channelworld/xml/dev/`.
- *XML-Arch*—`http://home.sprynet.com/sprynet/dmeggins/xml-arch.html`.
- *XML in HTML Meeting Report*—`http://www.w3c.org/TR/NOTE-xh`.
- *XML Object Model*—`http://www.microsoft.com/msdn/sdk/inetsdk/help/inet5017.htm`.
- *XML-Data Spec*—`http://www.microsoft.com/standards/xml/xmldata.htm`.
- *XML Linking Language (XLink)*—`http://www.w3.org/TR/NOTE-xlink`.
- *XML Linking Language (XLink) Design Principles*—`http://www.w3.org/TR/NOTE-xlink-principles`.
- *XML Pointer Language (XPointer)*—`http://www.w3.org/TR/WD-xptr`.
- *A Proposal for XSL*—`http://www.w3.org/TR/NOTE-XSL.html`.
- *HyTime Working Group FTP Archive*—This is the official working group's site for the interchange of files. You can get it at `ftp://infosrv1.ctd.ornl.gov/pub/sgml/WG8/HyTime/TC/`.
- *HyTime: ISO 10744 Hypermedia/Time-based Structuring Language*—This is a public copy of the official standard. You can find it at `http://dmsl.cs.uml.edu/standards/hytime.html`.
- *ISO/IEC 10744 HyTime (Second Edition)*—This is the unofficial, but as good as definitive, copy of the latest revision of the standard from Eliot Kimber (Dr. Macro). You can reach it at `http://www.drmacro.com/hythtml/is10744r.html`.
- *Unicode Home Page*—This is the official Unicode site, and can be reached at `http://www.unicode.org/`.

Information Sources

The following sites contain general information about SGML and XML:

- *SGML and XML Resources*—This is a very useful set of links and pointers. You can access it at `http://www.arbortext.com/linksgml.html`.

- *What Is XML?*—The Graphical Communications Association (GCA) are the main organizers of SGML and XML conferences around the world. This site has some useful pointers and can be reached at `http://www.gca.org/conf/xml/xml_what.htm`.

- *Commonly Asked Questions About the Extensible Markup Language*—This is maintained on behalf of the W3C and is the definitive site for a lot of those nagging questions that aren't answered by the official documents. You can access it at `http://www.ucc.ie/xml/`.

- *XML* (W3C site)—This is more or less the focus of all XML activity. You can reach it at `http://www.w3.org/pub/WWW/XML/`.

- *XML* (Robin Cover's site)—This SGML Web site is an Aladdin's cave of useful XML information. It can be reached at `http://www.oasis-open.org/sgml/xml.html`.

- *XML: The Extensible Markup Language* (James K. Tauber's site)—This very useful source of information be accessed at `http://www.jtauber.com/xml/`.

Software Packages

The following software packages are known to support XML:

- AElfred XML Parser:
  `http://www.microstar.com/XML/index.htm`

- Agave—SQml-Publisher:
  `http://www.agave.com/html/products/sqml_pub.htm`

- AgentSoft—XML Technology Demonstration:
  `http://www.agentsoft.com/xml/`

- Balise Home Page:
  `http://www.balise.berger-levrault.fr/current/index.htm`

- BCC XML Tools:
  `http://www.mygale.org/07/jcalles/XML/`

- Bjondi (Unicode Utilities):
  `http://www.bjondi.com/`

- Channel Maker—Download:
  `http://www.anyware.co.uk/anyware/cm/download.html`
- Chris Stevenson's Java Applets:
  `http://www.users.on.net/zhcchz/java.html`
- Chrystal Software Astoria & XML Bulletin:
  `http://www.chrystal.com/xml.htm`
- Clip XML Editor:
  `http://xml.t2000.co.kr/product/clip.html`
- Copernican Solutions Incorporated—XML Developer's Toolkit (XDK):
  `http://www.copsol.com/products/xdk/index.html`
- Crane Softwrights Ltd.—Shareware:
  `http://www.cranesoftwrights.com/shareware/`
- CSSize v0.9b1, Add CSS Attributes to HTML and XML Code:
  `http://lara0.exp.edf.fr/glazman/CSSize/cssize.en.htm`
- DataChannel—Datachannel RIO & WebBroker:
  `http://www.datachannel.com/`
- DTD2HTML, Perl Tools for Making DTDs Navigable:
  `http://www.ogc.uci.edu/indiv/ehood/PerlSGML.html`
- XML Import Filter for Lotus Domino:
  `http://www.digitome.com/download.htm`
- Docproc:
  `http://javalab.uoregon.edu/ser/software/docproc/`
- DSSSLTK, DSSSL toolkit:
  `http://www.copsol.com/products/index.html`
- Excosoft—Documentor XML/SGML editor:
  `http://www.excosoft.se/welcome/home_welcome.html`
- Expat (XML parser used in Mozilla):
  `http://www.jclark.com/xml/expat.html`
- EzDTD DTD editor:
  `http://www.download.com` (search for "ezdtd")
- Free XML tools:
  `http://birk105.studby.uio.no/www_work/xmltools/index.html`
- General Picture's CiaoXML Demo:
  `http://www.generalpicture.com/`

- GRIF S.A.—SGML and HTML Solutions:
  http://www.grif.fr/
- GroveWare Home:
  http://www.groveware.com/
- HEX—The HTML Enabled XML Parser:
  http://www-uk.hpl.hp.com/people/ak/java/hex.html
- HXA—Hubick's XML Analyzer:
  http://www.hubick.com/software/HXA/
- HyBrick (DSSSL viewer):
  http://collie.fujitsu.com/hybrick
- Hypermedic—XML Tools:
  http://www.hypermedic.com/style/tools/tools.htm
- IRIS XML Editor & DTD Generator:
  http://www.cabinfo.com/download.htm
- jade—DSSSL Engine:
  http://www.jclark.com/jade
- Scientific Information Components Using Java/XML:
  http://ala.vsms.nottingham.ac.uk/vsms/java/jumbo/ index.html
- Junglee Technology—Virtual Databases:
  http://wpreal.junglee.com/tech/index.html
- Java XML (jxml) Home Page:
  http://www.jxml.com/
- Lark—Non-validating parser:
  http://www.textuality.com/Lark/
- LTG Software—LT XML Tools and Developers' API:
  http://www.ltg.ed.ac.uk/software/xml/
- Majix (TetraSix)—MS-Word to XML Converter:
  http://www.tetrasys.fr/ProduitsFrame.htm
- The Microsoft XSL Processor:
  http://www.microsoft.com/xml/xsl/msxsl.htm
- Microsoft XML Parser in Java:
  http://www.microsoft.com/standards/xml/xmlparse.htm
- Microstar—Near&Far Graphic DTD Development Tool:
  http://www.microstar.com/Products-And-Technologies/index.html

B

- MONDO—Modeling Technologies:
  `http://www.chimu.com/projects/mondo/2`
- NXP XML Parser:
  `http://www.edu.uni-klu.ac.at/~nmikula/NXP`
- Object Design, Inc.—XML Downloads:
  `http://www.odi.com/content/products/pse/XMLDownload.htm`
- OmniMark Konstructor:
  `http://www.techmall.com/techdocs/NP980330-1.html`
- OVIDIUS MetaMorphosis SGML/XML Processor:
  `http://www.ovidius.com/efs-mm.html`
- QORX—Express and SQL Query as an XML Document:
  `http://www.griffinbrown.co.uk/tools.shtml`
- Roustabout, QuarkXPress-to-XML/SGML Translator:
  `http://www.attd.com/xml/products.html#roustabout`
- SAX—The Simple API for XML:
  `http://www.megginson.com/SAX/`
- SAX—DOM Bridge:
  `http://www.docuverse.com/personal/saxdom.html`
- SAXON—A Java class library for XML Applications:
  `http://home.iclweb.com/icl2/mhkay/saxon.html`
- SCHEMA.NET—For DTDs and Other XML Schemata:
  `http://www.schema.net/`
- Sean Russell's XML Package:
  `http://jersey.uoregon.edu/ser/software/`
- Silfide – EN – SXP – Frames—Xsilphide client/server environment for distributing language resources:
  `http://www.loria.fr/projets/XSilfide/EN/sxp/`
- Stilo WebWriter XML Editor:
  `http://www.pimc.com/WebWriter/download.html`
- Symposia Web Browser/Editor:
  `http://symposia.inria.fr/symposia/download-symposia.html`
- Tcl Support for XML:
  `http://tcltk.anu.edu.au/XML/`
- UWI.Com—The Internet Forms Company:
  `http://www.uwi.com/`

- Visual XML:
  `http://www.pierlou.com/visxml/`
- webMethods—Automate the Web:
  `http://www.webmethods.com/home.html`
- Web Publishers—Tools and Utilities Home Page:
  `http://www.webpub.com/tools/home.html`
- Woodstock XML Editor:
  `http://www.vtopia.com/`
- XML in Mozilla:
  `http://www.mozilla.org/rdf/doc/xml.html`
- XML Viewer Applet:
  `http://capita.wustl.edu/xmlres/examples/MSJavaParser/XMLViewer.htm`
- XML Application—Prototype:
  `http://www.cam.org/~pierlou/prototype/`
- XED—An XML Document Instance Editor:
  `http://www.ltg.ed.ac.uk/~ht/xed.html`
- XML::Parser:
  `http://www.netheaven.com/~coopercc/xmlparser/intro.html`
- XML Parser Component for Delphi:
  `http://www.icom-dv.de/xml.htm`
- XML Pro (Vervet Logic) XML editor:
  `http://www.vervet.com/`
- Xpublish (Mac):
  `http://interaction.in-progress.com/xpublish/index`
- XMLSOFTWARE.COM—The XML Software Site:
  `http://www.xmlsoftware.com/`
- XML Styler—Early XSL style sheet editor (now obsolete):
  `ftp://ftp.arbortext.com/pub/downloads/xmlstyler2c.exe`
- XML for Java—A collection of free IBM software for processing XML data:
  `http://www.alphaworks.ibm.com/formula/xml`
- XML Viewer Demo:
  `http://208.204.84.117/XMLTreeViewer/demo.html7`
- Xparse—XML parser in JavaScript:
  `http://www.jeremie.com/Dev/XML/index.phtml`

B

- Xpose XML Editor:
  `http://www.intravenous.com/products/`
- xslj—An XSL to DSSSL Translator:
  `http://www.ltg.ed.ac.uk/~ht/xslj.html`
- XSLProcessor—The first package to support the revised XSL (XSL2) proposal:
  `http://www.mygale.org/07/jcalles/XML/xslProcessor.html`
- XT—Free XML parser that implements the tree construction part of the XSL draft:
  `http://www.jclark.com/xml/xt.html`
- Zydeco—An XML Development Environment: `http://www.dn.net/zydeco/`

Software Companies

The companies listed here either already produce software that supports XML, have already announced software packages that support XML, or can be expected to release software that supports XML in the very near future (most of the software in the following list is discussed in Chapter 16):

- AIS Berger-Levrault—This company makes SGML and XML processing and database software. You can reach them at `http://www.balise.berger-levrault.fr/`.
- ArborText Inc.—They make SGML and XML editors, formatters, and conversion software. They can be reached at `http://www.arbortext.com/`.
- Chrystal Software Inc.—This document and component management software company can be reached at `http://www.chrystal.com/`.
- Copernican Solutions Incorporated—XML, DSSSL, and SGML software is produced here. You can reach them at `http://www.copsol.com/`.
- Grif S.A.—This manufacturer of SGML and XML editors, browsers and formatters can be accessed at `http://www.grif.fr/`.
- High Text—These Topic Navigation Map experts and SGML and HyTime consultants can be reached at `http://www.hightext.com/`.
- Inso Corporation—This manufacturer of SGML and XML conversion and browsing software can be reached at `http://www.inso.com/`.
- Language Technology Group—You can reach these makers of DSSSL and XML processing software at `http://www.ltg.ed.ac.uk/`.
- Microsoft Corporation—You can reach this manufacturer of XML (and other) software at `http://www.microsoft.com/`.

- SoftQuad—These makers of SGML editors and browsers can be accessed at `http://www.sq.com/` (an XML version of their HoTMetaL HTML tool, called XmetaL, has already been previewed at various conferences, a release is rumored for early 1999).

- STILO Technology Ltd.—These makers of SGML, HTML, and XML editors can be reached at `http://www.stilo.com`.

- webMethods—This is a manufacturer of WWW server software for XML. You can reach them at `http://www.webmethods.com/home.html`.

DSSSL

Pointers to the parts of DSSSL that are directly relevant to XML (such as the XS specification) can be found among the main lists of XML sites. The following addresses are for those with wider interests; the first is historical (a copy of the original DSSSL-o draft) and the others are for those who want to follow the development of the DSSSL specification (you will need to refer to this if you want to understand the XS specification):

- Norm Walsh is the developer of the DocBook DSSSL style sheets. His Web pages can be found at `http://www.berkshire.net/~norm/dsssl/`.

- *The DSSSL Documentation Project* is a voluntary initiative to (finally) create some large scale DSSSL documentation. The latest documents can be reached at `http://www.mulberrytech.com/dsssl/dsssldoc/`.

- James Clark, the developer of jade, keeps some DSSSL information on his Web site at `http://www.jclark.com/dsssl/`.

- The very first proposal for XSL (DSSSL-o), which is not just interesting for historical reasons, can be found at `http://sunsite.unc.edu/pub/sun-info/ standards/dsssl/xs/xs970522.ps.zip`.

- *The DSSSL Cookbook* is a collection of useful and instructive fragments of DSSSL code. It can be found at `http://www.mulberrytech.com/dsssl/dsssldoc/ cookbook/cookbook.html`.

- *DSSSL Online Application Profile*—This is the 1996.08.16 draft of the standard for the predecessor to XS. You can see it at `http://sunsite.unc.edu/pub/ sun-info/standards/dsssl/dsssl0/do960816.htm`.

- A *tutorial on DSSSL*—This is one of the best tutorials (and one of the few) that there is on DSSSL. You can access it at `http://csg.uwaterloo.ca/~dmg/ dsssl/tutorial/tutorial.html`.

- *Introduction to DSSSL*—Paul Prescod's very able introduction to DSSSL's style language can be reached at `http://itrc.uwaterloo.ca:80/~papresco/dsssl/tutorial.html`.

SGML

There are literally thousands of Web sites containing information concerning SGML. The following is an extremely select list of the most useful sites:

- *OASIS*—This is the organization for SGML vendors and other companies. You can see it at `http://www.oasis-open.org/`.
- *SGML FTP Archive*—Erik Naggum in Norway has been archiving the `comp.text.sgml` Usenet group for several years. The complete archive, containing more than 11,000 Usenet postings, can be found at `ftp://ftp.ifi.uio.no/pub/SGML`.
- *The SGML University*—This very useful repository for SGML bits and pieces can be found at `http://www.sgml.com/`.
- *The SGML Web Page*—This is probably the best online source for SGML information that there is. You can access it at `http://www.oasis-open.org/sgml/`.
- *ISO/IEC JTC1/SC18/WG8 Home Page*—This is the semi-official site for the ISO working group on SGML. You can reach it at `http://www.ornl.gov/sgml/WG8/wg8home.htm`.
- *Charles F. Goldfarb's Web Site*—As Charles is one of the inventors of SGML, this is one of the definitive sources for news and information on the subject. You can find it at `http://www.sgmlsource.com/`.
- *SGML on the Web*—This is a useful collection of pointers to Web sites that publish in SGML. You can reach it at `http://www.ncsa.uiuc.edu/WebSGML/WebSGML.html`.
- *W3C SGML Working Group Mailing List*—This is the public mailing list for the W3C SGML working group. The messages are archived at `http://lists.w3.org/Archives/Public/w3c-sgml-wg/`.

You should note that the Web addresses given here can change at any time. Although I have checked all of these addresses personally, and many have proved to be stable for a period of several years, I cannot absolutely guarantee that they are correct and, if so, for how long.

Usenet Groups

There are several Usenet discussions groups concerned with XML, either directly or by association.

Tip

Although it isn't my place to give anyone any lessons on Netiquette, there is nothing more embarrassing than making a fool of yourself in public. Usenet is public on a scale that few could imagine, and has astounding longevity. (I am constantly amazed—and sometimes embarrassed—to see some of my Usenet postings to SGML groups turning up on informative CD-ROMs many years after I made them.)

Generally, the standard of postings is extremely high and the audiences include the world's leading authorities. Before you leap into the fray, you'd be advised to check out the FAQ (frequently asked questions document) for that newsgroup to make sure your question hasn't been asked before. It also can't hurt to read a newsgroup for a couple of days before posting (known as *lurking*) to get a good feel for what is normal and permissible.

Don't let these admonitions put you off, though. Everyone is welcome to take part in the discussions, offer opinions, ask for help, and offer help. There is no such thing as a stupid question!

- `comp.text.xml`—This is the definitive group for all XML-related discussions.

- `comp.text.sgml`—This group carries some overflow and some misplaced discussions on XML (`comp.text.xml` is still too new for some newsgroup providers), but it's really the home for SGML and related-standard (for example DSSSL and HyTime). Most of the world's leading experts subscribe to this newsgroup, so although there are few postings, the quality is extremely high.

- `public.microsoft.xml`—One of the many of Microsoft's public Usenet groups.

Tip

If you do not have access to a Usenet feed, or if your provider does not carry these groups, point your Web browser to the Deja-News server, which carries almost every Usenet group there is and can be accessed through a normal Web browser at—`http://www.dejanews.com`.

B

Mailing Lists

There are quite a few mailing lists for XML and associated topics. Some are completely open, some are closed so that only subscribers can send messages, and a few are moderated to ensure that everyone stays on topic. In general, if you want to find out how to join a mailing list, send an empty email message to the address given (usually `majordomo`, which is in fact just a software package that responds automatically to certain trigger words) with the word `HELP` in the subject line.

- *XML Developers' Mailing List*—This is a public mailing list for extremely technical discussions about the development of XML and XML software. The following site keeps hyperlinked archives of all the messages sent to the list (and you will also find joining instructions here)—`http://www.lists.ic.ac.uk/hypermail/xml-dev/`.

- *XML EDI Mailing List*—This is a public mailing list for technical discussions about the use of XML for electronic data interchange (EDI). Send an email message to `majordomo@bizserve.com`.

- *Java-xml Interest Group*—This is a public mailing list for extremely technical discussions about using Java to process XML code. Send an email message to `majordomo@cybercom.net`.

- *Perl-xml Interest Group*—This is a semi-public mailing list for extremely technical discussions about using Perl to process XML code. Send an email message to `listmanager@ActiveState.com`.

- *XSL List*—This is a public mailing list for technical discussions about XSL. Send an email message to `majordomo@mulberrytech.com`.

- *Python-xml SIG*—This is a semi-public mailing list for extremely technical discussions about using Python to process XML code. Send an email message to `XML-SIG-REQUEST@python.org`.

- *DSSSL List*—This is a public mailing list for technical discussions about using DSSSL. Send an email message to `majordomo@mulberrytech.com`.

- *SGML-HL7*—This is a semi-public mailing list for extremely technical discussions about SGML or XML for medical records. Send an email message to `sgml-hl7@list.mc.duke.edu`.

- *Distributed Objects Mailing List*—This is a public mailing list for extremely technical discussions about the development of distributed object software. This site keeps hyperlinked archives of all the messages sent to the list. You can see it at `http://www.infospheres.caltech.edu/mailing_lists/dist-obj/`.

- *html-future Mailing List*—This is a W3C member-only mailing list but, although you cannot take part in any active discussions, the list is archived at `http://lists.w3.org/Archives/Public/html-future/`.

- *DSSSList—The DSSSL Users' Mailing List*—This is a public mailing list for the highly technical discussion of matters concerned with DSSSL. You can reach it at `http://www.mulberrytech.com/dsssl/dssslist/`.

Test Data

Once you start seriously experimenting with XML, you may find it useful to have a large amount of XML data to work with. You can either create this data yourself or, thanks to the generosity and hard work of a few individuals, a sizeable amount of public domain XML code can be downloaded from the Web.

- Joseph Conrad's *Heart of Darkness*—`http://home.sprynet.com/sprynet/ dmeggins/texts/darkness/ index.html`

- *The Bible*, *The Koran* and *The Book of Mormon*—`http://sunsite.unc.edu/ pub/sun-info/xml/eg/`

- *The Works of William Shakespeare* (all of his plays, not the sonnets)— `http://www.hypermedic.com/style/shakespeare/index.htm`

- *CSS2 Test Suite*, useful for checking what features of CSS2 your Web browser really supports and how well—`http://speckle.ncsl.nist.gov/~boland/css2/`

INDEX

Symbols

© (copyright symbol), 44

<!- tag, 43

_ (underscore), naming rules, 42

"" (quotation marks), attribute delimiters, 39

(pound symbol)
  document references, 233
  hyperlinks, 197

#FIXED keyword, 68

#IMPLIED element, 102

#IMPLIED keyword, 68

#PCDATA element, 64

#REQUIRED element, 102

#REQUIRED keyword, 68

% (percent sign), parameter entities, 133, 161

& (ampersand), debugging, 77

* (asterisk), element occurrence indicators, 62

+ (plus sign), element occurrence indicators, 62

> tag, 43

3D
  Chrome, 521
  Visual XML, 497

? (question mark), element occurrence indicators, 62

?>, 76

A

A element, 198

absolute references, 219

accented characters, 166

action sheets, 518-519

ActiveX Object, Object API, 254

actuate attribute, 208

actuation, 209

adding, XSL text formatting object, 477

Adobe, PGML, 512

Amaya browser, 498
  MathML, 501

ambiguities, 137-139

ambiguous content models, 60-61
  character content, 63
  element occurrence indicators, 62
  mixed content, 64

ampersand (&), debugging, 77

ancestor element,
   Omnimark LE, 314-316
ancestor relative refer-
   ence, 220
ancestry elements,
   matching (XSL),
   461-462
animating
   Chrome, 521
   VML, 515
appendData method, 354
applications, 496-497
   SAX, writing require-
      ments, 331
   SGML, 23-24
architectural forms, 123,
   132, 370-372
articles, XML resources,
   535-536
ASCII character set, 165
   case sensitivity, 30
   structured graphics, 513
asterisk (*), element
   occurrence indicators,
   62
attribute declarations,
   527
attribute markup, 39-41
attribute-list declara-
   tions, 527
attributes, 31, 527
   actuate, 208
   architectural forms, 371
   behavior, 209
   childNodes, 349
   content-role, 210
   DATAFLD, 233
   DCD, 368
   declaring, 64-65
      enumerated nota-
         tions, 157
   default values, 67

DTDs, 362
   creating, 108, 113
elements
   matching (XSL),
      462-463
   selecting, 223
ENTITIES, 66
ENTITY, 66
enumerated, 67
ID, 66
id, fragment identifiers,
   198
IDREF, 66
inline, 205
link elements, 198
NAME, 197
namespace conflicts,
   140
NMTOKEN, 67
Node object, 348
relational databases,
   131
remapping, 213
role, 212
   link descriptions,
      210
   Mozilla, 211-212
show, 207
string, 65
structured information,
   95
title, 210
tokenized, 66-67
vs elements, 132
XLink, 132
   attributes, 213
   form, 200
   lang, 40
automated processing,
   364
avoiding flow objects,
   XSL, 490-492

B

BACK element, 137
background property,
   CSS, 401
background-attachment
   property, CSS, 401
background-color prop-
   erty, CSS, 401
background-image prop-
   erty, CSS, 401
background-position
   property, CSS, 401
background-repeat prop-
   erty, CSS, 402
Bag element, 366
bags, 366
Balise, 304
behavior attribute, 209
behavior property, 520
behaviors, 517
   action sheets, 518-519
   CSS, 519-521
Berners-Lee, Tim, 8
binary entities, 154-155
binding, TABLE element,
   236
Bioinformatic Sequence
   Markup Language
   (BSML), 497, 537
bitmaps, image maps,
   507
block diagram DTD
   modeling, 124
block object (XSL), 468
   properties, 483-484
block-level elements, cascading style sheets,
   271-273
block-level-box object
   (XSL), 470
   properties, 488-489

BOF (beginning of file), 235
bookmarks, RDF, 366
books, XML resources, 533-534
books namespace, 365
books.xml, 296
border property, CSS, 402
border-bottom property, CSS, 402
border-bottom-width property, CSS, 402
border-color property, CSS, 402
border-left property, CSS, 402
border-left-width property, CSS, 402
border-right property, CSS, 402
border-right-width property, CSS, 402
border-style property, CSS, 403
border-top property, CSS, 403
border-top-width property, CSS, 403
border-width property, CSS, 403
box flow object (DSSSL), 426
braces {}, MathML, 504
brackets [], MathML, 504
browsers
    Amaya, 498
    character sets, 166
    checking versions, 292
    element markup, 38

extended link groups, 205
extended links, 203
HTML
    code validation, 9-10
    structure, 97
BSML, 497

C

calling macros, XSL, 481
CALS table model, 134
Cascading Action System (CAS), 518
cascading style sheets (CSS). See CSS
CASE Data Interchange Format (CDIF), 537
case sensitivity, 30
catalog files, 159
    jade, 414-417
catalog management packages, 161
CDATA section, 50-51, 528
CDF, 228, 496
CERN, 8
CGM, 508
Channel Definition Format (CDF), 496
Channel Definition Format. See CDF
character data, 165, 528
character entities, 152
    compared to parameter entities, 133
character entity references, 44
character flow object (DSSSL), 426

character object (XSL), 471
    properties, 484-485
character references, 528
character sets, 165-166
    CDATA section, 50-51
character strings, fragment identifiers, 198
CharacterData object, DOM specification, 354
characters, 528
    markup, 22
Charles F. Goldfarb Web site, 550
check bits, 165
Chemical Markup Language (CML), 497
child relative reference, 220
childNodes attribute, 349
childNodes property, 350
children elements 32
    matching (XSL), 463
Chrome, 521, 537
class selectors, CSS properties, 401
classes, Java
    example, 331-332
    interfaces, 332
classpaths, DXP parser, 82
clear property, CSS, 403
CML, 497
coding
    online help system, 270-271
    public domain XML resources, 553
color property, CSS, 403

commands
grep, 298
jade file conversion
HTML to RTF format, 415
XML to HTML format, 415-416
XML to MIF format, 415
comments, 43-44, 528
Computer Graphics Metafile (CGM), 508
computing, generated text, xls:value-of element, 476-477
Conceptual Knowledge Markup Language (CKML), 537
conditional markup, 136-137
conditional processing, XSL elements, 474-476
conditional sections, 528
conflicts, element selections, resolving (XSL), 464-465
construction rules, DSSSL style sheets, 433-434
containers, element structure, 111
content
automated processing, 364
creating DTDs, 109
distinguishing from markup, 26
element declarations, 57
public identifiers, 104

content formatting objects (XSL), 467-471, 483-489
block, 468, 483-484
block-level-box, 470, 488-489
character, 471, 484-485
graphic, 469
inline-box, 468-469, 488
link, 470, 489
list, 469, 485
list-item, 485-486
list-item-body, 486
list-item-label, 486
page-number, 470
queue, 467
rule-graphic, 469-470, 486-487
score, 470
sequence, 467
content models, 58-59, 528
ambiguous, 60-61
character content, 63
element occurrence indicators, 62
mixed content, 64
choices, 59
optional, 137-139
sequences, 59-60
content-oriented markup, 26
content-role attribute, 210
controlling
number elements, XSL, 477-479
whitespace, XSL, 481

converting
HTML to RTF format, jade commands, 415
SGML to XML, 106
tables, XML to RTF format, 440-442
XML to HTML
jade, 422-425
Omnimark referents, 316-318
scripting example, 318-330
XSL style sheets, 474
XML to HTML format jade commands, 415-416
XML to MIF, jade, 421
XML to MIF format, jade commands, 415
XML to RTF, jade, 419-420
copyright symbol (©), 44
Core portion, 344
CorelDraw, 513
countable actions, Omnimark LE, 310
country codes, ISO 3166, 41
Cover, Robin, 74
createTextnode( ) method, 357
cross references, 201
XML documents, creating, 446-450
CSS (cascading style sheets), 378, 519-521, 527
block-level elements, 271-273
code theft, 378
inline-level elements, 271-273

level 1, 378
level 2, 378
Mozilla 5, 268
  formatting specifica-
    tions, 270-271
  future support, 273
style sheet properties
  background, 401
  background-
    attachment, 401
  background-color,
    401
  background-image,
    401
  background-position,
    401
  background-repeat,
    402
  border, 402
  border-bottom, 402
  border-bottom-
    width, 402
  border-color, 402
  border-left, 402
  border-left-width,
    402
  border-right, 402
  border-right-width,
    402
  border-style, 403
  border-top, 403
  border-top-width,
    403
  border-width, 403
  class selectors, 401
  clear, 403
  color, 403
  display, 403
  first-letter, 403
  first-line, 404
  float, 404
  font, 404

  font-family, 404
  font-size, 404
  font-style, 404
  font-variant, 404
  font-weight, 405
  height, 405
  ID attributes, 401
  important, 405
  letter-spacing, 405
  line-height, 405
  list-style, 405
  list-style-image, 405
  list-style-position,
    405
  list-style-type, 406
  margin, 406
  margin-bottom, 406
  margin-left, 406
  margin-right, 406
  margin-top, 406
  padding, 406
  specifying, 400
  text-align, 407
  text-decoration, 407
  text-indent, 407
  text-transform, 407
  units, 399-400
  vertical-align, 407
  white-space, 408
  word-spacing, 408
viewing XML, 259-260
XSL style sheets,
  embedding, 395-399

D

**data binding, Data
  Source objects, 229**
data consumers, 229
  connected to Data
    Source Objects, 233
data interchange, 10

**Data Interchange
  Initiative, 537**
data islands, 248
  IE 5, 254-257
Data Object, 354
**data objects, well-
  formedness, 69**
data orientation, 16
Data Source objects
  IE 4, viewing XML,
    229-237
  IE 5, 248
databases
  delivery to, 297
  XML, 18
DATAFLD attribute, 233
**DCD (Document Content
  Description), 368-369**
debugging
  DXP parser, 81-84
  error messages, 89
  expat parser, 75-80
  online validation ser-
    vices, 85
  parsers, 74
  RUWF parser, 84
  XML files, 184-189
declaring, 29, 56
  attribute remapping,
    213
  attributes, 64-65
  conditional sections,
    136
  elements, 57
  empty elements, 58
  entities, location of,
    49-50
  external DTD subsets,
    103
  internal DTD subsets,
    100
  internal entities, 45
  link elements, 198

notations, 156
unrestricted elements,
    58
**default template rule,
    XSL style sheets**
overriding, 465
syntax, 465
Deja-News Web site, 551
delimiters, 37
delivery.xml, 295
**dereferencing, internal
    entities, 49**
**descendant relative refer-
    ence, 220**
developing DTDs, 105
from XML code,
    106-108
modifying SGML DTD,
    105
test case, 140-146
**Development Markup
    Language (DML), 497,
    537**
DHTML Behaviors, 519
**diagram DTD modeling,
    125**
**direct processing, XSL
    elements, 471-474**
directed graphs, 269
**display property, CSS,
    403**
**display-group flow object
    (DSSSL), 428**
displaying
CSS coding
    IE 5, 380-387
    Mozilla, 387-392
HTML coding
    IE 5, 380-387
    Mozilla, 387-392

XML coding
    IE 5, 379-387
    Mozilla, 387-392
XML/HTML hybrid
    coding, Web browsers,
    392-395
distribution, 16
**DML (Development
    Markup Language),
    497, 537**
**DOCTYPE declaration,
    56**
**Document Content
    Description (DCD), 368**
document element, 528
document entity, 34
Document Object, 239
DOM specification,
    352-353
IE 5, 250
properties, 239
**Document Object Model
    (DOM).** *See* **DOM**
**document type declara-
    tion, 50, 528**
**document type definition
    (DTD), 9**
**document types, declar-
    ing/debugging, 77**
**document-end event, rule
    syntax, Omnimark LE,
    312**
**document-start event,
    rule syntax, Omnimark
    LE, 311-312**
**documentElement prop-
    erty, 254**
**DocumentFragment
    object, 352**
**DocumentHandler inter-
    face (SAX), methods,
    332-333**

documents
adding extended links,
    204
element trees, 216-218
extended link groups,
    204
sample XML, 28-29
standalone, 100-102
DocZilla
development, 279
features, 279
Web site information,
    279
XML, viewing, 279
**DOM (Document Object
    Model), 238-239, 304**
background, 343
DOM 1.0, Mozilla 5
    support, 274-276
example, 355-357
future of, 357
implementation, 357
specification
    CharacterData
        object, 354
    Document object,
        352-353
    interface relation-
        ships, 345-346
    interfaces, 345
    NamedNodeMap
        object, 351-352
    Node object,
        347-350
    NodeList object,
        350-351
    structure, 344
double escaping, 47
**downloading, Mozilla
    Web browser, 388**

DSSSL (Document Style Semantics and Specification Language), 528
complexity of, 412
development environment
jade errors, 413
monitor resolution, 413
PFE, 413
jade
catalog file, 414-417
error messages, 417-418
knowledge of LISP language, 412
lack of documentation, 412
software packages
jade, 413
PFE (programmers file editor), 413
style sheets
advanced prefixing, 438
construction rule, 433-434
conversion from XML to HTML, 422-425
cross references, creating, 446-450
flow object trees, 431-432
flow objects, 425-431
parameters, 416-417
prefixing elements, 434-437
selection rule, 433
table of contents, creating, 442-446

XML to RTF conversion, 440-442
XML resources, 549-550
DSSSL (Document Style Semantics and Specification Language), SGML styling language, 376
DSSSL-Lite (Document Style Semantics and Specification Language), SGML styling language, 376, 412
DSSSL-o (Document Style Semantics and Specification Language) online, 412, 528
SGML styling language, 376
similarities to XSLVersion 1, 454-455
DTD Generator, 128
DTD2HTML package, 128
DTDHandler interface (SAX), 332
DTDs (document type definitions), 50, 99, 173, 362-363
ambiguous content model, 61
architectural forms, 371
checking with DXP, 174-182
checking with XML for Java, 183-184
checking XML files, 186
conditional markup, 136

creating, 108-109
assigning attributes, 113
element structure, 111-112
identifying elements, 109
presentation markup, 109-111
rule enforcement, 112
developing, 105
from XML code, 106-108
modifying SGML DTD, 105
test case, 140-146
element declarations, 57
elements vs attributes, 132
empty elements, declarations, 58
entities, 152
entity declarations, 49
extended links, 201
external, 103
external identifiers, 103
public identifiers, 104
home pages, 114-117
internal subsets, 100
link elements, declarations, 198
maintaining, 125
modular, 134-136
modules, 164
notations, 155
optional content models, 137-139
parameter entities, 133-134, 161

relational databases,
130-131
standalone documents,
100-102
string attribute type, 65
subsets, 50
declaring, 56
order read, 163
third-party tools,
128-130
unrestricted elements,
declarations, 58
validating documents
without, 97-98
validation, 98-99
visual modeling,
124-128
XML declaration, 29
dtdv.dtd, 175, 179, 182
dtdv.xml, 180
Dublin Core, 365
DXP parser, 81-84
checking DTDs,
174-182
checking XML files,
184-189
XML, SAX interface,
331
Dynamic HTML, 238,
379

E

e-commerce, 8
EBNF, 15
editors, 113
element construction
rules, 528
element content, 529
element event,
Omnimark LE, 313-316

element markup, 38
Element object, 355
methods, 240
properties, 239
element trees
branches, 216-217
code declarations, 217
groves, 217
nodes, 217
hidden, 218
relative locations, 220
roots, 216-217
structure, 218
element types, 529
ElementDef element, 368
elements
ambiguous content
models, 60-61
character content, 63
element occurrence
indicators, 62
mixed content, 64
architectural forms, 132
Bag, 366
CAS, 518
content models, 58-59
choices, 59
sequences, 59-60
declaring, 57
declaring attributes,
64-65
developing DTDs, 106,
122
DOCTYPE, 56
DTDs, creating, 109
Dublin Core, 365
ElementDef, 368
empty, declaring, 58
ENTITIES attribute, 66
ENTITY attribute, 66
events, 301
grouping, 111
ID attribute, 66

IDREF attribute, 66
IDREFS attribute, 66
KEYWORD, 110
link, 198-199
linking, 197
location, 208
locators, 198
logical structure, 32
matching (XSL)
by ancestry, 461-462
by attributes,
462-463
by children, 463
by ID, 461
by name, 461
by position, 463-464
by wildcards, 464
More, 370
nesting, 32
NMTOKEN attribute,
67
optional content mod-
els, 138
selection conflicts,
resolving (XSL),
464-465
selection methods
by attribute, 223
by instance numbers,
222
by node types, 222
ranges, 224
text, 223
selection rule, DSSSL,
433
SEMANTIC, 500
Seq, 366
sorting (XSL), 479-480
structure, 111-112
unrestricted, declaring,
58
validation, 98
vs attributes, 132

xref.list, 206
XSL
  conditional process-
    ing, 474-476
  direct processing,
    471-474
  restricted processing,
    474
**embedded links, actua-
tion, 209**
**embedded-text flow
object (DSSSL), 426**
embedding
  CSS properties
    in XSL style sheets,
      395-399
    in XSL style sheets,
      396-397
  HTML markup, in
    XML files, 490-492
empty elements, 31, 529
encoding declaration, 529
**encoding entities,
166-167**
end tags, 30, 529
  debugging, 78
entities, 33, 151-152
  benefits, 46
  binary, 154-155
  character data, 165
  character sets, 165-166
  dangers, 47
  declaring, 45
    location of, 49-50
  DTDs subsets, order
    read, 163
  encoding, 166-167
  entity resolution,
    161-163
  entity sets, 167-169

external
  public identifiers,
    159-161
  system identifiers,
    158-159
  internal, 153
  nested references, 34
  notations, 155-158
  parameter, 133-134,
    161
  predefined, 44-45
  references, 45
  synchronous structures,
    48
  troubleshooting, 47
  types of, 152
ENTITIES attribute, 66
ENTITY attribute, 66
entity declaration, 529
**entity management pack-
ages, 161**
entity manager, 161
entity references, 529
  debugging, 77
**EntityResolver interface
(SAX), 332**
**enumerated attributes,
67**
**enumerated notations,
157**
EOF (end of file), 235
equations, MathML, 498
error messages, 83
  checking DTDs, 184
  jade, 417-418
**ErrorHandler interface
(SAX), 332**
errors
  fatal, 83
  validity constraints, 178

escaping, 27
  entity references, 47
European languages, 166
**event-driven program-
ming, Omnimark LE,
310-311**
event handlers, 298
events
  document-end,
    Omnimark LE, 312
  document-start,
    Omnimark LE,
    311-312
  element, Omnimark LE,
    313-316
  processing instructions,
    Omnimark LE, 316
  processing XML as,
    298
executing
  jade, 414-417
  Omnimark LE, com-
    mand line syntax, 311
expat parser, 74-80
  installing, 75
**Extended Backus-Naur
Format (EBNF), 15**
**Extended Forms
Description Language
(XFDL), 540**
extended interfaces, 345
**extended link groups,
204-206**
**extended links, 199-204,
529**
  inline/out-of-line links,
    206
  location element, 209
**extended pointers
(XPointer), 215-216**
  absolute references, 219
  elements, selection
    methods, 222-224

implementing, 216
relative references, 219-221
XML Pointer Language, 216
extensibility, 16, 27
HTML, 11
Extensible Log Format Initiative, 537
Extensible Style sheet Language (XSL), 244
external DTDs, 103
declarations, 56
public identifiers, 104
subsets, 529
system identifiers, 103
external entities, 529
internal DTD subsets, 100
public identifiers, 159-161
system identifiers, 158-159
external files, checking DTDs, 176
external graphics files, 34
external parameter entities, modular DTDs, 134
external text entities, 152
external-graphic flow object (DSSSL), 426
external.pointer element, 50
EZDTD, 126
EzMath plug-in, 506

F

fatal errors, 83
file formats, 11
files, syntax checking, 76
filtering, extended links, 200
first-letter property, CSS, 403
first-line property, CSS, 404
float property, CSS, 404
flow object trees, 529
DSSSL style sheets, 431-432
flow objects (DSSSL style sheets), 529
avoiding, XSL, 490-492
box, 426
character, 426
characteristics, 429-430
display-group, 428
DSSSL, vs formatting objects (XSL), 466
embedded-text, 426
external-graphic, 426
heading-level, 430
horizontal-rule, 426
jade support, 425
line-field, 426
link, 428
over-mark-height, 430
page-balance-columns, 430
page-column-sep, 430
page-number-format, 430
page-number-restart, 430
paragraph, 425
paragraph-break, 426

score, 426
scroll, 425
sequence, 428
simple-page-sequence, 428
subscript-depth, 430
superscript-height, 430
table, 427
table-border, 428
table-cell, 427
table-column, 427
table-part, 427
table-row, 427
under-mark-depth, 431
vertical-rule, 426
following links, 197
following relative reference, 220
font property, CSS, 404
font-family property, CSS, 404
font-size property, CSS, 404
font-style property, CSS, 404
font-variant property, CSS, 404
font-weight property, CSS, 405
foreign language characters, 44
Formal System Identifier (FSI), 160
formats, PDF, 511
formatting objects (XSL), 482
content
block, 468, 483-484
block-level-box, 470, 488-489
character, 471, 484-485

graphic, 469
inline-box, 468-469, 488
link, 470, 489
list, 469, 485
list-item, 485-486
list-item-body, 486
list-item-label, 486
page-number, 470
queue, 467
rule-graphic, 469-470, 486-487
score, 470
sequence, 467
layout
page sequence, 466
simple-page-master, 466, 482-483
properties, 482
versus flow objects (DSSSL), 466
W3C status of, 482
forms, architectural, 370-372
FOSI (Formatting Output Specification Instance), SGML styling language, 376
fragment identifiers, 197-198
framework, 228
Frontier Syntax Checker, 86
fsibling relative reference, 220
function.xml, 90
function, ParseFloat(), 357

G

Gecko (Mozilla 5)
home page, 270
XML, viewing, 269-278
general entities, 65
generated text, computing (XSL), 476-477
generic identifiers, 529
getNamedItem() method, 352
global declarations, 163
graphic object (XSL), 469
graphics, structured, 506-508
PGML, 509-513
VML, 513-517
WebCGM, 508
graphs, directed, 269
grep command, 298
groves, 529
element trees, 217

H

Handheld Device Markup Language (HDML), 496, 538
HandlerBase class (SAX)
application writers, 333
subclassing, 334-337
hard copies, delivery to, 292
hash character (#), 63
HDML, 496
heading parameter, 133
heading-level flow object (DSSSL), 430

Health Level 7 (HL7), 496
height property, CSS, 405
helptopic.css, 259
helptopic.xml, 257-261
helptopic.xsl, 261
hexadecimal numbers, 165
hidden nodes, element trees, 218
hierarchies, 302-304
HL7, 496
home.page tag, 30
horizontal lines, DTDs, 110
horizontal-rule flow object (DSSSL), 426
HTML (Hypertext Markup Language), 9-11, 529
bad coding example, 25
CAS, 518
code theft, 378
compared to DTD, 362
data binding, 229
DOM, data islands, 256
image maps, 507
markup, embedding in XML files, 490-492
presentation-based, 26
RTF conversion, jade command, 415
structure, 96
XML conversion
jade, 422-425
jade command, 415-416
Omnimark LE referents, 316-318
Omnimark script example, 318-330

XSL style sheets, 474
XML hybrid coding, in Web browsers, 392-395
html( ) absolute reference, 219
HyBrick, 200
jade output viewer, 418
hybrid coding, XML/HTML, Web browsers, 392-395
hyperlinks, 196-197
HyTime, 370
locators, 198
Hypermedia/Time-based Structuring Language (HyTime), 370
Hypertext Management System (HTM-S), 537
HyTime, 123, 370, 530

I

ID attribute, 66
elements, matching (XSL), 461
fragment identifiers, 198
CSS properties, 401
id( ) absolute reference, 219
identifiers
notation, 156
public, external entities, 159-161
system, external entities, 158-159
IDL, 344
IDOMDocument Object, properties, 250

IDOMNode Object
methods, 252
properties, 251
IDREF attribute, 66
IE 4 (Internet Explorer)
CDF, 496
structured graphics, 513
viewing XML, 228-229
Data Source objects, 229-237
XML Object Model, 238-244
XSL processor, 244-248
XML Object Model, 239
IE 5 (Internet Explorer)
beta preview, Microsoft Web site, 380
CSS coding, displaying, 380-387
DOM, 357
Dynamic XML, 520
HTML coding, displaying, 380-387
viewing XML, 248
CSS, 259-260
data islands, 254-257
Data Source object, 248
Object API, 249-254
viewing directly, 257-258
XSL, 261-263
VML, 514
XML code, 28
displaying, 379-387
level of support, 379
image maps, 506
IMG element, 30, 198

implementing
extended pointers (XPointer), 216
modes, DSSSL style sheets, 445-446
important property, CSS, 405
Indelv Web site, 455
IndelvIT viewer/editor, 200
infinite links, extended link groups, 205
Information & Content Exchange (ICE), 538
information models, developing DTDs, 122
Infotek Web site, 535
inline attribute, 205
inline links, 199, 205-207
inline-box object (XSL), 468-469
properties, 488
inline-level elements, cascading style sheets, 271-273
Innovation Partner, 128
input streams, Omnimark LE, 318
Inso/Synex Viewport
anchors, 280
links, 280
navigators, 279
creating, 281
product support, 279
SGML, viewing, 288
style sheets, 279
defining, 280-288
webs, mounting/unmounting, 280

XML
relating, 281-288
viewing, 279-288
installing
expat parser, 75
jade, 413
Omnimark LE, 310
instance numbers, selecting elements, 222
Instructional Management System (IMS), 538
interfaces
classes, Java, 332
DOM specification, 345-346
internal DTD subsets, 530
internal entities, 45, 153, 530
declaring, 45, 49
internal subsets, 100
Internationalization and Localization Tools (ILE), 538
internationalization, HTML, 10, 16
Internet, 8-9
HTML, 9-11
Internet Explorer 5. *See* **IE 5**
Internet Open Trading Protocol (OTP), 496
ISO 10646 character set, 166
ISO 3166 country codes, 41
ISO 639 country codes, 40
ISO 8859 character set, 166
ISO SGML Web site, 550

ISO standards, 540-542
ISOcyr1, 168
item( ) method, 252

J

jade
catalog file, example, 414
error messages, 417-418
executing, 414-417
file conversion commands
HTML to RTF format, 415
XML to HTML format, 415-416
XML to MIF format, 415
flow object trees, 431-432
installing, 413
output, viewing, 418
package, downloading, 413
XML to HTML conversion, 422-425
XML to MIF conversion, 421
XML to RTF conversion, 419-420
Jade DSSSL processor, 200
James Clark Web site, jade availability, 413
Java, 81
classes, 331-332
DXP parser, 81
Java Speech Markup Language (JSML), 496, 538

JavaScript
childNodes attribute, 349
Element object, 240
Node object, 348
output_doc function, 241
ParseFloat( ) function, 357
traverse function, 242

K - L

KEYWORD element, 110
keywords
#FIXED, 68
#IMPLIED, 68
#REQUIRED, 68
NDATA, 157
NOTATION, 67, 157
Koala XML Validation Service, 85

language codes, ISO 639, 40
Lark parsers, XML, SAX interface, 331
law of entropy, 123
Law of NINO, 122
layout formatting objects (XSL), 466
page-sequence, 466
simple-page-master, 466, 482-483
legacy data, 13, 123
legal characters, 165
length property, 252
letter-spacing property, CSS, 405
line-field flow object (DSSSL), 426

line-height property,
   CSS, 405
link elements, 198-199
link flow object (DSSSL),
   428
link object (XSL), 470
   properties, 489
linking
   HTML, 11
   namespaces, avoiding
      conflicts, 139
   transclusion, 139
links
   behavior attribute, 209
   behavior of, 207
      effects, 207-208
      timing, 208-209
   descriptions, 210
      role attribute,
         211-212
   extended, 199-204
   extended groups,
      204-206
   inline, 205-207
   out-of-line, 205-207
LISP language, DSSSL
   implementation, 412
list object (XSL), 469
   properties, 485
list-item object (XSL),
   properties, 485-486
list-item-body object
   (XSL), properties, 486
list-item-label object
   (XSL), properties, 486
list-style property, CSS,
   405
list-style-image property,
   CSS, 405
list-style-position property, CSS, 405
list-style-type property,
   CSS, 406

listings
   action sheet document,
      518
   binary entity reference,
      154
   books.xml, 296
   catalog file, 160
   childNodes attribute,
      349
   client-side image map,
      507
   container elements, 112
   convert to Canadian
      currency, 356
   cross-referencing, 201
   data islands, 254
   data sets, position of,
      235
   Data Source Object,
      231
      data consumers, 233
      IE 5, 249
   databases, 131
   DCD, element defini-
      tions, 369
   delivery.xml, 295
   DHTML, 519
   DOM, IE 5, 252
   dtdv.dtd, 175, 179, 182
   dtdv.xml, 180
   dynamic HTML, 520
   email message, 57
   helptopic.css, 259
   helptopic.xml, 257,
      259, 261
   helptopic.xsl, 261
   "Hello World" docu-
      ment, 17
   HTML, Data Source
      Objects, 231
   HTML mimicing XML,
      94

inline links, 206
internal DTD subset, 56
internal entities, 46
   declaring, 49
ISOdia entity set, 168
JavaScript functions,
   243
MathML
   complex math, 504
   matrices, 502
   presentation markup,
      498, 500
   semantic markup,
      499
musicians.csv, 297
musicians.xml, 292, 299
NamedNodeMap object,
   352
navigating data sets,
   234
Node object
   attributes, 348
   methods, 350
notation declarations,
   169
OBJECT element, XSL
   control, 246-247
out-of-line links, 207
output_doc JavaScript
   function, 241
parameter entity, 133,
   135
PGML, 512
PostScript, converted to
   PDF, 511
PostScript file, 509
processing instructions,
   52
RDF file, 366
RDF resource file, 366
role attribute, 211
SGML notation declara-
   tions, 156

standalone documents, 100
structured data, 230
structured HTML, 96
TABLE element binding, 236
traverse JavaScript function, 242
VML
    animated Yin-Yang symbol, 515
    Yin-Yang symbol, 513
wf.xml, 80
wfq.xml, 75-77, 185-186
XML document, 17
local declarations, 164
locating
    Mozilla Web browser, 388
    Omnimark LE, 310
location element, 208
locators, 198, 530
    absolute references, 219
    extended pointers (Xpointer), 215-216
    link descriptions, 210
    relative references, 219-221
        ancestor, 220
        child, 220
        descendant, 220
        following, 220
        fsibling, 220
        preceding, 220
        psibling, 220
    URIs, 215-216
logical structure, 32-33, 530

M

machine-readable, 364
machine-understandable, 364
macros, calling (XSL), 481
mailing lists, XML resources, 552-553
Majix, 130
margin property, CSS, 406
margin-bottom property, CSS, 406
margin-left property, CSS, 406
margin-right property, CSS, 406
margin-top property, CSS, 406
Marius Garshol, Lar, 74
markup, 21-28, 530
    attribute, 39-41
    CDATA section, 50-51
    comments, 43-44
    conditional, 136-137
    declaring, 56
        elements, 57
        empty elements, 58
        unrestricted elements, 58
    delimiters, 37
    distinguishing from content, 26
    DTDs
        creating, 109-111
        elements, 109
    element, 38
    entities, 151-152
    escaping characters, 27
    generating, rule enforcement, 112

    minimization rules, 23
    naming rules, 42-43
    processing instructions, 52
    synchronous structures, 48
    troubleshooting, 47
markup languages, 12
matching elements (XSL)
    by ancestry, 461-462
    by attributes, 462-463
    by children, 463
    by ID, 461
    by name, 461
    by position, 463-464
    by wildcards, 464
Mathematics Markup Language (MathML), 497-506
matrices, 502
Megginson Web site, SAX resources, 340
meta languages, 12
metadata, 228
    Netscape Navigator, 268
    RDF, 364
methods
    appendData, 354
    createTextnode( ), 357
    Document object, 353
    DOM, 343
    Element object, 240
    getNamedItem( ), 352
    Node object, 252, 349
    NodeList object, 252
Microsoft Chrome, 537
Microsoft Web site, IE 5 beta preview, 380
Microsoft Word, 130

MIF (FrameMaker Interchange Format), 415
  XML conversion
    jade, 421
    jade command, 415
minimization rules, 23
mixed content, 530
  checking DTDs, 177
modeling
  databases, 130
  relational databases, 130-131
models, RDF, 365
modes, DSSSL style sheets, implementing, 445-446
modular DTDs, 134-136
modularity, 15
modules, 164
More element, 370
Mozilla 5
  cascading style sheets, 268
    displaying, 387-392
    formatting specifications, 270-271
    future support, 273
    support of, 270
  compiled binary retrieval, 269
  downloading, 388
  FAQ site, 269
  HTML coding, displaying, 387-392
  information types
    data, 268
    documents, 268
    metadata, 268
  metadata, Resource Description Framework (RDF), 268

role attribute, 211-212
standards support
  CSS 1.0, 270
  DOM 1.0, 270, 274-276
  XML 1.0, 270
transclusion support, Xlink syntax, 278
Web site, 269
XML, viewing, 268-278, 387-392
XML support levels, 270
MSUB element, 499
MSUP element, 499
MSXML parsers, XML, SAX interface, 331
multimedia, HyTime, 370
multiple declarations, attributes, 31
musicians.csv, 297
musicians.xml, 292, 299, 303

N

NAME attribute, 197
  namespace conflicts, 140
name characters, 530
name tokens, 530
NamedNodeMap object, DOM specification, 351-352
names, elements, matching (XSL), 461
namespaces, 34, 530
  architectual forms, 371
  avoiding conflicts, 139-140

RDF, 365
XML-Data, 364
naming
  authoring, 132
  rules of, 42-43
naming tags, 30
NDATA keyword, 157
Netscape Navigator. *See* Mozilla 5
News Industry Text Format Initiative (NTIF), 538
newsgroups (Usenet)
  posting etiquette, 551
  XML resources, 551
next case, 235
NMTOKEN attribute, 67
Node object, 251
  DOM specification, 347-350
  methods, 252
  properties, 251
NodeList Object, 252
  DOM specification, 350-351
  item( ) method, 252
nodes
  element trees, 217
    hiding, 218
  elements, selecting, 222
  IE 5 Object Model, 251
non-ISO standards, 540-542
non-validating parsers, 73
non-validating XML processor, 530
normalization, 31
notation, 530
  entity resolution, 163
NOTATION keyword, 67, 157

notations, 155-158
    checking DTDs, 178
**Nothing In, Nothing Out,
122**
**numbering elements,
    controlling (XSL),
    477-479**

O

Oasis Web site, 535, 550
**Object API, IE 5,
    249-254**
**OBJECT element, XSL,
    246**
object model
    IE 4, vs IE 5, 238
    IE 5, 249
    viewing XML, 238-244
objects
    DocumentFragment,
    352
    DOM, 343
    DOM interfaces, 345
    Element, 355
    Node, 251
    NodeList, 252
    standalone documents,
    102
occurrence indicators
    developing DTDs, 107
    optional content mod-
    els, 137
OFE, 496
Omnimark, 301
Omnimark LE
    command line execu-
    tion, 311
    common programming
    constructs, 318

conversion sizes, 310
countable actions, 310
    limit guidelines, 310
current version, 310
event-driven processing
    environment, 310
events
    document-end, 312
    document-start,
    311-312
    element, 313-316
    processing instruc-
    tions, 316
input streams, 318
installation, 310
locating, 310
output streams, 318
rules structure
    body, 310-311
    headers, 310-311
Samples Viewer, 330
Web site, 310, 330
XML conversion
    referents, 316-318
    scripting example,
    318-330
**online help system, XML
coding, 270-271**
**online validation services,
85**
Open Catalog (SOC), 159
**Open Financial
    Exchange Specification
    (OFE), 496**
**Open Software
    Description (OSD), 496,
539**
**Open Trading Protocol
    (OTP), 539**
OpenTag, 497, 539
opinion element, 200
**optional content models,
137-139**

**optional repeatable indi-
    cators, 108**
OR models, 124
**origin( ) absolute refer-
    ence, 219**
**OSD (Open Software
    Description), 496**
**OTP (Open Trading
    Protocol), 496**
**OurHandler class, SAX,
    document parsing,
    337-338**
**out-of-line link, 202,
    205-207, 530**
**output streams,
    Omnimark LE, 318**
**output_doc JavaScript
    function, 241**
**over-mark-height flow
    object (DSSSL), 430**
**overriding, default tem-
    plate rule, XSL style
    sheets, 465**

P

P3P, 497
packages, DSSSL
    jade, 413
    PFE (programmers' file
    editor), 413
**padding property, CSS,
    406**
**page-balance-columns
    flow object (DSSSL),
    430**
**page-column-sep flow
    object (DSSSL), 430**
**page-number object
    (XSL), 470**

page-number-format flow object (DSSSL), 430

page-number-restart flow object (DSSSL), 430

page-sequence object (XSL), 466

Panorama Pro, extended links, 203

Panorama SGML browser, 203

Panorama Web site, 154

paragraph flow object (DSSSL), 425

paragraph-break flow object (DSSSL), 426

paragraphs, element structure, 111

parameter entities, 133-134, 161

  conditional sections, 136

parameter entity, 530

parent elements, 32

  Omnimark LE, 314-316

ParseFloat( ) function, 357

parsers, 74

  SAX interface

    DXP, 331

    Lark, 331

    MSXML, 331

    OurHandler class, 337-338

    SXP, 331

    XML for Java, 330

    XP, 330

  XML, SAX interface, 330

PCDATA keyword, 63

PDF (postscript document format), 11

  PostScript displayed, 510

percent sign (%), parameter entities, 133, 161

Perl, expat parser, 74

PFE (programmers' file editor), package, downloading, 413

PGML, 509-513

physical structure, 33-35, 530

PICS, 365

pixels, 507-508

Platform for Internet Content Selection (PICS), 365

Platform for Privacy Preferences (P3P), 497

plug-ins, EzMath, 506

plus sign (+), element occurrence indicators, 62

pointers, out-of-line links, 207

positions, elements, matching (XSL), 463-464

Postscript, PGML, 509

preceding relative reference, 220

Precision Graphics Markup Language (PGML), 509

predefined entities, 44-45

prefixing

  advanced

    DSSSL style sheets, 438-439

  elements

    DSSSL style sheets, 434-437

preparent element, Omnimark LE, 314-316

presentation markup, 498

preserving whitespace, XSL, 481

previous element, Omnimark LE, 314-316

procedural markup, 23

Process Interchange Format (PIF), 539

processing

  XML as hierarchy/tree, 302, 304

  XML as series of events, 298-302

  XML as text files, 298

  XSL elements

    conditional method, 474-476

    direct method, 471-474

    restricted method, 474

processing instruction event, rule syntax, Omnimark LE, 316

processing instructions (PI), 29, 52, 531

processing XML

  database loading, 297

  delivery to multiple media, 292-294

  delivery to multiple target groups, 294-295

  reporting, 297

  restructuring information, 296

processing, transferring to client, **229**
processors
  elements vs attributes, 132
  entity encoding, 167
  optional content models, 138
programming, 16
prolog, 531
properties
  behavior, 520
  childNodes, 350
  CSS
    background, 401
    background-attachment, 401
    background-color, 401
    background-image, 401
    background-position, 401
    background-repeat, 402
    border, 402
    border-bottom, 402
    border-bottom-width, 402
    border-color, 402
    border-left, 402
    border-left-width, 402
    border-right, 402
    border-right-width, 402
    border-style, 403
    border-top, 403
    border-width, 403
    border-wop-width, 403
    class selectors, 401

clear, 403
color, 403
display, 403
first-letter, 403
first-line, 404
float, 404
font, 404
font-family, 404
font-size, 404
font-style, 404
font-variant, 404
font-weight, 405
height, 405
ID attributes, 401
important, 405
letter-spacing, 405
line-height, 405
list-style, 405
list-style-image, 405
list-style-position, 405
list-style-type, 406
margin, 406
margin-bottom, 406
margin-left, 406
margin-right, 406
margin-top, 406
padding, 406
specifying, 400
text-align, 407
text-decoration, 407
text-indent, 407
text-transform, 407
vertical-align, 407
white-space, 408
word-spacing, 408
Document Object, 239, 352
documentElement, 254
DOM, 343
Element object, 239
IDOMDocument object, 250

Node object, 251, 348
NodeList object, 252
protocols, XML compatibility, 13
psibling relative reference, 220
public domain XML coding, examples, 553
public identifiers, 159-161
  external DTDs, 104
Push Media, 496

Q - R

question mark (?), element occurrence indicators, 62
queue object (XSL), 467
quotation marks ("")
  attribute delimiters, 39
  entity references, 162

ranges, elements, string selectors, 224
raster graphics, 508
RDBMs, 228
RDF, 364-368
references, 45
  binary entities, 154
  entity resolution, 161
  internal entities, 153
  XML conversion, Omnimark LE, 316-318
Rein, Lisa, 74
relating, XML files, Inso/Synex Viewport, 281-288
relational databases, 130-131

relative references, 219-221
  ancestor, 220
  child, 220
  descendant, 220
  following, 220
  fsibling, 220
  keywords, 220-221
  preceding, 220
  psibling, 220
  steps, 220
remapping attributes, 213
rendering, 531
  terminology, 454
replacement text, entity resolution, 163
reporting, 297
reserved name character (RNI), 63
resolution, image maps, 507
resolving, selection conflicts with elements (XSL), 464-465
Resource Description Format (RDF), 539
Resource Description Framework (RDF), 364
  example, 268
  metadata
    properties, 268
    values, 268
  property types, 268
  resource terminology, 268
  values, 268
  Web site resources, 269
resource discovery, 364
resources (XML), 533
  applications, 537-540
  articles, 535-536

  books, 533-534
  DSSSL documentation, 549-550
  extended links, 200
  information sources, 543
  inline links, 206
  linking, 197
    descriptions, 210
  locators
    absolute references, 219
    relative references, 219-221
  mailing lists, 552-553
  RDF, 366
  SGML Web sites, 550
  software companies, 548-549
  software packages, 543-548
  standards
    ISO, 540-542
    non-ISO, 540-542
  test data, 553
  Usenet newsgroups, 551
  Web sites, 535
restricted processing, XSL elements, 474
reusability, HTML, 11
RFC 1766, 41
rich DTDs, 122
role attribute, 212
  link descriptions, 210
  Mozilla, 211-212
root element
  DTDs, 99
  logical structure, 32
root elements, 30
root( ) absolute reference, 219

RTF (Rich Text Format), 11, 415
  HTML conversion, jade command, 415
  XML conversion, jade, 419-420
  XML tables, converting, 440-442
RTF documents, 130
RTF format, markup, 22
RTF output, 292
rule body, Omnimark LE, 310-311
rule header, Omnimark LE, 310-311
rule-graphic object (XSL), 469-470
  properties, 486-487
RUWF parser, 84

S

SAX (Simple API for XML), 302, 330
  applications, writing requirements, 331
  conversion components
    event handlers, 339-340
    SAX distribution, 339-340
    SAX enabled parser, 339-340
  development, 330
  document parsing, OurHandler class, 337-338
  HandlerBase class
    interface implementations, 333
    subclassing, 334-337

interfaces
DocumentHandler, 332-333
DTDHandler, 332
EntityResolver, 332
ErrorHandler, 332
Megginson Web site, 340
SAXON variation, 340
variation on SAX, 340
XML parsers, 330
DXP, 331
Lark, 331
MSXML, 331
SXP, 331
XML for Java, 330
XP, 330
schemas, 105
namespace conflicts, 139
XML-Data, 363
XSchema, 369
score flow object (DSSSL), 426
score object (XSL), 470
scroll flow object (DSSSL), 425
SDML, 497
selecting elements
by attribute, 223
by instance numbers, 222
by node types, 222
ranges, 224
text, 223
SEMANTIC element, 500
semantic markup, 26, 498
Seq element, 366
sequence flow object (DSSSL), 428

sequence object (XSL), 467
sequences, 366
sequences of elements, 59
setting, DSSSL style sheets, parameters, 416-417
SGML (Standard Generalized Markup Language), 10, 12, 531
applications, 23-24
empty elements, 31
Inso/Synex Viewport, viewing, 288
modifying DTD, 105
style languages evolution
DSSSL, 376
DSSSL-Lite, 376
DSSSL-o, 376
FOSI, 376
XSL, 377
Web sites, 550
SGML FTP Archive Web site, 550
SGML University Web site, 550
shared data, 163
show attribute, 207
sibling elements, 32
Signed Document Markup Language (SDML), 497
simple links, 531
simple-page-master object (XSL), 466
properties, 482-483
simple-page-sequence flow object (DSSSL), 428
SMIL, 497

SoftQuad's Panorama SGML browser, 203
software
companies, XML technologies, 548-549
distributing, 9
XML resources, 543-548
sorting elements, XSL, 479-480
source code, SEMANTIC element, 500
source documents, Document Object, 239
spans, elements, selecting, 224
specifications, DOM
CharacterData object, 354
Document object, 352-353
interface relationships, 345-346
interfaces, 345
NamedNodeMap object, 351-352
Node object, 347-350
NodeList object, 350-351
structure, 344
specifying, CSS style sheet properties, 400
standalone documents, 100-102
start tag, 30, 531
attributes, 31
step element, debugging, 78
storage objects, 34
string attributes, 65
string selectors, elements, text selection, 223

structured graphics, 506-508
  PGML, 509-513
  VML, 513-517
  WebCGM, 508
structured information, 94-97
structures
  creating DTDs, 109
  synchronous, 48-49
  validation, 98
style languages (SGML), evolution
  DSSSL, 376
  DSSSL-Lite, 376
  DSSSL-o, 376
  FOSI, 376
  XSL, 377
style sheets, 517, 531
  CSS, unit property, 399-400
  DSSSL
    advanced prefixing elements, 438-439
    construction rule, 433-434
    flow object trees, 431-432
    flow objects, 425-431
    parameters, 416-417
    prefixing elements, 434-437
    selection rule, 433
  XSL
    default template rule, 465
    template rule, 459-460
Stylo Web Writer, 114
subclasses, HandlerBase class (SAX), 334-337

subscript-depth flow object (DSSSL), 430
subscripts, MathML, 500
subsets
  internal, 100
  order read, 163
superscript-height flow object (DSSSL), 430
superscripts, MathML, 500
SXP parsers, XML, SAX interface, 331
Synchronized Multimedia Integration Language (SMIL), 497
synchronous elements, 33
synchronous structures, 48-49
Syntax Checker, Frontier, 86
system identifiers, 158-159
  external DTDs, 103
system literals, 104
system object identifiers, 160

T

TABLE element, binding, 236
table flow object (DSSSL), 427
table of contents
  DSSSL modes, 445-446
  XML documents, creating, 442-446
table-border flow object (DSSSL), 428
table-cell flow object (DSSSL), 427

table-column flow object (DSSSL), 427
table-part flow object (DSSSL), 427
table-row flow object (DSSSL), 427
tables, XML to RTF conversion, DSSSL style sheets, 440-442
tabular modeling, 127
tag minimization, 24
tags
  attributes, 31
  comments, 43
  home.page, 30
  IMG, 30
  naming, 30
Tauber, James, 74
Techno 2000 Project XML Validation Service, 85
TEI DTD, 22
template rule, XSL style sheets
  element nodes, 459-460
  rendering action, 459-460
test data, XML resources, 553
Tetrasix, 130
TeX, 11
text
  character content, 63
  elements, string selectors, 223
  formatting objects, adding (XLS), 477
Text Encoding Initiative DTD, 164
text entities, 152
  encoding, 166
text files, processing XML as, 298

text-align property, CSS, 407

text-decoration property, CSS, 407

text-indent property, CSS, 407

text-transform property, CSS, 407

textual objects, well-formedness, 77

title attribute, 210

TMX, 497

tokenized attributes, 66-67

transclusion, 139
Mozilla 5 support, Xlink syntax, 278

Translation Memory Exchange (TMX), 497

traversal, 531

traverse JavaScript function, 242

traversing links, 197

types
enumerated, 67
strings, 65
tokenized, 66-67

typesetting mathematics, 498

U

UCS Transformation Formats (UTF), 166

UCS-2, 166

UCS-4, 166

under-mark-depth flow object (DSSSL), 431

underscore character (_), naming rules, 42

Unicode, 166
naming rules, 42

units, CSS properties, 399-400

universal resource identifiers. *See* URIs

unparsed entities, 34
notations, 155

unrestricted elements, 58

URIs (universal resource identifiers), 215
extended link groups, 204
hyperlinks, 197
system identifiers, 103, 158

URL Minder service, 42

URLs (Uniform Resource Locators), 15
system identifiers, 159

Usenet newsgroups, XML resources, 551

UTF-8, 167

UTF-16, 167

V

valid XML document, 531

validating
DTDs, 98-99
entity resolution, 163
modular DTDs, 136

validators, 97

validity constraints
checking DTDs, 178
declarations, 188

values, enumerated attribute types, 67

vector graphics, 508
VML, 513

Vector Markup Language (VML), 513-517

vertical-align property, CSS, 407

vertical-rule flow object (DSSSL), 426

viewers
extended link groups, 205
extended links, 203

viewing
jade output, HyBrick, 418
SGML, Inso/Synex Viewport, 288
XML
DocZilla, 279
Inso/Synex Viewport, 279-288
Mozilla 5, 269-278
Netscape Navigator, 268-269

viewing XML
IE 4, 228-229
Data Source objects, 229-237
XML Object Model, 238-244
IE 5, 248
CSS, 259-260
data islands, 254-257
Data Source object, 248
Object API, 249-254
viewing directly, 257-258
XSL, 261-263
XSL processor, 244-248

visual modeling, 124-128

Visual XML (VXML), 497

VML, 513-517
VXML (virtual XML),
497, 540

W

W3C (World Wide Web
Consortium), 531
CSS specifications, 378
CSS/XSL coding meth-
ods, 395
DOM specification, 344
URL Minder service, 42
Web site, 540-542
XSL formatting objects,
status of, 482
XSL proposal, 459
Web browsers
DocZilla, XML view-
ing, 279
HTML, bad code exam-
ple, 26
hybridization of XML
and HTML coding,
392-395
Inso/Synex Viewport
SGML viewing, 288
XML viewing,
279-288
Internet Explorer 5
CSS code, display-
ing, 380-387
HTML code, dis-
playing, 380-387
XML code, display-
ing, 379-387
Mozilla
CSS code, display-
ing, 387-392
downloading, 388

HTML code, dis-
playing, 387-392
XML code, display-
ing, 387-392
Mozilla 5, XML view-
ing, 269-278
Netscape Navigator,
XML viewing,
268-269
Web pages
behaviors, 517
CSS, 521
XML code, 28
Web resources, automat-
ed processing, 364
Web servers, system
identifiers, 159
Web sites
Charled F. Goldfarb,
550
data source objects, 229
Deja-News, 551
DOM, 344
DOM properties, 239
extended link software,
200
EzMath plug-in, 506
filtering with PICS, 365
Indelv, 455
Infotek, 535
Innovation Partner, 128
ISO SGML, 550
James Clark, jade avail-
ability, 413
Megginson, SAX
resources, 340
Microsoft, IE 5 beta
preview, 380
Mozilla 5 resources,
269
Oasis, 535, 550
Omnimark LE, 310,
330

Resource Description
Framework (RDF)
information, 269
SGML FTP Archive,
550
SGML University, 550
SoftQuad Panorama,
154
Tetrasix, 130
W3C, 550
XML standards,
540-542
XML, 535
editors, 114
examples, 537-540
XML Pro, 129
Web Writer, 115
WebBroker, 497
WebCGM, 508
WebTech's Validation
Service, 85
well-formed XML docu-
ment, 531
well-formedness, 69
DXP parser, 81
fatal errors, 83
well-formedness
checker, 86
wf.xml, 80
wfq.xml, 75, 77, 185-186
white-space property,
CSS, 408
whitespace, 98
controlling (XSL), 481
wildcards, elements,
matching (XSL), 464
WMF (Windows Meta
Format), 508
converting to structured
graphics, 513
wmfcnv.exe, 513
Word, 130

word-spacing property, CSS, 408
WordPerfect, markup, 22
writing, SAX applications, necessary requirements, 331
WWW (World Wide Web), 8-9
  HTML, 9-11
  speed of, 14

X

X-ACT (ActiveX XML), 540
XLink, 132, 363
  behavior of links, 207
  extended link groups, 204-206
  extended links, 199-204
  hyperlinks, 196
  inline links, 205-207
  link descriptions, 210
    role attribute, 211-212
  Mozilla 5, transclusion support, 278
  out-of-line links, 205-207
  form attribute, 200
XML (eXtensible Markup Language)
  advantages, 9, 13
  attributes, 31
  declaration, 29
  empty elements, 31
  features added, 15
  HTML conversion
    jade, 422-425
    jade command, 415-416

MIF conversion
  jade, 421
  jade command, 415
resources
  applications, 537-540
  articles, 535-536
  books, 533-534
  DSSSL documentation, 549-550
  information sources, 543
  mailing lists, 552-553
  SGML Web sites, 550
  software companies, 548-549
  software packages, 543-548
  standards, 540-542
  test data, 553
  Usenet newsgroups, 551
  Web sites, 535
root elements, 30
RTF conversion, jade, 419-420
sample document, 28-29
tables, converting to RTF format, 440-442
URLs, 15
XML editors, 113
XML files
  checking with DXP, 184-189
  checking with XML for Java, 189
  valid, 190

XML for Java, 183-184
  checking XML files, 189
  SAX interface, 330
XML Pointer Language, extended pointers, 216
XML Pro, 114, 129
XML Query Language (XML-QL), 497
XML Web site, 535
XML-Data, 363-364
XML-QL, 497
xmlwf application, 75
XP parsers, SAX interface, 330
XPointers, 363, 532
  locators, 198
xref.list element, 206
XSchema, 369-370
XSL (eXtensible Style Language), 377
  development, 412
  elements
    conditional processing, 474-476
    direct processing, 471-474
    matching by ancestry, 461-462
    matching by attributes, 462-463
    matching by children, 463
    matching by ID, 461
    matching by name, 461
    matching by position, 463-464
    restricted processing, 474
    selection conflict resolution, 464-465

sorting, 479-480
wildcard matches, 464
flow objects, avoiding, 490-492
formatting objects
content, 467-471, 483-489
layout, 466, 482-483
properties, 482
vs DSSSL flow objects, 466
HTML markup, embedding, 490-492
IE 5, 261-263
macros, calling, 481
numbering elements, controlling, 477-479
sample files, 455-459
SGML styling language, 377
sort element, attributes, 479-480
style sheets
default template rule, 465
embedding CSS properties, 395-399
template rule, 459-460
text formatting object, adding, 477
value-of element, computing generated text, 476-477
Version 1
code fragments, 454-455
similarities to DSSSL-o, 454-455
Version 2
publication date, 455
XSLProcessor, 455
W3C proposal, 459
whitespace, controlling, 481
XML to HTML conversion, 474
XSL processor, viewing XML, 244-248
XSLProcessor (XSL2), 455
Yin-Yang symbol, animated, 515